One of the key constitutional feature: s
that the political executive, or cabinet   .s
politically responsible to – the legisla   ·y
democracy democratic is that, once a k͟   ͟ne
new legislature has the power to dismiss the incu͟͟͟͟͟͟   nd
replace it with a new one. Moreover, it sits essentially as a court, passing
continual judgment on the record of the executive, and continuous sentence on its future prospects. That is how citizens, indirectly, choose and
control their government. But the relationship between legislature and
executive is not one-sided. The executive typically has the authority to
recommend dissolution of parliament and is usually drawn from the parliament. Executive personnel, therefore, have intimate familiarity with
parliamentary practices; and for their part, parliamentary personnel aspire
to executive appointments.

Surprisingly, little is known about the constitutional relationship between legislature and executive in parliamentary regimes; the present volume seeks to remedy this. Leading specialists on institutional politics in
the major parliamentary democracies have been encouraged to describe
legislative–executive interactions in terms of a common theoretical framework. The country-specific chapters have, as their central themes, cabinet
decision making and cabinet relationships with the parliament, parliamentary parties, and the permanent civil service. The editors have provided a theoretical overview at the outset and, in their conclusion, have
made theoretical sense of the empirical variation in parliamentary
practices.

CABINET MINISTERS
AND
PARLIAMENTARY GOVERNMENT

POLITICAL ECONOMY OF INSTITUTIONS AND DECISIONS

Editors
James E. Alt, *Harvard University*
Douglass C. North, *Washington University of St. Louis*

Other books in the series

James E. Alt and Kenneth Shepsle, eds., *Perspectives on Positive Political Economy*
Yoram Barzel, *Economic Analysis of Property Rights*
Robert Bates, *Beyond the Miracle of the Market: The Political Economy of Agrarian Development in Kenya*
Gary W. Cox, *The Efficient Secret: The Cabinet and the Development of Political Parties in Victorian England*
Leif Lewin, *Ideology and Strategy: A Century of Swedish Politics (English edition)*
Gary Libecap, *Contracting for Property Rights*
Matthew D. McCubbins and Terry Sullivan, eds., *Congress: Structure and Policy*
Douglass C. North, *Institutions, Institutional Change, and Economic Performance*
Elinor Ostrom, *Governing the Commons: The Evolution of Institutions for Collective Action*
Charles Stewart III, *Budget Reform Politics: The Design of the Appropriations Process in the House of Representatives, 1865–1921*
Gary J. Miller, *Managerial Dilemmas: The Political Economy of Hierarchy*
Jean-Laurent Rosenthal, *The Fruits of Revolution: Property Rights, Litigation, and French Agriculture*
Jean Ensminger, *Making a Market: The Institutional Transformation of an African Society*
Jack Knight, *Institutions and Social Conflict*
John Waterbury, *Exposed to Innumerable Delusions*

CABINET MINISTERS AND PARLIAMENTARY GOVERNMENT

Edited by

MICHAEL LAVER
University of Dublin

KENNETH A. SHEPSLE
Harvard University

CAMBRIDGE
UNIVERSITY PRESS

Published by the Press Syndicate of the University of Cambridge
The Pitt Building, Trumpington Street, Cambridge CB2 1RP
40 West 20th Street, New York, NY 10011-4211, USA
10 Stamford Road, Oakleigh, Melbourne 3166, Australia

First published 1994

Printed in the United States of America

Library of Congress Cataloging-in-Publication Data
Shepsle, Kenneth A.
Cabinet ministers and parliamentary government / Kenneth A.
Shepsle, Michael Laver.
p.   c. – (Political economy of institutions and decisions)
Includes index.
ISBN 0-521-43246-4. – ISBN 0-521-43837-3 (pbk.)
1. Cabinet system. 2. Cabinet officers. 3. Comparative
government. I. Laver, Michael, 1949–   . II. Title. III. Series.
JF331.S455   1994
321.8′043 – dc20   93-51079
                                                          CIP

A catalog record for this book is available from the British Library.

ISBN 0-521-43246-4 hardback
0-521-43837-3 paperback

Contents

v

Contents

List of tables and figure

TABLES

List of tables and figure

Series editors' preface

The Cambridge Series on the Political Economy of Institutions and Decisions is built around attempts to answer two central questions: How do institutions evolve in response to individual incentives, strategies, and choices, and how do institutions affect the performance of political and economic systems? The scope of the series is comparative and historical rather than international or specifically American, and the focus is positive rather than normative.

The theory of coalition formation has recently reemerged as a central area of theoretical innovation and development in comparative politics. In this first of two related volumes, Michael Laver, Kenneth Shepsle, and their collaborators provide the descriptive and empirical foundations for a pathbreaking "portfolio allocation" approach to party government and cabinet formation. The unifying claim of this approach is that both the partisan composition of the Cabinet and the partisan allocation of ministerial portfolios matter for policy outcomes in parliamentary systems. In keeping with the series' emphasis on rational decisions in institutional contexts, ministers are treated as optimizers promoting party policies within jurisdictions established by the structure of ministries, constrained by a wide range of institutional features. In this volume expert scholars describe how cabinet government works in fourteen countries, providing a unique, detailed study of such important constitutional and institutional variations as confidence votes, agenda control, veto powers, caretaker governments, and the roles of individual ministers, parties, and the civil service. Using these materials as a basis, in the next volume (provisionally entitled *Making and Breaking Governments*) Laver and Shepsle build an explicit, empirically testable theory of government formation and its effects on public policy in parliamentary systems.

Part I

INTRODUCTION

1

Cabinet ministers and government formation in parliamentary democracies

Michael Laver and Kenneth A. Shepsle

The efficient secret of the English Constitution may be described as the close union, the nearly complete fusion, of the executive and legislative powers. No doubt by the traditional theory, as it exists in all the books, the goodness of our constitution consists in the entire separation of the legislative and executive authorities, but in truth its merit consists in their singular approximation. The connecting link is *the Cabinet*. By that new word we mean a committee of the legislative body selected to be the executive body . . . The legislature chosen, in name, to make laws, in fact finds its principal business in making and in keeping an executive . . . The Cabinet, in a word, is a board of control chosen by the legislature, out of persons whom it trusts and knows, to rule the nation. (Bagehot, 1963: 66–7)

INTRODUCTION

Most Western countries, as well as many of the states in what used to be thought of as Eastern Europe, are parliamentary democracies. One of the key constitutional features of a parliamentary democracy is that the political executive derives its mandate from, and is politically responsible to, the legislature. What makes a parliamentary democracy democratic is that, once a legislative election has been held, the new legislature has the power to dismiss the incumbent executive and replace it with a new one. That is how the people, indirectly, choose their government. At any time during the life of a legislature, furthermore, legislators retain the right to withdraw their support from the executive and replace it with an alternative. In a very real sense, one of the main jobs of the legislature in a parliamentary democracy is to sit as a court passing continual judgment on the record of the executive, and continuous sentence on its future prospects.

This relationship is by no means one-sided. The executive typically has the power to recommend the dissolution of the legislature, and may in practice do this for no better reason than expected gains for the government parties at the ensuing election. In terms of personalities, further-

3

more, executive and legislature often overlap almost completely. Members of the executive typically are drawn from the legislature and very often continue to sit there, although France and Norway are notable exceptions to this. It is no exaggeration to say that a place in the executive is one of the main career goals of most ambitious legislators in any parliamentary democracy. All of this makes the intimate interaction between legislature and executive perhaps the most central political feature of parliamentary democracy; yet this interaction has been subjected to surprisingly little systematic analysis.

Most theoretical approaches to government formation, for example, in effect assume that governments in parliamentary democracies are controlled absolutely by their legislatures (Laver and Schofield, 1990). Early models were based upon the assumption that control over government was some sort of fixed prize to be shared by a winning coalition of legislators. A consequence of this assumption was the prediction that the cabinet would have as few parties as possible while still controlling a legislative majority (Gamson, 1961; Leiserson, 1966; Riker, 1962). The larger the number of actors involved in the government – and parties were seen as unitary actors – the smaller the share of the prize available to each. The nature of this prize was often left rather vague but, when made explicit, tended to be described in terms of a particular sack of political trophies, prominent among which were cabinet portfolios. Office-seeking political parties were thus assumed to be motivated to control as many cabinet portfolios as possible. As a result, authors who analyzed the payoffs of coalition bargaining often denominated these payoffs in terms of shares of a fixed set of cabinet portfolios (Browne and Feste, 1975; Browne and Franklin, 1973; Browne and Frendreis, 1980; Budge and Keman, 1990). It was sometimes assumed that, because of their policy interests, different parties might value the same cabinet portfolios in different ways – making portfolio allocation a variable sum game (Browne and Feste, 1975; Budge and Keman, 1990). Nonetheless, all "payoff theorists" treat cabinet membership as something to be consumed in and for itself. In effect, they treat the political game as ending, and the "payoffs" as being distributed, at the moment when legislative parties take control of their share of cabinet portfolios. They do not consider at all what happens in the cabinet after this moment, or how expectations about subsequent cabinet performance influence portfolio distribution in the first place. Specifically, payoff theorists have suppressed altogether the relationship between policy outputs and the allocation of cabinet portfolios.

Another group of theorists writing about the formation of coalition governments effectively ignore the cabinet altogether. They concentrate instead upon the policy position of the government that takes office, however this government might be construed (Baron, 1991; Baron and

4

Ferejohn, 1989; de Swaan, 1973; McKelvey, 1979; McKelvey and Schofield, 1986, 1987; Schofield, 1983, 1993). They, too, treat the political game as ending when the government is invested, assuming in effect that the incoming government takes office and immediately implements everything that it promised during the formation negotiations. In such models, indeed, the political identity of the cabinet is quite irrelevant. The equilibrium processes that are described are assumed to generate the same government policy output, whoever is in the cabinet.

It is only recently that political scientists have taken into account the constitutional relationship between legislature and executive. The behavior of sophisticated legislators is modeled as they calculate whether or not to defeat the incumbent executive and install some alternative (Austen-Smith and Banks 1988, 1990; Laver and Shepsle, 1990a,b; 1991). Whether legislators consciously perform these calculations or not, they must form beliefs about cabinet decision making in different potential executives so that they can forecast what each will do if given the keys to government buildings. This implies that any discussion of governance in parliamentary democracies must incorporate a systematic account of cabinet decision making. Without such an account, it is impossible to model the making and breaking of governments, because it is not possible to specify how legislators envisage the consequences of their actions.

This book is set firmly in this latter tradition. Its central theme is decision making in cabinets, set in the context of the more general political game in a parliamentary democracy. Most of the subsequent chapters are theoretically motivated descriptions of cabinet decision making in particular parliamentary democracies. The remainder of this present chapter sets out some of the main dimensions of this theoretical motivation by sketching a number of alternative models of cabinet decision making.

MODELS OF CABINET DECISION MAKING

Our choice of a model of cabinet decision making depends to a large extent upon the assumptions we make about the ways in which individual cabinet ministers are constrained by key political institutions. The most important of these institutions are: the legislature, the bureaucracy, political parties, and the cabinet itself as a collective entity. Essentially, as both Müller and Strom point out in this volume, different constraints generate different models of cabinet decision making.

Bureaucratic government

The rationale for a model of bureaucratic government depends upon the assumption that the effective power both to make and to implement public policy is located in the permanent civil service. The most typical justification for this assumption is that cabinet ministers are just politicians, more or less amateurs in particular policy fields, who move into and out of their jobs like birds of passage. Senior civil servants, in contrast, are more or less permanent professionals in a given field, with access to a vast pool of specialist expertise. If civil servants have a policy agenda of their own – whether this arises from particular personal tastes, a desire for professional advancement, or even from sincerely held views about what is best for the country – then they are in a very strong position effectively to determine government policy outputs. Strom, in his chapter, associates this model of bureaucratic government with Niskanen (1971). It is caricatured in the British "Yes, Minister" television series, in which the sophisticated and devious civil "servant" always gets the better of his amateurish and inept political "master." A key implication of the model is that the partisan composition of neither legislature nor executive has any real impact on public policy. In order to forecast government policy outputs, we simply need to know about the civil service.

Legislative government

If the executive is assumed to be constrained by the legislature rather than by the bureaucracy, then this assumption underpins a model of "legislative government." Under this assumption, all policy would be decided by the legislature, and the role of the cabinet would be that of mechanical implementation. We are aware of no substantive specialist in parliamentary democracy who has promoted this model. It is, as we have indicated, a model that implicitly underlies a number of formal approaches to government formation, emphasizing a policy equilibrium that is independent of cabinet composition.

If we assume that neither the bureaucracy nor the legislature determine government policy on their own, then we may assume that the executive itself plays a key political role. Four distinctive models of executive decision making, summarized by Muller in the following chapter, differ according to whether individual cabinet ministers are assumed to be constrained by the prime minister, their party organization, the cabinet as a collective entity, or none of these. The different assumptions generate models, respectively, of "prime-ministerial," "party," "cabinet," and "ministerial" government.

Prime-ministerial government

A model that Müller associates with Crossman (1963, 1972) involves a powerful collective executive dominated by a powerful prime minister.

External factors may impinge upon the cabinet to enhance prime-ministerial power. Such factors reflect the following considerations:

- Many constitutions designate the rights and duties of the prime minister in a far more extensive and explicit way than those of other ministers.
- Most government formation procedures designate a *formateur* or potential prime minister who first fulfils some investiture requirement and then presents a slate of ministers to the legislature.
- Most prime ministers have the subsequent formal power to hire and fire government ministers at will, subject only to the ultimate need to maintain the confidence of the legislature.
- The electoral role of a prime minister is becoming ever more important in what are increasingly treated by the media as "beauty contests" between leaders of the government and opposition.

Party government

In this model, associated with Rose (1976), a powerful executive consists of members who are subject to the discipline of well-organized political parties. Thus, although the legislature as a whole cannot tell the executive what to do, the caucuses of those parties who are in government can effectively impose policy upon "their" ministers. The most striking examples of the role of party caucuses in government can be seen in countries such as Britain that have a tradition of one-party government. The recent policy shifts by the British government on European monetary union, and the associated replacement of Prime Minister Margaret Thatcher by John Major, were all products of internal Conservative Party politics, subsequently imposed upon the entire British political system by virtue of one-party control of the cabinet. In such circumstances it becomes as difficult as it is unnecessary to determine whether it is the party or the cabinet that is deciding matters of policy. This highlights an important distinction between one-party cabinets that control a legislative majority on the one hand and coalitions or minority cabinets on the other. For one-party majority cabinets, internal party politics and cabinet decision making are intimately intertwined, and it is impossible to say where one begins and the other ends. When no party controls a legislative majority, internal party politics and cabinet decision making are quite distinct activities, the one often imposing itself on the other.

Cabinet government

A model Müller associates with Mackintosh (1969) implies a powerful executive that takes collective decisions binding all members. The prime minister may range from primus to inter pares, and individual ministers, while typically party members, are not effectively constrained by party caucuses. Many Western liberal democracies have constitutional doctrines of collective cabinet *responsibility*. Though it by no means automatically follows in principle, this is often taken to imply that cabinet *decision making* is also a collective activity. In practice, the doctrine of collective cabinet responsibility does indeed make it very difficult for political scientists to study the ways in which "collective" cabinet decisions are actually made. This is because the doctrine cloaks cabinet disagreements in a veil of secrecy, a matter that many of our country specialists will address.

Ministerial government

Ministerial government – a model related to the basic theoretical concerns that have inspired this book – implies a powerful executive in which individual ministers, by virtue of their positions as the political heads of the major departments of state, are able to have a significant impact on policy in areas that fall under their jurisdiction. This entails a division- and specialization-of-labor arrangement in which effective policy of any government depends upon the allocation of cabinet portfolios between politicians. A different allocation implies a different policy profile for the cabinet, and changes in portfolio allocations signal changes in government policy. Thus, a hard-line defense policy can be signaled by nominating a well-known hawk as defense minister. A credible policy shift to a softer line, it is assumed, involves changing the minister of defense. Knowing the policy preferences of cabinet ministers, and the process of interaction among them, it should be possible to forecast the policy outputs that will emerge from a particular cabinet once it has taken office.

MODELS OF CABINET GOVERNMENT: THREE KEY QUESTIONS

The choice between different models of cabinet decision making effectively turns upon the assumptions we make about the constraints upon individual cabinet ministers. Given the nature of the job of cabinet minister, these constraints can be difficult to determine directly. However, we can ask three key questions about cabinet decision making in a particular country, the answers to which give us strong hints about the most appropriate model of cabinet decision making. These questions are:

1. Is government policy affected by the partisan composition of the cabinet?
2. Is government policy affected by the allocation of cabinet portfolios between parties?
3. Is government policy affected by the allocation of cabinet portfolios within parties?

If the answer to the first question is "No, the partisan composition of the cabinet makes no difference to government policy," then the cabinet has no effective role in policy-making. This in turn may imply a model of bureaucratic or legislative government. Policy-making is dominated either by the civil service, which gets its way whoever the ministers are, or by the balance of forces in the legislature, which effectively imposes policy decisions on the cabinet. If the answer to the first question is "Yes," on the other hand, then the cabinet does make a difference.

If the cabinet does make a difference and the answer to the second question is "No, the allocation of portfolios between parties makes no difference to government policy," then this implies a model of cabinet or prime-ministerial government. Either cabinet policy-making is based on binding collective decisions, merely implemented at departmental level by individual cabinet ministers, or it is dominated by a single powerful actor in the cabinet, most likely the prime minister. If the answer to the second question is "Yes, it does make a difference which party gets which portfolios," then this implies a model of party or ministerial government. Either way, cabinet ministers make a difference. When there is party government, ministers act as agents of their party. When there is ministerial government, they need not.

The answer to the third question tells us something about the internal politics of the parties of government. If the answer is "No, the allocation of portfolios within parties does not make a difference," then this implies that parties are functioning as if they are unitary actors. To cast the argument in terms of individual decision makers, it implies that politicians are functioning as perfect agents of their party. If the answer is "Yes, the allocation of portfolios within parties does make a difference," then this implies that parties are not functioning as unitary actors. In this instance we need to look at politics within parties in order to understand cabinet decision making.

Much of the material in the chapters that follow addresses these questions. The general conclusions are rather consistent. There is no support whatsoever among our country specialists for the idea that partisan membership of the cabinet makes no difference to government policy. This implies no support for unreconstructed models of bureaucratic or legislative government.

Most authors discuss ways in which the prime minister can be powerful, and in which collective cabinet decisions are important, but most conclude that the allocation of portfolios between parties is important. This implies a qualified rejection of unreconstructed models of prime ministerial or cabinet government.

Most authors admit that the allocation of portfolios within parties can make a difference in certain special circumstances, but conclude on balance that it does not make a systematic difference. This implies a rejection of models that force a consideration of the effects of different policy positions within parties.

The net result – and this is a sweeping summary of some rich and complex arguments in the country chapters – is that portfolio allocation does make a difference between, but not within, parties. We return in more detail to this matter in the concluding chapter.

In qualification, however, it is worth alerting the reader at this stage to a general caveat offered by many of the authors. This is that there are not many cabinet ministers who are Tony King's "big beasts of the jungle" – fully autonomous decision makers ready and able to take decisions in defiance of all and sundry, including their party colleagues. Rather, ministers seem to operate within ministries as agents of their parties, with the job, more or less, of promoting party policy as far as they can in their particular niche of the government. This argument, as we shall see in the Conclusion, has far-reaching implications for how we might model cabinet decision making.

PLAN OF CAMPAIGN

The following chapters have been written by country specialists and deal with cabinet decision making in a series of parliamentary democracies. Some of these typically have one-party majority governments: Britain, Canada, Greece, and New Zealand. As we have just noted, in these countries the politics of cabinet decision making and the politics of intraparty decision making become intertwined in a complex web, and it is almost impossible to disentangle the two. The other countries covered have coalition cabinets, at least some of the time: Austria, Belgium, Finland, France, Germany, Ireland, Italy, the Netherlands, Norway, and Sweden. In these countries, the distinction between politics within parties and politics between parties is, analytically at least, much more distinct.

The original drafts of the chapters were presented and discussed at a workshop directed by the editors as part of the 1992 Joint Sessions of the European Consortium for Political Research, held in Limerick. In advance of these meetings the editors circulated theoretical arguments about portfolio allocation to the authors and asked each to complete a questionnaire on the relevance of these matters in his or her respective country. Each author was given an informal summary of the questionnaire responses and was asked to write a paper on cabinet decision making in his or her country, structured in terms of these issues.

The final chapter draws together some of the threads running through the country chapters, and attempts to lay some of the groundwork for a richer and more systematic theoretical treatment of cabinet government in parliamentary democracies. It also summarizes the authors' judgments on the main issues. These summaries are based in part on the chapters themselves, and in part on the results of the questionnaire. This enables us to give comprehensive coverage to themes – such as the role of caretaker cabinets or procedures for votes of confidence – that are very much neglected in the mainstream political science literature.

REFERENCES

Austen-Smith, David, and Jeffrey Banks. 1988. Elections, coalitions and legislative outcomes. *American Political Science Review*. 82: 405–22.
1990. Stable portfolio allocations. *American Political Science Review* 84: 891–906.
Bagehot, Walter. 1963. *The English Constitution*. London: Fontana.
Baron, David. 1991. A spatial bargaining theory of government formation in parliamentary systems. *American Political Science Review* 85: 137–65.
Baron, David, and John Ferejohn. 1989. Bargaining in legislatures. *American Political Science Review* 83: 1181–1206.
Browne, Eric, and Karen Feste. 1975. Qualitative dimensions of coalition payoffs: evidence for European party governments, 1945–70. *American Behavioral Scientist* 18: 530–56.
Browne, Eric, and Mark Franklin. 1973. Aspects of coalition payoffs in European parliamentary democracies. *American Political Science Review* 67: 453–69.
Browne, Eric, and John Frendreis. 1980. Allocating coalition payoffs by conventional norm: an assessment of the evidence for cabinet coalition situations. *American Journal of Political Science* 24: 753–68.
Budge, Ian, and Hans Keman. 1990. *Parties and Democracy: Coalition Formation and Functioning in Twenty States*. Oxford University Press.
Crossman, Richard. 1963. Introduction. In Walter Bagehot, *The English Constitution*. Glasgow: Collins.
1972. *The Myths of Cabinet Government*. Cambridge, Mass.: Harvard University Press.
de Swaan, Abram. 1973. *Coalition Theories and Cabinet Formation*. Amsterdam: Elsevier.
Gamson, William. 1961. A theory of coalition formation. *American Sociological Review* 26: 373–82.
Laver, Michael, and Norman Schofield. 1990. *Multiparty Government: the Politics of Coalition in Europe*. Oxford University Press.
Laver, Michael, and Kenneth Shepsle. 1990a. Coalitions and cabinet government *American Political Science Review* 84: 873–90.
1990b. Government coalitions and intraparty politics. *British Journal of Political Science* 20: 489–507.
1991. Divided government: America is not "exceptional." *Governance* 4: 250–69.
Leiserson, Michael. 1966. *Coalitions in Politics*. Ph.D. Yale University.
Mackintosh, John. 1969. A rejoinder. In Anthony King (ed.), *The British Prime Minister*. London: Macmillan Press.
McKelvey, R. D. 1979. General conditions for global intransitivities in formal voting models. *Econometrica* 47: 1085–1111.

McKelvey, R. D., and Norman Schofield. 1986. Structural instability of the core. *Journal of Mathematical Economics* 15: 179–98.

1987. Generalised symmetry conditions at a core point. *Econometrica* 55: 923–33.

Niskanen, William. 1971. *Bureaucracy and Representative Government*. Chicago: Aldine-Atherton.

Riker, William. 1962. *The Theory of Political Coalitions*. New Haven, Conn.: Yale University Press.

Rose, Richard. 1976. *The Problem of Party Government*. Harmondsworth: Penguin.

Schofield, Norman. 1983. Generic instability of majority rule. *Review of Economic Studies* 50: 696–705.

Schofield, Norman. 1993. Political competition and multiparty coalition governments. *European Journal for Political Research* 23: 1–33.

Part II

COALITION SYSTEMS

2

Models of government and the Austrian cabinet

Wolfgang C. Müller

INTRODUCTION

The aim of this paper is to explore the usefulness of a number of models of cabinet decision making with reference to Austrian cabinet behavior since 1945. The following models will be examined: cabinet government, prime-ministerial government, and party government. The bulk of the empirical evidence used stems from interviews with forty-four ex–cabinet ministers who served between 1959 and 1991.[1]

Austria has experienced various types of government since 1945. After an initial all-party government (1945–7),[2] a grand-coalition government between the People's Party (Osterreichische Volkspartei, OVP) and the Socialists (Sozialistische Partei Osterreichs, SPO) was established and was maintained until 1966. In that year, the OVP won an absolute majority of seats and eventually formed a single-party government led by Josef Klaus. In 1970 the SPO under Bruno Kreisky won a plurality of seats and formed a single-party government that was tacitly supported by the Freedom Party (Freiheitliche Partei Osterreichs, FPO). The SPO single-party government continued after the party won an absolute majority in 1971, which it successfully defended in 1975 and 1979. In 1983, the SPO fell short of an absolute majority and formed a coalition with the FPO that lasted until 1986. In 1987, Austria returned to grand-coalition government, this time led by the SPO and Chancellor Franz Vranitzky. The same arrangement was continued after the 1990 elections.

Predictably, each cabinet developed its own style of internal behavior. However, the greatest determinant of these different styles was the type of government composition. Moreover, the greatest distinction was between grand coalitions on one hand and single-party governments on the other. Accordingly, the main aim of this paper will be to examine cabinet behavior and the fit of the models investigated in these two types of government.

15

CABINET GOVERNMENT

Mackintosh (1969: 162) has probably provided the best definition of classical cabinet government:

> At a time when the area of government activity and therefore the civil service was small, these men (i.e., the cabinet members) could supervise and frame the entire policy of their departments and all important decisions were taken to and in the Cabinet. Thus the Cabinet collectively decided policy, defended it in the House and saw to its execution in practice. This was Cabinet Government, the forces were so balanced that while each Prime Minister's degree of authority varied a little, holders of the office could be described as primus inter pares.

Thus classical cabinet government was characterized internally by collective deliberation followed by collective decision making on the government's policy. The prime minister was a chairman rather than a chief (cf. Farrell, 1971); a primus, but still inter pares. Externally, the cabinet was dominant in its relations with the state apparatus and other political actors.

Although numerous writers in the 1960s and early 1970s claimed the continuation of more or less classical cabinet government in the United Kingdom, most subsequent observers seem to agree that it is a phenomenon of the past. This is not to say, however, that the cabinet has been reduced to a purely formal institution that only ratifies decisions made elsewhere. A number of authors have identified important issues that are still decided by the cabinet in a substantive way, and have stressed the role of the cabinet "as court of appeal for *both* ministers radically out of sympathy with a general line, *and* for a premier confronted by a ministerial colleague who insists on ploughing her or his furrow" (Dunleavy and Rhodes, 1990:11). If a cabinet deliberates, decides important issues and also functions as court of appeal, then we can speak of postclassical cabinet government.

The Austrian constitution subscribes to the principle of cabinet government. Politically, the most important government decisions have to be made by the cabinet. They include agreeing on government bills; approving reports to be sent to Parliament; issuing proposals that the federal president act in a specific matter; passing what amounts to a suspensive veto against *Land* parliament laws that the government deems to exceed or contradict the relevant *Landtag*'s powers; formally bringing matters before the federal constitutional court; passing all decrees issued in accordance with the emergency powers law; and calling elections, supervising their conduct, and calling the two houses of Parliament into session. All cabinet decisions have to be made unanimously; thus, each minister has absolute veto power.[3]

Table 2.1. *The political relevance of cabinet meetings*

Question: Were cabinet meetings (including preparatory meetings in single-party governments) the place in which important issues were discussed in detail?		
Type of government	Yes	No
Grand coalition (N = 14)	7%	93%
Single party (N = 25)	64%	36%

My interviews with ex–cabinet ministers included questions on the political relevance of cabinet meetings and their individual role in cabinet decision making. The results are presented in Tables 2.1 and 2.2.

According to Table 2.1, grand-coalition government fulfills neither the conditions of classical nor postclassical cabinet government. The cabinet meeting is reduced to a ritual. Matters on which the parties had agreed beforehand may be formally decided; the parties' opposing standpoints may be briefly repeated without trying to solve the problem in the meeting; or the controversial issue may be postponed to another cabinet meeting without any discussion. Substantive discussions and negotiations are conducted elsewhere. They may take place in bilateral talks between the minister sponsoring the cabinet proposal and the representative of the coalition partner in the respective policy field, who may be another minister, an MP, or the party's spokesperson. Whereas this is the lowest level of achieving interparty consensus, the "coalition committee" is the intermediate one. It is composed of a small number of high-ranking politicians from both parties, some of whom hold important cabinet positions; others are represented because of their parliamentary and party positions. If no consensus can be achieved at either of these levels, the matter is transferred to the top – to the chancellor and vice-chancellor. They normally do not engage in detailed discussions over the subject matter but try to overcome the political difficulties and then leave it to lower functionaries to conduct the detailed discussions and negotiations.

Although the answers of ministers who served in grand-coalition governments were remarkably consistent, those of ministers in single-party governments were not. One possible explanation for the differences is that single-party governments of the SPO behaved differently from that of the OVP. Whereas only four of sixteen SPO ministers denied that cabinet meetings were the place where important issues were discussed in detail, five out of nine OVP ministers did so. Moreover, all four SPO ministers referred to the last years of the SPO single-party government. At that time, Chancellor Kreisky's dominance and his illness had already transformed the character of the cabinet meetings. They had been reduced in length and

Table 2.2. *The cabinet ministers' role in cabinet decision making*

Question: How did you conduct yourself at cabinet meetings? Did you limit your contribution to matters concerning your own department, or did you also actively participate in matters that related solely to other departments?

Type of government	Limit contribution to own department	Participate in matters related to other departments
Grand coalition (N = 12)	75%	25%
Single party (N = 27)	81%	19%

increasingly became a Kreisky monologue rather than a debate between the cabinet members. In the case of the OVP, the different opinions about the relevance of cabinet meetings can to a large extent be attributed to the individual perspectives of the interviewees. In particular, those who had also participated in the narrower circles of cabinet decision making denied that detailed discussions were held in cabinet meetings. Overall, therefore, there is much more support for the cabinet government model in single-party governments than in grand-coalition governments.

Table 2.2 reveals remarkable congruence between grand-coalition and single-party governments. The overwhelming majority of cabinet ministers limited their contribution in cabinet meetings to their own department. Most of them in the interviews referred to an "unwritten rule" to restrict oneself to one's own department, or hinted at the reciprocity of such behavior ("I would not have liked it either if another minister had interfered in the affairs of my department"). The remaining one-fifth or one-fourth of cabinet ministers who reported their participation in matters related to other departments, were to a large extent "central people" – cabinet members who occupied high party office and/or central cabinet positions, in particular the minister of finance. A few more ministers mentioned their participation in "general political discussions," mainly concerning broad lines of government policy and party strategy, but not directly related to particular departments. Thus, according to Table 2.2, collective deliberation and decision making do not characterize the bulk of decisions by the Austrian cabinet. Only a few cabinet members act in a nondepartmental manner.

This is not to say, however, that cabinet decision making is totally dispersed. First, since many cabinet proposals affect departments other than the sponsoring one, these other ministers also exercise their departmental role by participating in decision making, watching over the interests of their departments (but not interfering beyond that point). Second, the exchange of papers before the cabinet meeting, as well as the meeting itself, is an essential way for cabinet members to inform their colleagues about their policies. In single-party governments, where the cabinet members tend to have similar political ideas, this has some coordinating effect. Third, in single-party governments there is some collective deliberation about general political issues or, in a more restricted core group, about some of the more important departmental policies. In the SPO government these deliberations were used to communicate the chancellor's general policy to the cabinet members without issuing formal directives. Though substantive decision making in the cabinet meeting itself occurred only rarely, the chancellor's and the other cabinet members' reactions to proposed policies were very important for the policies that were eventually implemented.

The second feature of postclassical cabinet government, the cabinet as a court of appeal, found little support in my interviews. Although the cabinet has occasionally had this role, normally the chancellor or, in coalition governments, the chancellor and vice-chancellor together have exercised this role.

In concluding this section, it can be said that there is almost no evidence for the cabinet-government model in grand-coalition governments; single-party governments, however, come close to a weak version of postclassical cabinet government.

PRIME-MINISTERIAL GOVERNMENT

According to a number of writers, cabinet government has been transformed into prime-ministerial government (Crossman, 1963, 1972). In this model, collective deliberation and effective decision making in the cabinet are replaced by monocratic decision making by the prime minister, whereas the external capacities of government remain high. Dunleavy and Rhodes have identified three different modes of prime-ministerial government: (1) a generalized ability of the prime minister to decide policy in all issue areas in which he or she takes an interest; (2) the ability of the prime minister to decide key issues that subsequently determine most remaining areas of government policy; and (3) the ability of the prime minister to define "a governing ethos, 'atmosphere' or operating ideology which generates predictable and determinate solutions to most policy problems, and hence so constrains other ministers' freedom of manoeuvre as to make them simple agents of the premier's will" (Dunleavy and Rhodes, 1990: 8).

As we have seen, the Austrian constitution has adopted the principle of cabinet government. However, it also contains some provisions that hint at the possibility of prime-ministerial government (Gerlich, Müller, and Philipp, 1988; Welan and Neisser, 1971). First, the federal chancellor

(Bundeskanzler) is the chairman of the cabinet and the coordinator of its work (Article 69). This clause, however, legally makes the prime minister only the first among equals, chairing cabinet meetings but not entitled to issue orders to cabinet ministers. Second, the federal chancellor differs from cabinet colleagues in having a unique capacity to control the composition of the cabinet. It is the federal chancellor who makes proposals for appointment and dismissal of cabinet ministers to the federal president. Third, the chancellor controls the civil servants' promotions and the government's constitutional law branch that gives expert opinons on the constitutionality of legislative proposals. Moreover, the prime minister's office provides the best access to the mass media. Fourth, the chancellor's power is influenced by party political factors. As the party chairman[4] he or she certainly enjoys power in cabinet decision making that goes beyond what the constitution and the distribution of bureaucratic resources would grant. At the same time, however, party politics limit the constitutional power of the chancellor to control cabinet composition (Müller, 1991a: 121). In coalition governments the formal power of the chancellor to nominate cabinet members is de facto split between him and the vice-chancellor, with both being in charge of those cabinet positions allocated to their respective party in the coalition negotiations. In the selection and, in particular, deselection of cabinet members of their respective party, the chancellor and the vice-chancellor are limited in their discretionary power by the rules or conventions of intraparty decision making. According to these, the party executives at least formally make these nominations; moreover certain cabinet positions have to be filled with representatives of specific intra-party groups.[5] The intraparty power of the chancellor and the vice-chancellor, of course, varies. It is greater in the more centralized and disciplined SPO than in the more factionalized OVP, and in both parties it is increased by electoral success.

Because of these party political factors nobody would expect a pure form of prime-ministerial government in coalition cabinets. If prime-ministerial government exists, it has to be conceptualized as a kind of dual leadership, with the chancellor and the vice-chancellor exercising the leadership role vis-à-vis the members of their respective parties as far as possible, and exercising the role together where the consensus of the coalition partners is required.

Although virtually every minister was ready to certify that the chancellor, and in coalition governments the vice-chancellor, were important for cabinet work in general, Table 2.3 contains the answers to a question that should allow us to get at the core of the prime-ministerial government concept, namely the chancellor's (and vice-chancellor's) impact on government departments.

According to Table 2.3, the people at the top of government were very

Table 2.3. *Significance of the federal chancellor (or vice-chancellor) for decisions relating to individual ministers' departments*

Question: How important was the federal chancellor (or vice-chancellor) in determining matters related to your department?

Type of government	Very important	Not very important
Grand coalition (N = 10)	60%	40%
Single party (N = 26)	85%	15%

important in the departmental affairs of most ministers. The chancellor in single-party cabinets had a greater impact on the individual government departments than the combination of chancellor and vice-chancellor in coalition cabinets. This is not necessarily what one would expect, since in grand-coalition governments, the same number of ministers is almost equally divided between two parties, increasing the chancellor's and vice-chancellor's capacity to control the activities of their respective party's ministers. However, decision making in coalition governments is more complex. The need to achieve a consensus with the coalition partner seems to leave less room for leadership by the chancellor or vice-chancellor. If they exercise influence on departmental matters it is often in their role as crisis managers of the coalition.

Can we, on the basis of Table 2.3, classify the Austrian cabinet, during the period of single-party executives, as operating under a form of prime-ministerial government? Before answering this, an important qualification concerning the information contained in Table 2.3 needs to be made. Almost every minister who defined the chancellor or vice-chancellor as having been very important for his or her departmental matters added that this was restricted to a small number of cases, which, however, usually were seen as very important. Having said this, which of the three modes of prime-ministerial government identified above might be relevant in Austria?

The essence of the first version of prime-ministerial government is a generalized ability of the chancellor to decide policy across all issue areas in which he takes an interest. Obviously, there are limits to what a single person who is otherwise heavily burdened can do. Nevertheless, most cabinet ministers give prior notice to the chancellor (or vice-chancellor) about those departmental policies that they consider might be politically "hot" and/or that will require political backing, for example to convince the minister of finance or a coalition partner. The chancellor (or vice-chancellor) in these cases may approve the minister's plans as they are, or may recommend modification (or even cancellation). The suggestions of

21

the chancellor (or vice-chancellor) in these important matters are as a rule accepted by the ministers. The chancellor (or vice-chancellor) may also invite ministers individually to report on a more or less regular basis about their departmental activities. In this respect, chancellors and vice-chancellors have varied substantially in their level of activity. Klaus and Vranitzky, for instance, applied a systematic style, whereas Kreisky was less systematic but probably more insistent on those issues which attracted his attention.

To summarize this discussion, it can be said that the chancellor in single-party governments approves most important departmental policies. In coalition governments, the chancellor and the vice-chancellor do this for their own ministers, and may also act as interparty negotiators of departmental policies if a consensus cannot be found at a lower level. Although all this hints toward prime-ministerial government, there are also important limitations. Even the major departmental policies are not initiated by the chancellor (or vice-chancellor), nor are they selected by them from a number of alternatives provided by the ministers. Moreover, the usual pattern is one of approval rather than of change of the ministers' proposed policies, and there are almost no examples of rejections. Thus, one might speak of "negative prime-ministerial government" in which the chancellor (or vice-chancellor) makes sure that policies across all issue areas under the jurisdiction of his party do not violate general party policy, or endanger party strategy.

In the second version of prime-ministerial government, control is achieved by the chancellor (and/or vice-chancellor) by deciding on key issues that subsequently determine most remaining areas of government policy. There have been few issues of such importance, but examples can be found. They include Kreisky's policy to combat unemployment in the 1970s, and the incumbent grand coalition's decisions to reduce the budget deficit substantially over a number of years and to apply for European Community (EC) membership. These issues certainly have set the agenda to a large extent for most government departments. However, without denying that Kreisky, Vranitzky, and Mock played key roles in initiating and making these decisions, the choices cannot be attributed to them alone. Rather, they were decisions made within narrow leadership circles of the respective parties and in negotiations between the coalition partners.

Finally, what is the evidence for the "ideological-authority version" of prime-ministerial government, in which the chancellor defines general principles that generate predictable and determinate solutions to most policy problems? To some extent the examples just cited can also be seen as implying a certain ideological authority for the prime minister. In addition, Chancellor Klaus in his single-party cabinet wanted to introduce a "style of pertinence" in which "emotions, opportunism and solutions for the day" were to be replaced by "pertinence, systematic and lasting solutions" (Pelinka and Welan, 1971: 331). This attempt was soon frustrated by the practice of the factionalized OVP government. It is also necessary to point out the limits of the more successful ideologies. The incumbent government's decision that in principle government spending has to be reduced, does not prevent cabinet members in practice from seeing their particular department as an exception that requires more and not fewer financial resources, as annual fights over the budget demonstrate. In contrast, Kreisky's ideology of fighting unemployment by massive deficit spending did not cause such uncomfortable consequences for the individual departments. For a number of years almost everything that could be argued to preserve or create jobs was financed. This could then be seen as a very successful ideology, though it may not constitute a hard test for the ideological-authority version of prime-ministerial government.

PARTY GOVERNMENT

The party government model focuses on the accountability of government (Kelsen, 1929: 19–20). According to Richard Rose (1976: 371),

Party government exists only in so far as the actions of office-holders are influenced by values and policies derived from the party. Where the life of party politics does not affect government policy, the accession of a new party to office is little more significant than the accession of a new monarch; the party reigns but does not rule.

Richard S. Katz (1986: 45) distinguishes between the *partyness of government*, meaning "a narrow institutional sense of party government as party control of the formal government apparatus," and *party governmentness*, which refers to "a broader sense of party government as a general social characteristic." Of the two, we will be concerned mainly with the former. The key question is thus to what extent political parties can control cabinet behavior. Although the parties' abilities to exercise this control will be influenced by many factors, three seem to be of particular importance. They are: (1) party programs; (2) the selection of cabinet members; and (3) control of cabinet members by the party.

Party control of the cabinet will be enhanced in situations where party programs not only clearly state the intentions of the party, but also specify appropriate means to the desired ends. In such circumstances, ministers will for their part have clear targets, whereas the party itself will have a yardstick for measurement of the performance of its cabinet personnel.

Party control of the cabinet will be enhanced where cabinet ministers have internalized, and acted upon, party values. A minister who acts as a party representative, who gives priority to party goals in making departmental and cabinet decisions, can be expected to implement existing party programs. Where relevant party programmatic commitments are lacking, he would be expected to act in accordance with what he might reasonably assume the party's position to be. The extent to which a minister's internalization of party values leads to party influence over the actual behavior of the cabinet and of the department concerned will of course depend upon the minister's political skill. His ability to control his department is a necessary precondition for party government, because otherwise the best intentions may lead to nothing, and the bureaucracy's conventional wisdoms will prevail over party goals.

However, the most crucial requirement for party government is secure control of cabinet members by the party. The mere existence of explicit and implementation-oriented party programs does not of itself guarantee that cabinet members are willing or able to put them into practice. Similarly, although the fact that a minister holds high party office may well increase the likelihood that he or she knows what the party wants, and even shares that desire, it does not guarantee the implementation of party policies. The most important means of achieving party government seems to be the maintenance of permanent control of the minister by the party. The more ambiguous a party's program and the less a party's governmental team is composed of high-ranking party functionaries, the more important such control is.

The Austrian constitution of 1920 (as amended in 1929 and still valid today, albeit in amended form) mentions political parties only briefly, and mainly in a negative sense – by excluding their functionaries and employees from being members of the constitutional court. Since 1945, however, the official constitutional doctrine as elaborated by academic lawyers and upheld by the courts has been that, though the constitution had not prescribed the role of political parties, it had proceeded from the assumption that parties exist and are essential for the functioning of the constitutional system. In 1975, a new party law was passed that contained a constitutional clause stating that the existence and the variety *(Vielfalt)* of political parties compose major elements of the democratic order of the Republic of Austria. This law states that the function of political parties includes participation in the development of the public's political will *(Willensbildung)*. Although it can be argued that these constitutional provisions provide a legitimation of party government, MPs are constitutionally not bound by a mandate from any individual or group, including their political party. Similarly, the constitutional position means that cabinet ministers' individual responsibility can also not be restricted by reference, for example, to party policy.

Party programs

Unfortunately, there is little systematic research on the practical relevance of party programs, though the limited evidence available suggests that party programs do not greatly determine the actual behavior of their parties when in government (Hroch, 1983). In general, opposition parties tend to have more detailed programs than governing parties. The latter's programs often amount to little more than stressing the importance of continuing the government's allegedly successful policy and are rarely very detailed about specific issues and measures. For their part, opposition parties often produce voluminous programs, as was the case with the SPO between 1966 and 1970, and with the OVP at each election since 1970. However, even when these two parties returned to government, the extent to which their respective policies were determined by their official party program seems to have been relatively low.

Selection of cabinet members

Between 1945 and 1987, an average of 42 percent of cabinet members (including secretaries of state) were or had been members of the executive body of their respective party. However, the individual parties practiced very different recruitment policies. During the first period of grand-coalition government, the SPO clearly had a much higher proportion of cabinet members with a "strong" party background than did the OVP. Similarly, during the SPO single-party governments of 1970–83, 43 percent of cabinet members had been elected to the party executive before their first cabinet appointment, whereas the figure for the single-party OVP government of 1966–70 was a mere 23 percent (Müller and Philipp, 1987: 285–6). Thus, one can conclude that "partyness" had a higher priority in the recruitment of cabinet members for the SPO than for the OVP. On that basis, a higher degree of party "governmentness" can be ascribed to the SPO's government-selection process and thus expected of the behavior of its government team.

The second characteristic that we stated that cabinet members ought to display in order for their government to rank highly in terms of "partyness" related to ministers' political skills. The preministerial careers of 72 percent of all Austrian cabinet members appointed between 1945 and 1990 included experience in directing large organizations, including businesses, branches of the state bureaucracy, quasi-governmental agencies, and trade unions. Accordingly, it could be argued that nearly three-quarters of all postwar Austrian ministers can be expected to have possessed the skills necessary to ensure that they controlled their respective government and were less susceptible to being "captured" by their civil servants (Müller, Philipp, and Steininger, 1987: 158–60).

Permanent control

One necessary precondition for permanent control of government through the party is the existence of party structures that can exercise such control. The job of cabinet members is full-time and requires them to be involved in a wide range of very complex subjects. Effective and ongoing party control would thus require the party to possess appropriately extensive and specialized structures and resources to provide it with the capacity to cope with the complex subject matter dealt with by its ministers, and thus to monitor cabinet behavior. All parties have committees that specialize in specific policy fields and that in part correspond to the remit of government departments. However, they lack permanent staffing and almost all of them are chaired by the respective cabinet minister (should the party happen to occupy the relevant position). Moreover, these committees by and large interpret their role as relating to the long-term development of party policy in their specific policy area. In short, they are primarily party oriented, as opposed to government oriented. Accordingly, they can hardly be regarded as instruments for providing the executive bodies of the parties with detailed information about the "partyness" of its ministers' record in office, let alone for holding the government minister to account.

Though party executives thus lack systematic reports about the purely party-related performance of their cabinet team, they do have other, more limited, sources of information at their disposal. They can evaluate their ministers' performance by reference to ad hoc information derived, for example, from the media or party loyalists within the state bureaucracy, as well as on the basis of party briefings prepared by the cabinet members themselves. The latter as a rule attend party executive meetings, whether or not they are elected members of these bodies. The number of party executive meetings has varied over time. In the SPO it declined after the party reform of 1967. Since then, the meetings are quite infrequent, with the full party executive *(Bundesparteivorstand)* meeting less than once a month and the smaller party presidium *(Bundesparteipräsidium)* meeting not more than once a month. The analogous meetings in the OVP are even less frequent: in 1989 there were in total no more than ten meetings of all three of its leadership bodies (Müller, 1991b: 231). The relative infrequency of party executive meetings suggests that these bodies could hardly be expected to exercise much control over the daily work of cabinet members, especially since those meetings are also (and often predominantly) concerned with purely party-related rather than government-

Table 2.4. *Frequency of ministers' reports to their party executive*

Question: How frequently did you report to your party executive on your work in the government?

Party	Frequently	Seldom/never
SPO (N = 19)	0%	100%
OVP (N = 10)	30%	70%

Table 2.5. *Party control of cabinet ministers*

Question: Did you ever receive, in your capacity as a government minister, directions from your party executive?

Party	Yes	No
SPO (N = 21)	0%	100%
OVP (N = 13)	38%	62%

related matters. Notwithstanding this caveat, it must be acknowledged that the party executives have at their disposal within the party a degree of policy-related capacity and a level of information on the activities of their ministers sufficient to enable them to deal effectively with strategically important issues concerning the direction of policy in their ministers' brief. Even at once a month or less, the party executives as a rule meet sufficiently often to enable them to give their cabinet ministers clear directives in such cases.

According to Table 2.4, however, the overwhelming majority of ministers rarely report to their party executive at all ("seldomly" means once a year or slightly more often). Some of these rare occasions occur at the initiative of the ministers who want to brief their party about important and/or politically "hot" issues, whereas in the other cases questions from party executive members provoked the ministers' statements. The three OVP ministers who reported their frequent involvement in discussions at the party executive level in their capacity as cabinet members either occupied central departments that allowed them to speak about government policy *tout court*, or frequently were not in line with their party. Ministers who commented on the infrequency of their reporting to the party executive stressed that none of the members of this body would be interested in routine departmental decisions. In any case the ministers seem to have applied a rather strict definition of what were important departmental matters worth reporting to the party executive.

Table 2.5 contains the answers of former ministers to the question,

"Did you ever receive, in your capacity as a government minister, directions from your party executive?" There is no evidence for party government with respect to the SPO and only little with respect to the OVP. In the latter case the picture becomes even more unambiguous when taking into account that three of the five ministers who received instructions from their party executive did so only once. Thus, permanent control of the cabinet by the party seems not to exist on any relevant scale.

Of the three possibilities by which parties can exercise control over their teams in government, therefore, only the selection of cabinet members seems to lead to a consequential degree of "partyness" of government in the case of the SPO. In the case of the OVP, the "partyness" of the selection process is considerably lower, but this may be compensated by the higher degree of permanent control. Nevertheless, measured against the concept of party government, the overall control of party over government seems to be low. Can we, therefore, conclude that party government hardly exists or is very weak in Austria, a country that probably has the most extensive party organizations of any Western democracy, and where the parties reach further into citizens' lives than in most other West European states?

Before answering this question some of the empirical evidence should be reconsidered. Let us start with the impact of the party executive meeting on the policy of cabinet members. Although it is true that the party body almost never issued directives to the ministers, many of them reported that individual members of the party executive made suggestions or requests concerning their policy or even criticized it. As a result of the heterogeneous party structure, OVP ministers seem generally not to have given much attention to these interventions. In the SPO, however, if they were seen to represent a relevant intraparty constituency, the respective ministers often conceded that the discussions in the party executive increased their sensitivity to an issue, and that they were taken into account in their departmental policy, if possible.

More generally, ministers' party contacts were not restricted to the party executive. Attending the meeting of the party in Parliament, holding functions at lower levels, and participating in party meetings all over the country on a regular basis, provided them with similar reactions to the government's policy from within the party. Since all of the SPO ministers saw it as important to live in harmony with their party, this certainly had an impact on government policy. However, this was not a one-way street. Each SPO minister can rely on being given significant room to maneuver by the party, and can, if he or she is ready to invest sufficient time and energy in intraparty work, carry the party with him or her to a considerable extent. Finally, it is worth mentioning that at the very top there is usually identity between the party and the government. The positions of chancellor and, in coalitions, vice-chancellor, are occupied by the party chairmen. They should know best what the party wants and, seen from the other side, what the party will accept. Thus, what has been discussed under the heading of prime-ministerial government is also relevant in the context of party government.

On the basis of this discussion we may speak of a "weak" version of party government in Austria. This is achieved by the recruitment of many high-ranking party functionaries into the cabinet and by the party's permanent feedback into their policies, rather than by permanent control.

As with the other two models of government already discussed, the party government model is of British origin, meaning that it is based on a two-party system. The party that wins a parliamentary majority takes over governmental power entirely and can implement its program. The translation of intraparty politics into government policies is more complex in coalition governments, because there are at least two government parties with different values and policy proposals. This is particularly relevant in grand-coalition cabinets when both parties are of almost equal size. Although the individual parties can follow the strategies outlined vis-à-vis their own government teams, it is also necessary to achieve a consensus with the coalition partner. This can be done in several ways: (1) by working out a coalition treaty; (2) by interparty negotiations during the government term, for instance within a coalition committee; and (3) by negotiations within the government.

A high degree of party government could be achieved by

- the parties' dominance in negotiations for the coalition treaty (as opposed to that of the governmental teams)
- an important role for the coalition treaty in determining government policies
- and/or frequent interparty negotiations over the government policy during the term of office.

All of the coalitions we have dealt with in this chapter were based on detailed coalition agreements that were negotiated by teams of high-ranking party officials and potential government members. All coalitions had their own forum for permanent interparty negotiations, namely, the coalition committee, which consisted of a small number of high-ranking politicians from both parties, some of whom held important cabinet positions, whereas others were represented because of their parliamentary and party positions. Moreover, the parties decided on the continuation or termination of coalitions. All these factors speak for party government.

It is interesting, however, to compare the old grand coalition (until 1966) with the new one (since 1987) in this respect. Whereas the coalition treaties of the first dealt almost entirely with the division of the spoils and the rules of the game (that is, with the working of the coalition), more than 95 percent of the treaties' contents in the new grand coalitions are devoted to policies (Müller, 1993). Although the extent to which the treaties determined government policies increased in the recent period, the "partyness" of negotiations over the treaty decreased. The most important change, however, concerns interparty negotiations during the term of the government. Not only has the importance of decision making within the coalition committee declined vis-à-vis decision making within the cabinet institutions, but its "partyness" has also declined.

We can conclude this section by stating that the party factor is central for cabinet decision making in coalition governments. Until 1966, the parties exercised their influence in a more direct way than they have since 1987.

CONCLUSION

Our empirical investigation has found that none of the three models of government – cabinet government, prime-ministerial government, or party government – exist in a pure or even almost pure form in postwar Austria. Moreover, the empirical fit of none of the models is so dominant that the Austrian cabinet could best be characterized by making reference to one model exclusively. On the other hand, each of the models helps us to understand certain aspects of cabinet behavior.

The cabinet government model that, even in its postclassical form, is furthest from the actual practice of cabinet work, has not disappeared altogether in Austria. The cabinet in single-party governments has maintained important residual functions as a mechanism of mutual information, sounding out, and coordination. Moreover, although this is mostly (but not necessarily) restricted to the "core people," it is a forum for collective deliberation, thereby de facto preempting later decision making on important issues.

The prime-ministerial government model has a much better empirical fit in Austria. The chancellor (and the vice-chancellor) can normally prevent ministers from making important decisions that would undermine general strategy or damage party fortunes. Moreover, the chancellor's (and vice-chancellor's) intense involvement in major government decisions that subsequently influence departmental decisions increases their impact considerably. Nevertheless, we had to make qualifications to all three versions of the prime-ministerial government model. Its empirical fit varied with government type. The most favorable conditions for prime-ministerial government are single-party government by the SPO with a strong leader.

There is very little evidence to support the party government model in its "hard core" version. This would consist of party programs that are unambiguous and detailed, and that thus provide clear targets for the cabinet members; some party mechanism to measure ministers' performance; the selection of cabinet members who have internalized the values of the party and who are skilled enough to put them into practice; and, most important, permanent control of the cabinet members by the party. However, our discussion has revealed that, besides a more or less party-centered recruitment into the cabinet, only more indirect means exist to ensure that the government teams do not diverge too much from the party. In coalition cabinets, the coalition treaty and the coalition committee are means of direct party influence on the government as a whole. This influence, however, has decreased in recent years.

At the risk of oversimplification, we may conclude our discussion of the three competing models of cabinet behavior by summarizing their respective merits as follows. The party-government model sets the broad framework for cabinet behavior. For each party there is a "policy corridor" within which the actions of its team in government have to remain. Usually this corridor is not precisely defined by party programs or explicit permanent control of the cabinet members by the party. Nevertheless it exists and cannot be strayed from on a permanent basis. The cabinet government model, since it is laid down by the constitution, forces cabinet members to look at least for the lowest common denominator, or may even lead to a collective deliberation and determination of important government policies and strategies. Alternatively (or in addition to this), the policy corridor of the cabinet members is further narrowed by the chancellor (and/or vice-chancellor), as outlined by the prime-ministerial government model. The chancellor (or vice-chancellor) sets important parameters and exercises a sufficient amount of control over departmental policies to ensure that nobody seriously violates the cabinet policy or image desired.

These models constitute the limits of another model, which in quantitative terms must be seen as the dominant one: ministerial government. The bulk of departmental decisions is made by the respective ministers within their jurisdiction without any interference from the cabinet, the chancellor (or vice-chancellor), or the party. Departmental decisions that need the approval of the chancellor (or vice-chancellor) and/or the cabinet, or that get the attention of the party bodies, are usually shaped to a high degree by the individual ministers.

Thus, this evidence supports the portfolio-allocation model of Laver and Shepsle. To begin with, despite a considerable convergence between the major parties during the postwar period, almost nobody would deny that the party composition of cabinet makes a difference to government policies. The portfolio-allocation model proceeds from the assumption that ministers enjoy a high level of autonomy over policy outputs within their jurisdiction. This means that in coalition governments the ministerial autonomy is used for the sake of the party goals of the respective minister (Laver and Shepsle, 1990a). As we have seen, there are limits to ministerial autonomy, and these limits are more significant when decisions are important from a party political perspective. Nevertheless, the occupation of specific government departments provides the best chance for a party to influence the respective government outputs. This is also clear from the behavior of the parties themselves, which are keen to occupy both those departments considered to have particular influence (Finance), and those that correspond most closely to the respective party's clientele.

In its intraparty version the portfolio-allocation model proceeds from the assumption that cabinet ministers even of the same party differ in their policy preferences and make different decisions when occupying the same portfolio (Laver and Shepsle, 1990b). Although limited, the autonomy of Austrian cabinet ministers also serves this purpose. Otherwise the intraparty factions – such as the leagues within the OVP and the trade unionists within the SPO – would have no rationale for claiming those departments that correspond most closely to their clientele. Although in most of these cases there was a high degree of congruence between the minister's behavior and the goals of his respective faction, we are more skeptical about the predictability of ministerial behavior in general. Although there have been cases in which ministers performed exactly as a well-informed spectator would have predicted, for most ministers the picture would be less clear.

NOTES

1 Since not all questions could be asked to all of the ministers or could be coded from their answers, the population represented in Tables 2.1 to 2.5 varies somewhat, explaining the differences in the N's and n's. The total number of cabinet ministers serving during this period is ninety-eight, of whom twenty died in office or before the interviews started and another eighteen still occupy high executive office, and for this reason could not be interviewed. Additional information was provided by interviews with secretaries of state, cabinet and ministerial officials and party leaders, analyses of private papers, memoirs, party materials, and newspaper reports.

2 In the provisional government all three parties, the Socialists, the People's Party, and the Communists, were represented roughly equally. After their electoral debacle in December 1945, the Communists were represented with only one minister and could no longer exercise much influence on cabinet decision making.

3 For an extensive treatment of all questions of constitutional law relevant in the context of this chapter see Adamovich, 1971; Walter, 1972; and Welan and Neisser, 1971.

4 Except for short periods, the positions of chancellor (or vice-chancellor) and party chairman have always been in the same hands.

5 In the SPO the minister for social administration has to be a trade unionist, and in the OVP the minister of agriculture and the minister of economic affairs have to be representatives of the Farmers' League and the Business League respectively.

REFERENCES

Adamovich, Ludwig. 1971. *Handbuch des österreichischen Verfassungsrechts.* Vienna: Springer, 1971

Crossman, Richard H. S. 1963. Introduction. In Walter Bagehot, *The English Constitution.* Glasgow: Collins.

1972. *The Myths of Cabinet Government.* Cambridge, Mass.: Harvard University Press.

Dunleavy, Patrick, and R. A. W. Rhodes. 1990. Core executive studies in Britain. *Public Administration* 68: 3–28.

Farrell, Brian. 1971. *Chairman or Chief? The Role of the Taoiseach in Irish Government.* Dublin: Gill & Macmillan.

Gerlich, Peter, Wolfgang C. Müller, and Wilfried Philipp. 1988. Potentials and limitations of executive leadership: the Austrian cabinet since 1945. *European Journal of Political Research* 16: 191–205.

Hroch, Fridrich. 1983. Möglichkeiten rationaler Wahlentscheidung und Politikkontrolle anhand von Parteiprogrammen. Ph.D. diss., University of Vienna.

Katz, Richard S. 1986. Party government: A rationalistic conception. In Francis G. Castles and Rudolf Wildenmann (eds.). *Visions and Realities of Party Government.* Berlin: de Gruyter.

Kelsen, Hans. 1929. *Vom Wesen und Wert der Demokratie.* Tübingen: Mohr.

Laver, Michael, and Kenneth Shepsle. 1990a. Coalitons and cabinet government. *American Political Science Review* 84: 873–90.

1990b. Government coalitions and intraparty politics. *British Journal of Political Science* 20: 489–507.

Mackintosh, John P. 1969. A rejoinder. In Anthony King (ed.), *The British Prime Minister.* London: Macmillan Press.

Müller, Wolfgang C. 1991a. Regierung und Kabinettsystem. In Herbert Dachs, Peter Gerlich, Herbert Gottweis, Franz Horner, Helmut Kramer, Volkmar Lauber, Wolfgang C. Müller, and Emmerich Tálos (eds.), *Handbuch des politischen Systems Österreichs.* Vienna: Manz.

1991b. Die Osterreichische Volkspartei. In Herbert Dachs, Peter Gerlich, Herbert Gottweis, Franz Horner, Helmut Kramer, Volkmar Lauber, Wolfgang C. Müller, and Emmerich Tálos (eds.), *Handbuch des politischen Systems Österreichs.* Vienna: Manz.

1993. Koalitionsabkommen in der österreichischen Politik. In Georg Becker, Friedrich Lachmayer, and Günter Oberleitner (eds.), *Gesetzgebung zwischen Bürokratie und Politik.* Vienna: Osterreichischer Bundesverlag.

Müller, Wolfgang C., and Wilfried Philipp. 1987. Parteienregierung und Regierungsparteien in Osterreich. *Osterreichische Zeitschrift für Politikwissenschaft* 16: 277–302.

Müller, Wolfgang C., Wilfried Philipp, and Barbara Steininger. 1987. Sozialstruktur und Karrieren österreichischer Regierungsmitglieder (1945–1987). *Osterreichisches Jahrbuch für Politik* 1987: 143–63.

Pelinka, Anton, and Manfried Welan. 1971. *Demokratie und Verfassung in Oster-reich.* Vienna: Europaverlag.

Rose, Richard. 1976. *The Problem of Party Government.* Harmondsworth: Penguin.

Walter, Robert. 1972. *Osterreichisches Bundesverfassungsrecht.* Vienna: Manz.

Welan, Manfried, and Heinrich Neisser. 1971. *Der Bundeskanzler im Öster-reichischen Verfassungsgefüge.* Vienna: Hollinek.

3

The political role of Norwegian cabinet ministers

Kaare Strom[1]

Representative democracy implies that the few will make decisions on behalf of the many; its legitimacy is predicated on popular acceptance of this arrangement, on public willingness to delegate authority to make collective decisions to a team of leaders. The problems of delegation are myriad and well known: it is difficult to ensure that any representative, or agent, faithfully and systematically acts in the interests of his (or her) principal. Nevertheless, some residual belief in the possibility of delegation distinguishes representative democracy from mere oligarchy or autocracy, where in practical terms all authority is vested in the Leviathan.

This chapter examines such delegation problems in Norway. The analysis will focus on the logic of delegation between the cabinet and the individual minister, and shall examine the extent of autonomy enjoyed by individual cabinet ministers in the process of governance. The paper consists of seven parts. In the first section after the introduction, I present an overview of the problems of delegation and their application to parliamentary government. Thereafter, attention is shifted to the Norwegian political system, some of whose most salient characteristics are described. The third section describes in greater detail the cabinet decision-making process in Norway. In the following part, I examine in greater detail the political role of the individual cabinet minister. Constraints on ministers from outside the cabinet are analyzed in the fifth section. In the sixth section I discuss in more general terms how agency losses between coalition leaders and ministers can be contained. The seventh section summarizes and concludes the analysis.

PARLIAMENT, GOVERNMENT, AND DELEGATION

Delegation of authority is a central feature of any contemporary democracy. Most important political decisions are made not in a plebiscitary way by the citizens themselves, but rather by bureaucracies, committees, cabinets, and legislatures. A key characteristic such entities have in common is the delegation of authority from the individual or individuals in whom it was originally vested – the principal – to one or more agents (Kiewiet and McCubbins, 1991; Tirole, 1986). Members of parliamentary committees, for example, act as agents of the representatives at large, and in the classic model of parliamentary democracy, the cabinet serves as the agent of Parliament. Delegation allows such organizations to acquire such great specialization and to fulfil their tasks at much-reduced costs in time and money.

Parliamentary government

Modern democracies differ in their delegation regimes. In parliamentary government, constitutional authority is delegated through a single chain of command. Parliamentarism, also frequently referred to as a system of "fused" powers, is "the form of constitutional democracy in which executive authority *emerges from* and is *responsible to* legislative authority" (Lijphart, 1984: 84, emphasis in the original). Parliament delegates authority to a prime minister (or chancellor, etc.), who selects a team of cabinet members who are given specialized tasks. Each minister in turn leaves implementation to a bureaucracy of civil servants. Constitutions based on parliamentary government typically embody the principle of popular sovereignty, but just as typically the legislative branch is directly elected by the people (who in this case are the principals). All other organs of state are thus designed to be responsible to the elected representatives of the people through a single command structure. This differs from presidential regimes, which are characterized by overlapping jurisdictions and mutual checks and balances. In these latter systems, each agent frequently serves multiple principals, and each principal may employ many agents.

The ideal-typical single-chain delegation regime of parliamentary government has been modified by the emergence of political parties and the practice of coalition government (Palmer, 1992). Parties can be explained as an effective way in which the agents in the executive branch are "bonded" to their principals in the legislature, and by which these individuals in turn make themselves accountable to the electorate (Cox, 1987; Palmer, 1992). Cabinet members thus come to serve several masters: the legislature, the prime minister, and the extraparliamentary political parties. The potential conflicts involved in these relationships are especially salient under coalition government. In the following analysis of Norwegian cabinet ministers, I shall thus recognize the somewhat ambiguous identity of their immediate principals by referring to them as "coalition leaders."

Agency problems

Any delegation of authority creates the risk that the intentions of the principal may not be faithfully executed by the agent. This may be because the agent has interests and incentives that are not perfectly identical to those of the principal, and because the principal lacks the means (information and mechanisms of enforcement) to monitor every action the agent takes. Delegation thus generates agency problems, driven by conflicts of interest between those who hold the ultimate authority to make decisions and the individuals acting in their place. Agency problems may take the form of omission, commonly known as "shirking," when the agent simply fails to act in the best interest of the principal, or commission, when the agent takes some positive action contrary to the will or interest of the principal. Agency problems are likely to be exacerbated under conditions of hidden action (principals cannot fully observe the actions of their agents) and hidden information (principals do not fully know the competencies or preferences of their agents to the exact demands of the task at hand).

Containing agency losses

In order to safeguard against agency losses, principals engage in various forms of oversight of their agents. These oversight activities are in themselves costly to the principal. The literature on delegation identifies four major measures by which agency losses can be contained: (1) contract design, (2) screening and selection mechanisms, (3) monitoring and reporting requirements, and (4) institutional checks (Kiewiet and McCubbins, 1991). Contract design typically seeks to establish shared interests, or incentive compatibility, between principals and agents, for example by giving the agent a share of the principal's gain. Screening and selection represent efforts by the principal to sort out good agents from bad before entering into any relationship with them. Monitoring and reporting are designed to force the agent to share with the principal information that the latter might not otherwise receive. Finally, institutional checks subject particularly critical agent decisions to the veto powers of other agents. Among the control mechanisms discussed here, the latter two are the only ones that operate ex post facto.

Institutional variations

Different delegation regimes engender different agency problems. Agency problems even vary from one country to the next. I focus on delegation processes that most directly involve cabinet ministers, primarily on the

Figure 3.1. *Models of delegation under parliamentary government*

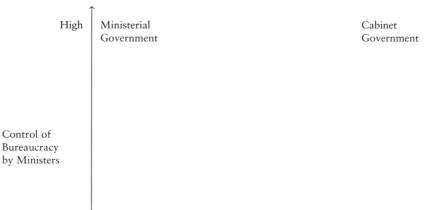

relationship between prime minister and individual cabinet member, and also on that between the minister and his or her civil servants. Each of these relationships can be characterized according to the degree of control exercised by the principal over the agent. Figure 3.1 presents a schema characterizing different delegation patterns under parliamentary government. The horizontal axis represents the extent to which individual ministers are controlled by coalition leaders, such as the prime minister or other party leaders. The vertical axis, on the other hand, stands for the control these individual ministers enjoy vis-à-vis the bureaucracy (here treated as a homogeneous entity).

Situations in which coalition leaders exercise a high degree of control over individual ministers, and in which the latter effectively oversee their respective civil servants, correspond to the classical model of cabinet government. Where bureaucracy is similarly checked, but individual ministers are largely autonomous vis-à-vis coalition leaders, we can speak of ministerial government. Finally, where cabinet members, collectively or individually, effectively fail to control their civil servants (for reasons suggested by Niskanen [1971]), we find bureaucratic government.

38

Delegation and coalition theory

Only very recently has coalition theory begun systematically to consider the implications of political delegation for government formation and maintenance. This is none too early, since agency problems are highly relevant to parties considering government participation, especially to the extent that these parties are policy seekers (Budge and Laver, 1986; Strom, 1990). Implicitly policy-based coalition theory has assumed a model of cabinet government in which individual ministers and civil servants are effectively controlled by party leaders. Laver and Shepsle (1990) have very fruitfully brought attention to this issue by suggesting instead that the appropriate model might be one of ministerial government, where individual ministers enjoy autonomy from the coalition leaders. If the actual situation more resembles the bureaucratic government model, however, no policy-based coalition theory may be of much value in explaining government behavior. That is to say, if civil servants ultimately decide policy as they like, it makes little sense to assume that parties are in the coalition game because they care about public policy. In this case, only the more cynical postulates of office-based (or "policy blind") coalition theory, irreverently expressed by Laver and Schofield (1990), remain plausible, that is, party leaders seek office in order to ride the back seats of fancy limousines and consume state dinners in exotic places.

Thus, delegation problems under parliamentary government are of great and direct relevance to the theory of government coalitions. This paper assesses the autonomy of individual cabinet ministers in Norway. Before we do so, however, we shall describe the main features of the Norwegian party system and the institutions within which cabinet ministers and party leaders operate.

POSTWAR NORWEGIAN PARTIES AND GOVERNMENTS

Electoral law and party system

From the end of World War II through the 1950s, Norway had a stable five-party system pitting the dominant Labor Party (Arbeiderpartiet, A or DNA) against a noncohesive bloc of four nonsocialist parties: the Conservatives (Høyre, H), the Liberals (Venstre, V), the agrarian Center Party (Senterpartiet, SP),[2] and the Christian People's Party (Kristelig Folkeparti, KRF). After the onset of the Cold War, the Communist Party (Norges Kommunistisk Parti, NKP) gradually faded into oblivion, losing its parliamentary representation in 1961. The 1960s and 1970s brought two new parliamentary parties: the Socialist Left Party (Sosialistisk Folkeparti, SF, later to become part of Sosialistisk Venstreparti, SV), and the Progress

Party (Fremskrittspartiet, FRP) on the far right. The Liberals declined precipitously and then in 1972 acrimoniously split into two parties, both of which have since disappeared from parliamentary politics.

Norway has a proportional representation (PR) electoral system tainted with considerable malapportionment, and until 1989 there were no supplementary seats in the Storting (the Norwegian parliament). The resulting legislative disproportionality has consistently been among the highest of all PR countries, which has given the nonsocialist parties (and particularly the smaller ones) strong incentives to form electoral coalitions in the form of joint lists. Such preelectoral coalition building clearly has facilitated nonsocialist cabinet coalitions as well. Effectively, the postwar development of the Norwegian party system can be broken down into three periods: one of Labor Party predominance from World War II until 1961; a phase of stable two-bloc competition from 1961 until the EC referendum in 1972; and finally, a time of polarization and fractionalization from that time until the present.

The post-1945 governments

The postwar record of Norwegian governments similarly falls into two distinct periods. Prior to 1961, Norway experienced stable, single-party, majority governments. The 1961 election deprived the Labor Party of a parliamentary majority, which it has never recaptured. After this, Norwegian cabinets have typically been less stable, more often than not "undersized," and in several cases, coalitions. Since 1961 Norway has had fourteen minority and only three majority governments. Seven of these governments have been true coalitions, whereas ten have consisted of only one party. Subsequent Labor governments have relied on legislative coalitions for their survival.

Although the composition and numerical basis of Norwegian governments have changed substantially over the postwar period, other patterns of government formation have remained stable:

1. All Norwegian governments have been either socialist or nonsocialist.
2. The Labor Party has eschewed coalitions not only with nonsocialist parties, but also with any of the smaller parties to its left. Thus, a socialist government has meant a cabinet of Labor alone. Since 1961, therefore, a socialist government has also meant a minority government.
3. Nonsocialist governments, on the other hand, have tended to be coalitions, though not necessarily majority coalitions. In all but one case, nonsocialist governments have included at least three parties.

The role of Norwegian cabinet ministers

To this day, parliamentary government has no place in the written constitution of Norway. Nonetheless, this principle has been virtually unchallenged since 1884. Yet many features of the 1814 constitution have never been repealed, giving Norway an idiosyncratic parliamentary constitution (Hernes and Nergaard, 1989).

The cabinet

The cabinet is formally recognized in the 1814 constitution as the Council of State. Article 12 of the constitution prescribes that the cabinet consist of a prime minister and at least seven other members. In practice the number of cabinet members in Norway has since 1945 varied between thirteen and nineteen, with a secular trend toward larger size. The cabinet normally meets three times a week, with all formal decisions (Royal Resolutions) being made on Fridays in the Council of State, where the king is present. Council of State meetings are largely ritualistic, typically lasting only thirty to forty-five minutes and containing no real debate on the issues under consideration. Decisions of the Council of State require the signatures of both the king and the prime minister. More substantive discussions take place in the king's absence in cabinet meetings on Mondays and Thursdays, which last two to three hours, as well as during informal cabinet luncheons on Fridays.

Cabinet formation

Since the Norwegian constitution never has been amended to reflect the introduction of parliamentary government in 1884, it contains few guidelines or restrictions concerning government formation. According to Article 12, the king formally selects his cabinet at will, but in practice he has exerted no personal influence on cabinet formation since 1928 (Björnberg, 1939). He normally follows the advice of the outgoing prime minister in designating a *formateur*. Only very rarely (in 1928, 1935, and 1971) has Norway experienced complicated cabinet crises, and even then negotiations were not protracted. There is no formal investiture requirement. Rather, a government remains in office until it demonstrably lacks the support of the legislature. This permissive interpretation of the parliamentary principle facilitates minority government formation.

The Norwegian constitution does not recognize any particular rules or constraints concerning caretaker governments. Such cabinets are most common after parliamentary elections, when there is a period of about one month between the election date (mid-September) and the date the

Parliament is convened (mid-October). Since the Norwegian legislature, alone among Western European parliaments, cannot be dissolved before the end of its four-year term, such dates are fixed and predictable. The incumbent government remains in office during this time even when it is clear that it will not receive a renewed mandate in the Storting. Incumbents are not expected to resign when a new head of state accedes to the throne, as in January 1991, when King Harald the Fifth succeeded his late father, King Olav the Fifth.

Cabinet authority

The cabinet (Council of State) enjoys extensive powers under the Norwegian constitution. It is the supreme, collective leadership of the central administration. In the form of bills and white papers, it initiates and prepares most legislation that is subsequently adopted by the Parliament. It can issue decrees with the force of law when Parliament is not in session. It is routinely granted broad implementation powers through regular legislation. It is in charge of a large system of public enterprises, for example in the important and largely nationalized oil sector. It is an institution to which appeals can be made by citizens under certain circumstances, and it enjoys other constitutional prerogatives, such as appointment powers. Within certain limits, the cabinet can delegate authority, most commonly to the individual ministries. Nevertheless, some decisions, such as certain appointments, are constitutionally required to take place in the Council of State.

The prime minister

The prime ministership is the only cabinet office established by constitution. Nevertheless, the Norwegian prime minister is, in the words of Johan P. Olsen (1983: 81), a "political organizer but no superstar." The prime minister is the head of the cabinet but his or her powers are otherwise vaguely described. Responsibilities include countersigning all decisions of the Council of State, preparing the cabinet agenda, chairing meetings, and casting a double vote in case the king is absent (rarely the source of any real power). The prime minister has the right to request information from any cabinet member, but cannot issue orders, change ministerial jurisdictions, dissolve Parliament, or, technically, dismiss ministers. In reality, there has been substantial variation in the freedom of choice enjoyed by prime ministers in selecting and dismissing cabinet members. At one extreme, Einar Gerhardsen is considered to have been the "strongest" prime minister of the postwar period in the discretion with which he could select his cabinet team. At the other extreme, prime ministers in coalition cabinets have had no opportunity to select the members representing the other parties (Eriksen, 1988b; Olsen, 1983).

The prime minister is in charge of the prime minister's office, a relatively small operation. The prime minister had virtually no administrative help until 1956, when his office was reorganized. By the mid-1980s it had a staff of approximately thirty, which is still comparatively modest (Berggrav, 1985).

Cabinet members

The general rule, spelled out in Article 2 of the standing orders of the cabinet (Regjeringsinstruksen), is for each cabinet member to be the administrative head of some ministry. (The prime minister heads his or her own office, but after World War II no prime minister has been in charge of any regular ministry.) Occasionally, though, ministers without portfolio have been appointed. This was most notably the case in the years of reconstruction immediately following World War II, when as many as three ministers without portfolio were included in the cabinet simultaneously. It is even rarer for any department to be represented by more than one cabinet member, although this again has occasionally happened in periods of administrative reorganization. Thus, Norway neatly fits one favorable condition for ministerial autonomy: being the head of a ministry is for all intents and purposes a necessary and sufficient condition for membership in the cabinet.

Though cabinet members may have close ties to Parliament, they cannot serve as representatives while they hold cabinet office. Nor is it expected that cabinet members have prior parliamentary experience. Between 1945 and 1978, 52 percent of all Norwegian cabinet ministers had no prior parliamentary experience (Olsen, 1983: 93). This proportion was especially high in the early postwar Labor governments under Gerhardsen. Particularly in ministries with distinctive and well-organized clienteles (such as Agriculture or Fisheries), it is considered much more desirable for cabinet members to have good interest-group ties than to have parliamentary experience. Prime ministers and finance ministers, however, tend to have extensive previous parliamentary experience.

Other political appointments

In addition to the cabinet members, there are two other principal types of political appointments in the Norwegian executive branch, namely undersecretaries of state (*statssekretær*) and personal secretaries to the minister (*personlig sekretær*). Undersecretaries of state, according to Article 14 of the constitution, are appointed by the Council of State as assistants to

43

individual ministers. Ministers may choose to delegate authority to their undersecretaries, who can then make formal decisions on the minister's behalf. However, the responsibilities of undersecretaries of state are meant to be political rather than administrative. They may be asked to attend cabinet meetings to report on matters under their jurisdiction, but have no voting rights. Surveys of political appointees reveal that ministers use their secretaries in a variety of ways. About half of all ministers delegate sub-areas of their own jurisdiction to their undersecretaries, whereas the other half put their undersecretaries in charge of general preliminary work on all kinds of matters. Under either arrangement, however, there is no question that the minister always retains the final authority (Eriksen, 1988a).

Personal secretaries, on the other hand, are formally appointed by the minister they serve. The minister cannot delegate authority to such appointees, who are meant to be more strictly political assistants to the minister. In practice, ministers do not always get the undersecretaries or the personal secretaries they desire. A little less than half the time ministers are able to handpick the persons they want, whereas just as often they end up with someone they do not know (Eriksen, 1988a; Olsen, 1983). The total number of political appointments (including ministers) has risen from twenty-two in 1947 to fifty-seven in 1988. Typically, each ministry has one undersecretary and one personal secretary, although there have been cases of multiple undersecretaries, especially in the Willoch coalition governments (1983–6). All undersecretaries and personal secretaries must resign with the minister to whom they are assigned.

Cabinet rules and procedures

Cabinet decision-making rules and procedures have evolved to reflect the practice of parliamentary government. Since the formal constitution still reflects the formalities of the cabinet as the "king's council," there are virtually no hard-and-fast rules for cabinet decision making. Certain conventions can be identified, however. All cabinet meetings are chaired by the prime minister, who is also in charge of preparing the agenda. Nevertheless, any minister can request that the prime minister put an issue on the agenda, and such requests are not denied. This represents a change since the early Gerhardsen days, when there was no set agenda and when cabinet members spoke in declining order of seniority. In those days, the most junior ministers sometimes had to leave without having an opportunity to present even the most pressing matters (Olsen, 1983).

In matters of dispute, it must be assumed that the cabinet could make its decisions by majority vote (Berggrav, 1985: 31). A quorum of more than half the cabinet members must be present for a formal decision to be made. On the other hand, that decisions of the Council of State require the signature of the prime minister technically gives this person veto powers. In practice, however, the influence of the prime minister is never exercised in this way, nor do we know of any prime minister who has threatened to veto a cabinet decision. The implicit decision rule practiced most commonly seems to be unanimity. Decision-making processes in the cabinet are characterized by a strong search for consensus. Formal votes are rarely taken, although they do occur. In order to avoid divisive votes, ministers make use of extensive consultations before controversial issues are brought before the cabinet. There is indeed a norm not to bring controversial issues (those known to be contested by at least one other minister) before the cabinet until all other means of resolution have been exhausted.

If disagreements persist after cabinet debate, recourse is generally taken to one of five mechanisms of resolution: reconsideration by the minister responsible for the issue; further extracabinet negotiations between the ministers involved in the dispute; referral to a committee of undersecretaries of state or civil servants; the appointment of a cabinet committee, often including the prime minister; or in the case of a coalition government, negotiations between party leaders (Eriksen, 1988b: 191). A formal protocol is kept of Council of State decisions, and individual ministers can request that their dissent from cabinet policy be registered in this document. This is the only way they can escape *legal* responsibility for cabinet decisions they consider "unconstitutional or injurious to the realm." However, except for parliamentary scrutiny, the cabinet protocol is confidential, and a registered dissent is no *political* excuse for public criticism of cabinet decisions.

Not all cabinet decisions are formally binding. Technically, cabinet ministers and their subordinates are bound only by the formal decisions of the Council of State and not by the more informal agreements reached in other cabinet meetings; yet this distinction must be considered more formal than real. Individual cabinet members would be ill-advised to ignore or sabotage any cabinet decisions, regardless of whether they had been ratified in the Council of State.

CABINET MINISTERS AND THEIR ROLES

Cabinet ministers play multiple roles in the Norwegian system. They are the legal heads of their respective ministries and thus administrators and specialists. They are generalists by virtue of their membership in the cabinet and through their participation in the collective decisions reached in that forum. Finally, they are partisans in the sense that they represent their particular political parties in the cabinet and in their own ministries. This latter is of course especially important for members of coalition cabinets. We shall examine the formal contents of each of these responsibilities and then the practical interpretations that Norwegian cabinet ministers tend to make of their roles.

Formal authority and responsibilities

Ministers have final authority in all matters decided within their ministries. All ministerial decisions are formally made in the minister's name and under his authority. As already mentioned, the undersecretary of state is the only person to whom the minister can formally delegate. Article 5 of the cabinet standing orders specifies certain matters that can be decided autonomously within each ministry without cabinet approval. Such matters include: (1) spending and accounting for funds already appropriated, (2) implementation of existing laws passed by the Storting, (3) matters delegated to the ministry by parliamentary action or cabinet decree, (4) appointments of commissions of inquiry and short-term appointments of delegates, and (5) other matters that traditionally have been decided by individual ministries.

On the other hand, Article 28 of the constitution specifies certain decisions (such as appointments) and other "important" matters, a notoriously ill-specified category, that *must* be made in the Council of State and cannot be delegated. In between these Article 5 and Article 28 categories, there is a considerable gray area where jurisdiction is a matter of balancing prime-ministerial demand and ministerial initiative and compliance. The long-term trend has been toward more and more matters being exempted from cabinet deliberation. Nevertheless, a royal resolution of 1982 requires cabinet approval before preparations of legal or administrative reforms, commissions of inquiry, white papers, or government proposals to the Storting can be initiated (Berggrav, 1985: 40).

On matters that come before the cabinet, the reporting minister is responsible for properly briefing the other cabinet members. Brief "cabinet notes" (*regjeringsnotater*) describing the issue and recommending a course of action are circulated before the cabinet meeting by the minister in charge. Such papers relating to issues involving government expenditure must be presented to the finance ministry before they are circulated to other cabinet members. Similarly, in matters that directly involve the jurisdictions of more than one ministry, all affected parties must be notified before the issue makes it onto the cabinet agenda.

Ministers bear two kinds of responsibilities for their actions and those of their subordinates. One is a *constitutional* responsibility for any illegal or unconstitutional behavior on the minister's part, including any non-compliance with acts of Parliament or withholding of information to which Parliament is entitled. A minister may also be constitutionally responsible for the actions of a subordinate, such as a civil servant, if negligence is shown in the instruction or oversight of this subordinate. Violations of the constitutional responsibilities of ministers are punishable by impeachment, but since the dramatic and unsuccessful impeachment proceedings against Prime Minister Abraham Berge in 1926–7, this extreme instrument has fallen into disuse. In recent years, ministers guilty of major violations of the law have tended to resign and face regular criminal prosecution. Thus, two ministers (one Conservative and one Labor) have during the 1980s resigned and subsequently been convicted of embezzlement.

A more pressing concern for most cabinet ministers is their *parliamentary* responsibility to the Storting. This is a collective responsibility shared by all members of the cabinet and all other political appointees in the ministries. Whereas ministers can escape some forms of constitutional responsibility by registering their dissent from Council of State decisions, there is no way for an individual minister to exempt himself from his parliamentary responsibility.

Ministerial norms and behavior

Surveys of ministers show that most of them focus their energies on matters pertaining to their own ministries. Eriksen (1988a) reports from a survey of thirty-five ministers that on average they devoted almost two-thirds of their time to departmental matters, whereas an average of 22 percent of their time was spent in or in preparation for cabinet meetings. Most ministers thus choose the role of specialist, but some exceptions apply. Occupants of the ministries of Finance, Municipal Affairs, and Environmental Affairs tend to spend more time on issues pertaining to other ministries. And the prime minister, of course, does not even have his or her own ministry. Also, ministers from small parties in coalition cabinets are more likely than ministers in single-party governments to spend more time on matters outside their own jurisdiction. This appears particularly to have been the case with ministers from the Center Party in the Willoch cabinets of 1983–6 (Eriksen, 1988a: 44).

The prevailing specialist orientation is reinforced by the work load cabinet ministers are under, by patterns of recruitment and experience, and by the norms of cabinet discussions. Most cabinet members feel severely overworked, and many report that they have little time to invest in matters concerning other ministries. Between 1945 and the late 1970s, three-quarters of all ministers served in only one ministry during their political careers, while only seven persons have served in three or more ministries, the prime ministership included. There was substantial variation across ministries, however, as 73 percent of all finance ministers had headed at least one other ministry, as had more than half of all prime ministers and ministers of defense, trade, justice, and foreign affairs (Olsen, 1983: 92).

The informal norms of cabinet meetings do not favor freewheeling discussions involving all members of that collective. Excessive questioning of the proposals of other ministers is not likely to win a cabinet member friends and goodwill, and most ministers largely confine themselves to debates involving their own jurisdictions. Exceptions must be made for the prime minister and the finance minister, however, as well as for party leaders in coalition cabinets. The prime minister and the finance minister are by virtue of their offices forced to be generalists. The prime minister is expected to be an impartial arbiter in disputes between other ministers, except that he or she is also expected to side with the finance minister when the latter attempts to impose fiscal discipline (Olsen, 1983).

CONSTRAINTS IMPOSED BY OTHER INSTITUTIONS

We now consider ties to other institutions or agents that might constrain the freedom with which cabinet ministers can make policy in their respective jurisdictions. We first consider ties to Parliament, second, those to the minister's party, and third (and briefly) the constraints imposed by the bureaucracy.

Parliament

The Norwegian Parliament enjoys a glorified role in the national mythology of parliamentary government. Parliament's hard-fought position as the defender of the people and their national heritage is still reflected in Norwegian norms and expectations concerning parliamentary government. The Storting is jealous of its constitutional powers and tends to look askance at any cabinet member who is not sufficiently deferential. The Parliament can be counted upon to be especially sensitive to perceived violations of the constitutional and parliamentary responsibilities of cabinet members. The Storting is a relatively egalitarian institution, but its proceedings are led by a board of presidents, which has six members. Membership on this board is proportional to party strength, and the government enjoys no special privileges. Nor does the government have any formal powers to set the parliamentary agenda, though in fact almost all legislation originates in the executive branch.

No-confidence motions against a member of the cabinet can be pressed by any member of Parliament, and there is not even a requirement of a second sponsor. Crises of parliamentary responsibility are relatively rare in Norway, as only three post-1945 cabinets (two in 1963 and one in 1986) have lost confidence votes. Two of these motions (those concerning Lyng and Willoch) were initiated by the government itself (Hernes and Nergaard, 1989). Parliament is quick to react, however, when it feels that there has been a breach of constitutional responsibility. In cases involving noncompliance with acts of Parliament, failure to inform the Storting, or unauthorized expenditures of public funds, Parliament often will be insistent on at least an expression, in a plenary session, of apology and contrition. Two recent cases will serve as illustrations.

In 1988, the Storting expressed its displeasure at the high salary given to the new president of the state-owned Post Office Savings Bank. When Consumer Affairs Minister Anne-Lise Bakken reported to Parliament on the matter, she blamed the civil servant in charge, without expressing any regret that she herself had approved this salary raise. Irked by the minister's defiant attitude, the opposition parties, which at this time commanded a parliamentary majority, immediately agreed to press a motion of no confidence against Bakken. A few hours later, Bakken again took the floor and expressed her regret. The opposition parties backed down and Bakken survived, but soon thereafter she was unceremoniously sacked by Prime Minister Brundtland.

In January 1992, Defense Minister Johan Jørgen Holst had to answer to Parliament for his failure to move aircraft control inspection from the Oslo area to Kongsvinger near the Swedish border. This move had been legislated by Parliament but the Defense Department had for reasons of cost and efficiency failed to follow through by the date established by Parliament. Nor had Parliament, in its own opinion, been properly informed of this lack of implementation. Holst's position was exacerbated by the fact that he had shortly before been in hot water over his authorization of extraordinary compensation to a high-ranking officer, without parliamentary approval. Holst's unrepentant arrogance provoked clear threats of a no-confidence vote, until his own parliamentary leader urged him to express his regrets. When Holst did so, the matter subsided (*Aftenposten,* 30 January 1992).

Such dramatic occasions clearly represent the most extreme forms of parliamentary oversight. Cabinet members regularly report to Parliament under less stressful circumstances through floor debates, question time, and similar procedures. Surveys of parliamentarians show that most report regular contact with one or more cabinet members. The proportion of representatives that report to be in contact at least once a month increased from 75 percent in 1966 to 97 percent in 1977. Much, but by no means all, of this contact is facilitated through the system of permanent committees in the Storting. These committees are the main foci of legislative activity and tend to have intimate contact with both ministers and civil servants in their respective jurisdictions. Such contact is facilitated by the fact that the jurisdictions of legislative committees tend to correspond to those of ministries. Members report most frequent contact with the ministry corresponding to their own committee (members serve on only one committee). In addition, representatives frequently enjoy good contacts with such ministries as Municipal Affairs and Education, presumably because they tend to be highly salient to local constituency interests (Hernes and Nergaard, 1989).

Political parties

Norwegian government is very much party government, and there has never been a nonpartisan administration since the introduction of parliamentary government. Nor is it customary for Norwegian cabinets to contain individual nonpartisan ministers. In fact, when the Labor Party occasionally has appointed ministers without long-standing party membership, it has caused bitter criticism. Many cabinet members can claim considerable seniority in party politics at the local level, and in the postwar period about two-thirds of all ministers have had experience from local politics (Olsen, 1983: 94). Undersecretaries and personal secretaries are no less partisan than their superiors, and in almost all cases they come from the same party as the minister, even in coalition cabinets. Willoch's last coalition cabinet (1985–6) is an interesting exception, where two Conservative ministers had two undersecretaries each, one from their own party and one from one of the two smaller coalition parties (Eriksen, 1988a: 47–8).

Party politics impinges on cabinet politics in a number of ways. The prime minister is normally the effective leader of his or her party, though the exact party office held can vary. The least successful prime ministers have also been those whose control of their own parties was least secure. In the Willoch cabinet, there was a deliberate policy of giving all three party leaders important cabinet responsibilities. The Willoch coalitions were also noted for the fact that the parliamentary leaders of the respective parties participated in cabinet meetings on important issues (Berggav, 1985: 31). Party policy considerations evidently matter in cabinet negotiations. Olsen (1983: 104) notes that cabinet members strengthen their bargaining position on contested issues when they can refer to party policy commitments that support their position. In the Willoch coalitions, major policy issues were often decided by a subcommittee of the cabinet, consisting of the prime minister, the other two party leaders, and the finance minister.

The civil service

Norway has a civil service with high formal standards of professionalism and neutrality. As we have seen, government ministries contain very few political appointees relative to the number of career civil servants. There are no prestigious schools of public administration, however, and the civil service may not enjoy quite as much ésprit de corps as those in some other countries. Relationships between ministers and civil servants are on the whole favorable, and surveys show little evidence of distrust or bureaucratic infighting. Ministers generally do not describe civil servants as partisan or obstreperous, although they occasionally complain of rigidity and lack of initiative. Eriksen (1988a: 135) reports that only four of thirty-two ministers interviewed had experienced what they described as lack of loyalty. Ulltveit-Moe (1991) arrives at similar results in an informal survey of cabinet ministers.

The most important civil servant with whom ministers have to deal is the permanent secretary (*departementsråd*), of which each ministry has one. Though some of these officials have well-known political preferences, Ulltveit-Moe presents a generally favorable picture of the experiences cabinet ministers have had with these civil servants.

CONTAINING AGENCY LOSSES

We have now largely completed the survey of the terrain in which Norwegian cabinet ministers must operate. As we have seen, the institutional context is complex, and it is difficult to draw any simple conclusion concerning the policy-making autonomy of individual cabinet ministers. To approach this question, however, let us briefly step back into the theoretical literature and consider the general mechanism by which principals can attempt to control agency losses. We use these categories to address the control cabinet leaders can exercise vis-à-vis individual ministers.

Contract design can, in the context of cabinet-level politics, be understood as referring to the creation of shared interests ("bonding") between cabinet leaders and ministers. Common party membership would seem to be the most common such mechanism, as members of the same party stand or fall together electorally. The relevance of such party connections is certainly high in Norway, where, as we have noted, it is extremely rare for nonpartisans to be given cabinet assignments. The institutions of parliamentary government and collective cabinet responsibility are the mechanisms by which party success matters for individual ministers. A common interest in party unity and electoral success thus may help keep ministers in line with party-leader preferences.

Likewise, *screening and selection* take place in large part through political parties and the extensive background Norwegian cabinet ministers tend to have in local politics. On the other hand, it is interesting to note that Parliament seems to play a less-important role in screening and selection than in many other Western democracies, especially those built on the Westminster model. There is also much less of an internal hierarchy of ministerial positions than, for example, in the United Kingdom. Politicians are not expected to advance through the ranks of executive appointments, which reduces the usefulness of lesser offices in screening and selection.

Monitoring and reporting are largely performed by institutions other than the party organization. There is little direct oversight of ministers by their parties. Cabinet meetings and parliamentary scrutiny, however, are meant to fulfill such needs. Given constraints of time and information, there is little reason to believe that cabinet or parliamentary oversight consistently functions effectively if ministers are intent on escaping control. Finally, undersecretaries of state have sometimes been given monitoring tasks in coalition cabinet, as in the last Willoch government already mentioned.

Institutional checks are provided in a variety of ways. One is through cabinet committees, which have been used with varying intensity by different administrations. A more important check may be Finance Ministry approval. Survey evidence suggests that Finance Ministry interference is perceived by many ministers as a real obstacle. The problem with this kind of check, of course, is that it concerns only expenditure decisions. Other ministries, such as Municipal Affairs and Environmental Affairs, have been given more limited roles as institutional checks on other units.

In more general terms, however, the plasticity of the ministry structure itself provides opportunities for institutional checks or contract design. Table 3.1 shows the major changes that have taken place in the Norwegian ministry structure since World War II. As we see, only two ministries, Agriculture and Defense, have escaped major changes in their organization or jurisdiction. Institutional changes have been particularly frequent in such policy areas as labor, family affairs, trade, education, and consumer affairs. Ministerial reform was particularly rampant in the period from 1945 to 1955, and again since the early 1970s (see Roness, 1979). Of course, there is no evidence that the majority of these changes were deliberate attempts to extract compliance from individual ministers. On the contrary, most changes in ministerial structure have probably been motivated by efficiency concerns and social change. Nevertheless, their very frequency warns us that ministerial jurisdictions should not be treated as fixed or exogenous.

Table 3.1. *Changes in Norwegian ministerial structure, 1945–92*

Ministry	Established[a]	Abolished	Divided	Merged	Other major change[b]	No change
Agriculture						X
Church & Education	1972		1982		1990, 1991	
Consumer Affairs	1982				1990, 1991	
Cultural Affairs						X
Defense	1972					
Environment						
Family Affairs	1956, 1990, 1972				1991	
Finance			1955			
Fisheries	1946					
Foreign Affairs			1984			
Foreign Aid	1984			1988		
Industry	1947		1978			
Justice			1948			
Labor		1946				
Labor & Admin.	1990					
Municipal Affairs	1948		1990			
Oil & Energy	1978	1950				
Reconstruction		1950				
Social Affairs			1948			
Trade		1988	1947		1945, 1955	
Transportation	1946					
Wages & Prices	1955	1972				

[a]Ministries without listed date of establishment existed as of the first postwar partisan government, which was formed November 5, 1945.
[b]These changes involved the transfer of substantial jurisdictions into or out of the listed ministry.

CONCLUSIONS

Cabinet-level decision making consists of a complex set of authority relationships, in which delegation is both a pressing need and at the same time a frequent source of controversy. In this analysis I have discussed some of the mechanisms of delegation and oversight in Norwegian ministerial decision making. Are Norwegian cabinet ministers autonomous? Can cabinet leaders effectively control them through the mechanisms we have identified? Though it is obviously difficult to answer these questions in the abstract, political parties are clearly the most effective vehicle of oversight and control. Ministers in single-party governments are far from autonomous, though some (such as Foreign Minister Halvard Lange under Gerhardsen) may enjoy considerable discretion within their jurisdictions. Nevertheless, disciplined parties led by powerful prime ministers provide formidable checks.

In coalition cabinets, on the other hand, we can safely say that it *does* matter which party controls which ministry. Prime ministers in such governments have been more constrained in their ability to check ministers representing a different party. Portfolio allocation between coalition parties also suggests obvious differences in preferences, and presumably, therefore, some measure of ministerial autonomy. Moreover, although Norwegian party politics tends to be consensual, there have been clear policy differences between socialist and nonsocialist governments, particularly in the 1970s and 1980s. Thus, Norway is at least not a clear case of bureaucratic government. Norwegian cabinet ministers do make a difference politically, though not to the extent of jeopardizing representative democracy.

NOTES

1 I thank Tom Christensen, Mathew McCubbins, Stephen Swindle, and Michael Thies for sharing valuable insights and ideas that have helped me develop this chapter. None of these individuals, of course, bears any responsibility for my interpretations and errors.
2 The Center Party was known as the Farmer's Party (Bondepartiet) until 1959.

REFERENCES

Aftenposten. 30 January 1992.
Berggrav, Dag. 1985. Regjeringen. In Trond Nordby (ed.), *Storting og regjering 1945–1985.* Oslo: Kunnskapsforlaget.
Björnberg, Arne. 1939. *Parlamentarismens utveckling i Norge efter 1905.* Stockholm: Almqvist & Wiksell.
Budge, Ian, and Michael J. Laver. 1986. Office seeking and policy pursuit in coalition theory. *Legislative Studies Quarterly* 11: 485–506.

Cox, Gary. 1987. *The Efficient Secret.* Cambridge University Press.

Eriksen, Svein. 1988a. *Herskap og Tjenere.* Oslo: Tano.

1988b. Norway. In Jean Blondel and Ferdinand Müller-Rommel (eds.), *Cabinets in Western Europe.* London: Macmillan Press.

Hernes, Gudmund, and Kristine Nergaard. 1989. *Oss i mellom: konstitusjonelle former og uformelle kontakter Storting – Regjering.* Oslo: FAFO.

Kiewiet, D. Roderick, and Mathew D. McCubbins. 1991. *The Logic of Delegation.* University of Chicago Press.

Laver, Michael, and Norman Schofield. 1990. *Multiparty Government: The Politics of Coalition in Europe.* Oxford University Press.

Laver, Michael J., and Kenneth A. Shepsle. 1990. Coalitions and cabinet government. *American Political Science Review* 84: 873–90.

Lijphart, Arend. 1984. *Democracies.* New Haven, Conn.: Yale University Press.

Niskanen, William A. 1971. *Bureaucracy and Representative Government.* Chicago: Aldine-Atherton.

Olsen, Johan P. 1983. *Organized Democracy: Political Institutions in a Welfare State – The Case of Norway.* Bergen: Universitetsforlaget.

Palmer, Matthew S. R. 1992. The Economics of Organization and Ministerial Responsibility. Unpublished manuscript.

Roness, Paul G. 1979. *Reorganisering av departementa.* Bergen: Universitetsforlaget.

Strom, Kaare. 1990. *Minority Government and Majority Rule.* Cambridge University Press.

Tirole, Jean. 1986. Hierarchies and Bureaucracies: On the Role of Coercion in Organizations. *Journal of Law, Economics and Organization* 2: 181–214.

Ulltveit-Moe, Johannes. 1991. Statsråden som departementsleder. *Report 1991*:13. Oslo: Statskonsult.

4

The Netherlands: ministers and cabinet policy

Rudy B. Andeweg and Wilma Bakema

PARTY COMPOSITION AND CABINET POLICY

The evidence does not look promising for those who look at the party composition of coalitions in the Netherlands for clues to predict public policy. Much attention has focused on the impact made by parties of the left on the development of the welfare state. After examining government expenditures in the Netherlands since 1900, Hoogerwerf (1977) concluded that there has been no relation between Social Democratic participation in government and the growth of the public sector. Cameron (1978) studied the expansion of the public sector in eighteen developed liberal democracies between 1960 and 1975 and found a 0.60 correlation between the proportion of the government's electoral base composed of Social Democratic parties on the one hand and the increase in the percentage of gross national product (GNP) represented by all governmental revenues. He concluded that leftist domination of governments was a sufficient but not necessary condition for the expansion of the public sector. The Netherlands represents his clearest example of a country with a high rate of public-sector growth and a low level of Social Democratic participation in government.

However, it would be too simple to conclude on the basis of such evidence that the party composition of the coalition does not matter. Comparative studies of the policy impact of parties are easiest to conduct on the basis of rather crude quantitative data such as the percentage of GNP taken by the state. It is likely that party impact is greater in other policy areas: culture, education, mass communication, and public health, for example. Such policy areas are more qualitative and therefore difficult to analyze systematically. Furthermore, we never have the ideal experimental situation with different governments in place in the same country at the same time. Fortunately, recent Dutch history does provide us with the next-best solution. In 1977, the election results were widely interpreted as endorsing the continuation of a Social Democratic / Christian Democratic coalition led by Den Uyl. However, negotiations were extremely difficult and broke down on several occasions – over plans for a profit-sharing scheme for employees, liberalization of abortion, the distribution of portfolios in the new cabinet, and the nomination of a Christian Democrat as minister of economic affairs. Eventually, compromises were found on all matters except the last. After 163 days of negotiations, cabinet formation had to start anew, this time aiming at a coalition of Christian Democrats and Conservative Liberals. These parties were able to reach agreement and, after 207 days, a new government led by the Christian Democrat Van Agt was sworn in by the queen. Both the abortive and the successful cabinet formation resulted in a government program. Hence, we can compare at least the policy intentions of a coalition of Christian Democrats and Social Democrats with those of a coalition of Christian Democrats and Conservative Liberals.[1]

To a considerable extent the agreement between the Christian Democrats and the Conservative Liberals is a copy of the earlier agreement between Christian Democrats and Social Democrats. There is, for example, no difference in the text on abortion. On abortion, however, Social Democrats and Conservative Liberals – both secular parties – think alike. On many other issues the change in coalition partner did leave an imprint on the government's policy program. On housing there is a clear change in emphasis from rent protection to the stimulation of house ownership. Compensation for expropriations was to be based on the market value of the real estate, not on its user value. On education, the previous government had set in motion the development of comprehensive secondary education. The Christian Democrats and the Conservative Liberals decided to stimulate experiments with alternatives to comprehensive education. They also added measures to protect small schools in less densely populated areas. The plans for a profit-sharing law agreed upon by Christian Democrats and Social Democrats allowed for trade union involvement in the management of the new funds. This provision disappeared in the program of Christian Democrats and Conservative Liberals. The latter program is also more firm in its commitment to national defense.

These are only a few examples of the differences between the two policy agreements. It seems safe to conclude from this evidence that the party composition of the cabinet does provide clues to the policies that the cabinet will pursue.

MINISTERS AND CABINET POLICY

If the government parties can make a difference to cabinet policy, do individual ministers matter too? At first sight the notion of "ministerial autonomy" or "departmentalism" – of ministers wielding de facto power over policy outputs in their jurisdiction – seems very well suited to the Dutch cabinet. As we shall see, however, it does require modification.

Autonomy at first sight

Several factors point toward a considerable degree of autonomy for individual ministers: a constitutional emphasis on individual ministerial responsibility, a tacit rule of mutual "nonintervention" in cabinet sessions, limited ascendency for the prime minister, and the absence of a strongly united civil service.

Individual ministerial responsibility. The Dutch cabinet developed as a rather loose combination of individual advisers to the king, each heading one of the departments of state. A few years after the introduction of ministerial responsibility in 1848, the Standing Orders of the Council of Ministers were adapted to replace the final decision by the monarch with collective decisions. The constitution, however, continued to recognize only individual heads of departments. In 1901 a minister referred to this when refusing to discuss cabinet procedures in Parliament: he could not be required to debate the procedures of a nonexistent entity! It is only since 1983 that the constitution allows that "the Ministers shall together constitute the Council of Ministers. . . . The Council of Ministers shall consider and decide upon overall government policy and shall promote the coherence thereof." Despite this new provision, an all-party Committee on Political and Administrative Reform (Deetman Committee) complained in its 1991 report that "the current constitutional order prevents any encroachment on external individual ministerial responsibility." The constitutional legacy is reinforced by the fact that ministers are recruited for one particular portfolio: it is rare for a minister to move from one department to another.[2]

The effect of this tradition of autonomy for individual ministers has long been visible in cabinet decision making. Zijlstra, a former minister of economic affairs, of finance, and prime minister, reminisces:

> In general, we held back. Each of us had his own responsibility and we respected that, also when the dossier was controversial politically. Take Cals's education reform. My party had many objections against that bill. In cabinet we warned Cals, and we put the objections to him. But we did not say: "You should do this or shouldn't do that, or else we shall resign." Out of the question. It was and it ultimately remained a matter for the minister of education to decide.[3]

In 1958, for example, Parliament rejected a fiscal proposal, despite the Social Democratic minister of finance's threat of a cabinet crisis. The Social Democratic ministers resigned but, to their anger, the Christian Democratic ministers did not join them. As one of the Christian Democrats in that cabinet recalls:

> The Social Democratic ministers remonstrated with us that we too had agreed to the fiscal proposal in cabinet. Our point of view was that we had not agreed to it, we had agreed not to object to it. . . . It was Hofstra's portfolio and if he thought he needed that measure it was not for us to stand in his way. But to us it was not worth resigning over." (minister, 1950s)[4]

Examples such as these testify to a strong tradition of individual ministerial responsibility.

The tacit rule of nonintervention. A tacit rule of nonintervention seems to operate during cabinet sessions. It is often frowned upon when a minister intervenes in debates that are not pertinent to his own portfolio: "One is not supposed to nag one's colleagues unnecessarily," as one minister explained to us. To a large extent this rule follows from the constitutional legacy of individual ministerial responsibility, but other factors also play a role:

> A minister who feels a need for a colleague's support on the next item is probably reluctant to argue against that colleague's proposal. Especially when the minister of finance had a conflict with another colleague, which was rather frequently the case, one was wise to assume a low profile: if you were to support your colleague, the minister of finance would retort, "Do you want to contribute financially?" Or, the other way around, were you to support the minister of finance, your colleague would think: "I'll get you for this." (minister, 1970s)

In our interviews, ministers often mentioned that noninterventionist behavior was produced not just by reciprocity or by the sanctity of an individual minister's portfolio, but also by the way ministers are briefed. Dutch ministers have no "cabinet ministeriel," and are briefed on cabinet items emanating from other departments only by their own departmental civil servants.

The role of the prime minister. Compared to his counterparts in other countries, the Dutch prime minister is still predominantly a primus inter pares.[5] He has no influence on the nominations of ministers other than from his own party. The prime minister lacks the power to dismiss ministers and cannot even reshuffle his cabinet by assigning ministers to other portfolios. The prime minister's role in terms of policy-making is mostly reactive. He cannot issue any directives to an individual minister. The prime minister casts the deciding vote in case of a tie, but our analysis of cabinet minutes for 1945–69 reveals only one case in which a prime minister has used this prerogative, and then on only a minor issue.

The Dutch prime ministership developed late: until 1922 the chair of the Council of Ministers rotated on an annual, or sometimes even a trimester, basis. Until 1937 the prime minister also had the responsibility for one of the departments of state, but lacked a staff to assist him in his responsibilities as chairman. Some commentators claim to observe a clear trend toward a stronger premiership in more recent years. It is primarily the increased visibility and external duties of the prime minister that are cited as evidence of such a development: a weekly press conference and television interview, EC summit meetings, and so on. Increased visibility, however, does not necessarily imply greater power.

A more promising line of argument, however, suggests that, as the need for coordination increases with the complexities of modern government, so does the demand for a strong coordinator in the form of the prime minister. A skillful prime minister may use his coordinating role to leave his mark on government policy but remains a mediator, a conciliator, or an arbitrator at most: he still cannot initiate proposals. Ministers who are wary of prime-ministerial interference defend their own departmental turf by doing their own coordinating or by resorting to even more drastic measures. During the 1973–77 government, for example, Prime Minister Den Uyl decided to reconnoiter the estuary where a controversial dam was being planned. For this purpose he commissioned a Customs ship. The minister of public works, angered by this unannounced interference, managed to obtain an even faster ship, and chased the prime minister out of his "territorial waters." Although there can be no doubt that the prime minister's hand has been strengthened somewhat as a result of the increasing need of coordination, it is still a very limited encroachment on the autonomy of individual ministers.

A disunited civil service. The autonomy of individual ministers vis-à-vis the civil service seems well protected by the constitution, or rather by the conception of political–bureaucratic relations that underlies some of its provisions. Policy decisions are to be made by Parliament and the cabinet. Bureaucratic decision making, in turn, is accounted for by members of the cabinet. In line with this "primacy of politics," Dutch bureaucracy has traditionally conformed rather well to features of the rational bureaucratic type: hierarchy, specialization, expertise, and political neutrality (Daalder, 1971; see also Kooiman, 1973).

Obviously this neatly structured pattern, in which ministers are "bosses of bureaucracy," does not preclude actual decision-making power in the hands of the civil service. There is ample proof that civil servants are important policy actors. About three-quarters of all MPs, questioned in the Dutch Parliamentary Survey of 1990, agreed with the statement, "It often is difficult for Cabinet Ministers to press their point when senior bureaucrats dissent."[6] Without resorting to generalizations of "Yes, Minister" caliber, many other writers have observed detrimental effects of bureaucratic actions: delay, obstruction, or unintended policy outcomes. As one senior civil servant has noted:

Essentially the cabinet of course has to decide what the policy is. If that is the policy with which the body of civil servants cannot agree, then they [civil servants] have the tools to, let's say . . . to slow down. You always are able to come up with technical problems and difficulties which make it desirable that a certain decision of the minister is postponed for half a year . . . I do not want to use the word sabotage but . . . the influence of certain higher civil servants can be fairly large. (quoted in Eldersveld, Kooiman, and Vander Tak, 1981: 73)

In some cases administrative powers are institutionalized. One example of structured administrative influence is the Central Economic Commission (CEC), an advisory body on economic and monetary policy consisting of senior economists from various departments as well as from the Dutch Bank and the Central Planning Bureau. The CEC is known to exert considerable influence not only on the annual preparation of the budget but also in the process of drafting the government program during coalition formation. In 1986, the CEC succeeded in having several of its proposals literally copied into the government agreement, causing the president of the Second Chamber to dub this advisory body a "pseudo cabinet."

However, the manifest role of the administration in political decision making does not necessarily contradict ministerial autonomy. There is not one single, unified "fourth branch of government" in the Netherlands. One of the most visible features of Dutch bureaucracy is its "sectorization," its fragmentation according to specific policy areas. Dutch bureaucracy lacks a typical civil service: even top bureaucrats are hired by and within a department. In general Dutch civil servants tend to be departmental specialists and to have their career within that one department. Except for a few homogeneous departments, sectorization can also be observed within departments. This internal sectorization often provides ministers with divergent advice and an opportunity to divide and conquer.

Constraints on closer inspection

At first sight the assumption of ministerial autonomy seems well supported in the Dutch case. Our description so far, however, is one-sided because it is out of date and incomplete. It is out of date because collective decision making in the cabinet has been strengthened in recent decades; it is incomplete because so far we have ignored the substantial contribution parliament makes to policy-making.

Internal constraints: the cabinet agenda. Until now we have failed to discuss the cabinet's agenda and the crucial question of how much a minister can keep from being debated in cabinet. In the past, interdepartmental conflicts constituted the most important items requiring referral to the cabinet. This is no longer the case, as this minister found out when consulting a prewar ex-minister:

When I was appointed I asked Oud how he had dealt with the question of what should or should not go to cabinet. His recommendation was that a minister should bring as few of his proposals as possible before the cabinet. The minister is individually responsible anyway. And if the minister would put an item on the agenda, the cabinet might actually want to discuss the proposal! . . . The Standing Orders, however, told me a different story, so I have not been able to follow Oud's advice. Considerably less than in the past does a minister have a choice of what he would and would not like to see discussed in cabinet. Such a choice exists only in a formal sense. As soon as a dossier involves more departments it is brought before cabinet. (minister, 1960s)

The most important clause in the Standing Orders of the Council of Ministers is Article 4.2, which lists the kind of items a minister cannot decide autonomously, but for which he needs cabinet approval:

-all proposals for legislation or decrees;
-all treaties;
-all white papers and all requests for advice from advisory councils that may have political or financial consequences;
-all publications of policy plans that may have political or financial consequences, or that may have an impact on other ministers' policies;
-the creation and/or composition of advisory councils;
-the creation and/or composition of interdepartmental committees that are permanent or that may eventually have political or financial implications; publication of the reports of advisory councils and interdepartmental committees;
-important items of foreign policy;
-the composition of and instructions to delegations to international conferences;
-all crown appointments (with a few listed exceptions).

Because of this nearly exhaustive list, neither the prime minister nor the other ministers have much room to manipulate the agenda. When a proposal is not covered by this list, the situation is less clear. If a minister even doubts whether proposal might have a bearing on general government policy he or she is required to consult the prime minister. Only if both of them agree that it is not a cabinet matter can the proposal be kept from the agenda. In our interviews, most ministers were unable to give a clear definition of general government policy. "It is what the prime minister says it is," was one typical answer. "The permanent secretary took care of that," was another. Expected political controversies seem to be the most important determinants of referral to the cabinet of dossiers not covered by Article 4.2:

Whenever I thought a decision – even when it was within my purview to make – could have political consequences, I talked it over with the prime minister, and sometimes I sent a memorandum to the cabinet: for example, when a decision could lead to an interpellation in Parliament. (minister, 1950s and 1960s).

If you keep something from the cabinet, you should make sure that the cabinet does not find out some other way:

A lot is formally required by the Standing Orders. Then there is a gray area, where you can make a mistake, but only once. After such a mistake you get a roasting; the prime minister will take you aside, or he will telephone; other colleagues complain in cabinet (minister, 1970s and 1980s).

Internal constraints: nonintervention reconsidered. The potential scope of collective decision making is wide but, as long as ministers follow the rule of nonintervention, such collective decision making seems largely pro forma and does little to encroach upon an individual minister's autonomy. A detailed study of one of the most recent years for which the cabinet minutes are available (1968), shows that about 80 percent of all contributions to the discussions in the cabinet can indeed be traced back to the speakers' own portfolios (Andeweg, 1990a). The same study showed that 79 percent of all the proposals come through discussions in the cabinet unscathed. However, one may also turn these figures around: one in five proposals is altered by the cabinet, and one in five sentences in the minutes does cross the boundaries of ministerial autonomy. Moreover, that was in 1968; since then developments have taken place that stimulate, or at least legitimize, one minister's interference with another's portfolio.

In the first place, the cabinet is no longer a gathering only of department heads; it has also become a coalition committee of leading party politicians. Recruitment of Dutch ministers has never been as apolitical as it is sometimes depicted, but the emphasis decidedly was on technocratic expertise in the policy area for which the new appointee was to be responsible (Bakema and Secker, 1988; see also Secker, 1991). Between 1946 and 1967, 72 percent of all ministers had such expertise when first appointed, whereas only 57 percent had previous political experience. Between 1967 and 1986 the percentage with technical expertise dropped slightly to 65, and the percentage with political experience rose sharply to 73. Meddling in another minister's portfolio may not be accepted for a head of department, but it may be perfectly legitimate for a party politician.

The politicization of the cabinet is also evidenced by the development from government program to coalition agreement. Before the 1960s, the coalition agreement negotiated by the party leaders was small and confined to a few principal issues. When the ministers met for the first time, they added to the coalition agreement to create the government program. Since the 1960s, and especially in the 1980s, the coalition agreement has become even more detailed and encompassing. There is little or no room for the ministers to add to or subtract from this agreement: it is now the government program (Bovend'Eert, 1988). In the first phase of this development, its role should not be overestimated: "It is referred to when there is a conflict, but after three or four months most of the assumptions underlying the coalition agreement was outdated anyway" (minister, 1970s).

Apparently, the coalition agreement now plays a much more important role: "The coalition agreement has gradually assumed greater significance. Eventually we have come to regard it as something like a law" (minister, 1970s and 1980s). The coalition agreement also provides ministers with a legitimate excuse to interfere in a colleague's portfolio.

Finally, a system of weekly political consultations has been set up. Each Thursday night, a party's ministers meet with their parliamentary party leader and the party chairman to discuss the next day's cabinet agenda. At these meetings junior ministers are also present. Often junior ministers are appointed at the department of another party's minister. Sometimes they are intended as political watchdogs, but they function more often as liaisons between their department and their party's ministerial team. Such meetings emphasize a minister's role as his party's bridgehead in the cabinet, and thus legitimize interventionist behavior.

In addition to the politicization of the ministers, there has been a second development that is likely to have weakened the rule of nonintervention. Until the early 1970s, budget negotiations resembled a non–zero-sum game: the public sector was expanding and each minister almost automatically got an annual budget increase. In these days of negative growth and retrenchment, ministers sometimes think it advantageous to interfere with other portfolios:

Later I did intervene by proposing additional cuts in the estimates of other colleagues. It is very dangerous, because you run a risk that they will reciprocate likewise. I made quite a study of the defense estimates, so that I could ask questions like, "Is it really necessary that we build this frigate next year?" [Question: Why did you do that?] "To maximize my own budget." The more you cut back elsewhere, the more money is available for education. So you pick a budget that is without party-political risks and of which you are convinced that there is still some slack. But I was cautious, because it is dicey. Before you knew it, he would hit back. (minister, 1970s and 1980s)

Despite the risks, a study of financial decision making in cabinets between 1975 and 1986 concluded that the rule of nonintervention was no longer as strictly adhered to as it was in the past (Toirkens, 1988).

Internal constraints: enforcing cabinet decisions. One could argue that collective decision making does not detract from an individual minister's autonomy if the implementation of cabinet decisions is not monitored and policed. In the Dutch case, a few mechanisms exist to enforce cabinet decisions. One of them consists of the progress reports prepared by the cabinet secretariat on the implementation of each cabinet decision. At this moment, too little is known about this instrument to ascertain its effectiveness.

A second mechanism consists of the cabinet minutes. These are detailed, nearly verbatim records of the discussions in cabinet, taken by the semi-autonomous cabinet secretary and one of his deputies: in recent years they have amounted to about twenty-four hundred densely printed pages each year. Officially, the minutes are secret, but they are distributed to all ministers and junior ministers. In practice, senior officials in most departments have easy access to complete minutes, and junior civil servants can get pages relevant to their work. Journalists sometimes get access to "leaked" extracts. This relatively wide circulation makes it difficult for a minister to ignore a cabinet decision.

Third, many cabinet decisions have financial consequences, and these turn the minister of finance into an active law-enforcement officer. If a minister "forgets" a particular cabinet decision, then the minister of finance may very well remind him of it during budget negotiations. Note that the minister of finance has his own army of informers in all the departments: the Inspectorate of Finance.

Finally, Parliament has to be informed about many cabinet decisions. Occasionally a minister finds himself defending in Parliament a policy that he fought in the cabinet:

Roolvink was very much opposed to a wages policy, and really wanted to abolish wage control altogether. Most other ministers were not ready for that yet. This led to a sharp confrontation in the cabinet. Although Roolvink fought ferociously and even threatened to resign, it was decided eventually that we should issue a decree restricting wage increases. We had to defend this decree in the Second Chamber. It appeared that an overwhelming majority of the Second Chamber was against the wage decree; the cabinet did not stand a chance of getting that through Parliament. Yet, Roolvink defended the controversial decree vigorously and without once acknowledging the insinuation made by the opposition, that he himself had always been opposed to such a decree. The cabinet went down as a whole, all flags flying. The morning after, we had a brief postmortem in the cabinet. All Roolvink said was, "Mr. President, you do understand that I am full of bitter sentiments." (minister, 1960 and 1970s)

How effective these policing mechanisms are is unknown: ministers who have successfully ignored cabinet decisions are unlikely to celebrate in public. It seems unlikely, however, that such evasions take place on any significant scale. The Dutch cabinet, it would seem, is to a large extent a functioning collective decision making institution (cf. Baylis, 1989; 148–53). Recent developments have strengthened collective decision making at the expense of individual ministerial autonomy.

External constraints: Parliament. As in all parliamentary systems, executive–legislative relations are governed by two basic rules: ministerial responsibility and parliamentary confidence. However, whereas in most parliamentary systems ministers are part of the representative body, in the Netherlands they are not. Dutch ministers have no seat and no vote in Parliament. This incompatibility of ministerial and parliamentary roles is but one symptom of a more general distance between the cabinet and Parliament.

According to the constitution, laws shall be passed jointly by government and the States General (the two houses of Parliament). To this end legislative interactions have been regulated rather specifically. Bills can be submitted to the Second Chamber by either the cabinet or an MP, and are scheduled for discussion whenever Parliament wishes. Although cabinet cannot control the legislative timetable, it does dominate the legislative agenda by taking the initiative. Of all bills submitted to Parliament in the period 1965–85, about 97 percent were initiated by cabinet ministers.

Despite its initiating role, the cabinet is by no means predominant in legislative affairs. The process of legislation is characterized by an intricate system of checks and balances, allowing MPs to interfere at several points in the process. One such point is the "preparatory enquiry" of bills by a parliamentary committee. In committee meetings the bill is discussed by the responsible minister and a small number (about twenty) of technically informed MPs. Minister and MPs interact in writing as well, through the exchange of various legislative reports. There is not much research done on this topic, but our impression is that, even in this early stage of legislation, substantive deals and concessions are being made both by the MPs and by the minister.

In the next phase, the plenary session, every MP can propose amendments to the bill that are decided upon by majority vote. At this point, there is not very much a minister can do to avert an unwanted parliamentary amendment to his bill except informally squeezing the MPs belonging to his party. As a last resort he can declare the proposed amendment unacceptable. By using this traditional formula the minister indicates that the acceptance of the amendment by a majority of MPs will either cause him to withdraw the bill or to resign. In practice it is quite common for

Second Chamber MPs to change government bills by means of parliamentary amendments. Each year hundreds of amendments are proposed, of which about one-third are actually enacted into law.

Apart from its legislative role, Parliament oversees cabinet policies. To this end, ministers are responsible to Parliament, which can dismiss them at will. Since 1848 ministerial responsibility has been a written part of the constitution, but the exact content is a matter of debate. Constitutional scholars tend to agree on at least four categories to which individual responsibility of ministers before Parliament applies: deeds of the royal family, decisions and nondecisions of ministers themselves, and those of their junior ministers and their civil servants.

There are three ways in which Parliament can make ministers respond. First, by asking for information (written questions, question hour, interpellations); second, by confronting ministers with parliamentary policy proposals (motions); and third, by investigating government acts (parliamentary inquiries). Constitutionally, ministers are required to convey any information asked for by Parliament, except for matters touching the "interest of the state." As a rule, parliamentarians tend to jealously guard their right to know. Accusations of having transmitted incomplete or inadequate information may cause a minister to resign.

Each MP may put a policy proposal to the vote, provided it is supported by at least four colleagues. Interestingly, parliamentary motions, passed by majority vote, do not bind the cabinet. A minister may disregard them, taking the risk of subsequent parliamentary action.

A strong weapon in the hands of parliament is the so-called right to inquire. A majority of MPs can decide to invest a parliamentary investigative committee with semilegal powers to question witnesses. Since 1977 ministers are required by law to submit themselves to public interrogations by such a committee. The danger of a parliamentary inquiry to cabinet life is testified to by the fact that inquiries held in the last ten years caused the defeat of two cabinet ministers, two junior ministers, and at least two senior administrators.

There is no investiture in the Netherlands: confidence is assumed to exist unless Parliament decides otherwise. There is no specified procedure for censuring individual ministers or the government. Any motion intended or interpreted to express distrust or disapproval may cause the resignation of one or all ministers, or the dissolution of Parliament and early elections.

It is difficult to assess the extent to which formal powers of parliamentary oversight actually constrain individual ministers. One clear-cut measure is the degree to which Parliament uses its power to dismiss either the cabinet or an individual minister. The Dutch Parliament has acted rather modestly in this respect. Eight of the twenty postwar cabinets have fallen prematurely, four because of conflicts within the cabinet itself, and four as a result of an overt act of Parliament. Moreover, individual postwar ministers have been relatively spared compared to earlier times when ministers were "consumed by parliamentarians like artichoke leaves." Out of the 157 postwar ministers, 33 have resigned individually. Parliament is but one of the causes: eleven resigned for personal reasons (including disease and decease), ten because of the appointment to another noncabinet position, five as a result of an internal conflict in the cabinet, and seven because of a conflict with Parliament.

Things are more complicated, however. At least two other processes affect the impact of Parliament on the cabinet (Andeweg, 1990b). One is the set of interactions between cabinet ministers and parliamentary coalition parties. Government decision making is guided by the contents of the government agreement, to which both ministers and parliamentary coalition parties are tied. Policy-making is further facilitated by party discipline and by the practice of mutual consultations through weekly "precooking" meetings between ministers and parliamentarians belonging to the governing parties. In this model one cannot realistically speak of ministerial autonomy. The ability of ministers to set policy is seriously constrained by the contents of the government agreement, which – it should be remembered – is a written "treaty" between parliamentary parties on future policies.

A second process concerns the role of distinct "policy circuits," particularly important to agricultural decision making but also relevant to such divergent sectors as social security, education, health, and defense. In such policy circuits a minister, acting as head of a department, deals primarily with a small number of specialized MPs in a parliamentary standing committee, as well as with advisory bodies and interest organizations relevant to the policy area. From this perspective of sectoral decision making in rather closed policy subsystems, a minister may have a considerable degree of autonomy with respect to other ministers. Yet, within each sector and subsystem, he or she is but one actor, and maneuvering room is constrained by various sectoral interests.

Overall, several different factors constrain a minister's freedom of action: Parliament as such in legislative affairs; the governing parties in Parliament through the government agreement and precooking mechanisms; and specialized parliamentary committees acting within policy circuits.

CONCLUSION: DUTCH QUESTIONS TO THE PORTFOLIO-ALLOCATION APPROACH

The portfolio-allocation approach addresses three basic questions. Do cabinet policies change when parties in government change, when parties reallocate portfolios among themselves, and/or when individual ministers change portfolios?

In the Dutch case, the answer to the first question is "Yes." We found evidence that parties do make a difference, at least in determining government policy intentions. The answers to the second and third questions depend on the degree of ministerial autonomy or departmentalism – on the extent to which ministers can control policy outputs in their jurisdiction.

Our *tour d'horizon* of opportunities for, and constraints on, ministers in Dutch coalition governments does not provide a clear answer to the question of ministerial autonomy. The constitutional legacy of individual ministerial responsibility, the tacit rule of nonintervention, the less-than-commanding role of the prime minister, as well as the absence of a unified "fourth branch of government," seem to point to a considerable degree of autonomy for ministers within their own portfolios. The gradual strengthening of collective cabinet decision making, due in particular to the politicization of ministerial office and the fact that the Dutch Parliament is less docile than is normally the case in parliamentary systems of government, all provide powerful constraints on ministerial autonomy. Some of these constraints (for example, the coalition agreement or the weekly political consultations) provide alternative means for the parties to ensure the implementation of their policies. The underwriting of the program through portfolio allocations is one of the instruments to influence policy-making in the cabinet, but not the only one.

Complications arise, however, when we look into the second and third question more closely. If parties are to control departmental policy outputs through the allocation of portfolios, at least two more conditions have to be met: parties must allocate portfolios to ministers in order to underwrite their intended policies; ministers must live up to party expectations. The Dutch case prompts certain questions with regard to these additional conditions; we shall conclude with a brief discussion of them.

An empirical question: the neglect of nominators' motives

In our interviews with former cabinet ministers, we asked why they thought they were chosen. Some of the answers clearly support the portfolio-allocation approach:

I was my party's parliamentary spokesman for development aid; I had written the paragraph on development aid in the election manifesto; defended that paragraph at the party conference; I was part of the team that negotiated with the other parties. This meant that I could carry out what I had conceived, but that was more or less accidental. (minister, 1970s and 1980s)

Very occasionally one of the coalition parties vetoes someone nominated by another party. In 1952, for example, the Catholic Party objected to the appointment of the Social Democrat, Hofstra, as minister of finance, because he had just published a book on taxation that they considered Marxist. In that same year the Social Democrats objected to the appointment of the Catholic, Luns, as Minister of Foreign Affairs. As all the foreign secretaries in the budding European Community were Catholics, the Social Democrats feared a "papist" Europe. A compromise was eventually found by appointing an additional minister of foreign affairs, the nonpartisan Beyen. Note that such a veto also provides support for the portfolio-allocation approach.

However, the interviews also reveal cases that do not fit: "I did not like the move to Housing, especially after that conflict with Parliament. I also had different ideas about a solution for the housing shortage; I expected more from a market approach, but Parliament would not let me" (minister, 1950s). In this case the motive for the nominators was to find another portfolio for a sitting minister, whose "old" portfolio fell to another party during cabinet formation. There are many more examples of party "elephants" who have to be found a portfolio. The opposite situation also occurred, when a party landed a particular portfolio and was desperate to find anyone willing and able to fill it. In 1959 the portfolio of the navy was assigned to the Catholic Party. To a considerable degree the Dutch Catholics are concentrated in the two southern, landlocked provinces, and Catholic sailors are a rare breed. After an elaborate search, the party discovered a Catholic submarine commander and literally helicoptered him from his ship to a position as junior minister. The party leaders often meet with refusals, and their final nominations may not always be their first choices. Appointments can be rewards for loyal service to the party or its leader: one of the ministers interviewed owed his appointment to the fact that he always drove his parliamentary party leader home in his own car. The appointments also provide the party with a bridgehead in the cabinet, regardless of portfolio:

In the first place, Romme [the party leader] wanted me because he knew that I would give as good as I would get – in that whole cabinet there was no KVP minister with parliamentary experience. In the second place [it was] because he would be able to get a message to cabinet through to me. (minister 1950s, and 1970s)

Finally, some appointments may have a largely symbolic value. When, in 1989, the Christian Democrats exchanged the Liberals for the Social

Democrats as coalition partners, they appointed the chairman of the Christian Employers Association, Andriessen, as minister of economic affairs, to allay any fears of a radical shift to the left.

A theoretical question: the neglect of institutional roles

The portfolio-allocation approach assumes that ministers live up to the expectations of the nominators, and that their behavior as minister can be predicted from past actions and positions. But institutional norms, rules, and payoff structures also mold a minister's role and thereby his behavior. Elsewhere we have argued that the Dutch cabinet actually contains two institutions: a meeting of heads of departments and a coalition of party prominents (Andeweg, 1988a, 1990). Ministers have to switch constantly between their partisan and their departmental roles. We described how the civil service as such does not significantly constrain ministerial autonomy. Often, however, there is no need for the civil service to obstruct or sabotage; ministers "go native" anyway:

It is nearly always the case that the departmental role of a minister is emphasized. That is because the department is a minister's "home," where he is pampered and consoled. The secretary, the car, the messenger, the chauffeur, the whole outfit is provided by the department. A minister is sucked into a tradition that also encompasses moments of camaraderie. From the very first day the minister is made to understand that he will be judged by the degree to which he is successful in bringing the department more money and prestige. Only the very strong are able to withstand that pressure. In nine out of ten cases the minister returns as a specific defender of the specific interests of that department. (minister, 1960s, 1970s, and 1980s)

Most ministers have the tendency to get hooked on their department. For the governing of the country it is extremely detrimental. That is what the mocking phrase, "un Jacobin ministre n'est pas encore un ministre Jacobin" is all about. (minister, 1960s, and 1970s)

Whether it is in the first days or later, there is considerable evidence that most ministers turn out as ambassadors of their departments in the cabinet rather than as ambassadors of the cabinet in their departments. To the extent to which this process cannot be predicted in advance, it may be difficult to forecast the policy impact of nominating a particular minister to a particular portfolio.

NOTES

1 See Andeweg, Dittrich, and Van der Tak (1977).
2 Analysis of an international dataset on ministerial careers shows that 70 percent of Dutch ministers are one-post ministers. Only Austrian ministers are less mobile (see Bakema, 1991: 90).

3 Interview by W. Breedveld in Van Drimmelen (1987: 212).
4 Unless indicated otherwise, the quotations are from interviews with seventy-eight former cabinet ministers, conducted by Rudy Andeweg. These former ministers were promised that they would remain anonymous in publications based on these interviews.
5 For a more elaborate discussion see Andeweg (1991).
6 Results from the Dutch Parliamentary Survey of 1990, conducted among all MPs of both houses.

REFERENCES

Andeweg, R. B. 1988. Centrifugal forces and collective decision-making: the case of the Dutch cabinet. *European Journal of Political Research* 16:125–51.
   1990a. Tweerlei ministerraad. In R. B. Andeweg (ed.), *Ministers en Ministerraad*. The Hague: SDU.
   1990b. King in Parliament. Paper presented to the ECPR joint sessions, Bochum.
   1991. Not just chairman, not yet chief? *West European Politics* 14, no. 2:116–32.
Andeweg, R. B., K. Dittrich, and T. Van der Tak. 1977. *Kabinetsformatie*. Leiden.
Bakema, W. E. 1991. The ministerial career. In J. Blondel and J. L. Thiébault (eds.), *The Profession of Government Minister in Western Europe*. London: Macmillan Press.
Bakema, W. E., and I. P. Secker. 1988. Ministerial expertise and the Dutch case. *European Journal of Political Research* 16:153–70.
Baylis, T. 1989. *Governing by Committee: Collegial Leadership in Advanced Societies*. Albany, N.Y.: SUNY Press.
Bovend'Eert, P. T. 1988. *Regeeraccoorden en regeringsprograms*. The Hague: Staatsuitgeverij.
Cameron, D. R. 1978. The expansion of the public economy: a comparative analysis. *American Political Science Review* 72:1243–61.
Daalder, H. 1971. On building consociational nations: the cases of the Netherlands and Switzerland. *International Social Science Journal* 3:355–70.
Deetman Committee, 1991. *Rapport bijzondere commissie vraagpunten*. The Hague.
Eldersveld, S. J., J. Kooiman, and T. van der Tak. 1981. *Elite Images of Dutch Politics*. The Hague: Nijhoff.
Hoogerwerf, A. 1977. De groei van de overheid in Nederland sinds 1900: aspecten van omvang, ontwikkeling, onevenwichtigheid en overbelasting. *Bestuurswetenschapen* 31:111–25.
Kooiman, J. 1973. The Higher Civil Servant in Holland: Role, Status and Influence. Paper presented to the ECPR joint sessions, Mannheim.
Thomassen, J. J. et al. (eds). 1992. *De geachte afgevaardigde: hoe Kamerleden denken over het parlement*. Muiderberg: Coutinho.
Toirkens, S. J. 1988. *Schijn en werkelijkheid van het bezuinigingsbeleid, 1975–1986*. Deventer: Kluwer.
Van Drimmelen et al. 1987. *Voor de eenheid van beleid*. The Hague: Staatsuitgeverij.

5

The political role of cabinet ministers in Ireland

Brian Farrell

MAIN FEATURES OF THE IRISH CABINET SYSTEM

In large measure, the Irish cabinet system is a replica of the early twentieth-century British model, though there are some differences. It is subject to a rigid written constitution, although this has rarely curtailed the accretion of executive power. It is dependent upon a single-transferable-vote system of proportional representation in elections, which has generated a significant range of possible governments, from single-party majority through to wide coalitions (Farrell, 1987a), and might be expected to strain the conventions of an inherited Westminster–Whitehall model. Nevertheless, perhaps the greatest differences are found in the size, structure, and relative underdevelopment of the Irish cabinet system.

Size

In terms both of political and bureaucratic personnel, only a small number of people have participated in the Irish core executive. The Irish Free State constitution of 1922 limited membership of the Executive Council (cabinet) to not less than five and not more than seven, with provision for up to five "extern" (noncabinet) departmental ministers.[1] The subsequent and still-current constitution, *Bunreacht nah Eireann*, specifies that the government shall consist of not less than seven and not more than fifteen members (Article 28). In fact governments were remarkably slow to reach these constitutional maxima. Moreover, in earlier decades the limited access to cabinet membership was further reduced by low turnover rates and excessive ministerial longevity (Coakley and Farrell, 1989).

Structure and underdevelopment

Constitutionally, legally, procedurally, and in practice, the doctrine of collective responsibility reigns supreme in Ireland. Article 28. 4.2 declares,

"The Government shall meet and act as a collective authority and shall be collectively responsible for the Department of State administered by members of the Government." The convention is invoked to justify the concentration on the cabinet as the focus of decision making and as a continuing institution. This insistence on the cabinet as the source of authoritative decisions has had a stultifying effect on institutional reform and adaptation. In particular there has been no development of a cabinet committee system, nor any extension of the powers of individual junior ministers, either of which might be expected to reduce the burden of cabinet decision making. Noncabinet ministers of state are dependent on "their" cabinet ministers in submitting matters for cabinet consideration (Penniman and Farrell, 1987: 150–2). There have been occasional efforts to identify the functions and specify the responsibilities of individual ministers but it appears that no Taoiseach (prime minister) to date has been able to offer junior ministers access to the cabinet without the prior approval of the relevant cabinet minister.

Similarly there has been no elaboration of formal cabinet committees, although ad hoc committees are used to resolve specific issues. There are some exceptions to this general rule, and some delegation appears to occur in dealing with the problems of estimates and budget allocations. Nevertheless, ministers (including prime ministers) and officials rarely accept the absence of a committee system as a defect. On the contrary, they argue that there is no need for a committee system in a government that is small and whose members meet frequently; that it is difficult enough to organize the attendance of ministers at cabinet meeting without attempting additional committee meetings; that the experience of cabinet committees has been at best mixed;[2] that informal meetings between ministers who may be in disagreement are an adequate substitute.

LEGISLATIVE–EXECUTIVE RELATIONS

Constitutionally in Ireland there is a separation of powers between legislature and executive, and the government is responsible to the Dáil (the popularly elected lower house), which nominates one of its members to be Taoiseach (Farrell, 1988). In reality the deputy selected is typically the head of the strongest party grouping in the house, and the government can effectively control the legislature as long as its party support remains solid.

This control extends to the parliamentary agenda. A government with a secure parliamentary majority, or even a working minority, has virtually total control over the legislative timetable. Although the party whips coordinate the parliamentary program, the government is in the dominant position. Dáil Standing Order 25 states the position clearly: "The Taoiseach shall have the right to determine the order in which Government business shall appear on the Order paper and by announcement at the commencement of public business, the order in which it shall be taken each day." Standing Order 86 allows "a minister to move, without notice, at the commencement of public business" that private members' time (that is, opposition time) be preempted.

Opposition parties can (and occasionally do) refuse to cooperate with a government that is seen to be overbearing. The protests are typically marked by constant challenges on the Order of Business, frequent calls for a quorum, or divisions and withdrawal of pairing arrangements with government ministers. Effectively these can disrupt legislative business, embarrass the government, and compel the excessive use of guillotine motions in public business.

Such negative tactics cannot be applied indefinitely. Nor do they equate with according a positive role in policy-making to the Dáil. The legislature cannot impose policy decisions upon either an unwilling cabinet or an unwilling individual minister. It may resist ministerial proposals – rarely with any significant effect – but has no effective means of translating its own proposals into executive action. Standing Orders 122–5 (endorsing the virtual monopoly of the executive regarding public expenditure enshrined in Article 17.2 of the constitution) require that bills involving the imposition of charges upon the people or the appropriation of revenue or other public moneys, and implementing resolutions voting money or imposing taxation as well as motions covering grants of money for the public service, may be moved only by a member of the government, and this greatly reduces the scope for parliamentary initiatives. Government control of sessional dates and the timetable is a further obstacle to policy-making by parliament.

Even the answerability of government to Parliament is severely curtailed. Deputies may address oral and written questions to specific ministers but successive chairmen have ruled that it is open to the minister (or Taoiseach) to direct the question to a colleague. The chair disallows questions involving internal cabinet arrangements and collective responsibility, and permits ministers, if they wish, to link two or more questions together in a composite reply. There is a well-established principle that the chair has no power to compel a minister to answer a question or a supplementary question.

The ultimate threat is a direct challenge to the executive by the legislature that put it in place. A motion of no confidence in the government, once moved, is normally converted into a motion of confidence and given precedence in government time in the Dáil. Were the government to refuse

Table 5.1. *Legislative activity, 1985–91*

Year	Government bills		Private members' bills				
			Introduced		Discussed		
	Introduced	Passed	Dáil	Seanad	Dáil	Seanad	Passed
1985	44	24	3	1	1	2	0
1986	45	39	9	0	2	1	0
1987	50	34*	9	3	4	1	0
1988	30	35	13	1	5	1	0
1989	33	32	13	2	8	0	1
1990	35	28	13	0	6	0	0
1991	32	32	11	2	8	1	1

*includes a bill to amend the constitution.
Source: I am indebted to Ms. Marie Kennedy, bills officer, Leinster House for these data.

time, the opposition parties could agree to give the motion priority in private members' time. The normal exclusion relating to reopening issues already determined by the Dáil does not apply to confidence motions.

However, the reality is that any legislative challenge to the executive remains empty as long as the government's party support in the Parliament remains secure. Government defeats on substantive motions are extremely rare. Narrower majorities that have characterized election results in the 1980s have forced governments into deals with individual deputies, or into coalitions with small party groups, but they have not enhanced the policy-making capacity of the Parliament. In essence the Parliament provides an arena for opposition, but its deliberative and revising function are minimal. Legislation is drafted within the executive and ratified by the Dáil and Senate. Overwhelmingly it is government bills that are passed into law. Since 1958 only two private members' bills have been passed;[3] more usually, if the government accepts the principle of such a bill, the deputy is invited to withdraw the proposal on the understanding that a government bill will be drafted and presented. Although there has been some increase in the number of opposition bills discussed, this has little effect on the government's virtual monopoly in lawmaking, as Table 5.1 indicates.

Nor can it be suggested that efforts to develop a parliamentary committee system have had more than a peripheral effect on public policy-making. A study of the committees in the twenty-fourth Oireachtas, 1983–7, concludes: "It was never reasonable to expect the fledgling new Irish committee system to enjoy powers of command over the executive. Its function was not to set up alternative cabinets but rather to channel informed opinion and analysis into the parliamentary chamber" (Arkins, 1988: 97).

The concentration on the cabinet itself as the clearinghouse for information and the center of all government decision making severely restricts the independence of individual ministers.

Although the Ministers and Secretaries Act (1924, and subsequent acts) provides that "the powers, duties and functions" of specified departments "shall be assigned to and administered by the minister," and that "each of the Ministers, heads of the respective Departments of State . . . shall be a corporation sole under his style or name," even the internal departmental autonomy of ministers is severely restricted. In particular, stringent controls are exercised by the Department of Finance, reinforced by the obligations of departmental accounting officers (usually the secretary of the department).[4] Extensive interviews with ministers in a variety of Irish administrations indicate that they are very restricted in regard to policy-making.[5] In effect, with the rarest of exceptions, they will always seek cabinet approval in policy matters. Ministers were asked, "In matters relating to your own department, what kind of decisions did you not feel able to take on your own?" Responses fell into four categories: issues involving cost, innovation, coordination, or those regarded as politically sensitive. A small number of ministers mentioned security matters.

Finance and control

Ministers were unanimous in identifying the Department of Finance as a major constraint on their capacity to run their own departments, let alone advance new policy proposals.[6] A number gave examples of the minute scrutiny of expenditure. A minister recalled that in the easier financial circumstances of the 1960s minor transfers (he suggested £50,000–£100,000) between budget subheads were tolerated and gave a minister some leeway; he mentioned, with some pride, an additional departmental expenditure of some £70,000 for postage, which he personally approved without prior financial sanction. On the other hand, another minister recalled a cabinet discussion in the 1980s about whether postage in a particular department should be £80,000 or £90,000 in a given year. It is also clear that the increased stringency required by the state of the public finances now prevents ministers making internal switches of monies between subheads in their own departments. A minister who had served in a number of departments (and subsequently in Finance) offered a sweeping judgment that echoes the views of many: "Everything involving finance is a near-impossibility for any minister off his own bat."

Innovation

The capacity of individual ministers to innovate is severely restricted by the emphasis on collective responsibility and tight financial control. There have been some notable exceptions. Perhaps the most spectacular happened in 1966, when the minister of education announced to a journalists' conference a proposal for free secondary education, which had not been cleared with either the Department of Finance or the cabinet. There is strong evidence to indicate that the speech had been shown in advance to the Taoiseach (Farrell, 1991: 106–7; O'Buachalla, 1988: 278). Nevertheless, this was totally atypical.

A large number of ministers identified policy innovation as requiring prior cabinet approval. Some gave specific examples: a scheme to standardize various provisions to supply free fuel within the Department of Social Welfare was brought to the cabinet. Another spoke of the inability to restructure schemes within another department; he found that "anything that's new, any scheme that's not been approved beforehand – even if it is on a pilot basis" had to go to the cabinet.

Coordination

The scope for independent ministerial initiatives is also severely restricted by the demands of interdepartmental coordination. Ministers do not operate in a vacuum; new departures in one area quickly affect others. Ministers and senior civil servants are alert to developments that are seen as interfering with their turf, and act accordingly. In his memoirs, Garret FitzGerald records the efforts of the Department of Finance to enter into negotiations with the Northern Ireland civil service without reference to his own Department of Foreign Affairs (FitzGerald, 1991: 225). Another minister of foreign affairs reported forcing the revision of a policy affecting aliens inaugurated by the Department of Justice without prior clearance.

Even bringing initiatives to the cabinet without previously consulting the relevant ministers is a virtual recipe for failure. A minister who served as a whip commented, "It was futile to bring things to the cabinet table without prior agreement. I could sit back and see that . . . if you hadn't squared it off, you were silly. It was a bad minister who tried." However, other ministers appeared to ignore this strategy: "I never lobbied colleagues in advance to get people on side," said a minister with experience in several departments.

Politically sensitive issues

Ministers were also acutely conscious of possible political repercussions of their decisions, and tended to play safe by using the cabinet as a clearinghouse. They were also aware that ministerial colleagues might have useful experience to offer. One, who had served in a central policy department, put the point in a general context:

I didn't want to appear to upstage colleagues. Even if you knew you were right, bring it up . . . Although on the face of it "corporation sole," in practice if you pushed your luck on that, there was always the danger that colleagues would say, "Well, if you want to be that smart and do it yourself, goodbye if anything goes wrong." So, if there was any significant innovation, any significant political element, it was better to try and carry colleagues with you.

Collective responsibility and collective decision making

It is evident that the principle and practice of collective responsibility in the Irish system extends to collective decision making. Particular ministers may be energetic in pursuing policy initiatives, but they do not win all their battles (Farrell, 1991; Hussey, 1990; Valiulis, 1985; Whyte, 1980). Ministerial and/or departmental proposals are not simply "noted" at cabinet. Although most ministers expressed varying degrees of dissatisfaction with the extent to which major issues were debated, none of them suggested that the cabinet was a mere rubber stamp; it was regarded as a genuine and comprehensive constraint on individual ministerial autonomy. It was also clear that the Taoiseach's role is highly influential: failure to manage the cabinet creates log jams throughout the decision-making process, whereas an early and clear expression of approval by the Taoiseach can greatly expedite a positive cabinet outcome on a ministerial proposal.

THE ROLE OF THE TAOISEACH

The Taoiseach plays a pivotal role in the Irish political system. He is chairman of the cabinet, manager of ministers, and increasingly seen as chief executive of the state. His dominance further limits the capacity of individual ministers – or even groups of ministers – to control public policy.

Chairman of the cabinet

Procedure, practice, and power makes the Taoiseach master of the cabinet. Indeed any weakness in chairing affects the efficiency of the cabinet – a Fianna Fail minister reported that there were considerable periods under an unassertive Taoiseach in which internal disagreements on contentious issues were "put on the long finger." During the FitzGerald coalition it was evident that the Taoiseach's preference for discursive discussion was an obstacle to decision making. However, in practice, although ministers may complain of being bullied or delayed, they do not challenge the Taoiseach's control of the agenda and of cabinet business.

This is not to suggest that there is an impenetrable wall. Whereas the cabinet secretariat has no compunction about rejecting a ministerial memorandum if it is not related to his or her area of responsibility, a minister has a virtually complete right to submit and have accepted for the agenda a properly processed item within the jurisdiction of the ministry concerned. However, experienced observers have noted that typically a sensitive issue will not have reached the point of being put on paper until the minister has discussed the matter with the Taoiseach.

The Taoiseach is also extremely influential in determining the outcome of cabinet discussions. All ministers acknowledged this as a fact of cabinet life. "Really you can't get an item discussed for five seconds at a cabinet meeting if the Taoiseach isn't with you," was a typical comment. The Taoiseach's position is strengthened by well-established conventions. Votes are rare, dissent recorded even more rarely.[7] There is no fixed quorum; the Taoiseach can, in effect, summon a snap meeting, and this small set of ministers will nevertheless be regarded as a cabinet meeting. Although he is accorded no formal veto, it is evident that his open opposition can delay, substantially modify, or ultimately destroy a ministerial proposal. Even his indifference to a contentious issue at cabinet may defer decision indefinitely.

Manager of ministers

Central to the Taoiseach's dominance over ministers is that he nominates them and allocates their portfolios. Subject to Dáil approval, they are appointed by the president. Article 28.9.4 provides that "the Taoiseach may at any time, for reasons which to him seem sufficient, request a member of the Government to resign; should the member concerned fail to comply with the request, his appointment shall be terminated by the president if the Taoiseach so advises." Although sackings are extremely rare and are even more rarely provoked by policy disagreement, this is an important weapon in the Taoiseach's armory.

There is no formal hierarchy of ministers, although the Tanaiste (deputy prime minister) has a constitutional role. Finance is recognized as the most powerful office after the prime minister, and Foreign Affairs is particularly prestigious. It is clear that senior politicians can and do hold out for particular appointments.[8] It is also certain that a strong-minded Taoiseach can refuse.

The criteria for ministerial selection and deployment are far from clear in the Irish system. There is no obvious emphasis on specialized skills or competence. Even previous experience as a front-bench spokesperson in a particular area carries no predictable right of succession. Typically appointments are made from the senior political ranks, although the emphasis on parliamentary service has recently become less pronounced. Overall, however, it appears that loyalty and proximity to the party leader is a dominant consideration in cabinet selection (for a fuller discussion see Farrell, 1987a,b). Although Taoisigh insist that choices are based on merit and capacity, they show a remarkable tendency to surround themselves with loyalists. The allocation of specific portfolios to particular ministers frequently seems secondary.[9]

Chief executive

The general trend in Western Europe has been for the prime minister's role as chief executive to become more important, and Ireland is no exception. Ireland, as a member of the EC, has also had to confront demands on the role of prime minister as the country's representative on a range of intergovernmental bodies. Inevitably, there have been political and administrative adjustments as a result of this.

Lynch originally initiated change by appointing an independent economic adviser. Subsequently elected to the Dáil in 1977, this adviser was made minister in a newly created department of economic planning and development. Haughey abolished the department when he became Taoiseach two years later, but absorbed many of its senior personnel into the prime minister's department. This move (accompanied by a formal separation of the functions of secretary to the cabinet and secretary of the department) considerably strengthened his capacity to act as chief executive. This is illustrated by the fact that the departmental secretary in large measure negotiated and then chaired monthly meetings overseeing two successive national understandings on pay, taxation, and other aspects of public policy that were agreed between the government and the major social partners. Haughey also created a minister of state in his department, with special responsibility for the coordination of government policy and EC matters.

All of these developments have enhanced the executive role of the Taoiseach, increased his capacity to probe proposals by other ministers, strengthened his coordinating function, entrenched his mastery of the cabinet, and further circumscribed ministerial autonomy.

MINISTERS AND POLITICAL PARTIES

In Ireland, political parties appear to have only minimal influence on ministerial policy-making. Since the Taoiseach is typically the head of his party, this role may become an additional source of influence for him vis-à-vis a group of recalcitrant cabinet colleagues. In one of the abortive efforts to deprive Charles Haughey of leadership, for example, he threatened to appeal over the heads of his parliamentary party to the party at large. Ministers are expected to attend the regular meetings of the parliamentary party (usually weekly when the Dáil is in session) and are regarded as foolish if they neglect backbenchers. Equally, ministers are typically aware of grass-roots opinion; controversial issues are often left unresolved, or left to the courts to determine, simply because of a ministerial reluctance to tackle entrenched attitudes in the party.

Neither Fianna Fail nor Fine Gael show any evidence of either a capacity or a desire to constrain their ministers. Ministers, or spokespersons, hold powerful positions in the upper echelons of the party. They largely control decision making in regard to the formulation of policy for party programs, at annual conference, and in elections; they also supervise most aspects of electoral organization (including chairing conventions for nominating party candidates).

Typically, government policy and legislation is at an advanced stage, having been processed through the administration and cabinet, before being presented to the parliamentary party. On occasions, amendments by party colleagues are considered; on rarer occasions, broad issues of policy that are regarded as politically sensitive (family legislation, licensing laws) are given a wider airing. A determined minister backed by the prime minister is scarcely ever constrained by the party, however.

Smaller parties that have participated in government (most recently the Labour party and Progressive Democrats) frequently claim to be policy driven. They appear to be able to exercise more constraint on their ministers in regard to some aspects of their portfolios. However, this may be largely a function of the small parliamentary membership of such parties and the correspondingly greater influence of the party structure. As with larger parties, ministers, and especially leaders, are powerful within the smaller parties but – perhaps as a function of size – tend to be closer to their parliamentary colleagues. On the other hand, as coalition has come to be more accepted, the negotiation of policy options and priorities has become more detailed. To that extent, parties have some say in defining government strategy.

CIVIL SERVANTS AND MINISTERS

A populist myth frequently propounded in Irish political journalism identifies the civil service as the "permanent government." It portrays senior civil servants as an entrenched, professional and protected elite group of puppet masters manipulating the transient, part-time, and vulnerable amateur ministers, who are no more than titular lords of their departments. This representation is as unrealistic as the opposite image, the conventional dichotomy between politics and administration in which elected politicians make policies and civil servants administer them. Campbell and Peters (1988: 81–2) have noted that "as persistent as this dichotomy has been it is being eroded in both the world of scholarship and the world of government. . . . to the extent that it continues to survive, it survives as a convenient fiction rather than a description of any reality."

By and large this convenient fiction has been maintained in the formal behavior of the Irish civil service. They uphold the legal principle of the minister as corporation sole – itself, of course, a convenient escape from public accountability. They are careful to defer to the "master" in public and take trouble to establish, as far as possible, a good working relationship with the minister. Their success can in part be measured in ministerial responses to a question about their experience and relationship with the civil servants. Irrespective of party, most ministers regarded a good level of collaboration as "usual"; none found it unsatisfactory. Most Fine Gael and Labour ministers thought civil servants "never" oversold policies, though Fianna Fail ministers split half and half between those who opted for "never" and those responding "sometimes." There were similar party differences between those who thought civil servants "never" blocked ministers and those who thought they sometimes did, but only a handful thought this obstruction was "usual."

As already noted, however, most ministers were critical of the dominant role of the Department of Finance. One particularly outspoken Labour minister said of a secretary in Finance that he "cultivated this relationship with secretaries of line departments" and claimed that this secretary barely spoke to the minister of finance. Most ministers obviously shared Gemma Hussey's (1990: 12) experience, that ministers of finance "rarely agreed to any spending proposal and fought the battles at full cabinet." Clearly, on many of these occasions, the minister of finance voiced a departmental rather than personal point of view. The need to struggle against predictable negative responses from the Department of Finance is seen, however, not so much as specific civil-service backing, but as part of the whole governmental system.

Within their own departments, ministers were prepared to deal with some degree of resistance to new ideas. Much obviously depended on the personalities involved. A particularly popular and experienced minister said it all depends on "your own personality and temperament," but mused that "some people like internal tension. . . . but if a minister chooses to set up tension, they [the civil servants] are in such a position within the machine that they can block you or thwart you or harass you or hassle you. They can cause a lot of bother. I've seen it happen to ministers." FitzGerald quotes examples of civil-service obstruction to plans to develop multidenominational education and to reduce hospital waiting lists. He regards these as "exceptions," possibly due to "a marked reluctance on the part of some civil servants to contemplate changes in existing policies, about which they had become very defensive, and from a tempo of activity at administrative level very far removed from that of a businessman or a politician" (FitzGerald, 1991: 385–6).

Fianna Fail ministers (frequently having longer experience in government) seemed more alert to civil servants pushing their own policy preferences. One of the most critical suggested that the elected minister made only a small impact on the departmental view as expressed in memoranda and observations: "I'd say if you checked the last hundred bills, say since 1980, that the submissions regardless of the minister – whether he was right wing, left wing, an ideological person or not – its probably the same view." Of overselling, a Fine Gael minister asserted confidently that "you could spot it a mile away." An experienced Fianna Fail minister said that promotion of policies by civil servants "goes on all the time, by all of them" and recalled stiff resistance to his efforts to divest his department of an "out office" that, in his view, contributed nothing to the portfolio and had only about ninety junior staff involved.

Perhaps the most comprehensive comment on relations between ministers and civil servants came from a senior minister with substantial business experience: "All the dodges are there . . . the big file on Friday evening. If you don't plant your authority on the department on day one, you're in trouble. They don't stop blocking. You have to blast the first blockage. A good private secretary is the key: he knows the department."[10]

Overall it is clear that Irish ministers are at a significant disadvantage in seeking to impose themselves on their departments and drive them in new directions. It requires energy, persistence, expertise, and a degree of luck to go beyond what one minister called "keeping the show on the road." Some effort has been made to use ministerial advisers to facilitate ministers anxious to achieve change, but their expertise in a particular policy area is likely to be offset by their inexperience in dealing with the administrative apparatus and its personnel. Besides, they can fight only individual battles; they cannot hope to take on the massed battalions of the bureaucracy. There is the added problem that time is a scarcer resource for the part-time and transient minister than for the full-time and permanent civil servant. One might fairly conclude that the Irish civil service is extremely resistant to substantive (and especially to structural) change; it is adept at slowing change's pace, but ultimately yields to a minister who has the will, capacity, tenacity, and time to press for change.

CONCLUSION

On the basis of the evidence in this chapter, in the Irish political system ministerial autonomy is severely restricted, collective cabinet responsibility is rigorously upheld, the prime minister is influential in all areas of policy, the civil service (and in particular, the Department of Finance), is entrenched and powerful, the Parliament and party are ineffective in promoting or obstructing policies and in controlling the executive, and the selection of ministers and party spokesperson is rarely, if at all, related to substantive policy issues.

A number of further points must be noted in relation to the allocation of cabinet portfolios in Ireland. First, there is an almost complete lack of predictability in regard to the likely effects of particular ministerial appointments. Second, the assumption of rationality and self-interest among decision makers is contradicted daily. As one Irish minister commented, "Life is untidy." The life of a cabinet is far more subject to immediate and urgent pressures than to the considered evaluation of long-term policy outcomes. This general problem is exacerbated in the Irish system because of the failure to develop structures that might alleviate the burdens placed on an overloaded cabinet agenda. A third point to note is that policymaking is not the principal purpose of cabinet life in Ireland. A major concern of Irish politicians is the simple maintenance of the government in office.

At the same time, the three questions posed in the introduction to this book reveal hitherto neglected aspects of the Irish political system.

The party composition of the cabinet does make some difference to government policy outputs. Because of the frequently noted convergence in most policy areas between the two main parties, Fianna Fail and Fine Gael, and because of the failure of these parties to detail, cost, and prioritize their policies, this factor has been underestimated. Coalitions with two policy-driven parties – the Progressive Democrats and the Labour Party – and the consequent increasing emphasis on the negotiation of agreed government programs, highlight that the party composition of the cabinet has more effect on policy outputs when there is a change of government. In contrast, governments remaining in office over a number of elections seem more subject to the disciplines of administrative continuity and less likely to initiate policy change.

It follows from this that the allocation of cabinet portfolios between different parties also has some impact on policy outputs, and minority parties in coalitions are particularly concerned to secure control of specific departmental responsibilities. It is notable that the finance portfolio is always retained by the major party and, over a relatively short period of time (and not without a degree of managerial care by the Taoiseach) party differences between ministers tend to be submerged in the collective consciousness of the cabinet as a whole. Ministers come to share a "them-and-us" mentality in which party colleagues outside the cabinet club are placed on the other side. However, it seems likely that in any foreseeable coalition pact, the bargaining over the allocation of portfolios will become more acute.

The allocation of portfolios within parties does not appear to make a major difference to overall governmental policy outputs. Certainly the capacity, skill, personality, and circumstances of individual ministers can have a striking influence in particular areas. As indicated, both ministers and civil servants acknowledge the impact of individual appointments. Ministers do matter – but only sometimes.

NOTES

1 Constitution of the Irish Free State, Articles 51 and 55. No extern ministers were appointed after 1927.
2 Some particularly unhappy experiences with cabinet committees may be noted. The long struggle to extract a proposal on children's allowances from a cabinet committee is detailed in Farrell (1991: 62–3). Much of the problem that exploded in the Arms Trial Crisis of 1970 (in which four senior ministers either left or were sacked) can be traced to a cabinet committee – significantly not chaired by the Taoiseach – established to deal with Northern Ireland.
3 They can be seen as an extension of the "Tallaght Strategy" (in which Fine Gael promised broad support for a minority Fianna Fail government committed to common pursuit of severe budgetary constraints). For comment see Collins (1992: 138).
4 Departmental secretaries in their role as accounting officers are responsible directly to Parliament, not to their minister. See O'Halpin (1991: 295).
5 This paper draws on many years of informal interviews with senior political and administrative personnel. In particular, it cites quotations from a series of formal interviews with thirty-six ministers and former ministers (eighteen Fianna Fail, fourteen Fine Gael, and four Labour) conducted in the late 1980s as part of a cross-national survey spearheaded by Professor Jean Blondel.
6 A recent account by the current secretary of finance in S. Cromien (1991: 336–64).
7 There were two instances of recorded dissent in the 1920s, a refusal to record dissent in the First Inter-Party Government and a minister who claimed to have his dissent recorded in a Fianna Fail government in 1980.
8 In 1979 Haughey's rival for the party leadership was able to demand the

position of Tanaiste (deputy prime minister) and a veto on appointments to the security portfolios of Justice and Defense.

9 For a contrary view see FitzGerald (1991: 429, 621–5).

10 Cf., "It is sometimes suggested that a new minister in his early days in a department, has to show 'who's boss!' I find this a childish misconception; no minister of quality needs to do this, any more than an abbot in a monastery" (Whitaker, 1983: 163).

REFERENCES

Arkins, Audrey. 1988. The committee of the 24th Oireachtas," *Irish Political Studies* 3: 91–8.

Campbell, Colin, and B. G. Peters. 1988. The politics/administration dichotomy: death or merely change? *Governance* l:l.

Coakley J., and B. Farrell. 1989. Selection of Cabinet Ministers in Ireland, 1922–1982. In M. Dogan (ed.), *Pathways to Power: Selecting Rulers in Pluralist Democracies*. Boulder, Colo.: Westview.

Collins, Stephen. 1992. *The Haughey File*. Dublin: O'Brien.

Cromien, Sean. 1991. The power of the purse. *Administration* 38:4.

Farrell, Brian. 1987a. Government formation and ministerial selection. In H. Penniman and B. Farrell (eds.), *Ireland at the Polls, 1981, 1982 and 1987: A Study of Four General Elections*. Durham, N.C.: Duke University Press, for American Enterprise Institute.

1987b. The aftermath: forming a government. In M. Laver, P. Mair, and R. Sinnott (eds.), *How Ireland Voted: the Irish General Election of 1987*. Dublin: Poolbeg.

1988. Ireland: more British than the British themselves. In J. Blondel and F. Müller-Rommel (eds.), *Cabinets in Western Europe*. London: Macmillan Press.

1991. *Sean Lemass*. 2d ed. Dublin: Gill & Macmillan.

FitzGerald, Garret. 1991. *All in a Life*. Dublin: Gill & Macmillan.

Hussey, Gemma. 1990. *At the Cutting Edge: Cabinet Diaries 1982–1987*. Dublin: Gill & Macmillan.

O'Buachalla, S. 1988. *Education Policy in Twentieth-Century Ireland*. Dublin: Wolfhound.

O'Halpin, Eunan. 1991. The civil service and the political system. *Administration* 38: 4.

Valiulis, M. G. 1985. *Almost a Rebellion: the Irish Army Mutiny of 1924*. Cork: Tower.

Whitaker, T. K. 1983. The Department of Finance. In T. K. Whitaker (ed.), *Interests*. Dublin: Institute of Public Administration.

Whyte, J. H. 1980. *Church and State in Modern Ireland, 1923–1979*. 2d ed. Dublin: Gill & Macmillan.

6

Finland: *ministerial autonomy, constitutional collectivism, and party oligarchy*

Jaakko Nousiainen

CENTRIPETAL AND CENTRIFUGAL FORCES

Everything considered, the single most important influence on cabinet decision making is probably the partisan complexion of the government, a factor that significantly affects the relationship between ministers and the collective cabinet. In a single-party cabinet there is a direct link between party preferences, government declarations, and cabinet and ministerial agendas. The actual division of decision-making powers is a practical question. Coalitions, in contrast, lack these direct links. Coalition policies are harder to formulate, because collective decisions cannot be derived directly from the preferences of any background group; instead, they unfold outside the confines of the cabinet, in ad hoc settings. The problem is that in coalition governments the primary reference group of a minister is not the coalition but his or her own party. There is a perpetual conflict between coalition preference and party preference, and the latter assumes priority in the ministerial norm hierarchy.

As a consequence, decision making in coalition cabinets tends to approximate a federalist model, with separate spheres of authority for the central power (cabinet) and various subsystems (ministries). Naturally, there is constant tension between these levels. A minister defends his – or his party's – dominion, whereas other participants will keep an eye on him and try to force the common line upon him. The key question as far as this book is concerned, then, is this: how extensive is the personal policy-making space of a minister? How easily can she detach herself from the coalition, the party, or both?

Historically, Finnish government has been shaped primarily by the collective principle. Even today, centripetal forces dominate cabinet decision making. Among Western European parliamentary regimes, therefore, this country represents a setup that heavily restricts the freedom of individual ministers to shift policy outputs within their jurisdiction toward the particular alternatives they themselves prefer. The relevant centripetal features of the policy-making environment can be summarized in terms of a tradition of bureaucratic collectivism; a situation of extreme legal regulation; a tradition of heterogeneous nonbloc coalitions; unitary, disciplined parties; and the role of permanent civil servants.

The tradition of bureaucratic collectivism

Modern Finnish parliamentary government was preceded by the nineteenth-century Senate that resolved administrative matters in its weekly plenary sessions, following procedures characteristic of a court of justice. Individual members of the team were not vested with much decision-making authority. The Constitution Act of 1919 sanctioned the same norm (Article 40): "Matters devolving upon the council of state shall be handled in plenary session, excepting when matters of a specific nature have been committed by decree of a minister for decision in his capacity as head of the relevant ministry." In the course of time more and more routine matters have been transferred to the ministries, but even today the cabinet handles about a hundred items in a single formal meeting – in round figures forty-five hundred items every year. In reality it makes effective decisions on only a small number of issues on the agenda, but the necessity to bring even minor matters to the whole cabinet for ratification tends to stretch the effective reach of the collective agenda down to the administrative level. At least the formal decision-making authority of ministers is heavily curtailed.

Extreme legal regulation

As far as formal decision-making powers are concerned, in most Western European countries there is a large "gray zone" within which the minister or the leading circle of the cabinet is able to decide *in casu* which issues should be brought to the full cabinet for deliberation. This is not formally the case in Finland. In the spirit of strict Weberian rationality, the authority lines between different levels of public decision makers are drawn rigidly through legislative action. Laws and decrees regulate in detail the division of decision-making power between the president, the cabinet and individual ministers, other central offices, and provincial and local authorities. All authorities know, as a matter of principle, which matters belong to their jurisdiction; conflicts of competence are rare, and as a rule the vertical division of duties cannot be changed by a simple decision of a higher authority. The same applies in the horizontal direction: a change in law is required to establish a new ministry or to transfer matters from one ministry to another.

It is conceivable that this arrangement has a centrifugal effect: in a legal and egalitarian administrative culture a minister is able to do what he or she is entitled to do without anybody having much to say about it. This is to a great extent the case in Finland. The pressure toward conformity is weak in a coalition. Nevertheless, the individual minister's freedom of movement is in any case limited to the lower part of the governmental agenda, and the power he wields is party power rather than individual power.

Heterogeneous nonbloc coalitions

The dominant type of government in Finland is a majority coalition that transcends conventional bloc boundaries; this type of coalition has been in power 85 percent of the time from 1965 to 1991. In most cases the parliamentary base of coalitions has been broadened by including some of the small parties, which have had to be content with a minimal payoff of one or two portfolios.

Governmental functioning in these circumstances is colored by perpetual conflicts and competition – both ideological and practical – for policy outputs. The total policy field does not become easily segmented in terms of partisan control because portfolios change hands between parties in successive cabinets, and because there is an effective built-in system of mutual watch and control. The breadth of formal collective handling is instrumental in this respect, which explains why parties have been reluctant to curtail it in a decisive way. As a consequence the effective agenda tends to broaden to encompass many unimportant matters, and it easily becomes politicized and subject to bargaining between parties. The importance of routine administration and middle-level issues in day-to-day governmental process is emphasized, and a slow, deliberative, and incrementalist style of decision making becomes dominant.

Unitary disciplined parties

Most Finnish parties are, in good Scandinavian style, compact and disciplined structures in the organizational arena as well as in parliamentary and governmental ones. Larger parties cannot, of course, avoid having dissenting groups and wings, but serious factional disputes soon lead to a formal breakaway as the minority finds it cannot survive inside the party. Conservatives as well as Agrarians, Social Democrats, and Communists have experienced party splits after World War II. Functional centralization combined with the parties' clear-cut interest profile enhances the individual minister's role as agent of his group.

Finland: autonomy, collectivism, and oligarchy

Changing ministers, permanent civil servants

During the past sixty years the average life of cabinets has been about twelve months. Only in the 1980s did two governments stay in office from one general election to the next, a full four-year period. Of the 132 ministers who served in 1964–87, 65 made only one – in most cases a short – visit to the State Council. Half of the reappointed stayed in two governments only (Nousiainen, 1991: 69–70).

Civil servants, on the other hand, are extremely well protected against removal from office. Once appointed, a person cannot be easily dismissed or assigned to a lower post, nor even moved to another post with equal rank, without his or her consent. Civil service careers are accordingly very stable, and shifts from one ministry to another are quite unusual. In particular, permanent secretaries have achieved a very influential position during the past two decades. The highest officials are appointed by the president or the cabinet; a minister is allowed to fill only lower positions in his department. It is worth mentioning that the minister's personal staff consists of one person only – his political secretary.

RECRUITMENT, CAREERS, AND MINISTERIAL PROFILE

The first phase of the government-formation procedure consists of negotiations, headed by an *informateur,* over the partisan scope of the coalition. After that, the head of state nominates a *formateur* who opens discussions about the government program. These deliberations typically last from two to four weeks.

As the program talks advance, the question of the division of portfolios between participant parties is raised. The Center Party has always been interested in the Ministry of Agriculture, and the minister of social affairs has often come from the Social Democratic Party. Otherwise the assignment of portfolios to parties is so complicated that it does not allow the formation of solid interest fortresses. Small support parties demand important departments for their few ministers. Big parties also want to control these same ministries. In the ensuing adjustments, the seat shares of parties as well as the substantive importance and political visibility of different portfolios are weighed very carefully. At this stage there is not yet any serious talk of ministerial candidates.

The nomination of specific persons to assigned posts is an internal party affair; only an experienced and strong *formateur* can use a veto to block the candidacy of an unsuitable person. The only exceptions are the foreign minister and minister of defense; their nominations presuppose the consent of the president of the republic. At this phase it is a matter of chance

91

Table 6.1. *Expertise of Finnish ministers*

Type of expertise	First appointment	All appointments
Political	46%	68%
Sectoral	31%	54%

whether a party has specialists and spokespersons of the relevant issue areas to put forward, and competing intraparty criteria for selection make everything even more complicated. The party organization leadership prefers both its own members and technocratic-area specialists; the parliamentary party, as a central counterweight, defends the quota of senior MPs; and the largest party districts claim the right of an area representation of their own. In the final team, the party profile is significant as far as policy expectations are concerned. The personal policy profile of a minister is visible only in a secondary way, from behind his or her party.

Assuming that the capacity of a minister consists of political skills and professional/technical expertise (see Bakema and Secker, 1988), their combination produces four ministerial types: politico–specialist (political and technical); professional politician (political); specialist (technical), and amateur (neither political nor technical).

From 1964 to 1987 there were 217 ministerial appointments in Finland; 113 of them were first appointments for the persons in question. The number of persons involved was 132, excluding all prime ministers as well as three short-lived caretaker cabinets of the period. The percentage of ministers with one or the other type of expertise was as shown in Table 6.1. It could be expected that in a fragmented multiparty system, where every single group is represented by only a few ministers and where parties have distinctive interest profiles, most ministers would be experienced politicians and professional experts. However, when we look at the persons receiving their first appointment, this expectation is not fulfilled: only about half of the newcomers may be regarded as professional politicians and one-third as experts in their respective policy fields. Coalition politics places an emphasis on partisan representativeness in the selection process, and it is purely a matter of chance whether top ministerial candidates are familiar with the issue areas of the portfolios that have been entrusted to the party. In spite of this, cabinet posts seem to be easily accessible to people outside the small circle of leading politicians.

Portfolio reshuffles during the life of an administration are extremely rare, primarily because of the short duration of cabinets. Even in reshuffles, the quotas allocated to parties are kept intact because a change in the equilibrium would only exacerbate strained relations. Individual minis-

Table 6.2. *Overall role orientation of ministers*

Level of orientation	Politico–specialist	Specialist	Professional politician	Amateur	All
Cabinet generalist	1		15	9	25
Head of department	4	9	2	1	16
Both roles			1	5	6
Total	5	9	18	15	47

ters resign only when they are offered another high post in public or private life. In this case the party in question nominates the new minister. The only situation that leads to new negotiations between partners and a cabinet reshuffle is when all members of some party resign.

In a study of Finnish cabinets and ministers between 1965 and 1987 (Nousiainen, 1991: 72–5; 1992) the forty-seven ex-ministers interviewed were asked to recall how they generally perceived their position after the first appointment. Were they to be first and foremost general politicians and representatives of their parties in the government, or did they see themselves as specialized leaders oriented primarily to the matters of their ministries? It is not surprising in a country such as Finland, as Table 6.2 reveals, that most ministers enter government as party representatives rather than with sectoral policy-making in mind. The tone of everyday life in large coalitions is set by party competition and conflict. Ministers constantly keep an eye on each other and are not free to concentrate on ministerial policies. All sensitive issues are submitted to arbitration between party groups. As has been indicated, general political skills rather than specialized skills are stressed in the recruitment process.

Table 6.2 shows that the subjective evaluation of the ministers' approach to the job closely follows the objective classification of ministers. Almost without exception person · with substantive knowledge of the field said they entered the government as departmentally oriented experts, whereas professional politicians and amateurs said they were party representatives equipped with more general resources.

MINISTERS AND THE COLLECTIVE CABINET

Scope of the cabinet's jurisdiction

In 1988, the State Council in eighty-one formal plenary sessions handled 4,472 agenda items (the figures from two previous years were 4,649 and 5,060). An analysis of these data reveals that 31 percent of the items applied to legislation, other parliamentary business, and government decrees; 2 percent to national planning and other forms of policy steering; and roughly the same share to important aspects of foreign relations. This suggests that, of all the issues presented in official cabinet meetings, almost two-thirds involved individualized administrative decisions.

The collective cabinet in Finland has both a formal administrative agenda and an effective political agenda. As we have seen, a host of matters – roughly a hundred items in a single meeting – must be handled in the formal system. It is safe to say that a large majority of the issues are administrative, typically prepared in the ministries under the leadership and responsibility of a single minister. Administrative routines are given formal ratification in these official cabinet settings. (The actual participation and influence of a minister is discussed later in this chapter.) This collective handling, though often pro forma, nevertheless has significance in the coalition system. First, ministers and party groups are informed of what is happening in other parts of the government complex. Second, party groups are given a last opportunity to present their vetoes if a question becomes controversial.

However, the borderline between purely administrative and politically laden issues is far from clear, and thus items on the administrative agenda are also submitted to political and institutional checks. It is habitual in large coalitions that a ministerial group assigns its members to monitor ministries led by other parties. One of the most important tasks of the ministers' private secretaries is to read agenda papers and to draw the minister's attention to matters that seem sensitive from the point of view of the ministry or the party. Administrative issues may unexpectedly get a party-political tone; typical examples are civil-service appointments that have not been submitted to the collective preparation of the cabinet. In this case the conventional norm requires that the minister contact this colleague before the meeting and ask him or her to reconsider the matter.

Effective administrative control is also carried out by the six-member Cabinet Finance Committee. It meets every week, and its most important task is to supervise the use of budget appropriations. It issues an opinion on budgetary matters in advance of their resolution in cabinet. The real influential members of this committee are the prime minister, the minister of finance, and the highest officials of the Ministry of Finance. Small matters such as personnel administration aside, almost half of the items resolved in plenary cabinet sittings have gone through this committee (Tiihonen, 1989).

The process of agenda determination

To understand the peculiar decision-making style of the Finnish government it is necessary to be aware of certain basic features of the process of

agenda formation in broad, heterogeneous coalitions. Two different interpretations may be entertained on this.

According to the first interpretation, the effective agenda of heterogeneous cabinets is established in the coalition agreement, which has been
worked out carefully and in considerable detail. On the one hand the
agreement excludes from discussion the issues most likely to generate
conflict, and on the other hand it determines the policies to be carried out
during the cabinet's term in office. The core of the cabinet's action consists
of the implementation of what has been decided during the process of
government formation. The need for the involvement of the entire cabinet
is limited because implementation can be entrusted to individual ministers, who are autonomous actors in this very restricted sense.

According to the second interpretation, nonparticipation in government has a high cost, and therefore the party leaders' tolerance in
government-formation negotiations is broad. In an effort to be included in
the cabinet, party leaders are willing to compromise on their more gran-
diose objectives and limit their requirements to those principles of greatest
concern to their party (Luebbert, 1986: 44–53). In this case the coalition
agreement takes on a different tone: it is no longer a detailed listing of
measures to be implemented but instead a collection of mutually agreed-
upon principles, purposes, and broad goals. These principles are later
raised on the concrete agenda for specification and action that take place
in different arenas of the coalition system. Party leaders are well aware
that the real settlement of the issues takes place later; by including many
kinds of items in the declaration they seek tentative assurance of a voice in
that settlement (see Truman, 1964: 285).

Finnish practice is clearly closer to the second interpretation. Recent
coalition agreements, a mixture of action program and declaration, are
prepared in a "something for everybody" mode without the inclusion of
implementation schedules, cost estimates, or draft bills. The program of
the first conservative–socialist coalition – formed in April 1987 –
contained among other things one important new item for both partners:
tax reform for the Conservatives, and partial reform of industrial relations
for the Social Democrats. With respect to these general goals, the parties
reached an agreement easily, but the following year was filled with heated
discussion over the precise specification of these goals and the proper
means to achieve them. In more general terms, it is clear that a cabinet's
agenda can never be fully determined in advance. New problems, goals,
and solutions are introduced continually during a policy process. Most of
the time cabinets are forced to react to changes in their environment.

Management of the political agenda

One part of the political agenda is based on the government proclamation, a second part emanates from continuous talks between the parties, and a third part is generated by the administrative process. This last is the responsibility of the individual minister. A behavioral norm, learned through long collective experience, stipulates that far-reaching, costly, or politically "hot" issues must be brought at an early stage to the party-political arena for discussion and arbitration. Taking others by surprise with completed proposals at an official meeting is the surest way to ruin a good initiative. Suspicions arise and attitudes become rigid. The credibility of the minister in question is also adversely affected.

The cumbersome collective decision-making machinery has been able to remain functional only through the separation of policy deliberation from administration. Since the late 1930s, the cabinet has met on Wednesday evenings – before the official sitting on Thursday – to discuss unofficially the most important parts of its collective agenda: parliamentary business, the economic situation, development plans of various policy sectors, individual measures of general interest, and so on. A joint dinner – in summer perhaps a sauna – strengthens the cohesiveness and group spirit of a fragmented cabinet; after all, ministers do not see very much of each other. The meeting is jokingly called "the cabinet's evening class."

The agenda for the unofficial meeting is fixed by the prime minister on the basis of suggestions from ministers, who are often inclined to suggest relatively minor issues in order to secure their political acceptance in an early phase of preparation. The importance of these unofficial meetings is especially evident, however, in the case of a complete deadlock. The standard procedure is to set up an ad hoc working group consisting of the interested ministers or – for more important questions – representatives of all party fractions including the smallest. Party representatives receive instructions from their groups, but enjoy considerable latitude in making compromises. The agreement reached is ratified in the "evening class" and then returned to the ministry for final technical preparation. At this juncture the hands of the minister are tied. He or she is able to polish the details but not establish a new policy line.

The constitution entrusts the president with extensive powers to direct the foreign policy of the nation. According to Article 33, "The president shall determine the relations of Finland with foreign powers." This means that one can hardly speak of autonomous policy-making as far as the foreign minister is concerned. The president must make his formal decision in a cabinet meeting over which he presides, but foreign-policy leadership consists mostly of his own free action and not of legally regulated decision making. Although there is a cabinet-level foreign-affairs commit-tee, President Koivisto has effectively transformed it since 1982 into a presidential staff where major foreign policy decisions are made. Indica-tive of this is the public lament of a cabinet minister, Hannele Pokka, in October 1991, that the rest of the cabinet had to read in the newspapers about the important decision to acknowledge the independence of the Baltic states (*Helsingin Sanomat* 9 October 1991).

Most cabinet matters have an economic dimension. The Cabinet Fi-nance Committee concentrates on the everyday control of budgetary ex-penditures, whereas the parallel Economic Policy Committee discusses more far-reaching issues dealing with the public and national economy. In a formal sense the latter is only a preparatory organ, but during the past fifteen years it has been transformed into a coalition committee, com-posed of leaders of the government parties, that shapes economic policies and whose recommendations cannot be easily changed in the cabinet. It is perhaps an overstatement to call it an "inner cabinet," but it does fulfill the role of a policy-making working committee for the government.

The decision rule for collective cabinet decision making varies with the issue. In purely administrative matters the decision is recorded without most ministers giving it any attention. A decision is unanimous if minis-ters are fairly interested and familiar with at least the outlines of the problem and its solution. This level of the collective agenda is dominated by consensual decisions that have typically been reached through adjust-ment of conflicting goals or through a bargain.

Simple majority vote is a legitimate decision rule, though the signifi-cance of this procedure has diminished as the state council has been transformed from an administrative collegium to a political body. Political wisdom recommends that prime ministers avoid divisions in questions to which parties have become strongly attached; the prestige of a big group does not tolerate a public defeat on such issues. A voting decision is a comfortable and harmless way to clear an issue from the agenda on rela-tively unimportant questions such as civil-service appointments. (Only eleven votes were taken in the official meetings in 1989, and five in 1991).

The foregoing should establish that the Finnish cabinet is best thought of in terms of party groups rather than ministers equipped with personal ambition and goals. Moreover, its policy-making function is directed from the collective level. The policy process is slow and incremental, involving so many participants that it may be difficult to see the basic ideology of a new law or to establish whose interests are being served.

The decision rules of Parliament make things even more complicated: until 1992, one-third of the representatives could delay the adoption of most ordinary laws for between one and two years. As a consequence, in order to secure the passage of an important measure, the cabinet was often forced to negotiate with the opposition before submitting a proposal to Parliament.

The policy-making profile of individual ministers in these circumstances is by necessity relatively low. The collective machinery largely eludes the notion of individual ministerial responsibility. From 1965 to 1991 no individual minister resigned following a failure to push desired policies through. Such resignations take place en masse on a party basis. In 1971 and 1982, People's Democrats withdrew their three ministers, in 1978 the Swedish Party their sole minister, and in 1990 the Rural Party also removed their sole minister. For the sake of cabinet solidarity, a minister has to comply with party agreements. He or she must swallow a personal defeat, and the inter-party control system ensures that policies are implemented in the agreed way.

PRIME MINISTER: LITTLE POWER BUT SOME INFLUENCE

The prime minister inherited from the bureaucratic past a position that entailed little more than the chairmanship of the ministerial collegium. Later coalition parliamentarism blocked efforts to strengthen this formal role. Thus, for most of the modern period, a temporary and rotating leadership has prevailed in place of a real and lasting leadership. From 1950 to 1986 Finland had sixteen different prime ministers – compared with only five in Sweden and nine each in Denmark and Norway. The average duration of the premiership was only 2.3 years.

As the aura of national leader belongs to the president, the prime minister has the rather prosaic role of organizer and arbitrator rather than of a policy activist. A clear indication of the weakness of the inner ministerial hierarchy is that many prime ministers have returned later to the cabinet as ordinary ministers, some of them several times.

Most prime ministers find their power curtailed by the fact that they are unable to select ministers and appoint who they consider to be the right people to the right posts. Nor can they sack or reshuffle ministers without the consent of proper party organs. This applies in most cases even to ministers from their own party.

The prime minister does decide which issues are discussed at the cabinet's unofficial policy-deliberation meetings. However, this does not mean that the prime minister has the power in practice to set the collective political agenda. This is settled among coalition leaders, while parties arrange a careful follow-up to ensure that the government program is put into effect in a balanced way. In this respect the prime minister's party has no real practical advantage over other government parties.

The influence of the prime minister derives mainly from the fact that he is the most active person in the cabinet and is located at the intersection of information streams. He presides over cabinet meetings and the most important committees; he keeps in contact with the president about national policy problems; he bears the responsibility for both the initiation and the progress of incomes-policy negotiations; and his daily routine consists of settling disputes between ministers and government parties, reconciling and adjusting the demands of different partners to a policy package acceptable to all.

THE MINISTER IN HIS OR HER DEPARTMENT

Although the autonomous decision-making power of individual ministers is heavily restricted, they are still in charge of the preparation of policies in their respective fields. If a minister is unable to push through the policies she favors personally, she can still obstruct measures to which she is opposed by retarding their inclusion in the collective agenda. This will not help for long, however, because the ministerial collegium – not the prime minister alone – can force a rebellious minister to report an issue to the state council. But in fact, interparty agreements also set the schedule that binds the preparation process.

The minister's formal jurisdiction is not sufficient for autonomous policy-making. The first notable delegation of decision-making powers from the cabinet to individual ministers was put into effect in 1932. At the same time, however, the state council was authorized to prescribe that in certain matters the Finance Committee must be consulted before their resolution in the ministries. A minister cannot act alone contrary to the committee's opinion: if he is not willing to comply, the matter must be submitted to the full cabinet's decision. In the postwar years the list of such matters grew long, and the authoritative opinions have been mostly based on the bureaucratic fiscal interest of the Ministry of Finance. In case of disagreement, the individual minister has slim prospects of getting his view accepted. As a matter of principle the Finance Committee has an effective right of veto vis-à-vis the ministries, but in practice the widening of the economic policy-making space since the 1960s has diminished the importance of this control mechanism.

In addition to constraints on ministerial autonomy imposed by the finance committee, cabinet ministers are further constrained by the civil service in two ways, politically and bureaucratically. The uppermost layer of the civil service has become highly politicized since World War II (though the position of appointed officials is secured in spite of changes of governing coalitions). The bureaucratic tradition stresses loyalty to the political leadership, but in the preparation of highly controversial measures a minister often has to seek the cooperation of officials sympathetic to her own party. The ministers who are in the most awkward situation are those from the smallest parties: for them there are no trusted officials available and they may well have to face a permanent secretary with a different political orientation.

Irrespective of party politics, however, the heavy mass of administration keeps churning on, presenting – through established interests of bureaucracy – a major barrier to political innovation. As far as political ministers are concerned, however, agenda management and the creation of consensus obviously occupy a very important place in their goal hierarchies (see Gustafsson and Richardson, 1979: 417). This helps explain why a change of cabinet ministers and parties leads to only minor changes in policy. Between 1966 and 1982, the Communists participated in seven Finnish governments but failed to accomplish any significant reshaping of established policies in the ministries they controlled. For example the radical, Erkki Tuominen, minister of justice in Karjalainen's cabinet in 1970–1, was criticized for backing out of several agreements made between leftist groups, and adopting instead the policy line supported by his officials (Jyränki, 1971: 113–14).

At its best, ministerial leadership can be seen as "visionary realism," a behavior that combines transformative goal setting with a strong sense of political realities. It involves an ability to see beyond today's routines, as well as to adjust visions to existing circumstances and use one's skills and powers to "transform vision into action" (see Keren, 1988: 5–6). The latter component – a sense of political realities – necessarily dominates the pragmatic incentives of Finnish ministers; personal visions do not rank high. When asked, "When entering office, did you have a program or some clear personal objective?" eight ministers said they had no special objective, and five said they were concerned with small separate issues. The bulk, nineteen ministers, said they were concerned with middle-level issues, whereas eight ministers were concerned with general aspects of their policy field.

Politicians are certainly more inclined to overemphasize than to underrate the rationale and logic of their actions. Even so, several ministers felt they were not properly prepared, as they had no concrete action program or specified objectives when entering office. This is not surprising: in most cases access to the government and the portfolio are settled at the last moment and largely by chance. There is no time to study the field in detail. As noted earlier, portfolios in Finland are not distributed to sector specialists who would have gained mastery of the field and who would have specifically prepared themselves for the task. All partisan ministers, furthermore, apparently took it for granted that they would promote their parties' central objectives.

Only a small minority of ministers saw their goals in so broad a perspective that they were able to identify with the whole departmental field or with the general policies of the governmental program. The first type of attachment was typical of the area specialist, the second of top party leaders. Usually the minister set his or her personal objectives at the middle level on the political–administrative scale by selecting one problem complex, possibly a single policy project, in which he or she had been involved during earlier public life. For most short-term ministers, the implementation of this project was already a considerable achievement. "You can't expect a minister to carry through several reforms. You have to choose your priorities. There is such an inflow of issues that it is impossible to take a stand on all of them; you have to be selective and leave the rest to the officials" (specialist minister).

CABINET AND MINISTER IN LEGISLATIVE– EXECUTIVE RELATIONS

According to the constitution (Article 36), "The members of the State Council must enjoy the confidence of Parliament." Until 1991 that confidence was not measured in any kind of investiture but the cabinet, which was formed in negotiations between parties and formally appointed by the president, was presumed to have confidence until specifically denied this by Parliament.

The rights of individual representatives are well secured in the Finnish Parliament. They have an unlimited right to speak in plenary sittings, extensive rights of initiating legislation and fiscal bills as well as of suggesting amendments to government bills, and an opportunity make oral and written questions to the ministers.

There is no special motion of no confidence in a technical sense. The principle is that Parliament can, in connection with most issues considered and on the proposal of any two representatives, adopt a resolution that asserts that the cabinet has lost its confidence, or that criticizes its doings to such a degree that the cabinet cannot stay in place. The interpellation, which can be raised at any time by twenty representatives, is a special technique for this purpose; but a resolution overthrowing the cabinet can also be adopted, by a simple majority, in connection with ordinary bills, budget proposals, or government reports and messages. It is the substance, not the form, that is decisive. It is thus very easy for the opposition to put to the test the confidence enjoyed by the cabinet. In this sense the Finnish parliamentary system is extremely elastic.

In practical terms the relationship between Parliament and the cabinet varies sharply depending on the breadth of the coalition. The cabinet does not formally control the legislative agenda, although standing orders prescribe that government proposals must be considered before private members' bills. Resorting to its formal autonomy, Parliament can, during periods of minority government, propose independent policies and unilaterally impose its policy decisions upon an unwilling cabinet. This happened in earlier years. Cabinets tolerated the supremacy of Parliament for some time – on average no more than a year. After this they became exhausted and (as the popular saying goes) looked for a branch on which to hang themselves by making the adoption of a measure a "cabinet question."

During majority governments the unitary nature of parties, and the strict party discipline typical of the Nordic countries, secure for the cabinet a manifest supremacy and control of the legislature. In the loose coalitions of the 1950s, the government could still disintegrate in the parliamentary arena, but in the stable coalitions of the 1980s this was no longer the case. Parliamentary fractions today are closely steered by party leaders in the cabinet, and it is inconceivable that Parliament would act independently on any important question. The government orders the policy decisions it needs – and gets them. The chances of independent interventions are even smaller, as part of the economic and welfare legislation has been settled in annual incomes-policy agreements between the cabinet and the major labor-market organizations. In these circumstances the opposition has good formal rights to make initiatives but minimal opportunities to raise them to the effective agenda.

Since World War II the power of dissolution has been transformed into a personal prerogative of the head of state. He can now act only upon the prime minister's initiative, but is tied to the recommendation neither in law nor in practice. However, the dissolution of Parliament has not, in general, proved to be an expedient remedy for conflicts between government and legislature. In the past seventy-five years Parliament has been dissolved only seven times (four times after World War II). In all these cases the dissolution was the result of a coalition crisis, the failure of political parties to form a viable government. So it is almost a constitutional convention that the power of dissolution cannot be used as a weapon for regulating the relationship between parliament and the government.

In the case of a collective resignation, the president will ask the cabinet to stay in place until a new government is formed. The cabinet's formal position is not affected but it is unlikely to launch any important new projects. If the government has fallen due to internal conflicts, it will obviously have lost much of its internal cohesion and may no longer be able to control groups forming a majority in the legislature. So if important policy decisions have to be made, it may be necessary for advance consultations with parliamentary groups to be more intensive than normal.

Finland: autonomy, collectivism, and oligarchy

ARE FINNISH MINISTERS TOTALLY POWERLESS?

The critical question that follows from all that has been said is, "Are Finnish ministers incapable of individual policy-making?" As far as the government-formation process is concerned, the effective policy of a government may be made dependent on arrangements at three levels: the appointment of individual politicians to the leadership of policy sectors; the allocation of portfolios between participant parties; and the total partisan structure of the coalition. It seems that Finnish cabinet policies in different issue areas are conditioned primarily through the partisan structure of the coalition, less through allocation of portfolios between participant parties, and least of all through the appointment of individual politicians.

Ministers as individuals are of course not all the same. In fact, a generational change since the 1960s has produced a new and more efficient type of minister. To the extent that parties broadened their interest bases and oriented themselves increasingly to societal steering, the share of young, strongly party-political ministers began to increase. All of the cabinets of the 1980s had five to eight ministers with less than ten years' work experience outside Parliament. As one source writes, "The parties have adopted the view that governance requires ruthless party politicians" (Tiihonen, 1991b: 130).

The ministers of the new generation are not area specialists – in most cases are not even the party's best spokespersons in the field – but are experts in political management. They make the best use of their personal capacities primarily as agents of their parties in coalition politics. From the electoral point of view, political visibility is an inevitable requirement. However, it is difficult to avoid the conclusion that these ministers lack the means for policy-making that is independent of their party. Striving for autonomy would lead to a more passive role and isolation from the ministry.

Portfolios are allocated in the first instance to different parties, and policy forecasts are based more on the minister's party affiliation than on his or her individual views. It is not of crucial importance whether the Conservative A or B has been appointed minister of finance; but a Conservative minister of finance is expected to have a different policy line than a Social Democratic minister, and an Agrarian minister of labor is expected to push different employment policies than a Communist minister. (Among major policy fields, the presidential role in foreign policy is again an exception.)

The collective decision-making machinery is dependent on initiatives and materials coming from the ministries. Nevertheless, many items on the government agenda are fixed in the coalition agreement, and all new items of any importance must be submitted to a joint processing at an early stage. As was observed earlier, the bringing along of completed proposals to a cabinet meeting is a sure way to destroy a promising undertaking. However, the parties have not been able permanently to "colonize" the ministries within their areas of interest; portfolios change partisan hands. Since the 1970s, ministers of labor have represented Communists, Conservatives, and Center Party populists; their policy objectives have been varied, but the coalition lathe has rubbed off the edges.

The experience of Communist ministers provides a good example of how difficult it is to make partisan policies in large coalitions. The extreme left once kept the important portfolios of the ministers of interior and justice. However, forced into the role of a "captive party" in coalition with the two big groups, the Center Party and the Social Democrats, it had to compromise its principles more than any other party (see Hakovirta, 1973: 125–31).

The historian of the State Council (Tiihonen, 1991a: 73–4) summarizes the prevailing decision-making style as follows:

In its role as the decision-making arena of short-lived and conflictual multiparty governments, the collegial plenary sitting is slow, inflexible and formal. Its decisions are consensus decisions. The interests of all partners are reflected in the most important governmental solutions; the decisions have been balanced with respect to administrative units, parties, policy fields, geographical divisions, and the needs of different population groups . . . Centralized collective decision making pushes political responsibility into the background. No single decision maker can be found . . . the other side of the system is that the autonomous decision-making power of a minister is restricted to minor issues. All major political issues are decided by the president or by the whole cabinet. Governmental matters proceed through many hierarchical layers and varying preparation stages. The minister in charge of the preparation will not necessarily even recognize the final product. It would also be difficult to consider him solely responsible for it.

Assuming that this is a correct summary of the governmental decision-making process, then the effective policy of a government in separate departmental fields depends primarily upon its overall political complexion. Individual ministers have little more than a residual role.

It is again important to note that Finnish coalitions are not based on any division between left- and right-wing blocs. The key position has always been held by the large Center Party which, within the frame of its agrarian interest, has been willing and prepared to cooperate with groupings on both the left and the right. The consecutive coalitions differ from each other only in shades; they do not manifest strictly divergent worldviews and interest profiles. Finnish governmental policies are thus directed to the smooth middle road, and a new cabinet can, even in its major policies, follow the directions taken by its predecessor. A strong corporatist element in national policy-making contributes further to the stability of government policies, beyond changes of coalition structures.

REFERENCES

Bakema, W. E., and I. P. Secker. 1988. Ministerial expertise and the Dutch case. *European Journal of Political Research* 16: 153–70.

Gustafsson, Gunnel, and J. J. Richardson. 1979. Concepts of rationality and the policy process. *European Journal of Political Research* 7: 415–36.

Hakovirta, Harto, and Tapio Koskiaho. 1973. *Suomen hallitukset ja hallitusohjelma, 1945–1973*. Helsinki: Gaudeamus.

Jyränki, Antero. 1971. *Valta ja vallan siirto*. Helsinki: Kirjayhtymä.

Keren, Michael. 1988. Introduction. *International Political Science Review* 9: 5–6.

Luebbert, G. M. 1986. *Comparative Democracy: Policymaking and Governing Coalitions in Europe and Israel*. New York: Columbia University Press.

Nousiainen, Jaakko. 1991. *Ministers, Parties and Coalition Policies*. University of Turku.

Tiihonen, Paula. 1989. *Budjettivalta: budjettisäännökset ja suunnittelukäytäntö*. Helsinki: Lakiniesliiton Kustannus.

Tiihonen, Seppo. 1991a. Muuttumaton, luja hallitusvalta. *Politiikka* 33: 72–4.

1991b. The professionals of government. In Matti Wirg (ed.), *The Political Life of Institutions*. Jyväskylä: Finnish Political Science Association.

Truman, David. 1964. *The Governmental Process*. New York: Knopf.

7

Cabinet ministers and policy-making in Belgium: the impact of coalitional constraints

Arco Timmermans

INTRODUCTION: THE BELGIAN CABINET

Government formation

Postwar Belgian elections show that Belgium is a country of political minorities. Of the thirty-six cabinets that have held office since 1945, thirty-two were coalition cabinets, nearly all of them majority governments.[1] Only between 1950 and 1954 did Belgium have a short experience of Christian Democratic single-party government based on a narrow parliamentary majority. Not infrequently, furthermore, Belgian cabinets are formed without an election taking place. Although this practice ended in the mid-1960s in the Netherlands, such *fliegende Wechsel* of coalition partners still occurred in the 1980s in Belgium.

Cabinet formations in Belgium often are quite lengthy – usually taking two or three months and sometimes even longer. This situation is similar to that in other relatively fragmented multiparty systems such as Finland, Italy, the Netherlands and Israel. For the most part, these formations are not simply cumulative processes; often several attempts by a *formateur* or *informateur* are made in which the parties involved may change. These interparty negotiations seem to involve more than just the formulation of general goals and exchange of symbolic payoffs before the parties start talking about the other payoff currency, cabinet portfolios. Bargaining on coalition policy is a serious affair in Belgium, and the results usually are written down in a coalition agreement. When completed, the agreement is submitted to official party bodies for approval, which does not always involve mere ratification. The support of extraparliamentary parties for these agreements ranges from unanimity to majorities of less than 60 percent of the vote.

A minimal winning coalition is typically the outcome of these formation negotiations in Belgium (Strom, 1990: 246–7). However, special parliamentary majorities are required on certain bills, such as those in community policy. For this reason, cabinets sometimes are extended to "surplus majority" status in order to avoid being dependent on one or more opposition parties.

Despite the protracted formation process, Belgian cabinets do not last long, they averaged 1.4 years between 1945 and 1985 (Frognier, 1988b: 71). The cause of cabinet termination is most typically an internal dispute within the cabinet, which is more common in Belgium than elsewhere (see Budge and Keman, 1990: 160–1). However, average duration has increased in the past decade, mainly because two cabinets almost completed their full legal term of four years (though both did ultimately break down). For the entire postwar period before 1982, only two cabinets remained in office for their full term.

In contrast to the short duration of cabinets, individual ministers remain in office for 3.8 years on average (for the period 1945–85), although for the most part not continuously and/or with the same portfolio (Frognier, 1988b: 71). Christian Democratic ministers have the longest periods of continuity in office (partly due to their party's permanence in power); some members of the Dehaene cabinet, including Prime Minister Dehaene himself, have been in office for more than twelve years, surviving ten different cabinets.

General features of the Belgian cabinet

The Belgian cabinet is formally labeled the Council of Ministers. This constitutional body includes only ministers, not state secretaries – who are, however, formally included in the government. Since 1970, the constitution requires that, with the possible exception of the prime minister, the Council of Ministers comprise an equal number of French-speaking and Dutch-speaking ministers. This is one way in which the community issue was dealt with, clearly in an accommodating manner. Ever since, the language/community issue has had major consequences for the building of political institutions in Belgium, as the arrangement of the Council of Ministers shows.

Partly as a response to the increasing size of cabinets, standing committees were established to deal with certain policy areas. Though the significance of these committees tends to vary from cabinet to cabinet, some have acquired considerable weight. The most long-standing is the Committee for Economic and Social Coordination (Senelle, 1983: 53–63). In certain instances, the CESC may even formally replace the Council of Ministers in deliberating on policy decisions. Other standing committees considered important are the Committee for Institutional Reforms and the Committee for Foreign Policy. Mostly, the prime minister himself chairs these committees, which include other ministers according to their jurisdiction. The most central committee, at least for some time, has been the Committee for Overall Policy, first established in 1961 and including the most prominent ministers, including the deputy prime ministers.

Apart from formal cabinet committees, there are other arenas for ministerial decision making. In the beginning of the 1980s, the important Committee for Overall Policy was practically replaced by a group composed of the prime minister and the deputy prime minister who led the coalition parties. (The post of deputy prime minister was introduced in 1958. Since then, cabinets have included one or more deputy prime ministers. Since October 1980 all coalition parties minus that of the prime minister have obtained such a post in the cabinet.)

The following sections deal with the composition and working of the Belgian cabinet. They concern the extent to which coalition parties in Belgium constrain the cabinet and individual cabinet ministers, and to what degree ministers have autonomous decision-making power in their respective jurisdictions. In Section 2, the procedures and patterns of portfolio allocation between the coalition parties are discussed, together with the selection of ministers and possible constraints on party leaders making this selection. Section 3 deals with policy-making. In Belgium, policy bargaining between parties starts during government formation and continues once the government has taken office.

PORTFOLIOS AND MINISTERS

The allocation of portfolios: the interparty level

Government formation really becomes cabinet formation when the allocation of cabinet portfolios between the coalition parties is discussed by party spokespeople. Portfolio allocation has a quantitative and a qualitative aspect. In quantitative terms, and within the general constitutional constraint of language parity in the Council of Ministers, cabinet formation in Belgium tends to result in an overrepresentation of smaller coalition parties (Laver and Schofield, 1990: 176). It must be said, however, that this "relative weakness effect" is not very strong in Belgium (see also Budge and Keman, 1990: 128–31).[2]

In qualitative terms, particular parties tend to prefer some portfolios to others. When different parties claim the same key portfolios, things become more complicated and deals must be struck. Often, the less-crucial portfolios are used as side payments in such deals, but parties may have preferences on these as well.

Bargaining over the allocation of portfolios is somewhat peculiar in

Belgium, in that it does not always take place in one arena involving all coalition parties at the same time. Sometimes, especially in the last decade, the sequence of negotiations is that an initial qualitative distribution is first made between the linguistic groups of the prospective coalition parties, after which these party groups start the allocation of the available set of portfolios in separate meetings.[3] When one party is dominant in either group, the result may be that the portfolio allocation within the coalition turns out to be unbalanced (or in any case unsatisfactory to one or more coalition parties). This happened, for example, in May 1980, when the dominant position of the Parti socialiste (PS) in the French-speaking group enabled that party to take hold of the key portfolios of Budget, Internal Affairs, and Justice; this was judged as a major flaw by the Christian People's Party (CVP) in the ensuing cabinet (De Ridder, 1982: 76–7). Parties that fear they are deprived in this way may want to use subsequent cabinet reshuffles to remedy the situation.

Language may also be decisive in another respect. Apart from portfolios that in Belgium are split into two along the ethnic/linguistic dimension (such as Education, Cultural Affairs, Regional Affairs, and Institutional Reform), it sometimes happens that a "neutral" portfolio is deliberately allocated to a minister from one language group rather than to one from the other. For example, in May 1988, during the formation of the Martens VIII cabinet, the Ministry of Internal Affairs was allocated to a Dutch speaker in order to prevent a French-speaking candidate from being appointed as mayor of a largely Flemish-speaking commune on the language border. This seemingly trivial matter had great symbolic importance and had already triggered the fall of several cabinets since the early 1970s.

Considering the overall pattern of the distribution of key portfolios since 1945, some posts do appear to be occupied by one party rather than another. First, the Finance and Budget portfolios (which are separate in Belgium) are usually held by the Christian Democrats when in coalition with the Socialists, but mostly held by the Liberals when they participate in government. The same pattern applies to the portfolio of Justice. When in office, one of the Socialist parties usually obtains the portfolio of Labor, which otherwise goes to the Christian Democrats. The Christian Democrats for the most part also hold Social Affairs, irrespective of which other parties are in the coalition. The portfolios of Internal Affairs and Foreign Affairs tend to change hands from Christian Democrats to Socialists and vice versa, which thus means that when incumbent, the Liberals rarely or – in the case of Foreign Affairs – never take these portfolios. Finally, the portfolio of Institutional Reform, which is important in Belgium and split into one post for a Dutch speaker and one for a French speaker, is the key portfolio that circulates most among parties.

Party factions and portfolios

In the process of bargaining over cabinet portfolios, those who defend the interest of their party face at least one major constraint – the presence of party factions. This is most relevant to the Christian Democratic family, which has by far the most institutionalized factions within its ranks. Within the CVP and Christian Social Party (PSC), the workers' factions, the middle-class factions, and the farmers' factions claim representation not only in Parliament but also in the cabinet. In fact, only a minority of Christian Democrat parliamentarians and ministers is *sans famille* – not affiliated with any faction (see, for instance: Dewinter, 1989: 714–23).[4] Indeed, the Christian Democrat family's almost continuous presence in government has enabled the different factions to obtain a firm hold on certain portfolios.

Thus, the influential workers' faction of either the CVP or the PSC supplied the ministers of social affairs between 1974 and 1988. The Labor portfolio also was held by a member of this faction, except in coalitions including the Socialists. Though the Agriculture portfolio ceased to be a ministerial post in 1981, it was most of the time held by a minister linked to the farmers' faction within the CVP. More generally, when the portfolios are in Christian Democratic hands, the workers' factions tend to control Public Health, Transport, and the civil service, whereas middle-class factions tend to control Internal and Foreign Affairs (Dewinter, 1989: 723). Finally, the office of prime minister (a Christian Democrat since 1958 except for a one-year interruption in 1973) has never been strongly related to a faction.

Given these patterns of portfolio allocation between and within parties, it is difficult to maintain that Belgian parties take an interest in cabinet portfolios only for the sake of being in power. It is of course true that being in power, and occupying certain ministries, provides a coalition party with many possibilities to distribute patronage appointments and other spoils within its own ranks. However, straightforward policy motivations also play an important part in portfolio allocation in Belgium.

The selection of individual ministers: party notables and ministrables

For a long time, it was the cabinet *formateur* who first complied a list of eligible ministerial candidates and then went to the king to have these candidates appointed. Today, the *formateur* still makes his (thus far not her) way to the king, but the actual selection has been taken over by the coalition parties. The party presidents, as leaders of the extraparliamentary parties, are most influential in this, at least on an intraparty rather than an interparty level. The criteria they use for nominating party members to ministerial posts are first of all party political, considering departmental expertise only as a secondary matter. With the party presidents holding the cards in the ministerial-selection process, the position of ministerial candidates vis-à-vis these figures is clearly decisive, in terms of both personal relations and policy positions.

Sometimes, however, practical politics mean that party presidents can often avoid nominating a particular person (perhaps a rival) to a particular portfolio only by actually declining the portfolio in interparty negotiations. This is what PS president André Cools did in May 1980, to avoid giving his party rival and incumbent minister of foreign affairs, Henri Simonet, another term of office (De Ridder, 1991). If the party president himself has high ministerial aspirations and a party rival happens to be the *formateur* (who still has a say in the selection process within his own party and is likely to be the new prime minister), the situation can become very complicated. In December 1981, for example, *formateur* Wilfried Martens nominated his party president (and rival) Leo Tindemans for the foreign office, with the special provision that the party would reserve the post for him for the next ten years (De Ridder, 1991: 145).[5]

A more structural constraint on the selection of ministers is provided by party factions. The party president must make sure that each faction is represented in the party's group of ministers in the cabinet according to its relative strength. As we have already seen, factions within the CVP and PSC are also successful in demanding specific portfolios. Often, *ministrables* from these factions accompany the party president to the formation talks, so that part of the selection of ministers may be completed before the portfolios are allocated.

Whatever the constraints on selection, those who eventually become ministers tend to be recruited from higher party ranks. Between 1945 and 1985, some 38 percent of all cabinet ministers had previously been a party leader of some kind (Dewinter, 191: 48). Looking more specifically at party presidents we find that, since the Lefèvre cabinet of 1961, thirteen party presidents became a minister, four of whom acquired the office of prime minister and four that of deputy prime minister.[6] The Martens V cabinet (1981–85) stands out as the most extreme case in this respect: in a four-party coalition, three party presidents were in the cabinet. Generally, however, party presidents remain in their prestigious and powerful office much longer than the life of a cabinet – on average, nearly five years.[7]

Expertise in a particular policy arena does not seem to be a criterion for ministerial appointment in Belgium. Belgian ministers are typically not specialists trained in specific departmental matters; only one out of every five ministers can be so labeled (Blondel, 1988: 64–6). This is related to the rapid rotation of ministerial appointments in successive cabinets, which favors (and indeed guarantees) amateurs rather than specialists (Frognier, 1988b: 81). It is also significant that prominent ministers often obtain more than one portfolio at a time.

Party negotiators and cabinet ministers

The complex policy negotiations involved in government formation in Belgium mean that certain ministers may to some extent have been pre-selected as a result of their role as party spokespersons in the formation talks. Since the 1960s, party spokespersons have often become engaged in a process of policy prefiguration, whereby interparty agreements are made in different policy areas. Party negotiators who become ministers may thus contribute to their own policy "destiny," and perhaps to that of others.

It is rare, however, for the set of negotiators to be transformed en masse into the new cabinet. For one thing, there may simply have been too many party spokespersons to include them all in the cabinet. In the spring of 1988, for instance, no less than eighty-five negotiators, divided into several working groups, participated in cabinet formation (De Ridder, 1989: 186). Though this is an exception, finding ministerial posts for all party delegations would be a problem for even the most creative inventor of new cabinet portfolios. There are of course more substantial reasons that not everyone involved in formation bargaining enters the cabinet. We have already seen that party presidents, the top negotiators, often do not join the cabinet. This is probably because they do not see it as a promotion. Second, party negotiators may, for one reason or another, be kept outside the cabinet by their party presidents or by the *formateur*. Conversely, often (but certainly not always), cabinet ministers have been a party spokesperson in cabinet formation.

Negotiators who do become ministers do not systematically obtain portfolios directly related to the policy areas they were dealing with in formation bargaining. One reason is that, when party delegations are not large, a "negotiation portfolio" during the government-formation process is often more comprehensive than the jurisdiction of a single-cabinet portfolio. It may even cut across the jurisdictions of several different cabinet portfolios. Another reason is that at least two party representatives (and since 1973 always four or more) are involved in bargaining over one policy area. They obviously cannot all take the cabinet portfolio associated with this.

MINISTERS AND POLICY

Coalition bargaining and policy agreements

Chronologically, cabinet portfolios are allocated after the coalition parties have dealt with policy. As noted, interparty negotiations usually carry on for a few months and, despite frequent "re-starts" after a change of parties, policy bargaining between a given set of parties may result in extensive and detailed agreements. It has been persuasively argued that cabinet formation is a policy-making arena par excellence, as the extrainstitutional setting and secrecy of the meetings enables parties to deal with policy conflicts without too much pressure from party followers, and free from the formalities of legislative procedures (Peterson and De Ridder, 1986: 575; Peterson et al., 1983). Another motivation for making detailed policy agreements concerns mistrust between the parties. This mistrust provides an incentive to make mutual commitments, especially on controversial issues. This is very clearly the case with issues on the ethnic/linguistic policy dimension that, since the early 1960s, have produced a high level of uncertainty among the parties about each others' policy positions (Rudd, 1986: 136–8). For these reasons, coalition policy agreements are drafted and, since the 1960s, have gradually increased in size. The longest coalition agreement to date was formulated for the Martens VIII cabinet in the spring of 1988, and was forty thousand words long.

More important than their sheer length are the contents of coalition policy agreements. At a very basic level, these agreements are "part of the definition of issues as they are dealt with in subsequent steps" (Peterson et al., 1983: 74). Specific policy intentions can in principle be implemented, whereas general ones require further bargaining during the life of the cabinet; this may or may not give rise to conflict between the parties. In addition, agreements to disagree on a particular issue may, as a procedural rather than a substantive compromise, serve to postpone the decision in question.

Perhaps the most important aspect of coalition policy agreements, however, is their enforcement. When no substantial bargaining on controversial issues takes place during cabinet formation, none of the parties may seriously consider the subsequent enforcement of the coalition agreement. If the coalition agreement includes compromises on policies that are important to all parties, however, then things are different. Coalition parties may well have the incentive, if not the ability, to enforce the agreements.

The implementation of a coalition agreement may first be facilitated by the inclusion of the former negotiators in the cabinet. The proportion of ministers in this position varies from one cabinet to another. In this respect it is interesting that one cabinet in which only a few negotiators took a cabinet seat (the Tindemans V cabinet in office from June 1977 to October 1978) experienced a subsequent collapse over key provisions on community policy in the coalition agreement. This cabinet has been used as an example of how not to do things (see De Ridder, 1989: 109–22).

The key problem in enforcing any such agreement, of course, is that policy compromises on single issues are rarely equally satisfactory to all parties. One reason is that balance between parties is often established at a multi-issue level through package deals. Once a particular issue is on the cabinet agenda, some party may want to increase its payoffs by breaking the agreement. One of the main incentives not to break such an agreement is the fear of reciprocal action by others. A party that unilaterally breaks an agreement not only may expect reciprocal action from another party on a different issue but also may face the threat that the other party, through the collective resignation of its ministers, will bring down the entire cabinet. It is for these reasons that the norm of *pacta sunt servanda* (pacts must be honored) has emerged. When, as is common in Belgium, party leaders or cabinet ministers talk about the coalition agreement in terms of loyalty and faithfulness, they are stating this norm in a different way. It must also be said, however, that this rule becomes less relevant when one party becomes more motivated by the promising prospects of a new election than by the immediate pursuit of policy and the maintenance of the coalition.

Thus coalition policy agreements may set part of the agenda for the ensuing cabinet. This part may contain directly implementable policy decisions (sometimes even complete draft bills) or more general statements that have to be specified through further bargaining within the cabinet or elsewhere, as well as agreements to disagree that are meant to keep an issue away from the cabinet agenda. The enforcement of the agreement by the coalition parties is a matter of reciprocal control. This may reduce the relevance of the specific allocation of portfolios between the coalition parties. Moreover, it may give individual ministers very little leeway in policy-making.

The cabinet agenda

Although the coalition policy agreement is already on the agenda before the cabinet takes office, formal decisions on policy are made during the tenure of the cabinet. These may be made by individual ministers or by the collective cabinet.

The cabinet has few constitutionally prescribed decision-making powers. Indeed it has largely been the cabinet itself that has, as its own master, given decision-making powers to the Council of Ministers. This has been done, indirectly, by including in laws and royal decrees the explicit requirement that executive decrees be deliberated in the council (on the powers of the cabinet, see Lagasse, 1988; and Senelle, 1983). Major laws often contain numerous items for which deliberation by the cabinet is required. More directly, the cabinet is given competence on certain matters listed in the *Practical Instructions of the Council of Ministers*. According to these, the council is to deliberate and decide on "overall governmental policy." Next, it must be consulted in cases of a legislative initiative taken by a minister, or if royal or ministerial decrees drafted by an individual minister are likely to have important budgetary or political consequences. Within this category, we also find major appointments in the civil service or state-controlled agencies. Furthermore, consultation of the cabinet is necessary in cases of draft circulars involving significant rises in governmental spending, or if cabinet solidarity is at stake for any other reasons. Finally, some additional matters, such as high decorations and the presence of cabinet members at certain events, must be put to the weekly meeting of the cabinet (Senelle, 1983: 28–32).

Although decisions on all these matters should at least be formally submitted to the cabinet, it does not necessarily follow that these decisions are collective in the sense that every minister is actively involved. As Mackie and Hogwood have put it, "Cabinets are not devices which attempt to suck all important decisions in for collective decision-making" (1985: 4). In practice, many items are the objects of relatively routine decisions (decorations or naturalization, for example) that are usually passed by the cabinet on the nod. For quite different reasons, more substantial decisions may in reality be left to one minister or a few of the most involved ministers. Moreover, it is not always clear what matters actually must be dealt with by the cabinet as a whole; the phrases "overall governmental policy" and "important budgetary or political consequences" leave a certain freedom of maneuver.

In many instances cabinet decisions are in practice extensively prepared, or even "pre-cooked," by single ministers, by informal groups of ministers, by one of the standing committees within the cabinet, or by the inner cabinet. The prime minister plays a crucial role here, being the person who refers matters to such groups or to individual ministers, thereby determining the cabinet agenda and quite possibly keeping matters away from it.

In some cases, the *Instructions* even *require* policy decisions to be prepared at subcabinet level. Proposals for decorations, for instance, are first to be considered by the minister of foreign affairs. In the case of decisions with a major budgetary impact (as based on the Audit Act of 1963), matters are put on the cabinet agenda after the minister of the budget has formally agreed to do so (Senelle, 1983: 42).

Turning to constraints on the agenda of an individual cabinet minister, the most obvious is the practical need for consultation and cooperation between ministers. Many of today's policy decisions do not fall clearly or exclusively within the jurisdiction of one portfolio and, even if they formally do, decisions may affect other portfolios to such an extent that consultation between ministers becomes inevitable. Well-known examples are the annual fights between ministers of the spending departments and the minister of the budget.

A second constraint concerns the decision-making power of individual ministers on matters that are the object of interparty politics. If such matters give rise to tensions either between or within the coalition parties, then ministerial decisions may be controversial, and decision making may shift toward the collective body.

A third factor that may push cabinet decision making toward collectivity is the requirement for linguistic parity in the Council of Ministers. If the stakes are high on some issue where a qualified majority is required, especially in the field of community policy, only the involvement of all ministers from each language group can prevent a deadlock. The possibility of deadlock is not just theoretical; issues involving the language communities have triggered the fall of most cabinets since 1970.

To a large extent the prime minister can decide whether an item for decision should be on the cabinet agenda, the agenda of an individual minister, or that of an informal group of ministers. Prime Minister Martens was particularly renowned for his active role in using his agenda power to find ways out of conflicts. He often changed the formal arena of a decision from the cabinet to that of informal meetings with individual ministers or small groups of ministers, even, if necessary, their respective party leaders from outside the cabinet. However, Martens was also reluctant to suspend meetings of the full cabinet, as this "dramatized matters" and was "a public evidence that the cabinet had lost its cohesion" (Martens, 1985: 99–100).

Decision rules and decision-making practice

It is important to be clear about the decision rule used in the cabinet. The formal decision rule in Belgium is *consensus* (see, for instance, Senelle, 1983: 47). This term, however, is misleading. As one author has put it, the consensus rule "is defined more in terms of process than result" (Frognier, 1988a: 216). If this is true, then consensus seems to imply at least some space for collective decision making. Attempts to achieve consensus take the form of negotiations between groups of ministers, particularly between the deputy prime ministers who are the leaders of their parties in the cabinet. These deputy prime ministers may be constrained by extraparliamentary parties, in particular by party presidents. Though this last point is very important, it does not change the fact that consensus must be achieved within the cabinet itself.

The result of this method of achieving consensus need not be unanimity in the sense that everyone agrees with the decision made. However, each individual minister is expected to adhere to a decision once made, since ministers are collectively responsible for cabinet decisions. If a minister voices a different opinion in public, he or she infringes on the doctrine of collective responsibility and will be forced to resign or be dismissed by the prime minister. Given this, the decision rule of consensus should not be confused with unanimity, though each minister must behave as if these are the same thing. Each minister's knowledge that he or she will be held responsible for every collective decision reached must condition behavior during the process of achieving a consensus in the first place.

What, then, is the actual cabinet decision rule? Majority voting is not a very useful mechanism for arriving at policy decisions; it is, rather, an instrument for removing recalcitrant ministers from the cabinet. Majority decision making is also institutionally hindered, at least with regard to policies regarding the language communities, by the constitutional requirement of language parity in the Council of Ministers.

A decision rule that seems to conform better to Belgian reality is that of "hierarchy."[8] It must be emphasized in the case of the Belgian cabinet, however, that this is an informal decision rule, not a formal one, and that ministers remain collectively responsible. It is also important to note that hierarchy operates within cabinet parties, not between them. We have already noted that the deputy prime ministers, leaders of the cabinet parties, are prominent in decision making. The definition of decision making in terms of hierarchy implies that these party leaders discuss important policy questions with the prime minister and then compel ministers from their respective parties to adopt a particular decision, which then is ratified by the collective cabinet. The same procedure is followed when the cabinet is to implement or elaborate parts of the coalition agreement. As deputy prime ministers often have been involved personally in the drafting of these agreements, they may feel relatively committed to them and watch over their implementation or interpretation by other ministers.

Thus, at least with regard to relatively important issues, decision making in the cabinet is hierarchical. The hierarchy runs from the prime minister, through the deputy prime ministers, down to the ordinary ministers. The special position of the deputy prime ministers, who as a group have virtually replaced the Committee for Overall Policy (see previous section), is reinforced by the fact that they often are in charge of two or even three different portfolios at the same time. In the Martens VI cabinet (1985–87), the three deputy prime ministers together were in charge of eight out of twenty-one portfolios (with the cabinet consisting of fifteen ministers).

Deputy prime ministers for the most part acquire at least one portfolio from the following set: Economic Affairs, Institutional Reform, Budget, Justice, Internal Affairs, and Planning. These are all key portfolios (except the last), related to major fields of community and economic policy since the early 1960s. Thus, the deputy prime ministers acquire key portfolios in order to deal with important policy problems at the highest level and to ensure the implementation of policies already agreed on.

The decision-making hierarchy in Belgian coalitions may also be seen to extend beyond the cabinet to the extraparliamentary parties. Meetings between party presidents may take place when the parties are close to deadlock in formal decision-making arenas. Such interventions may even be at the request of the prime minister, as in September 1978, when Leo Tindemans appealed to the presidents of the coalition parties to replace the cabinet in the drafting of amendments to a contested bill on community policy (*De Standaard*, 11 September 1978). The 1970s and early 1980s in Belgium are often referred to as the period of the "junta of party presidents." That this characterization is not used regarding the past decade is probably more because the "junta" lost cohesion, than because of the withdrawal of party presidents from decision making.

Party presidents become involved in coalition policy-making and cabinet affairs to press party policy as well as to break deadlocks. In fact, a party's group of ministers is not infrequently instructed to stand firm on a particular issue if the stakes to that party are high. The result of one party's team of ministers being intransigent may easily be a cabinet breakdown. This was, for example, the fate of Mark Eysken's cabinet in September 1981, after PS ministers had been instructed by their party president to "go on strike" until they had their way in the cabinet on substantial credits to the troubled steel industry in Wallonia (Platel, 1982: 283).

Yet, as with the allocation of portfolios and selection of *ministrables,* the power of the party presidents in policy-making during the tenure of the cabinet has limits. Party presidents are elected party officials and, to be reelected, must have sufficient support from the party rank and file and factions.[9] Although, in cabinet formation, internal differences may be suppressed by keeping the party delegation small enough (and by using the argument that the party loses bargaining strength if intraparty differences are displayed), things are less easily manipulated during the tenure of the cabinet, when confrontations between minister and party president become public more easily. A special case of this concerns the prime minister's party. We may find rivalry between prime minister and party president for the actual leadership of the party (Covell, 1982: 455). This rivalry is reinforced if the two belong to different wings or factions, which is usually the case.

Overall, we find the prime minister, deputy prime ministers, and the party presidents at the top of the decision-making hierarchy in Belgium. The deputy prime ministers often form a link between the extraparliamentary parties, especially party presidents and ordinary ministers in the cabinet. But when politically sensitive decisions must be made, deputy prime ministers are in turn dependent on their party presidents. Although the latter play an important role in deciding key policies, this does not always remove disagreement or enhance the stability of the coalition. The net result, however, is a very strong structuring of the decision-making process along party lines.

Individual ministers

Given the nature of the cabinet agenda and the cabinet decision rule, the policy-making latitude of the individual ministers is rather limited. We have also seen that there are some cases that are formally on the cabinet agenda, but in which the decision may be developed by a single minister. Where decisions are not explicitly on the cabinet agenda, a minister is most likely to have a free hand in dealing with departmental matters if they are "shopkeeping" activities or routine decisions. On more important decisions the minister is first constrained by colleagues from other ministries (given the need for interdepartmental coordination), though the unwritten rule of reciprocal nonintervention may reduce the extent to which ministers meddle in the affairs of others. Other important constraints are party political forces and constitutional provisions relating to the language cleavage. The coalition policy agreement may also play a role in limiting the scope of an individual minister.

Much less of a constraint on ministers are the civil service and Parliament. A Belgian minister is seldom "captured" by his or her civil service because the civil service itself is so politicized. This politicization is a multiparty affair; at least for those ministries that frequently change hands between parties, subsequent ministers may each appoint a contingent of party functionaries. As a consequence, departmental staffs are highly heterogeneous in Belgium, which reduces their grip on policy-making. For this reason, ministers appoint "ministerial cabinets" that consist exclusively of party affiliates, and thus form a kind of "shadow bureaucracy."

Turning to the power of parliament, the highly disciplined parliamentary groups of the coalition parties seldom vote against the cabinet or any individual minister. Only once has a cabinet failed to reach a majority in a formal vote of investiture, and this was in the case of a single-party minority cabinet in March 1946. Similarly, motions of no confidence are seldom introduced and, when either house is to vote on a government bill, the minister and cabinet can usually be confident that the required majority will be achieved.[10] With regard to substantive policy-making activities, Parliament mostly has to await the labors of ministers, which can really become a test of patience. Sometimes, a parliamentary majority (which must typically include one or more coalition parties) may get something done by threatening to hold up the examination of bills. This happened in 1988, for example, when several ministers seemed to be rather nonchalant in submitting their budget on time (Couttenier, 1987: 373). However, as soon as matters become party political, parliamentary parties usually show disciplined behavior. Finally, certain ministers, endorsed by the cabinet, not infrequently operate under a regime of special powers that allow the responsible minister to make policy decisions without these having to pass through the legislative process.

Thus, individual ministers face interdepartmental and other coalitional constraints on their decision-making power. These constraints are most pressing on ordinary ministers, who face coalitional constraints not only from outside the cabinet (from the extraparliamentary parties and the coalition policy agreement), but also from deputy prime ministers and the hierarchical nature of cabinet decision making. Nonetheless, though these coalitional constraints clearly limit the scope of ordinary ministers, the ministers' departmental agendas (including interdepartmental consultations) are often very full, and this may make them want to remain aloof from interparty politics. It is therefore typically only if an interparty problem within the governing coalition falls at least partly under his or her policy jurisdiction, that an individual minister may feel really constrained by the political role of his or her deputy prime minister.

CONCLUSION

The decision-making power of individual ministers is attenuated to the extent that policies depart from departmental routine and become more interdepartmental or coalitional. However, though certain forces push decision making toward the cabinet as a collectivity, in many cases genuinely collective, and thus often controversial, decisions are avoided. This is first of all done by the prime minister, who is responsible for the continued existence of the cabinet. Within the cabinet, moreover, decision making on politically important matters is hierarchical, with a prominent role played by deputy prime ministers. The top of the hierarchy, however, is often located outside the cabinet and comprises the extraparliamentary parties, represented by the party presidents. Party presidents also play an important role in political crises, when they can resolve, but may also initiate, coalitional conflict.

Policy-making in Belgian cabinets may also be viewed in terms of the relevance of portfolio allocation to coalition policy. As we saw in the second section, parties and factions have specific preferences for portfolios. It is evident that these preferences reflect a concern with specific policy areas. However, it is also evident that the portfolio preferences of parties are not always satisfied, and that portfolio bargaining itself is preceded by often-substantial negotiations on a coalition policy agreement. Both may have consequences for the effects of portfolio allocation on cabinet policy.

In examining the effects of portfolio allocation, three questions can be asked, outlined in the Introduction to this book. First, there is the question of whether the identity of the parties in cabinet makes a difference to policy outputs. In Belgium, the party composition of cabinets has indeed had an effect on policy outputs, but this is partly because cabinets are formed on the basis of distinct policy priorities in the first place. In the mid-1980s, for example, several Christian Democratic–Liberal cabinets implemented economic austerity measures that constituted a radical shift from the economic policy of preceding cabinets, in which the CVP and PSC governed with the Socialists. It can be argued, however, that the permanence in office of the Belgian Christian Democrats, and their ability to choose partners in successive coalitions, increases their bargaining power (Luebbert, 1986). This may reduce the effects on coalition policy of any other party in the cabinet. (Laver and Budge, eds., 1992).

The second question concerns the allocation of portfolios between parties and the effects this has on cabinet policy. Here, our discussions of portfolio preferences and the coalition agreement are relevant. If parties prefer different portfolios because their policy concerns differ, then portfolio allocation will not give rise to problems within the limits of the agreed numerical distribution. In reality, this situation does not arise for the key portfolios, but rather for portfolios covering policies such as agriculture, science, the middle classes or family affairs. As the related issues are salient only to particular parties, these parties face few coalitional constraints in policy-making within the jurisdictions of these portfolios. Hence, with this type of portfolio the interparty allocation does make a different to policy outputs.

In contrast, if a portfolio is desired by two or more parties with different policy intentions, then allocation problems will arise. The consequence of one party acquiring a particular portfolio may be that another party will look for ways to influence policy-making within that particular jurisdiction. One result of this can be that decision making in the cabinet becomes more collective. It must be noted, however, that part of this allocation problem is located at the top of the cabinet, where the political role of the deputy prime ministers is precisely to negotiate the more-important policies. If we also take into account the possibility of coalition policy agreements that are specific enough to be implemented, then portfolio allocation may weigh less heavily on the cabinet. In fact, one of the incentives to formulate a coalition agreement is to reduce such problems, since the parties' joint commitment to those policies included in the coalition agreement may reduce the relevance of having some particular party in charge of a key portfolio.

The third question concerns whether the allocation of portfolios within parties makes a difference to policy outputs in Belgium. Here, we must consider factions as well as individual ministers. Though it is true that the factions within the CVP and PSC relatively often acquire particular portfolios, they also have only limited decision-making power during the tenure of the cabinet. Constraints on individual ministers apply with equal force here, so that the effects on policy of particular factions being in charge of particular portfolios may also be reduced.

Thus, while individual ministers within parties in Belgium may put their mark on more routine and unambiguously departmental matters, they are, given party and coalitional constraints, relatively exchangeable when important decisions must be made. This may also explain the high frequency of intraparty reshuffles in Belgium.

The general conclusion to be drawn from the answers to these three questions is that Belgian cabinets to a large extent are an arena for interparty politics, in which the extraparliamentary parties rather than the ordinary ministers are predominant when matters become serious. This becomes especially clear when we consider the role of extraparliamentary parties in bargaining over coalition policy, and the limited impact on this policy of portfolio allocations to individual ministers.

NOTES

1 Only three were minority governments. These were in office for only a very short period, either because they had caretaker status or because they soon were extended with another party to obtain majority status. This may illustrate the salience of the parliamentary-majority requirement in Belgium.

2 If a regionalist party leaves the cabinet, it does not produce a collective resignation of the whole cabinet. In such a case, the portfolio(s) in question is (are) reallocated to one or more ministers from the same language group. In Belgium, cabinet reshuffles (and thus portfolio reallocations) are relatively frequent. In fact, Belgium in this respect scores highest of all countries in which coalition governments prevail.

3 Note that since 1970, the quantitative distribution between these groups is constitutionally determined at equality.

4 This author also rightly points to the presence of a (less institutionalized) division within the CVP and PSC, as well as within the other traditional parties, into a *unitarist* and a *federalist* wing. Since the early 1980s, the moderately federalist wings have largely crowded out the unitarists within these parties.

5 Tindemans indeed remained minister of foreign affairs in four successive cabinets, until June 1989, when he resigned to become a member of the European Parliament.
6 In Belgium, the offices of party president and minister are incompatible.
7 Excluding interim party presidents (calculation based on Maes, 1990: 56–62).
8 The distinction between unanimity, majority, and hierarchy as decision rules is borrowed from Scharpf (1989).
9 Though often there is only one candidate in the election of a party president (Maes, 1990: 54). Still, the incumbent party president must manage to become that candidate.
10 An important deviant case, however, occurred in April 1980, when the Martens II cabinet was defeated in the Senate on a constitutional amendment requiring a two-thirds majority. Here, the earlier-mentioned internal division within the CVP on federalization generated a sufficiently large group of MPs to dissent.

REFERENCES

Blondel, Jean. 1988. Ministerial careers and the nature of parliamentary government: the cases of Austria and Belgium. *European Journal of Political Research* 16: 51–71.
Budge, Ian, and Hans Keman. 1990. *Parties and Democracy: Coalition Formation and Government Functioning in Twenty States*. Oxford University Press.
Couttenier, Ivan. 1987. Belgian politics in 1986. *Res Publica* 29: 359–82.
Covell, Maureen. 1982. Agreeing to disagree: elite bargaining and the revision of the Belgian constitution. *Canadian Journal of Political Science* 15: 451–69.
De Standaard (Flemish newspaper).
Dewinter, Lieven. 1989. Parties and policy in Belgium. *European Journal of Political Research* 17: 707–30.
 1991. Parliamentary and party pathways to the cabinet. In Jean Blondel and Jean-Louis Thiébault (eds.), *The Profession of Government Minister in Western Europe*. New York: St. Martin's.
Frognier, André-Paul. 1988a. The mixed nature of Belgian cabinets between majority rule and consociationalism. *European Journal of Political Research* 16: 207–28.
 1988b. Belgium: a complex cabinet in a fragmented polity. In Jean Blondel and Ferdinand Müller-Rommel, *Cabinets in Western Europe*. London: Macmillan Press.
Laver, Michael, and Ian Budge (eds.). 1992. *Party and Coalition Policy in Western Europe*. London: Macmillan Press.
Laver, Michael, and Norman Schofield. 1990. *Multiparty Government: The Politics of Coalition in Europe*. Oxford University Press.
Luebbert, Gregory. 1986. *Comparative Democracy: Policymaking and Governing Coalitions in Europe and Israel*. New York: Columbia University Press.
Mackie, Thomas, and Brian Hogwood. 1985. Decision-making in cabinet government. In Thomas Mackie and Brian Hogwood (eds.), *Unlocking the Cabinet: Cabinet Structures in Comparative Perspective*. London: Sage.
Maes, Marc. 1990. De formele aanstelling van de partijvoorzitters in België, 1944–1990. *Res Publica* 32: 3–62.
Martens, Wilfried. 1985. *Een gegeven woord*. Thielt: Lannoo.

Peterson, Robert, and Martine De Ridder. 1986. Government formation as a policy-making arena. *Legislative Studies Quarterly* 11: 565–81.

Peterson, Robert, Martine De Ridder, J. Hobbs, and E. McClellan. 1983. Government formation and policy formulation: patterns in Belgium and the Netherlands. *Res Publica* 25: 49–82.

Platel, Marc. 1982. Martens IV – Eyskens I – Martens V. *Res Publica* 24: 273–303.

Ridder, Hugo De. 1982. *De keien van de wetstraat.* Leuven: Davidsfonds.

1989. *Sire, geef me honderd dagen.* Leuven: Davidsfonds.

1991. *Omtrent Wilfried Martens.* Tielt: Lannoo.

Rudd, Chris. 1986. Coalition formation and maintenance in Belgium: a case-study of elite behavior and changing cleavage structure, 1965–1981. In Geoffrey Pridham (ed.), *Coalitional Behavior in Theory and Practice.* Cambridge University Press.

Scharpf, Fritz. 1989. Decision rules, decision styles and policy choices. *Journal of Theoretical Politics* 1: 149–76.

Senelle, Robert. 1983. *De ministerraad in België.* Deventer: Kluwer.

Strom, Kaare. 1990. *Minority Government and Majority Rule.* Cambridge University Press.

8

The role of cabinet ministers in the French Fourth Republic

François Petry

INTRODUCTION

Three related sets of considerations influence the role of cabinet ministers in parliamentary systems. One is the type of decision making in the cabinet. At one extreme is "pure" collective cabinet decision making, under which cabinet ministers have no differentiated role, no individual decision power. At the other extreme is "pure" individual ministerial decision making, which implies a complete absence of collective cabinet responsibility in government. This chapter will attempt to determine the position of the cabinets of the French Fourth Republic on the collective–individual decision-making continuum.

Another consideration concerns the power of cabinet relative to other decision makers – the civil service, Parliament, and political parties. Cabinet ministers have a significant role in shaping policy outcomes only to the extent that they can push their projects past these other decision makers. This paper will examine the relationship between cabinet ministers, Parliament, bureaucrats, and party leaders in the French Fourth Republic and draw some implications for the role of ministers in shaping policy.

A final consideration is of what individuals are appointed to which portfolios. The portfolio-allocation approach to government formation (Austen-Smith and Banks, 1990; Laver and Shepsle, 1990a,b) associates particular policy outcomes with specific ministerial appointments. This chapter thus asks whether it was possible to forecast the consequences of allocating a portfolio to a given minister in the governments of the French Fourth Republic.

CABINET DECISION MAKING IN THE FRENCH
FOURTH REPUBLIC

The cabinet met every Wednesday morning at the Elysée, the residence of the president of the republic. Junior ministers (state secretaries) did not normally take part unless the cabinet agenda included items directly of concern to them. The president chaired the cabinet meeting and kept its minutes. These powers were far from negligible, considering that the president continued in office far longer – and was therefore more experienced and better informed – than most individual cabinet ministers, including the prime minister of the day. The president had an active role in cabinet deliberation, but that role was only participatory. He was not tied by collective cabinet responsibility, and consequently his opinion had no formal impact on cabinet decisions. However, in practice, the president's views could carry weight, especially in the fields of defense and foreign affairs.

The cabinet was a collegial body. Its deliberations were characterized, at least in theory, by collective decision making under the leadership of the prime minister. According to the constitution, only the prime ministers and members of Parliament could propose legislation. In other words, and in accordance with the principle of collective cabinet responsibility, ministers could not individually make decisions involving legislation, or seek Parliament's approval on government decisions.[1] However, the *Rules and Procedures of the Cabinet* did expressly mention the right of cabinet members other than the prime minister to prepare legislation. According to these rules,[2] proposals for cabinet consideration had to be submitted to the cabinet secretariat several days in advance, for review and circulation to ministers. Members of the government directed their observations about the proposed legislation to the minister who proposed it. These observations were transmitted to the prime minister, who decided when the proposed legislation would be included in the cabinet agenda. The prime minister had the power to stop the process whenever he wanted, and to make his own proposals. After a proposal was discussed in the cabinet, it was presented to Parliament with the signature of the prime minister and the countersignature of the ministers concerned.

Procedural rules as well as parliamentary practice required cabinet decisions to be prepared by a single minister or by a group of ministers. The focus of cabinet meetings was primarily on final decision making or the confirmation of earlier decisions that had been made by ministers individually, in the Cabinet Council[3] or in some ad hoc inner cabinet (*conseil restreint*) charged with the preparation of a given question. Instances of ministers simply walking into cabinet meetings and requesting cabinet agreement on some unannounced decision were rare. Cabinet members knew that the cabinet would be suspicious of walk-ins and therefore likely to reject their request. Walk-ins most often resulted from a tactical decision by the prime minister (for example, over announcement of the Suez invasion) designed to eliminate the risk of leaks.

The process of preparing legislation to be eventually decided by the cabinet was often collective in the sense that a decision could involve more than one minister. This collective ministerial involvement in government decisions was primarily a consequence of the increasing complexity of policy problems addressed by the cabinet. A number of problems cut across ministerial jurisdictions and needed interministerial coordination and agreement.

The fact that most items presented before the cabinet had been prepared in advance did not necessarily imply that everything went smoothly in cabinet meetings. Cabinet deliberations were not always harmonious. Ministers did not hesitate to defend their position and to argue with one another or with the prime minister on points of policy. Several factors explain the particular atmosphere of cabinet meetings during the French Fourth Republic. First, there was the impact of ideological differences between ministers who often acted as delegates of their respective parties and were consequently inclined to voice partisan preferences in the cabinet. Second, inner cabinet and interdepartmental committee meetings often failed to produce any decisive outcome, so that their usefulness remained somewhat limited. Policy disagreements among ministers – and interdepartmental rivalries that should have been smoothed out by those precabinet meetings – were bound to come into the open at cabinet meetings. Third, the prime minister lacked the authority – and often the charisma – necessary to settle policy differences between cabinet ministers. The inability of many prime ministers to make a final decision on issues that divided the cabinet was partly responsible for the endless nature of some cabinet meetings, which were brought to a close only by the mutual exhaustion of the participants. Thus, the cabinet meeting of August 27, 1948, lasted fourteen hours, following a Cabinet Council meeting that had itself lasted for six hours (Arné, 1962: 91).

The cabinet decision rule has been variously described as "consensus" or "unanimity" (Arné, 1962: 91). By this is meant that the prime minister made the final decision after having heard the opinion of all interested members of cabinet. In accordance with his role as a broker or conciliator, the typical prime minister of the French Fourth Republic tried to read the mood of the meeting and summarize the views of his ministers. Insofar as the decision reflected the general mood of the cabinet, ministers were not expected to express contrary opinions; if they did, these were not recorded. As a general rule, there was no vote in the cabinet.[4] However, when differences on issues were important, it was not rare for cabinet

127

members to openly express their disagreement with a government decision, and this amounted to a vote.

Once the cabinet had decided on a bill, and the bill was presented before Parliament, ministers were expected to support it. However, some ministers could not refrain from attacking cabinet decisions of which they did not approve, in speeches or in the media. Normally a minister who publicly criticized a cabinet decision had to resign, although there were a few instances in which a minister who had publicly criticized a cabinet decision did remain in government (Williams, 1964: 397; Arné, 1962: 75).

THE IMPACT OF PARTIES ON CABINET MINISTERS

One cannot study the role of cabinet ministers in the governments of the French Fourth Republic without examining the impact of political parties on their behavior. The actions of ministers from the disciplined mass parties (Communist, Socialist, and also the Popular Republican Movement, or MRP) were severely constrained by the policies or strategic decisions of their respective parties (Williams, 1964; MacRae, 1967). Ministers from weak and divided groups (the Moderates and Radicals, for example) had more freedom of action. As a general rule, however, there was a strong identification between parties and cabinet members,[5] undermining collective decision making in the cabinet but not enhancing ministerial autonomy.

Collective cabinet decision making was most severely constrained by party politics at the beginning of the French Fourth Republic. The period of *tripartisme* (1946–7) was characterized by a more or less systematic colonization of ministries and civil service by the three parties that took office immediately after World War II (Communists, Socialists, and MRP). In January 1946 these three parties signed a treaty distributing the governmental spheres of influence within which they would conduct their distinct policies. Each party was to control its own sector of government, staffed with its own ministers. The cabinet was a forum in which party delegates conducted their business. The prime minister acted as a mere broker between the parties. One reliable author even reports that the distribution of ministries in the Ramadier cabinet of 1947 had been agreed by the three parties before the president had even called upon a candidate for the premiership (Williams, 1964: 390).

Parties had exclusive power not only over ministerial appointments but also over how policies would be administered. Official appointments were openly made in the interest of the party controlling the relevant ministry. Absent ministers were replaced not by colleagues from allied departments but by another minister from the same party. A reliable observer could say in 1948 that "in any given department if you know the political outlook of the minister . . . you almost certainly know also the party loyalty of most senior officials of the ministry – even of the technical services."[6]

After the collapse of *tripartisme,* parties lost their political monopoly over specific sectors but, for many years to come, their influence was felt at the level of senior-level appointments.[7] They continued to exercise control over the appointment and behavior of cabinet ministers. Parties often laid down their conditions before joining a coalition government. This often involved demanding specific ministerial posts and vetoing appointments outside the party. Party vetoes were not always successful, however. Sometimes a prime minister with a strong personality would insist on, and succeed in, appointing cabinet members of his own choice against the will of the parties.

One consequence of the strong identification of parties with their delegates in the cabinet was the lack of a sense of collective cabinet responsibility in the governments of the French Fourth Republic.[8] Ministers did not feel bound by the obligation of ministerial solidarity; many considered that their prime responsibility was to their party, and after this only to their government. A related consequence was mutual suspicion between coalition partners in cabinet. Cabinet ministers from different parties had a tendency to consider each other rivals rather than partners. This naturally helped to limit the scope of cabinet collective decision making. The ability of ministers to take individual initiatives was also diminished by mistrust among cabinet members. From the beginning of the period, sensitive policy areas (for example national defense) were divided among several ministerial portfolios, each given to a different party so as to avoid monopolization by one party. Cabinet appointments (such as colonial or diplomatic posts) were often allocated on the basis of proportional representation among the parties in government. Being mutually suspicious, parties in government kept a close eye on each other's activities in and out of the cabinet. As a consequence, it was unlikely that a minister could make an important decision within his jurisdiction without seeking cabinet approval. Conversely, a minister could not ignore a cabinet decision affecting his jurisdiction without his rivals taking notice.[9]

THE CLASH OF TWO CONCEPTIONS OF THE ROLE OF CABINET MINISTERS

According to the constitution of 1946, the prime minister was much more than primus inter pares in the cabinet (in contrast to his predecessor in the Third Republic). The constitution gave him broad powers over his ministers, who were assigned a subordinate role. On the other hand, ministers, and the parties to which they belonged, were determined to keep a high degree of autonomy vis-à-vis the prime minister. In these conditions, clashes between governments and parties were inevitable. These started to surface early in the period and gave rise to parliamentary practices that are peculiar to the French Fourth Republic. Two in particular are of direct interest in a discussion of the role of cabinet ministers: one, the practice of "double investiture," regulated the very formation of government; the other was the "informal vote of confidence," which often resulted in a cabinet crisis and eventual collapse.

According to the constitution, the prime minister was personally invested by Parliament on the basis of his program. The investiture rule was meant to underscore the fact that the prime minister was personally invested, independently of his ministers, and that he could appoint and dismiss them at will. The selection of cabinet members was to come only after the prime minister had been invested. The intention of the constitution makers was clear: by instituting a personal investiture before cabinet selection could start, they hoped to prevent bargaining over cabinet spoils (*les marchandages*) that could only weaken the authority of the prime minister. However, the hopes of the constitution makers were destroyed almost immediately after the regime was put in place. Early in the period, prime ministers began to ask for legislative approval of their cabinet immediately after they themselves had been invested. This second investiture was not required by the constitution – indeed it was against its very spirit – but parties demanded it nonetheless. In practice only two prime ministers dared to choose their cabinets without consulting the party groups in Parliament, and they both failed to receive majority approval for the composition of their cabinets. In fact many prime ministers, rather than seeking a double parliamentary investiture, preferred to make the composition of their cabinet known at the time of the first investiture debate. As a general rule, the overall composition of the cabinet was decided before the investiture (Arné, 1961: 196). After the constitutional revision of 1954, Parliament was to invest the prime minister only after he had formed his government.

The practice of double investiture takes on a special significance in the light of the portfolio-allocation approach. The constitutional rule of personal investiture required Parliament to approve a prime minister's policy program before it could be underwritten by ministerial appointments. This was consistent with the idea of pure collective cabinet decision making. Constitution makers saw no need for the parties to know the names and policy preferences of individual ministers before investiture because they anticipated a strong executive capable of enforcing collective cabinet decisions. With pure collective cabinet decision making, the partisan identity of individual ministers is virtually irrelevant. However, in practice the situation was quite different. From the start, ministers were delegated by their parties to ensure that party policies would be implemented in the cabinet. The political identity of individual ministers mattered a great deal to the parties.

The situation that resulted was that the prime minister and his cabinet ministers – at least some of them – had widely divergent expectations of where individual ministerial decision power ended and where collective cabinet decision making started. The resulting uncertainty made it all the more difficult to predict the consequences of allocating a given portfolio to a particular minister. It was also a major factor in cabinet instability.

Another parliamentary practice relevant to this discussion was the "informal vote of confidence." According to the constitution, the government needed to resign only if defeated in a vote of censure proposed by the opposition, or by a vote of confidence proposed by the prime minister. In both cases an absolute legislative majority against the government was needed to defeat it. The government could dissolve Parliament after two government crises had occurred within eighteen months, provided the government had been defeated by a formal vote of confidence or of censure. Prime ministers relied heavily upon confidence votes to ensure that their policies would pass in the National Assembly, so much so that the solemn confidence-vote procedure soon became an obstacle and was ignored. Instead the prime minister used the informal vote of confidence which, unlike the formal procedure, did not involve the threat of dissolution. A number of votes of confidence were triggered by policy disagreements within the cabinet.[10] The practice of informal votes of confidence was designed to make individual ministers, and the parties that had delegated them in the cabinet, face their responsibilities without risking serious frictions that might put even further strain on already-tense interparty relations within the cabinet. The practice was self-defeating, however. By making the threat of dissolution a remote possibility, it removed from the prime minister a powerful sanction against ministers who refused to obey his authority.

All too often policy disagreements between key ministers could not be contained within the cabinet. In accordance with the doctrine of collective cabinet responsibility, ministers who threatened to defy cabinet decisions publicly were dismissed. However, a ministerial resignation was likely to lead to the collapse of the entire cabinet. Quite often, a situation of policy disagreement within the cabinet resembled a game of chicken between a particular minister and the cabinet (embodied by the prime minister). The most likely outcome of this in a cabinet in the French Third Republic was that the minister would get his way. During the French Fourth Republic, however, the prime minister and a recalcitrant minister often came into head-on conflict. The minister knew that if he publicly criticized a cabinet decision he would be sacked; but he nonetheless had little incentive to remain loyal to the cabinet because he knew that his dismissal would provoke the collapse of the entire cabinet, and it was likely that he would not be invited to join the next government.

Policy disagreement among cabinet members became so severe in the last years of the French Fourth Republic that it was necessary to create a new extraconstitutional organ called the Committee of the Majority, better known as a series of "roundtable conferences," to work out government policies on issues already before Parliament. A roundtable on Algerian reform, held in 1957, was the first of a series called to resolve disagreements that directly threatened the life of the government.[11] Each failed to achieve its purpose, however, because if the prime minister was incapable of imposing the discipline of collective decision making within his cabinet, he apparently could not impose that discipline outside government.

MINISTERIAL TURNOVER

Between 1945 and 1958, there were 227 ministers and secretaries of state in twenty-four successive governments. These numbers refer to first appointments to a governmental position without distinguishing between full ministers and secretaries of state, and do not count reappointments unless they involved a promotion from secretary of state to minister. Among the 227 members of government to the French Fourth Republic, 9 were only secretaries of state and never became full ministers, and 36 others were first appointed as secretaries of state and later promoted to full ministers. This leaves a relatively small pool of ninety-two people who were first appointed as full ministers. These ninety-two first appointments were of rather short duration, considering that the average life of a cabinet in the French Fourth Republic was only six months. However, people who had been appointed to the cabinet once had an excellent chance of being reappointed several times in the future. Dogan (1989) calculated that the 227 members of government were appointed to a total of 776 ministerial positions, but that 250 of those appointments went to only 23 men, each of whom participated in nine or more cabinets. Another sixty-six ministers each belonged to more than three and fewer than nine cabinets. The remaining 208 appointments went to 138 persons who participated in three governments or less. There was thus a governmental nucleus of about thirty personalities, who were regularly appointed to cabinets.

Frequent ministerial reappointment gave individual ministers more practical experience and political expertise and thereby contributed to their decisional autonomy. This was all the more true when a minister was reappointed repeatedly to the same portfolio, as was the case for Bidault and Schuman at Foreign Affairs, Petsche at Finance, or Moch and Brune at the Ministry of Interior.

Cabinets that followed elections (Blum, Ramadier, Pleven II, Mollet) tended to have high numbers of newcomers. Deep adjustments in the composition of the government were also needed between elections as the legislative support coalition changed. Thus, the unusually high number of newcomers in the Bidault II cabinet is explained by the Socialist move from office to opposition. Similarly, the high number of newcomers in the Laniel cabinet was in response to the "integration" of the Gaullists. Most changes of government, however, were rather like cabinet reshuffles, involving relatively small shifts in the composition of the government – except that the prime minister himself changed.

A change of government did not necessarily mean a change of the ministerial team, parliamentary majority, or political orientation. It was more like a new crystallization of the same parliamentary majority around a new group of ministers that included few newcomers, and that proposed a program in which only the order of priorities was changed. Cabinets with many newcomers were not necessarily the ones with important policy changes. Conversely, a change in government policy could happen without much change in the ministerial team. Thus the Pinay cabinet, with only one newcomer (Pinay himself), coincided with important changes in economic policies. In several instances, the new prime minister would take control of a department to better signal the change in policy. Thus, Pinay took responsibility for the Ministry of Finance in addition to being prime minister to better impress upon all that the financial policies of the preceding government were over. For similar reasons Mendès-France assumed the Foreign Affairs post in addition to that of prime minister.

MINISTERS, PARLIAMENT, AND CIVIL SERVANTS

An enduring theme in writings on French politics is that a strong administrative state substitutes for a weak political leadership in carrying out the nation's government. This interpretation, although excessive as a general historical statement, is probably more true for the French Fourth Republic than for other periods of French political history. Several factors accounted for the shift of policy-making power from cabinet ministers to civil servants. One was ministerial instability, which made ministers dependent upon the civil service for the expertise and competence that they could not acquire during their short tenure in office. This was compounded by the requirement that cabinet ministers keep their seat in Parliament. As a consequence, a minister had to devote a significant amount of time and energy to parliamentary and constituency affairs. These parliamentary obligations interfered with the ability of a minister to secure full control over the conduct of his ministry.

Ministerial dependence upon civil servants was aggravated by the lack of cabinet cohesion. The ideological divisions between coalition partners and the weak powers of the prime minister meant that a minister who wanted to push through a reform opposed by his civil servants could not hope for the support of the cabinet. The lack of cabinet support was especially serious in the areas of defense, security, and foreign affairs, in which the tension between officials and politicians was more or less permanent. In the last years of the regime, colonial administrators and army general officers openly defied the directives from their ministries in Paris.

Ministerial autonomy was also constrained by the threat of legislative sanction. In part as a reaction against the excessive use of special powers before World War II, the constitution of 1946 prohibited the National Assembly from delegating its legislative power to members of the government. This did not prevent ministers from asking and obtaining from Parliament the power to issue decrees having the force of law, just as their predecessors of the French Third Republic could; but some powerful safeguards were put in place against possible abuse of special powers by cabinet ministers. For example, decrees could be issued only by specific ministers for limited periods of time and subject to collective cabinet approval. In the last years of the regime, decree laws gave way to the *loi-cadre*. Unlike the *decret-loi*, the *loi-cadre* did not give a blank check to the cabinet, but required a close collaboration of the cabinet and Parliament on a precise agenda.

Apart from the limited instances in which it could be avoided, parliamentary control over the cabinet was tight. Committee chairs – not the relevant minister – were responsible for piloting bills through Parliament, and parliamentary debate on a bill opened with the committee's report by a *rapporteur* (or *rapporteur-général*) rather than by a ministerial declaration like in Britain. In the not-infrequent event that the committee opposed the government proposal, Parliament would hear the case *against* a cabinet minister's bill before hearing the case *for* it, thereby placing the minister in a position of weakness vis-à-vis the legislature.

Committees, like cabinets, were battlefields in which political parties fought out their differences. But the partisan composition of committees differed from that of the cabinet since it included nongovernment parties. Ministers responsible for a particular policy that had been adopted in the cabinet could never be sure that it would be also adopted by the relevant committee(s) in the National Assembly. Experienced ministers, however, could exercise their political skill by making sure that a favorable committee would be granted jurisdiction over their bill, or by playing committees against each other when their bill overlapped committee boundaries.

A powerful source of possible legislative sanction on ministerial autonomy was the Finance Committee of Parliament. The committee often did battle with the "spending ministries" (Defense, Education, etc.), but more often than not in these instances, the committee was an ally to the prime minister and the finance minister.[12] On some occasions the committee used its power to reject the government's budget and submit its own. Overall, however, the Finance Committee was less dangerous to the cabinet than the Finance Committee of the French Third Republic, which had the reputation of being a maker or breaker of governments. The Finance Committee was directly responsible in the defeat of only two governments in the French Fourth Republic (Faure, 1952, and Mollet, 1957, both on tax issues).

In general, committees were strong not because they had the power to control governments but because governments were weak and divided. The behavior of committees was more an irritant than a threat, and a determined cabinet minister was almost always able to persuade the National Assembly to disavow a recalcitrant committee. Members of Parliament could exercise scrutiny of the government by asking ministers to appear before committees. They could also seek explanations of ministerial decisions by way of written questions and interpellations. Questions were strictly limited in time and were never an important instrument for scrutiny of the cabinet. By contrast, interpellations gave members of Parliament a good opportunity to attack particular ministers because they ended with a vote, often qualified (*motivé*) by an expression of confidence in the government's policy. Like their predecessors of the French Third Republic, several governments of the French Fourth Republic were overthrown by the National Assembly on interpellations.

Cabinet ministers were not totally deprived of leverage in their relationship with Parliament and the civil service, however. As mentioned, a determined minister who enjoyed the support of cabinet often had the last word in case of conflict with a parliamentary committee or the civil service. Reinforcing ministerial autonomy was the typically French institution of the ministerial cabinet. Ministerial cabinets had evolved in the French Third Republic as instruments of coordination between ministries on the one hand and Parliament or the civil service on the other. But they not only were useful as coordination instruments; they also served to shield a minister from bureaucratic or partisan influences. Ministers of the French Third Republic were in the habit of hiring their cabinet from relatives and friends. One drawback was that ministerial cabinet members lacked technical competence. (Apart from being incompetent, they were sometimes venal.) Under the French Fourth Republic, ministers increasingly appointed senior civil servants to their ministerial cabinet. This was a guarantee of technical competence and probity. Many ministerial cabinet appointees were nonpartisan, and this contributed to increase a minister's independence vis-à-vis the party (King, 1960). Neutral ministerial cabinet members who had formal ties with neither the government nor the parties could be very useful to ministers in the conduct of difficult missions or negotiations.

CONCLUSION

This study has examined the role of cabinet ministers during the French Fourth Republic in the light of the portfolio-allocation approach. The central research question was: How significant a factor were cabinet ministers in affecting government policy outputs during the period? Several important points have emerged from the preceding discussion. First, there were some powerful factors limiting cabinet ministers' ability to influence policy outputs. Cabinets were often too weak and disunited to assume the leading role in the conduct of government policy. Other institutional factors – mainly parliamentary committees and civil servants – filled the power vacuum left by cabinet ministers. Second, cabinet instability made tenure in office too short to allow ministers to become fully effective in their departments. Third, cabinet ministers of the French Fourth Republic had less decisional autonomy than their Third Republic counterparts. The cabinets of the French Fourth Republic were several steps closer to using pure collective decision making than those of the Third Republic.

Second, each of the points developed in this chapter must be substantially qualified. Thus, the lack of a strong prime minister, although weakening the cabinet taken collectively, meant that individual ministers enjoyed some degree of decisional power in cabinet. Ministers of the French Fourth Republic had less decisional power than their predecessors in the Third Republic, but more than their successors in the Fifth Republic. Next, although it cannot be denied that the high ministerial turnover diminished the role of cabinet ministers overall, particular important departments enjoyed a remarkably low ministerial turnover.

A final point concerns the impact of political parties on the role of cabinet ministers. Aside from the prime minister, whose party origin was normally not of great importance politically,[13] ministers were strongly influenced by political parties. The impact of political parties on cabinet ministers appears contradictory. On the one hand, the strong identification of parties with ministers contributed to clarify the latter's role: the policy consequence of appointing a Socialist – rather than, say, a member of the MRP – in the Education portfolio was quite easy to predict. On the other hand, the identification of ministers with parties implied mutual suspicion between cabinet members from different parties. Ministers used their office to prevent the implementation of policies by rival groups just as frequently as to promote their own party's policy. Many new ministers, determined to make their mark, soon found their effort frustrated by the obstacles generated by a system of mutual obstruction.

NOTES

1 Collective decision making and collective cabinet responsibility became the rule only after World War II. Third Republic cabinet ministers enjoyed some degree of individual decision making backed up by the power to ask for a vote of confidence on individual ministerial policy (individual responsibility). See Arné (1962); Soulier (1939).

2 *Réglement intérieur des travaux du gouvernment* (II, and b. *Projets de loi*) as quoted in Arné (1962: 171–2).

3 The Cabinet Council (*conseil de cabinet,*) met infrequently (except under the premiership of Mendès-France). The prime minister took the chair of the conseil de cabinet and junior ministers participated.

4 The cabinet is reported to have formally voted on the decision to dissolve the National Assembly in December 1955.

5 Because cabinet members voted in Parliament, it was possible that the *mot d'ordre* by a minister's party was in conflict with the policy of the cabinet. Sometimes the party authorized the minister to vote with his cabinet colleagues. Ministers rarely voted against the party line without the authorization of their party.

6 Marcel Waline (1948) *Les partis contre la république,* quoted in Williams, (1964: 391).

7 Thus, the Education Ministry was a Socialist stronghold, and Foreign Affairs was monopolized by the MRP until 1954, whereas Interior remained a Radical fief, and Defense went to the Conservatives.

8 For development on the lack of a sense of responsibility among ministers of the French Fourth Republic, see Leites (1959).

9 The governments of the French Fourth Republic had a reputation for being unable to keep secrets. Grosser (1961) makes the interesting speculation that the failure by cabinet ministers to keep cabinet deliberations secret was due primarily to their role as delegates of political parties. Ministers, when pressed to justify their actions before party leaders, would inevitably give accounts of cabinet deliberation. These accounts were promptly leaked to the media.

10 The first two votes of confidence of the French Fourth Republic resulted from lack of ministerial discipline in the cabinet. In March 1947 the prime minister asked a vote of confidence to compel Communist ministers to observe ministerial responsibility or resign. The second vote of confidence followed in May of the same year to put pressure on the Socialist ministers, who had said they would not stay in government without the Communists.

11 Four additional roundtable conferences were called by Premier Félix Gaillard. They dealt with the national budget, constitutional reform, electoral reform, and medical insurance. See Andrews (1962) for a detailed discussion of roundtable conferences.

12 Members of the National Assembly could make proposals to spend public money. The Ministry of Finance could almost always count on the support of the Finance Committee in its constant battle to resist such proposals.

13 The prime minister was traditionally "above the parties." With two notable exceptions (Bidault, president of the MRP, and Mollet, general secretary of the Socialist Party [SFIO]), prime ministers were not party leaders.

REFERENCES

Andrews, W. 1962. Swan song of the Fourth Republic: the Committee of the Majority. *Parliamentary Affairs* 15: 485–99.

Arné, S. 1962. *Le Président du Conseil des ministres sous la Quatrième république.* Paris: Librairie de droit et de jurisprudence.

Austen-Smith, D., and J. Banks. 1990. Stable governments and the allocation of policy portfolios. *American Political Science Review* 84: 891–906.

Dogan, M. 1989. *Pathways to Power: Selecting Rules in Pluralist Democracies.* Boulder, Colo.: Westview.

Grosser, A. 1961. *La Quatrième république et sa politique extérieure.* Paris: Librairie Armand Colin.

King, J. B. 1960. Ministerial cabinets of the Fourth Republic. *Western Political Quarterly* 13: 433–44.

Laver, M., and K. Shepsle. 1990a. Coalitions and cabinet government. *American Political Science Review* 84: 873–90.

   1990b. Government coalitions and intraparty politics. *British Journal of Political Science* 20: 489–507.

Leites, N. 1959. *On the Game of Politics in France.* Stanford, Calif.: University Press.

MacRae, D. 1967. *Parliament, Parties and Society in France.* New York: St. Martin Press.

Soulier, A. 1939. *L'instabilité ministerielle sous la Troisième république.* Paris: Recueil Sirey.

Waline, M. 1948. *Les partis contre la république.* Librairie Rousseau.

Williams, P. 1964. *Crisis and Compromise: Politics in the Fourth Republic.* London: Longman Group.

9

The political autonomy of cabinet ministers in the French Fifth Republic

Jean-Louis Thiébault

The autonomy of cabinet ministers in France must be analyzed in the specific context of the "presidentialist" regime of the Fifth Republic. By its logic, this regime tends to be characterized by presidential domination in the exercise of political power, even if there was some limitation of this during the period of "cohabitation," 1986–8 (Duhamel, 1991; Duverger, 1985; Mény, 1991). In general, French ministers have very little autonomy within the framework of their relations with the president and the prime minister. On the other hand, their freedom of action toward Parliament, their protection against political parties, and their influence over the career civil service are stronger. This does not compensate, however, for their dependent position in relation to the president and prime minister.

INDIVIDUAL MINISTERIAL AUTONOMY

The autonomy of cabinet ministers over policy areas within their jurisdiction

Formally, French cabinet ministers have little autonomy; indeed, the constitution scarcely discusses the role of ministers. In principle, they jointly participate in the determination and management of government policy, and they are heads of their departments. But since the beginning of the Fifth Republic, more importance has been attached to their role in the management of ministerial departments than to their political and governmental functions (Thiébault, 1988). In France, the formal power structure is very hierarchical. All ministerial decisions must be countersigned by the prime minister, who signs some fifteen hundred decrees and seven to eight thousand interministerial orders per year. When a decree is necessary, the cabinet ministers must ask the prime minister for his advice on the draft. The cabinet ministers' power of regulation is therefore exceptional. It is often residual, divided and largely subordinate, in the strict context of

139

their prerogatives and for the strict implementation of legal texts. Ministers also write circulars explaining the regulations to those responsible for implementing them, or to those concerned with their consequences.

This autonomy is expanded in practice by policy-making resources in the jurisdiction of most ministers. Cabinet ministers are heads of a ministerial department. They have a bureaucracy at their disposal as well as a small group of personal advisers. They can appoint their own ministerial cabinet to advise them. They also have a budget at their disposal, though they have only limited power to take the initiative in the financial management of their department because the rules of public finance are inflexible.

Cabinet ministers, however, cannot formulate cabinet policy on their own. Although they participate in the making of policies within their field of responsibility, these policies are then presented in main interministerial meetings before being approved by the Council of Ministers. Indeed, the final decision on matters requiring legislation is normally reserved to the Council of Ministers.

The minister of finance is in a stronger strategic decision-making position than all other ministers. His function entails supervising the activities of other ministers. He shares with the prime minister an overview of all public spending and thereby of all governmental activities. One of the centers of power within the Ministry of Finance is the budget division, which supervises the implementation of every ministerial budget to ensure that expenditure accords with appropriations. Financial controllers play a major part in this task.

The threat of legislative sanction

Ministerial autonomy is not constrained by the threat of legislative sanction. Cabinet ministers are not at the mercy of Parliament. Indeed, Parliament may criticize an individual minister, but any attempt to demand a ministerial resignation tends to be translated into a general issue of confidence in the government.

Cabinet ministers have at their disposal many constitutional limitations on Parliament's legislative power. They benefit from the right of the government to control the parliamentary agenda (Article 48), which they use to give priority to bills they wish to push. Other elements of procedure and organization also strengthen the power of ministers. Government bills are discussed in the form presented by the government, not as amended by the relevant parliamentary standing committee. In addition, ministers benefit from the right of the government to move amendments of a bill under consideration. The government also has the power to force a final vote on a bill containing only those parliamentary amendments it has been willing to accept. Government ministers make frequent use of the so-called blocked or package vote (Article 44) to restrain the government's own supporters from voting for amendments. All in all, government ministers have a number of procedural weapons for pushing their policy proposals through Parliament.

The influence of political parties

The actions of ministers are not constrained by strategic decisions of their party. At the beginning of the Fifth Republic, General de Gaulle criticized the model of government based on political parties, and parties have systematically been kept separate from the government, which derives its legitimacy from its nomination by the president. The first governments included many senior civil servants (Duverger, 1986; Quermonne, 1987) and, since cabinet ministers must give up their parliamentary seat if they are members, rigid separation characteristizes relations between the whole government and the parties. Later, during his second term, de Gaulle appointed more cabinet ministers, who came from the majority parties. Nevertheless, the strict delineation between the government's and the parties' areas of activity was maintained. Ministers were therefore very autonomous from the policy or strategic decisions of their party. The Mitterrand presidency marks the first time in the Fifth Republic in which something close to "party government" has existed (Cerny and Schain, 1985).

A consequence of the separation between government and party is that few Fifth Republic ministers hold leadership positions in their party. The two positions of prime minister and party leader, for example, have rarely been merged. (The exception is Chirac, for the periods 1974–5 and 1986–8.) Refusal to merge these functions has deprived the party leaders of even sitting in the government. The rigid partition between the government and the political parties remain a feature of the Fifth Republic.

Relations between the government and the parliamentary party group are also limited. Since 1981, however, the Socialist parliamentary group has secured an agreement on the presidential program while it has been allowed free initiatives on detailed provisions. At a seminar gathering in July 1982, the Socialist ministers, the leaders of the parliamentary group, and the party executives decided to create joint working groups involving the party organization and the ministerial cabinets. The working groups were to write bills in specific areas, but this initiative failed. In addition, the Socialist parliamentary group can be a tool with which the president exercises influence over the prime minister and cabinet ministers (Portelli, 1987).

Ministers have less autonomy from political parties when relations between the presidential majority and the parliamentary majority are unstable. In these circumstances, parliamentary party leaders and extraparliamentary party heads play a much more active role in governance – either directly as part of government or indirectly as monitors of their parties' ministers.

The power of the career civil service

There is intensive participation by senior civil servants in the process of political decision making in France. Some ministers are forced to play the role of spokespeople for the civil service rather than of representatives of their party within the bureaucracy. The autonomy of cabinet ministers thus seems constrained by the career civil service. Nevertheless, the practice of power has considerably reinforced government control over the civil service. This has happened directly as a result of limited but significant powers of promotion and transfer of officials, and indirectly as a result of an interventionist policy style. The bureaucracy is no longer a "state within the state" but is now more accountable to ministers (Cerny and Schain, 1985).

In order to help cabinet ministers manage their departments, the ministerial cabinet has developed (De Baecque and Quermonne, 1981). These cabinets permit the minister to assemble a group of personal collaborators, who typically enter and leave the ministerial cabinet with the minister and thus serve as his personal team. Ministerial cabinets prepare the ministers' work. Their interventions increasingly short-circuit the activities of senior civil servants. Members of ministerial cabinets tend to take the place of senior civil servants, dealing with policy questions directly or leading negotiations by themselves.

Many interministerial meetings are held, with a member of the prime minister's personal staff as chairman. These provide the opportunity for members of ministerial cabinets to participate in the coordination of policies between different departments. The frequency of these meetings is a consequence of the involvement of the prime minister in issues formerly dealt with by a cabinet minister or even by the head of a department division. The development of this interministerial coordination suggests that ministerial powers have been restricted by the prime minister and his or her own advisers. These restrictions have underwritten the extension of prime-ministerial control to every ministerial department, and have secured the creation of an administrative network made up of senior civil servants, who discuss matters at the prime minister's official residence, the Hôtel Matignon. This has become a crucial element in decision making, because these ever-more frequent meetings allow Matignon management to extend over every central office (Quermonne, 1987).

The participation of senior civil servants in political power reaches a climax when ministerial posts are occupied by senior civil servants who are not members of Parliament. In France, civil servants constitute a key type of cabinet minister; between 1945 and 1985, 35 percent of all ministers had civil-service expertise when first appointed (Blondel and Thiébault, 1991). This practice was established in 1958 by General de Gaulle when his government included senior civil servants who were appointed to important ministries (Home Office, Defense, and Foreign Affairs). However, since de Gaulle, there has been a steady increase in the number of ministers sitting in Parliament at the time they acquired office. President Pompidou only exceptionally called for nonparliamentarians to sit in the government. Governments are nevertheless deeply influenced by the weight of senior civil servants, which has led to the suggestion that French governments are dominated by a "mandarinate" in which the grandes ecoles (such as the Ecole nationale d'administration and the Ecole polytechnique) play a large part (Dogan, 1986; Gaxie, 1986).

COLLECTIVE CABINET DECISION MAKING

Collective cabinet decision making takes place in the Council of Ministers. The constitution lists the types of item requiring referral and approval by the council: the discussion of draft bills; ordinances; some decrees; and the appointment of a wide range of senior members of the judiciary, civil service, and military. The president of the republic determines other matters that should be decided by the council of ministers. The agenda is first discussed at the Elysée by the general secretaries of the government and of the presidency. Both officials are then received by the president, who hears their proposals, makes appropriate changes, and finalizes the agenda.

The Council of Ministers meets every Wednesday at the Elysée. Discussion is led by the president. Draft bills and some decrees are first discussed. Agreement has usually been achieved beforehand and there is little discussion, because the cabinet ministers follow the principle of nonintervention. There is no interference of a minister with the portfolio of another minister.

The most time at council meetings is devoted to ministerial statements. Every week, the minister of foreign affairs makes a statement on the international situation. There are also other regular ministerial statements on aspects of European policies, on budgetary preparation and execution, and on parliamentary work. Normally the president makes his views known at the end of the discussion that follows these statements (Fournier, 1987). He asserts choices, indicates orientations, and gives directives to the cabinet ministers, either on the content, the form, or the timetable of decisions.

Traditionally, the Council of Ministers does not decide on a majority basis. The deliberations are said to be collegial and to involve all members of the government on the basis of collective ministerial responsibility. There are no votes. The president strives, before concluding the deliberations, to give the prime minister the last word (Thiébault, 1988). The Council of Ministers is therefore a collegial meeting with heads of ministerial departments and is an important stage (often the last one) in governmental decision making. Since it tends in practice to formalize decisions that have already been taken elsewhere – in interministerial committees at Matignon or interministerial councils at the Elysée – real debates are rare.

PRESIDENTIAL INFLUENCE

Within the framework of their relations with the president of the republic, ministers have limited autonomy. From the beginning of the Fifth Republic, General de Gaulle stressed presidential authority in the nomination of ministers, and some ministers respond to the president's wishes as much as to the prime minister's. Whatever the constitution says, the president has the final say in the choice of ministers. Although ministers are collectively responsible to Parliament, they are personally responsible to the president; every successive head of state has reinforced this dependence (Cabannes, 1990; Suleiman, 1980; Sung, 1988).

French government has thus become presidential government rather than prime-ministerial or cabinet government. Ministers are in effect ministers of the president, except during the period of "cohabitation" (1986–88). In April 1992, to give a telling illustration, the Beregovoy government included Bredin, Guigou, Royal, Bianco, Charasse and Vauzelle, all of whom were former Mitterrand advisers at the Elysée and closely linked with the president.

Since the beginning of the Fifth Republic, ministerial dependence on the president has affected the selection and implementation of foreign and defense policy. The president is charged by Article 52 of the constitution with the negotiations of treaties, and by Article 13 with the appointment of ambassadors. Above all, however, he engages in direct diplomacy with the leaders of foreign countries. He is in direct contact with the minister of foreign affairs, who is regularly received at the Elysée. Even the practice of power sharing during the period of cohabitation did not prevent the head of state from intervening in the nomination of the minister of foreign affairs. The nuclear arsenal also implies a concentration and personalization of power in favor of the president. A decree of January 1964 states the president's dominance over defense policy and gives him control over France's strategic nuclear deterrent. During cohabitation the president continued to affirm his predominance on the definition of great strategic options (Cohen, 1986).

Successive presidents of the republic have also intervened in other fields, but they cannot be concerned with all social and economic issues. They are obliged to select only those that may involve conflict or promise great rewards in the event of success. Sometimes the president sends a public letter to the prime minister (after consultation with him) setting out the program of government activities for the next six months. This takes the form of specifying the general objectives and guidelines of government policy, together with the particular issues upon which the interministerial meetings will concentrate their attention. Government decision making is thus guided not by the contents of party manifestos but by the contents of the presidential programs. The ability of ministers to set policies is constrained by the contents of these programs. Since 1981, therefore, the Socialist-dominated government has been guided more by Mitterand's presidential programs (the "110 propositions" or the *Lettre aux Français*) than by the Socialist manifesto (the *Projet Socialiste*). Only during cohabitation was government decision making guided by the coalition agreement of the two right-wing parties, UDF and RPR.

The president of the republic also makes occasional use of interministerial councils, whereby he and his staff take over the coordination and arbitration previously exercised by the prime minister and his staff – who in turn have been encroaching upon the decision-making autonomy of ministers. The president may also prefer bilateral meetings with "his" ministers, meetings that help him to get information directly from members of the government and express his views to them.

The number of the councils varies each year, according to the president in office. At a September 1965 press conference, for example, de Gaulle gave a summary of his numerous political contacts during his first seven-year term. He had convened the cabinet 302 times and interministerial councils 420 times. He had received the prime minister 505 times and other ministers 2,000 times (Hayward, 1973). Pompidou, by contrast, convened few such meetings but maintained especially close contact with key ministers. Decisions were often made at these informal meetings and were subsequently ratified in the council of ministers (Hayward, 1973). Particularly under President Giscard d'Estaing, the interministerial councils were almost as frequent as the councils of ministers and became the essential arena in which decisions were made. The same frequency occurred at the beginning of the first Mitterrand seven-year term of office. Since 1986, however, this practice has been greatly reduced.

PRIME-MINISTERIAL INFLUENCE

Since the beginning of the Fifth Republic, the cabinet ministers have also been constrained by the prime minister. The constitution accords the prime minister considerable powers. Article 20 states that "the government shall determine and direct the policy of the nation," and Article 21 adds that "the prime minister shall direct the operation of the government." No prime minister in the Fifth Republic, however, has sought to challenge the primacy of the president because, with the exception of the period of cohabitation, they belong to the same political coalition controlling a majority of seats in the Parliament. The prime minister cannot act against the wishes of the president. In terms of relations with cabinet ministers, however, the prime minister is no longer primus inter pares. He or she has authority over the other cabinet ministers, so that the conception of a horizontal or egalitarian government has been replaced by one of vertical or hierarchical government (Thiébault, 1988).

The prime minister can give instructions to other cabinet ministers. He or she leads governmental action by determining the rules of conduct ministers must follow. Prime-ministerial instructions are often invitations to have bill drafts ready in order to submit them to the Parliament, or instructions for the elaboration of a budget. Other instructions are simple letters to ask ministers to speed a reform, to tell them how to behave in EC negotiations, or to instruct them what not to concede when discussing wages with trade unions. The frequency and the precision of these instructions depends upon the personal authority of the prime minister.

In case of disagreements between the cabinet ministers, the prime minister can also use his arbitration power, and thereby enforce his decision on cabinet ministers. This arbitration power is one of the main instruments by which the head of the government can ensure his predominance (Quermonne, 1987; Tricot and Hadas-Lebel, 1985), and occurs in all fields. The budget is the most frequent matter to be referred to arbitration intended to reconcile the divergent positions of the minister for finance and spending ministers. But the minister of finance, always a powerful and influential politician, sometimes enjoys such power that the prime minister gives up budgetary arbitrations in practice and relies on his colleague. There are also arbitrations on the nomination of certain senior civil servants and on the elaboration of draft bills or decrees (Ardant, 1991).

The main instruments of the prime minister are the general secretariat of the government and his or her personal staff. The former prepares draft bills or decrees for the prime minister, informs him or her about all matters to be discussed, and follows up the implementation of cabinet decisions. The prime minister's personal staff are chosen for their competence and personal loyalty. They monitor the work of all ministers and interministerial committees to facilitate prime ministerial coordination and arbitration. Through the work of this staff, as well as through his or her position as the chair of many interministerial committees, the prime minister has the means to influence most areas of governmental policy-making (Elgie and Machin, 1991).

The proliferation of ministerial departments has increased the necessity for coordination, and the prime minister plays this coordinating role. The prime minister often calls interministerial committees, whose purpose is usually to allow the coordination of the governmental policy within a specific domain that falls under the responsibility of several different ministerial departments. Interministerial committees are very powerful instruments in the hands of the prime minister, who can use them to control ministers (Thiébault, 1988). Cabinet ministers themselves attend the meetings but they can also be accompanied by one or two collaborators. The prime minister relies in this coordination on a close relationship with the president. Cabinet ministers can also call upon the latter, though in these circumstances, the president normally decides in favor of the prime minister and against the cabinet minister.

LEGISLATIVE–EXECUTIVE RELATIONS

The responsibility of the French government to the national assembly can be tested in three different ways.

The first involves the situation when, after deliberation with the Council of Ministers, the prime minister tests legislative support for the government program or for a statement of general policy. At the beginning of the Fifth Republic, a newly formed government immediately presented itself to the assembly to ask for its program to be approved. The third Pompidou government (1966) did not conform with this requirement, however. The prime minister argued that at any time, opposition parties in Parliament were able to test support for the government by introducing a censure motion. He also stressed that the government is formed, and exists, the moment it has been appointed by the president, and does not need any preliminary investiture by Parliament. Nevertheless, since 1958, governments have always won a majority of votes in the legislature.

The second and third ways to test legislative support for the government imply a censure motion. This can be initiated by opposition parties, who choose the best opportunity to do it. The censure motion must gain an absolute majority of votes to be passed, a procedure that favors the government. Only once has such a vote succeeded: in October 1962, when the first Pompidou government was defeated. The procedure can also be initiated by the government. After deliberation within the Council of Ministers, the prime minister can test general legislative support for the government with a motion of censure when a bill is being passed, if this has great importance in his eyes. If no censure motion is introduced or if the censure motion does not get an absolute majority of votes, then the associated bill is said to be passed (Article 49.3 of the constitution). This provision also favors the government. It allows the adoption of a bill each time an absolute majority of representatives does not want to defeat the government. In fact, Article 49.3 has been fully used only very recently. This article is particularly effective when the majority is divided (as with the Barre governments) or when the government is a minority one (as with the Rocard, Cresson, and Beregovoy governments).

CONCLUSIONS

Since the beginning of the Fifth Republic, cabinet ministers have been very dependent upon the president and the prime minister. Ministers tend to relate to the president and the prime minister almost as if the former were civil servants. This is reinforced by the requirement that cabinet ministers must relinquish their parliamentary seats when they come to office, and by the fact that a large proportion of cabinet ministers come from the higher civil service. Political considerations must still be taken into account in the selection of cabinet ministers, but the government is no longer truly a center of genuine political power; it is, rather, primarily an administrative body. Governments are not threatened by votes of censure in Parliament, as the majority has become cohesive and disciplined. Government duration has thus tended to coincide more with the phases of the presidency. More importance has been attached by cabinet ministers to the management of their ministerial department than to political and governmental functions.

The notion of ministerial autonomy is of limited applicability in the French Fifth Republic. The main characteristic of the regime is presidential supremacy – government dominated by the president. Because he has the final say in the choice of cabinet ministers, governments are very close to the president. Moreover, government decision making is guided not by the contents of coalition agreements between majority parties, but by the contents of the presidential programs. Only during the brief period of cohabitation did cabinet ministers regain some of their powers. Even then, however, the constraints imposed by the power of the prime minister remained.

REFERENCES

Ardant, Philippe. 1991. *Le premier ministre en France.* Paris: Monchrestien.
Blondel, Jean, and Jean-Louis Thiébault (eds.). 1991. *The Profession of Government Minister in Western Europe.* London: Macmillan Press.

Cabannes, Jean. 1990. *Le personnel gouvernemental sous la Cinquième république*. Paris: Librairie général de droit et de jurisprudence.

Cerny, Philip G., and Martin A. Schain (eds.) 1985. *Socialism, the State and Public Policy in France*. London: Frances Pinter.

Cohen, Samy. 1986. *La monarchie nucléaire*. Paris: Hachette.

De Baecque, François, and Jean-Louis Quermonne (eds.) 1981. *Administration et politique sous la Cinquième république*. Paris: Presses de la Fondation nationale des sciences politiques.

Dogan, Mattei. 1986. Filières pour devenir ministre de Thiers à Mitterrand. *Pouvoirs* 36: 43–60.

Duhamel, Olivier. 1991. *Le pouvoir politique en France: droit constitutionnel 1*. Paris: Presses Universitaires de France.

Duverger, Maurice. 1985. *Le système politique français*. Paris: Presses Universitaires de France.

Elgie, Robert, and Howard Machin. 1991. France: the limits to prime ministerial government in semi-presidential system. *West European Politics* 14: 62–78.

Fournier, Jacques. 1987. *Le travail gouvernemental*. Paris: Presses de la Fondation nationale des sciences politiques.

Gaxie, Daniel. 1986. Immuables et changeants: les ministres de la Ve république. *Pouvoirs* 36: 61–78.

Mény, Yves. 1991. *Le système politique français*. Paris: Montchrestien.

Portelli, Hugues. 1987. *La politique en France sous la Vème république*. Paris: Grasset.

Quermonne, Jean-Louis. 1987. *Le gouvernement de la France sous la Vème république*. Paris: Dalloz.

Suleiman, Ezra N. 1980. Presidential government in France. In Richard Rose and Ezra N. Suleiman. (eds.), *Presidents and Prime Ministers*. Washington, D.C.: American Enterprise Institute.

Sung, Nak-in. 1988. *Les ministres de la Cinquième république française*. Paris: Librairie Général de droit et de jurisprudence.

Thiébault, Jean-Louis. 1988. France: cabinet decision-making under the Fifth Republic. In Jean Blondel and Ferdinand Müller-Rommel (eds.), *Cabinets in Western Europe*. London: Macmillan Press.

Tricot, Bernard, and Raphael Hadas-Lebel. 1985. *Les institutions politiques françaises*. Paris: Presses de la fondation nationale de sciences politiques.

10

The role of German ministers in cabinet decision making

Ferdinand Müller-Rommel

INTRODUCTION

The style of cabinet decision making in the Federal Republic of Germany depends upon a set of structural and behavioral variables. Among the structural variables one can distinguish the formal rules that lay down cabinet procedures and that are quite stable over time, and political factors that can change over time. There were, for instance, changes in coalition type as well as in party and parliamentary-fraction discipline that influenced the working of cabinet machinery in the Federal Republic. Likewise, personality characteristics such as the charisma of the chancellor or individual ministers have an impact on the cabinet system. Among behavioral variables, the leadership style of the chancellor seems to be most important in the German case. Decision making in the cabinet depends very much upon the way a chancellor coordinates cabinet work and relates this to bureaucrats, his party and parliamentary fraction, his coalition partner, and the media. Furthermore, whether or not cabinet ministers are politically autonomous certainly makes a difference for the effectiveness and efficiency of cabinet decision making.

This chapter summarizes basic information about formal procedures for cabinet decision making, individual ministerial autonomy, legislative–executive relations, and the impact of the chancellor and his office on policy-making in Germany. The available literature was supplemented as a source by interviews taken with former ministers. Thus, research findings about the functioning of the German cabinet system (until recently the research domain of public administration) are confronted with the assessment of cabinet life by former ministers.

German ministers in cabinet decision making

STRUCTURAL PATTERNS OF THE CABINET

Formal rules

It was not until the early nineteenth century that the first council of ministers was established in Germany. Due to personal problems in coordinating governmental policy, the king of Prussia appointed a group of equally ranked ministers to discuss policy and solve interdepartmental disputes. Although the various ministers who formed the first cabinet were largely independent of one another, they remained exclusively the ministers of the crown. They had direct access to the king and jointly advised the monarch on decision making.

This collegial principle (later referred to as the *Kabinettsprinzip*) changed with the appointment of a minister who was solely responsible for "the acts of the crown." This minister took on the role of an administrator heading the entire government. In 1867 the Imperial Chancellory was established. According to the constitution the chancellor was alone responsible for the policy of the empire (later referred to as the *Kanzlerprinzip*). Ministers were his administrative subordinates and the cabinet no longer existed.

The situation changed somewhat with the Weimar constitution. A cabinet was reestablished and ministers (now politicians rather than bureaucrats) were given some autonomy in conducting departmental policy (later referred to as the *Ressortprinzip*). However, the chancellor's primacy remained intact. He was responsible for national policy as well as the appointment and dismissal of ministers. However, the Weimar constitution gave the president of the republic the power to appoint or dismiss the chancellor. If a chancellor had to deal with too many parties in Parliament and could not find a majority to vote for a government, then the president could nominate a new chancellor. This constitutional regulation allowed President Hindenburg to appoint Adolf Hitler as a chancellor in 1933.

The constitution of the Federal Republic of Germany adopted most of the Weimar principles with two major differences: the government was no longer dependent upon the power of the president, and the link between Parliament and government was strengthened, so that the parliamentary majority has the power to dismiss a chancellor by a so-called constructive vote of no confidence (*Konstruktives Mißtrauensvotum*) provided that an alternative candidate is nominated. This procedure protects against unstable parliamentary alignments. In the Federal Republic, the vote of no confidence has been attempted twice: in April 1972 against Chancellor Willy Brandt (the motion failed); and in October 1982, when an absolute majority of members of Parliament voted against Chancellor Helmut Schmidt and replaced him with Helmut Kohl.

Thus, executive power in contemporary Germany is shared between the chancellor (*Kanzlerprinzip*), the cabinet government (*Kabinettsprinzip*) and the ministers (*Ressortprinzip*). Consequently, the power structure in the Federal Republic is dispersed rather than hierarchically arranged. Article 65 of the Bonn constitution begins:

The chancellor determines and bears responsibility for the general policy of the government. Within this policy, each minister conducts the affairs of his department independently under his own responsibility. The government decides on differences of opinion between ministers. The chancellor conducts the business of the government in accordance with the rules of procedure adopted by it and approved by the president.

The government in the Federal Republic is drawn from a parliamentary majority. They are appointed and can be dismissed by the chancellor. With the exception of the finance minister, all other ministers have equal rights in cabinet meetings (Braunthal, 1972; Dyson, 1978). The finance minister is in a superior position: "He has the power to veto all decisions of financial importance, including all legislative proposals with implications for public spending, provided the chancellor sides with him" (Mayntz, 1980: 158).

Besides the chancellor, all ministers, together with the state and parliamentary secretaries to the chancellor's office and the head of the federal press office, belong to the cabinet. In addition the chief of the president's office, the personal secretary of the chancellor and the keeper of the minutes attend cabinet meetings. In the absence of the relevant minister, the parliamentary state secretary will participate in cabinet meetings. Departmental state secretaries and heads of divisions at the chancellor's office (*Abteilunsleiter*) participate by invitation. Only the chancellor and the ministers are entitled to vote on policy decisions.

Cabinet size, party strength in cabinet, and type of cabinet government

Since 1949 West Germany has been governed by fourteen cabinets. The size of the cabinet has varied over the years. During the consolidation period it was rather low, increasing markedly in the 1960s. Although the number of ministries has been fairly stable over more than ten legislatures, the total number of persons who have significant influence on cabinet decision making has increased (Müller-Rommel, 1988b: 155). Interestingly enough, since 1969, the administrative and political elite of the ministries has become twice as large as that of cabinet. This suggests two things. First, the political influence of top civil servants (*Staatssekreatäre*) and parliamentary party elite (*Parlamentarische Staatssekretäre*) has grown, presumably because of the increasing number of activities of the modern state and the declining role of Parliament. Second, cabinet decision making has become increasingly dependent on a consensual bargaining process of a political-administrative character. One of the most important problems a contemporary German cabinet has to deal with is to integrate the constant demands of bureaucrats.

The number and the relative strength of parties in the cabinet is another central aspect of cabinet decision making. In contrast to the situation in New Zealand described elsewhere in this book, German governments composed exclusively of one party are more likely to be "hierarchical" or "oligarchical" than collective. It seems more likely that a "collective" structure will be found in a government composed of two or more parties. The Liberal Party (FDP) has been longest in government, having taken part in thirty-five of the forty-two years of postwar cabinet government in West Germany. This is despite the fact that the numerical strength of party representation was low in relation to that of the Christian Democrats and Social Democrats (Müller-Rommel, 1988a: 174).

It has often been claimed that the Schmidt cabinet was similar to the Adenauer cabinet in that both were hierarchical. Although the personality of the chancellor might partially explain this phenomenon, the structural conditions of party strength in the cabinet under both chancellors should also be considered. Helmut Schmidt and Konrad Adenauer (as well as Willy Brandt in his first cabinet) had a comfortable party majority in the cabinet, whereas Helmut Kohl, Ludwig Erhard, and in particular Kurt Georg Kissinger presided over cabinets in which the strength of their party was rather low. Consequently, the decision-making process under those chancellors needed to be more collective.

The coalition constellation is closely related to party strength in the cabinet. All postwar cabinets in the Federal Republic were composed of majority coalitions. Because of the country's prewar history there is still a certain fear among the public of a minority coalition government . Only in 1963 and 1982, when the ministers of the FDP withdrew from the cabinet, did the Federal Republic have a minority government – for one month. Generally, German political parties try to coalesce with their immediate ideological neighbors (for example, Christian Democratic Union (CDU) with Christian Social Union (CSU)) and add other adjacent parties until a majority government is formed. There have been three different types of majority cabinet since 1961: the Christian – Socialist coalition (grand coalition, 1966–9); the Christian–Liberal coalition (1961–6 and 1982–92); and the Socialist–Liberal coalition (1969–82).

BEHAVIORAL PATTERNS OF CABINETS

The aim of this section is to explore how those who actually took part in cabinet decision making (that is to say, the ministers themselves) assessed their role in government. The discussion is based on interviews with former German cabinet ministers, who held office between the mid-1960s and the mid-1980s.[1] The themes covered in the interviews included: informal cabinet structures; cabinet policy areas; individual preparation for cabinet meetings; specialization of ministers; the leadership style of the chancellor; and the ministers' relationship with their own parties, parliamentary groups, and civil servants. Experiences drawn from the interviews clearly support findings from earlier interviews with politicians in Western Europe (Headey, 1974; Aberbach et. al., 1981).

Collective cabinet decision making

Ministers in the Federal Republic have the autonomy to initiate policy proposals. These proposals formally have to pass the cabinet before going to Parliament. There appear to be three modes of interaction between political actors in the cabinet decision-making process before a proposal is officially dealt with by the cabinet. We might think of these as the political way, the administrative way, and the hybrid way.

The *political way* for the preparation of proposals involves bilateral communications between the chancellor and various ministers, who may come from different parties. Much reliance is placed on these informal ad hoc meetings, where proposals are discussed and then sent to departmental officials for implementation. The informal meetings may be between the chancellor and only one minister. However, most take place between the chancellor, some of his personal advisers, and one or two ministers. Under the Schmidt government, for instance, a small group of four executive leaders (the *Kleeblatt*) met frequently to prepare policy proposals. During the same period FDP cabinet members regularly had breakfast together before each cabinet meeting.

The *administrative way* involves communications between civil servants in the chancellor's office and those in ministerial departments, to discuss policy proposals. Since the agenda of cabinet meetings as well as the deadlines for the submission of proposals from different departmental ministries is supervised by the staff of the chancellor's office, the administrative links between those departments are essential. Civil servants from the chancellor's office and from the ministries bring together facts and knowledge about particular proposals and try to formulate compromises. If and when an agreement is reached, the outcome is usually accepted by the ministers concerned and the top political appointees in the chancellor's office. The proposal is then sent directly to the cabinet for approval. Such a procedure may therefore have the effect of reducing the extent of discussion at cabinet meetings.

The *hybrid way* is through cabinet committees. Although these are formally chaired by the chancellor, they are often taken over by the minister responsible for the issue under discussion. Sometimes, the minister sends a deputy, who is often a senior civil servant from the department. However, in contrast to England, cabinet committees do not play an important role in Germany. In fact, one should not refer to a "system" of cabinet committees in the Federal Republic, as the cabinet makes only limited use of committees as decision-making and coordinating bodies. Although there were only two cabinet committees in operation in the mid-1960s (Economics and Defense) a few ad hoc committees for special subjects emerged in the late 1970s. These committees met only occasionally and played no major role in cabinet decision making.

In sum, prior preparation of proposals has a strong impact on cabinet decision making. Consequently, the cabinet is only sometimes the arena for real debate on issues. Each proposal must, however, be approved by the cabinet before going to Parliament. (Note that, although the cabinet may reject ministerial proposals, it cannot give orders in the sphere of ministerial jurisdiction.) Since most problems over policy issues have been solved in the prior preparation of the cabinet meeting, only rarely are there serious conflicts between ministers in the cabinet. In cases of conflict, the chancellor has the right to formulate what he perceives to be the majority view (*Kanzlerprinzip*) and his suggestion becomes the cabinet decision. Formal voting in the cabinet is very rare.

How do ministers perceive decision making in the cabinet? Former ministers were asked what preparation for cabinet meetings they actually used. The answers to this question give a clear picture (see Table 10.1). First, the majority of respondents either agreed to proposals with other ministers or consulted with the chancellor on policy proposals before taking them to the cabinet; only rarely did ministers take issues directly to the cabinet. Second, with respect to the role of the chancellor's office, there seems to be some evidence that ministers of the Socialist–Liberal government consulted the chancellor's staff more often than ministers of the Christian–Liberal government. Obviously, this can be explained by the different leadership styles of the chancellors who deployed their staff more (or less) intensively in the formal process of policy-making (Müller-Rommel, 1993b). Third, in the view of the ministers, cabinet committees play only a minor role in the process of preparing cabinet decisions. Interestingly enough, cabinet committees fulfilled major functions in preparing cabinet matters only during the period of the Grand Coalition. Neither party membership nor type of government to which each minister

Table 10.1. *Ministers' strategies for taking issues to cabinet (in percentages)*

	N	Agreement beforehand with other ministers		Consultation with cabinet committees		Discussion with chancellor		Consultation with chancellor's office		Taking issue to cabinet (directly)	
		Yes	No	Yes	No	Yes	No	Yes	No	Yes	No
Party member											
Social Democrat	12	83	8	58	33	83	8	33	58	33	58
Liberal	4	75	25	50	50	50	50	25	75	25	75
Christian Democrat	8	87	12	37	62	62	37	12	87	12	88
Total*	24	83	12	50	46	71	25	25	71	25	71
Type of Government											
Christian–Socialist	4	100	0	75	25	75	25	25	75	25	75
Socialist–Liberal	12	83	8	58	33	75	17	33	58	33	58
Christian–Liberal	8	75	25	25	75	62	37	12	87	12	87
Total*	24	83	12	50	46	71	25	25	71	25	71

N = Number of cases.
* Numbers do not total 100 in each case because of "no replies."

Table 10.2. *Problem solving in the cabinet (in percentages)*

	N	By consensus		By chancellor's decision		By cabinet committee		By discussion among ministers	
		Yes	No	Yes	No	Yes	No	Yes	No
Party member									
Social Democrat	12	100	0	17	83	25	75	17	83
Liberal	4	25	75	50	50	25	75	25	75
Christian Democrat	8	100	0	12	87	25	75	0	100
Total	24	88	12	21	79	25	75	12	87
Type of government									
Christian–Socialist	4	100	0	0	100	50	50	0	100
Socialist–Liberal	12	92	8	17	83	25	75	25	75
Christian–Liberal	8	75	25	38	62	13	87	0	100
Total	24	88	12	21	79	25	75	12	87

N = Number of cases.

belonged made much difference to the way in which they assessed the process of preparing policy issues for cabinet meetings.

One of the main reasons for cabinet meetings is to decide on policy matters. After what has been said about the prior preparation of cabinet proposals, it is not surprising that, in the eyes of nearly all ministers, problems in the cabinet are solved by consensus (see Table 10.2). Only very rarely were problems solved by the chancellor, by cabinet committees, or by discussion among ministers in cabinet meetings.

However, there is an interesting variation in this overall finding: ministers from Socialist–Liberal governments assessed cabinet problem solving in a slightly different way than ministers from Christian–Liberal governments, feeling that there was a higher degree of problem solving by consensus. In their view, unresolved problems were delegated to cabinet committees. The chancellor very rarely resolved an issue by making a decision that then became the cabinet decision. Ministers from the Christian–Liberal governments, on the other hand, also stated that problems in the cabinet were solved by consensus, but said that the chancellor made decisions more often on his own, and that cabinet committees consequently did not play any role in resolving policy disputes. In sum, there is evidence for arguing that ministers feel a collective responsibility for cabinet decisions even though there is no collective decision making in the cabinet.

Individual ministerial autonomy

Cabinet ministers in the Federal Republic enjoy a wide range of autonomy in decision making (*Resortprinzip*) which they do not wish to forego. In fact, "The political system's capacity for active policy-making is largely a capacity of its ministerial bureaucracy" (Mayntz and Scharpf, 1975: 48). Federal ministers have to rely on the expert knowledge of the civil servants who provide them with information. Because ministers are usually deemed successful or unsuccessful by virtue of the way they manage their departments, those who are respected (not only by civil servants but also by their fellow ministers and the chancellor) are able to handle their departments and see to it that the cabinet approves the policy proposals and financial requests those departments have formulated. As pointed out before, every minister has to ensure that there is interdepartmental coordination on policy issues prior to cabinet meetings, especially when issues affect more than one department.

It can be argued that those ministers who have coordinated the prior preparation of policy proposals most effectively are most satisfied with cabinet decisions. In addition, they probably avoid having matters raised in cabinet meetings that have not been initiated by them, but that can affect their own departments. Ministers often have a vested interest in

Table 10.3. *Ministers' activities in cabinet (in percentages)*

| | N | Ministers act beyond own jurisdiction in cabinet | | | Other ministers act beyond jurisdiction in cabinet | |
		Yes often	Yes sometimes	Never	Yes commonly	Yes occasionally
Party member						
Social Democrat	12	42	58	0	25	75
Liberal	4	25	50	25	75	25
Christian Democrat	8	25	75	0	50	50
Total	24	33	62	4	41	58
Type of government						
Christian–Socialist	4	25	75	0	50	50
Socialist–Liberal	12	33	59	8	25	75
Christian–Liberal	8	38	62	0	62	37
Total	24	33	62	4	41	58

N = Number of cases.

neither interfering with nor criticizing the proposals of fellow ministers, and expect colleagues to behave in the same way when proposals for their own department come to the cabinet. In this way each also protects his or her own autonomy.

Ministers were asked to express their level of satisfaction with cabinet decisions. They were also asked whether cabinet ministers acted beyond their jurisdiction in the cabinet. The majority of ministers stated that they were satisfied (83 percent) or very satisfied (13 percent) with cabinet decisions. Only a small minority of ministers (4 percent) from the Social Democratic Party articulated dissatisfaction with cabinet decisions. The responses to the question about ministers' activities in cabinet meetings reveal that only 1 percent of the German ministers claimed that none of their fellow ministers went beyond their jurisdiction in cabinet meetings, whereas 58 percent suggested that colleagues did act beyond their jurisdiction occasionally, and 41 percent claimed that it was a common occurrence. As far as their own behavior was concerned, 4 percent of the ministers claimed that they never went beyond their own jurisdiction, whereas 62 percent did so sometimes, and 33 percent often went beyond their own jurisdiction. By and large, these results indicate that there is more activism among German ministers in cabinet meetings than the current literature in political science suggests.

Legislative–executive relations

The formal link between executive and legislature is straightforward: as mentioned, ministers are appointed and dismissed by the chancellor. They serve at his pleasure and not that of the Parliament. There is also a formal relationship between ministries and Parliament. In 1969, Chancellor Brandt imposed on each ministry a so-called parliamentary state secretary. Although the secretary of state in each ministry is, as a career civil servant, responsible for the continuity of departmental administration, the parliamentary state secretary is also a member of Parliament and is concerned with relations and communications between the ministries on the one hand, and between Parliament and party groups on the other. The parliamentary state secretary is expected to keep closer contact with the various party groups than the minister himself. In this way the legislature is constantly informed about, and also directly involved in, the preparation of policy proposals.

Another more informal relationship between legislature and executive consists of links between ministers and members of the parliamentary party fraction. More than two-thirds of all ministers in the Federal Republic between 1949 and 1990 were members of the national Parliament for at least one legislative session before they were recruited as ministers. In addition, eighty-six ministers were national party officials in various capacities prior to becoming a minister (Müller-Rommel, 1992). One might reasonably assume that ministers who have specialized in certain policy fields as member of Parliament may well be inclined to look after these issues in the cabinet and maintain close contact with members of Parliament who serve in the respective committees.

Respondents were asked whether they experienced cooperation or competition with the party executive and parliamentary fraction (see Table 10.4). Overall, the majority of the ministers (83 percent) closely cooperated with the parliamentary group, whereas only 62 percent felt there was a close cooperation with the party executive. There are, however, variations in the responses of ministers from different parties, and different types of government. Given the literature on the relationship between Social Democratic government and the Social Democratic Party in Germany, it is not surprising that only 67 percent of the ministers from the Social Democratic Party acted in close cooperation with the party executive. Among the Christian Democrats, the cooperation was even lower (37 percent). However, nearly all ministers (92 percent) of the Socialist–Liberal government claimed to have closely cooperated with the parliamentary fraction. This result leads to the conclusion that the parliamentary state secretary in each German ministry obviously fulfils his function as a communicator between the minister and the parliamentary party

Table 10.4. *Ministers' relations to party executives and own party fraction in Parliament (in percentages)*

	N	Minister: party executive				Minister: party fraction			
		Close cooperation		Competition		Close cooperation		Competition	
		Yes	No	Yes	No	Yes	No	Yes	No
Party member									
Social Democrat	12	67	33	17	83	83	17	17	83
Liberal	4	100	0	25	75	100	0	0	100
Christian Democrat	8	37	37	0	75	75	12	0	87
Total*	24	62	29	12	79	83	13	8	87
Type of government									
Christian–Socialist	4	75	25	0	100	75	25	25	75
Socialist–Liberal	12	67	33	25	75	92	8	8	92
Christian–Liberal	8	50	25	0	75	75	12	0	87
Total*	24	62	29	12	79	83	13	8	87

N = Number of cases.

* Numbers do not total 100 in each case because of "no replies."

groups. The finding also shows that ministers from the Christian Democratic Party feel themselves to be more autonomous from their party executive and parliamentary fraction than ministers from the Social Democratic Party.

The chancellor and his office

The chancellor plays a dominant role in cabinet decision making, in part because of his constitutional power (*Kanzlerprinzip*). He is in charge of ministerial appointments, he organizes the executive, and he formulates general policy guidelines. He also supervises the services of the press office and of the Federal Intelligence Service. Besides these formal tasks the chancellor has the power to set priorities among policy goals and to formulate directives for policy implementation.

The way in which the six federal chancellors have implemented policy has depended upon both their individual leadership style and the specific institutional setting within which they operated. Naturally, both factors are strongly interrelated. The leadership style of a chancellor is determined by the operating style of the cabinet and by the support he receives from his party, parliamentary group, and coalition partner(s), as well as by public image (see Müller-Rommel, 1993b). This last is particularly important on first coming to office, whereas support from the party and coalition partners is more significant for staying in office (von Beyme, 1983: 341).

More than half of the ministers interviewed (62 percent) did not believe that the chancellor has an important impact on the overall business of government, or an influence on coalition problems (the percentage among Christian Democrats is in both cases higher than among Social Democrats). Around two-thirds of all ministers did not view the chancellor as being influential in cabinet meetings on economic or defense issues, whereas the majority of ministers (79 percent) from all parties and types of government agreed that the chancellor influenced cabinet policy on foreign affairs. This result is consistent with what we know about the policy interests of the chancellors in the Federal Republic (Müller-Rommel, 1993b). The authority to formulate policy guidelines has been used by all chancellors. However, most of them have devoted themselves strongly to foreign-policy issues. German chancellors did not influence policy matters in the cabinet very strongly, and in that respect left a fairly high degree of autonomy for ministers in their jurisdiction. They nevertheless took initiatives to build consensus among cabinet members and, if necessary, talked to ministers individually. According to the ministerial interviews, chancellors Brandt and Schmidt had a closer direct contact to ministers during cabinet meetings than did chancellors Kohl or Kissinger.

Table 10.5. Chancellor's influence on cabinet decision making (in percentages)

	N	Overall government		Economy		Foreign affairs		Defense		Coalition problems		Build consensus		Talk to ministers individually		Decide on issues	
		Yes	No	Yes	No	Yes	No	Yes	No	Yes	No	Yes	No	Yes	No	Yes	No
Party member																	
Social Democrat	12	58	42	33	67	75	25	25	75	58	42	67	25	67	25	42	50
Liberal	4	0	100	25	75	75	25	75	25	0	100	50	50	75	25	25	75
Christian Democrat	8	25	75	25	75	88	12	25	75	25	75	75	25	37	62	25	75
Total*	24	37	62	30	70	79	21	33	67	37	62	67	29	58	37	33	67
Type of government																	
Christian–Socialist	4	75	25	0	100	50	50	0	100	50	50	100	0	50	50	0	100
Socialist–Liberal	12	42	58	42	58	83	17	33	67	50	50	58	33	75	17	42	50
Christian–Liberal	8	12	87	25	75	87	12	50	50	12	87	62	37	37	62	37	62
Total*	24	37	62	30	70	79	21	33	67	37	62	67	29	58	37	33	67

N = Number of responses.

* = Numbers do not total 100 in each case because of "no replies."

In addition, as expected, all chancellors only very rarely decided on issues in the cabinet.

To carry out both policy aims and administrative tasks the chancellor is aided by the chancellor's office. In fact, the office has become a key institution for the chancellor in the last forty-two years. In the early 1950s the chancellor's office was purely responsible for the political security of Chancellor Adenauer. In the 1960s it developed into a letter box for passing proposals to the cabinet. Under Brandt, the office became an institutional watchdog over the ministries, and a clearinghouse for bills submitted by ministries to the cabinet (Dyson, 1974: 364).

Today, the office supplies the chancellor "with advice and information on the consideration of policy issues and links him with ministers and their departments" (Johnson, 1983: 64). In general, the chancellor's office had a major part to play in structuring cabinet decisions in accordance with the chancellor's views. However, the office is by no means a cabinet secretariat; the cabinet as such is without an administrative infrastructure.

The staff of the chancellor's office has come to play a large part in German politics, a part that is sometimes regarded as excessive in that it appears to undermine the collective character of cabinet decision making. The functions of the staff are both administrative and political. The chancellor's staff members act administratively in that they organize the meetings of the cabinet and in particular the flow of business between the chancellor and the ministers. They are concerned with gathering, circulating, and, to an extent, controlling ministerial proposals. They also deal with the cabinet agenda, record and monitor cabinet decisions, and supervise the implementation of these decisions. They often play a part in the development of long-term ideas about cabinet activities. In doing so, the chancellor's staff can be said to exist in order to improve the efficiency of the cabinet. Nonetheless, staff members never act entirely administratively. They also have political functions: they make suggestions to the chancellor on policy questions and may develop their own policy proposals.

The office of the German chancellor has a staff of 450, only a small minority of whom are political appointees (the head of the office, the heads of the six divisions into which the office is divided and the three state secretaries). These political appointees direct between fifty and sixty higher civil servants and their supporting and technical staff, spread over forty-one policy units. Each of these policy units mirrors a policy field in one of the departments of the government; there are, as already mentioned, strong links between civil servants in the chancellor's office and their counterparts in the various ministries.

How do German ministers assess the role of the chancellor's staff in the process of cabinet decision making? Respondents were first asked whether the chancellor's staff played an important political role. Second, they were asked to specify the precise nature of the role of the chancellor's office in the cabinet government. In this respect, respondents were asked whether members of the office give personal advice to the chancellor, prepare the cabinet agenda, control policy proposals coming from the ministers, and develop their own policy proposals. As Table 10.6 shows, five-sixths of the ministers viewed the staff of the chancellor as generally important in the policy-making process. In addition, ministers perceived the function of the chancellor's staff as both administrative and political. Nearly all ministers claimed that the chancellor's office prepares the cabinet agenda and advises the chancellor politically. Only a minority (12 percent) believed that the chancellor's staff develop their own policy proposals, whereas nearly two-thirds of the ministers expressed the view that the staff in the chancellor's office controls ministers' proposals.

Thus, ministers perceived the chancellor's staff as an important feature of cabinet decision making. Nevertheless, it is remarkable to note that ministers, whether Socialists or Christian Democrats, view the chancellor's staff as helpful in cabinet life; they do what they are expected to do, namely, provide a means of smoothing cabinet decision making without questioning the autonomy of every single minister.

DO MINISTERS MAKE A DIFFERENCE?

In the Federal Republic the party distribution of the key portfolios does not make a difference to overall government policy once a coalition has been formed. Although ministers in Germany maintain the autonomy of their departments, they are nevertheless bound to the coalition policy "treaty," which is a very precise agreement over draft bills and leaves hardly any room for deviation or interpretation. Bureaucrats in the ministries as well as in the chancellor's office constantly control and monitor the implementation of this coalition treaty. In other words, in the Federal Republic, we find bureaucrats more often than ministers in the driver's seat for implementing the main governmental policies.

In very exceptional political situations, the chancellor and his staff – rather than the ministers – become most important in formulating government policy. It was, for instance, on the instructions of Chancellor Helmut Kohl that the treaty of union between the Federal Republic and the former German Democratic Republic was carried out by bureaucrats in the chancellor's office. Because the relevant ministers were not even asked for their opinion in the case of all passages of the draft, the chancellor earned much criticism, but no minister has seriously questioned his authority in setting the guidelines for this treaty. Similarly, the handling of work on the *Ostverträge* under Chancellor Brandt, and the preparation of the draft for

Table 10.6. *The impact of the staff in the Chancellor's office (in percentages)*

	N	Important role in policy process		Prepare cabinet agenda		Control ministers proposals		Advise chancellor politically		Develop own policy proposals	
		Yes	No	Yes	No	Yes	No	Yes	No	Yes	No
Party member											
Social Democrat	12	100	0	83	17	75	25	100	0	25	75
Liberal	4	75	25	100	0	50	50	75	25	0	100
Christian Democrat	8	63	37	100	0	50	50	100	0	0	100
Total	24	83	17	92	8	62	37	92	8	12	87
Type of government											
Christian–Socialist	4	100	0	100	0	75	25	100	0	0	100
Socialist–Liberal	12	92	8	83	17	58	42	100	0	25	75
Christian–Liberal	8	100	0	100	0	63	37	75	25	0	100
Total	24	96	4	92	8	62	37	92	8	12	87

N refers to the number of cases. Cell entries give percentages.

the European monetary system under Chancellor Schmidt, took place in the chancellor's office. The *Bundesbank* and interested ministers were informed of the process, but the details of the government policy had been worked out by the chancellor's staff in his office.

In sum, the cabinet of the Federal Republic cannot be defined as a "working cabinet." Its role is essentially limited to that of a final political check on the general lines of governmental policy. Decisions are approved, rather than made, in the cabinet meetings. Although the partisan composition of the government affects the nature of policy outputs, the allocation of key portfolios between parties and within parties does not matter substantially in governmental policy-making. What matters most, in the end, is the negotiated coalition treaty. But of course, what can reasonably be negotiated is ultimately dependent on the partisan complexion of the coalition, and on anticipated reactions about what roles the parties of government will subsequently play in the making and implementing of policy.

NOTES

1 Between 1966 and 1985, eighty-two ministers served in executive offices. Of these, forty-four were still in office in 1987, or had died before the interviews were conducted. Among the remaining thirty-eight former ministers, we interviewed twenty-four.

REFERENCES

Aberbach, Joel D., Robert D. Putnam, and Bert A. Rockman. 1981. *Bureaucrats and Politicians in Western Democracies.* Cambridge, Mass.: Harvard University Press.

Braunthal, Gerard. 1972. *The West German Legislative Process.* Ithaca, N.Y.: Cornell University Press.

Dyson, Kenneth. 1974. The German federal chancellor's office. *Political Science Quarterly* 89: 364–71.

   1978. *Party, State and Bureaucracy in Western Germany.* Beverley Hills, Calif.: Sage.

Headey, Bruce. 1974. *British Cabinet Ministers.* London: Allen & Unwin.

Johnson, Nevil. 1983. *State and Government in the Federal Republic of Germany.* Oxford: Pergamon Press.

Mayntz, Renate. 1980. Executive leadership in Germany. In Richard Rose and Ezra N. Suleiman (eds.), *Presidents and Prime Ministers.* Washington, D.C.: American Enterprise Institute.

Mayntz, R., and F. Scharpf. 1975. *Policy Making in the German Federal Bureaucracy.* Amsterdam: Elsevier.

Müller-Rommel, F. 1988a. The center of government in West Germany. *European Journal for Political Research* 16: 171–90.

   1988b. Federal Republic of Germany: A system of chancellor government. In Jean Blondel and Ferdinand Müller-Rommel (eds.), *Cabinets in Western Europe.* London: Macmillan Press.

1992. *Politische Karrieren und politische Entscheidungen in Bonner Kabinetten.* Lüneburg: mimeo.

1993a. Ministers and the role of the prime ministerial staff in Western Europe. In Jean Blondel and Ferdinand Müller-Rommel (eds.), *Governing Together.* London: Macmillan Press.

1993b. The chancellor and his office. In Stephen Padget (ed.), *From Adenauer to Kohl: The Development of the Federal German Chancellorship.* London: Hurst.

von Beyme, Klaus. 1983. Governments, parliaments and the structure of power in political parties. In Hans Daalder and Peter Mair (eds.), *Western European Party Systems.* London: Sage.

11

Cabinet ministers and parliamentary government in Sweden

Torbjörn Larsson

INTRODUCTION: THE STRUCTURE OF SWEDISH GOVERNMENT

The structure of the Swedish government differs somewhat from that of most other countries, perhaps with the exception of Finland. Swedish ministries are small. Less than three thousand civil servants, divided among thirteen ministries, help the cabinet formulate its policy. The ministries, together with the cabinet office, form a chancery, which is at the cabinet's disposal. The government has, to a large extent, the freedom to create its own organization and to decide the lines along which the work should be carried out. The constitution stipulates neither a fixed set of ministries, nor the area of responsibility for any given ministry. The allocation of so much freedom to the cabinet stems from a firm belief that different types of cabinets have different needs (*Constitution of Sweden*, 1989: 20). A coalition government, for example, may need to operate in a completely different way from that of a one-party government.

There are two main explanations for the humble size of Swedish ministries. One is that governmental policy on the highest level is to a large extent carried out by semi-independent agencies. On the lower level it is implemented by local and regional governments. Exactly how much independence these administrative authorities have in reality is debatable (Tarschys, 1990). However, the fact is that the constitution guarantees them a level of freedom that is unparalleled in most other countries. "Neither any public authority, nor the Riksdag [Parliament], nor the body of a local government commune may determine how an administrative authority shall make its decision in a particular case concerning the exercise of public authority against a private subject or against a commune or concerning the application of law," to use the words of the constitution. This means that directives may be given only in the form of general rules or guidelines. In other matters the cabinet has greater freedom to control and supervise the administrative agencies. Nevertheless, because the Swedish agencies are always directly responsible only to the cabinet as a whole, not to the minister in charge, this limits ministerial powers. This is a somewhat delicate matter to which I will return later in this chapter.

The second reason Swedish ministers do not function as the heads of a large administrative bureaucracy has to do with how policy is made in Sweden. Most of the preparatory work preceding the introduction of a bill in Parliament is not done by the ministries but rather by royal commissions. These commissions are set up by the government, and their position is similar to that of the administrative agencies. A royal commission is answerable to the cabinet as a whole and is directed by way of general guidelines. Royal commissions normally include civil servants from agencies and ministries, as well as representatives from different interest groups, and members of Parliament. The commission should be, and often is, a forum for knowledgeable and experienced people to vent their opinions and learn to compromise. Participating in a commission, furthermore, is one of the best chances the political opposition can have to influence government policy.

The effect of this system is that a large part of Swedish government policy is "precooked" – that is, the foundation for it is laid in the commissions. At best, Swedish policy-making can therefore be described as a melting pot, in which the outcome is decided mainly in terms of what is technically possible and politically desirable, and also in terms of which particular interest group is the strongest at the time (Johansson, 1992).

THE RELATIONSHIP BETWEEN PARLIAMENT AND GOVERNMENT

Only since 1974 has Sweden had a constitution stipulating a system of parliamentary government, though in practice it was a parliamentary democracy long before that. The most important aspect of parliamentary control over the government consists of the right to appoint and to dismiss the prime minister. The constitution of 1974 stipulates that it is the speaker of Parliament – not the King – that plays a leading role in the process of selecting a new candidate for prime minister should the incumbent die or resign. Once the new prime minister has been elected by Parliament, he or she is responsible for selecting the rest of the cabinet. The king, though still head of state, does not take any part in this process.

The speaker of the Parliament, after consulting with all of the party leaders in the house and the three deputy speakers of Parliament, presents a candidate for the prime minister. Parliament then votes on the suggested candidate, and a majority of "No" votes is required to stop the candidate from being elected. That is, 175 or more of the 349 members of Parlia-

Table 11.1. *Percentage of all Swedish ministers who were previously members of Parliament*

	1840–1905	1905–32	1932–76	1976–82	1982–90
Parliament, local					
government	33	45	49	72	48
<omostru	6	7	15	8	14
Civil servant	51	36	20	10	17
Private enterprise					
interest groups	3	5	13	4	17
Other	7	7	3	6	3
N	156	149	110	47	29

Source: Att styra riket, 1990: 192.

ment must oppose the speaker's nomination. There is no stipulation as to the number of "Yes" votes – the only pertinent constitutional concern is how many MPs are opposed to the candidate. If the candidate is rejected by Parliament, then the speaker is allowed three more attempts to produce an acceptable candidate (the same candidate can be proposed more than once). Should Parliament fail, after voting four times, to appoint a prime minister, it is automatically dissolved and a new election is held within three months. In practice, the speaker has always had his first candidate accepted, and consequently there has never been any need to nominate more than one candidate. One can thus say that every new cabinet in Sweden faces an immediate vote of no confidence.

Once elected, the prime minister has the right to appoint and dismiss the other ministers. The constitution of 1974 strengthened the prime minister's position (*Constitution of Sweden,* 1989: 20), making the old expression primus inter pares obsolete. Every Swedish prime minister since 1974 has stated clearly the intention to fight, if necessary, for the right to select ministers. However, the prime minister's power to appoint and dismiss ministers is somewhat curbed in a coalition government. In these cases, when the cabinet consists of more than one party, the party leaders will first negotiate about the distribution of ministerial portfolios. Thereafter, each party leader decides who shall hold portfolios allocated to his or her party (Bergström, 1987). When looking for suitable cabinet candidates, the prime minister need not restrict himself to members of parliament, although many ministers have had some experience as an MP before being promoted to the cabinet, as can be seen from Table 11.1. The gradual introduction of a parliamentary government in Sweden since the beginning of the nineteenth century has meant an increase in the proportion of ministers with a background as politicians at the expense of those trained as civil servants. It is also worth noticing that, during periods in which the Social Democrats have been the dominant party in power (1932–76, 1982–90), the proportion of ministers recruited from private enterprise or interest groups has been larger than otherwise.

The prime minister's choice of ministers is limited by important representative and managerial factors. Despite that a minister is appointed and not elected, the prime minister cannot afford to neglect the representative aspects of his choice (Bergström, 1987; Ruin, 1986). Once appointed, every minister in Sweden has equal status in the cabinet (which at present consists of twenty-one ministers). Each minister has a seat in Parliament and is granted the right to make speeches but not to vote. A member of Parliament who is promoted to a ministerial post will be given a new seat in Parliament on the government benches, but will have to give up his or her original seat to an alternate member. Consequently, ministers tend to appear in Parliament these days only when their own issues are being debated, or on special occasions. Before 1970, when ministers were more often than not full-time members of Parliament, they were in the house most of the time – a practice that made it easy for MPs to set up meetings with them.

When a cabinet resigns, it is automatically transformed into a caretaker cabinet. There is only one difference, according to the constitution, between a caretaker cabinet and a normal one: a caretaker cabinet cannot dissolve Parliament. In reality, caretaker cabinets have always avoided presenting bills to Parliament and have confined themselves to administrative matters. Sweden has had very little experience of a caretaker cabinet that has remained in office for a long time. It is, however, reasonable to expect that a caretaker government that was forced to stay in power for several months or longer would operate more and more like an ordinary cabinet.

MINISTERIAL DISCRETION IN POLICY-MAKING

The first distinction made in this context is between the minister as a policy maker in sectors within the jurisdiction of his or her department, and the minister as someone who represents general cabinet policy. I think we can safely assume that a minister usually acts on behalf of his or her policy sector, even when dealing with general political issues. When he or she is acting as a government representative, however, it must be kept in mind that particular departmental interests are only a small part of the overall picture. The second distinction to be made is between policy-making inside the chancery as opposed to politics outside it. Within these two distinct arenas, different forces and actors impinge on the decision-making ability of a minister; we use these to structure subsequent discussion in this chapter.

From an internal point of view, Swedish government falls into several units or actors. The cabinet as a collective body is a natural focus of interest, but both the prime minister and the chancellor of the Exchequer also play important roles as counterparts to ministers. Also of significance is the core of civil servants in a minister's own department.

The cabinet as a collective body

The collective responsibility of the Swedish cabinet is laid down in the constitution and is given a wide definition. Almost every decision made by the government, according to the constitution, falls within collective decision-making. There are only four types of decision for which collective responsibility is not applicable: some decisions made by the minister of foreign affairs; a few issues for which the minister of defense is responsible; organizational issues and questions regarding personnel management inside the ministries; and a few special, small, and unimportant matters that can be taken care of by an individual minister if delegated to do so by the cabinet. A Swedish cabinet will thus make about twenty thousand collective decisions a year; individual ministers make a few hundred decisions. Formally, the autonomy of an individual minister is quite limited; a minister literally needs cabinet approval for almost each decision made.

As a result, the Swedish cabinet meets more frequently than almost any other cabinet in the world. Formal cabinet meetings are held once a week when Parliament is in session. During these meetings, hundreds of decisions are made in about half an hour. Obviously this is made possible only by a rather ritualistic procedure, and cabinet meetings are normally simply the formal registration of decisions already made elsewhere. Every minister and ministry has been provided with an advance agenda for these meetings, but only the title and the suggested decision is mentioned in that agenda. Minutes must be kept of all cabinet meetings, including the recording of dissenting opinions. (Recorded dissent rarely happens today – once in the past twenty years – but in the nineteenth century it was not uncommon for some ministers, sometimes all of them, to oppose the king's decision this way.)

These formal cabinet meetings are normally followed by a more informal general cabinet meeting (*allmän beredning*) in which more important matters are deliberated. Any difference of opinion between ministers is normally settled during these meetings, if bilateral or other negotiations have failed. The agendas for these meetings are usually distributed a few days in advance, but sometimes matters may be brought up on shorter notice. The items on the agenda at general cabinet meetings are mostly presented by civil servants from the ministries concerned, who will also answer any questions, but who have to withdraw before the discussion starts. The only "outsider" present is the undersecretary to the prime minister or, in a coalition government, the undersecretaries to the party leaders. Recently, the leader of each party group has also been present in the Parliament. No minutes are kept and votes are seldom taken.

At most, 1 percent of all formal cabinet decisions are discussed in these general meetings. Social Democratic one-party governments seem to have brought up a larger number of matters for discussion in general meetings than non-Socialist coalition governments. With a coalition government, it is only natural that more matters have to be discussed, and more disputes settled, by informal deliberations between the parties involved, as a full cabinet meeting may not be the best arena for these discussions (Larsson, 1986: 235–6).

In addition to this, all members of the cabinet meet each weekday for lunch, with the exception of ministers not in Stockholm. During this "lunch deliberation," matters of political importance, but of relatively limited substance, are discussed; appointments are a typical subject. There are no civil servants present at these lunches, which have no predetermined agenda (Feldt, 1991: 485). These lunches used to be well attended, but in recent years there has been less participation. Currently, it is said that two lunches, those on Tuesday and Wednesday, are more important than others. Every cabinet also holds a retreat for a day or two every year in order to get away from everyday chores and discuss more long-term and strategic policy matters.

Cabinet committees or inner cabinets have not been common in Sweden – every minister has equal status. The Social Democrat government that fell from power in 1991 organized its cabinet into committees during its last two years in power, but this example was not followed by the succeeding non-socialist government.

One informal way of controlling individual ministers and ministries is "sharing." Sharing means that all directives to royal commissions, parliamentary proposals, and answers to questions put forward in Parliament are distributed to every minister and ministry before they are published. All ministers must give clearance before action can be taken in these matters. Administrative matters, on the other hand, do not have to be dealt with in this way. In reality, however, it is very rare for a minister to read a proposal that has been submitted as part of the process of sharing. This work is instead done by civil servants who will inform their minister or undersecretary only if they feel there is anything in the material indicating another minister or ministry is trespassing on their territory.

In short, Swedish ministers meet a lot – although this does not necessarily imply that they influence each other a lot. Having a position in the cabinet means – in Sweden as elsewhere – fighting for your corner, but this is not always done in the open. Coordination and influence are to a large extent achieved by anticipating the reactions of others. This is especially true for some Social Democrat governments of the past, where the same people were appointed ministers for decades. A minister with years of experience can often guess well in advance what another minister or ministry is going to say on a specific issue. There are traditional areas of conflict between ministries that go back a long time, and an intelligent minister generally tries to avoid these minefields. Thus, the fact that overt conflict is not observed does not mean that underlying conflict does not exist.

Overall, despite the high level of collective decision making at the formal constitutional level, in reality ministers and ministries will to a large extent be left alone to formulate the policy of the cabinet in their own area of responsibility, as long as the policy does not have economic implications or great political importance. Therefore, ministers' primary concern is not with the work of their cabinet colleagues, but rather with the chancellor of the Exchequer or the prime minister, usually in that order.

The prime minister

The organization and operation of Swedish government is very much a product of the long regime of the Social Democrats, who were in power for more than fifty years during the twentieth century. A Social Democratic prime minister would often let individual ministers make decisions regarding future policy in their respective areas of responsibility (Carlsson, 1990). The job of consolidating ministerial policy into cabinet policy was to a large extent in the hands of the chancellor of the Exchequer. Only after 1965 did the prime minister really start to build an office of his own (Ruin, 1990). Today that office consists of about thirty people, most of whom are political appointees. In the prime minister's office, six to eight people have the special assignment of scrutinizing the work of ministries and ministers.

The situation is a bit different when there is a coalition government. The group of supervisors in the prime minister's office will then have equivalents in other parts of the chancery. Every government party, in order to achieve day-to-day coordination, sets up a small unit of political appointees. These units try to supervise not only the work of ministers from the other parties but also that done by ministers from their own party. Members from these cabinets meet on a regular basis, or whenever necessary, to coordinate policies or to solve conflicts (Koalitionsregerandets villkor, 1983).

The level of influence of the prime minister is largely a product of whether there is a conflict or not. It is not only conflicts inside the cabinet that activate the prime minister. Conflicts inside the chancery are often solved by other means, but whenever there is a conflict with the political opposition the prime minister must play an active role. The prime minister is the first and foremost defender of government policy. Much of his time is taken up by this work, and by other forms of governmental representation. The work of the prime minister consists to a large extent of either managing crises or preventing them from occurring in the first place, as the late Prime Minister Tage Erlander once said (Ruin, 1990). Because the emergence of crises is often decided by forces outside his control, there is little room for the prime minister to choose the sectors which to concentrate his influence upon.

The prime minister can, of course, solve conflicts between two or more ministers without involving the cabinet as a whole, especially in a one-party government. In a coalition government the prime minister typically forms an informal inner cabinet together with the other leaders (Larsson, 1986: 427–9). The prime minister is also the chairman of the cabinet and the person who tries to distill the essence of the collective decision when discussions there are over. The cabinet seldom votes on issues; as a result, the prime minister's position as chairman of the cabinet and caller of the cabinet consensus contributes to his influence. The prime minister decides to a large extent which matters will be discussed in the cabinet, but he cannot stop a minister from bringing up a matter for discussion. Ministers are free to take any matter for discussion to a lunch deliberation.

To conclude: the prime minister can exert a strong influence on an issue, but has great difficulties in deciding on what matters this power will be exercised. Added to this, his office is understaffed, which means it is not possible for him to acquire the information needed to supervise all of the work of his ministers. The influence of the prime minister will therefore be exerted on a more ad hoc basis, in contrast to the influence of the chancellor of the Exchequer, whose organization is much better equipped for controlling the ministers.

The chancellor of the Exchequer

Ministers must always negotiate with the Ministry of Finance in matters that have, or may have, economic or organizational implications. This means that the vast majority of governmental matters come under the scrutiny of the chancellor of the Exchequer and his or her civil servants. The chancellor has a much larger organization than the prime minister in order to fulfil this mission. About forty people are employed in a bureau in the Ministry of Finance with the sole task of scrutinizing the work of other ministries. Members of this bureau, the bureau of budget, divide their work so that each ministry is scrutinized by three or four civil servants. These civil servants are very effective, and sometimes the Bureau of Budget is called the "central intelligence" of the chancery. Because of this, the minister of finance is usually very well informed on every issue; sometimes he or she knows the matter better than the minister formally in charge.

The power of the chancellor is also determined by his or her dominance in deciding the general economic policy of the government. By being the minister with more or less of a monopoly on information and knowledge in macroeconomics, the chancellor of the exchequer sets the limits to the rest of the government's maneuvering. He or she is typically supported in this by the prime minister. Both know that they are tied to each other because they have the main responsibility for government policy as a whole (Feldt, 1991: 142–3).

Civil servants

Another aspect of the chancery to be considered by a minister who wants to implement policy is the civil service. As we have seen, the civil service is very small; furthermore, very few civil servants are political appointees. Besides the minister himself, the only persons in the ministries recruited on political criteria are the undersecretary, the information officer, and one or two special political advisers. Consequently they are the only ones who will be forced to leave the ministry if the government should resign.

Given the relatively few people working in each ministry, ministers are normally acquainted with every civil servant working for them, and hierarchical relationships within the ministries are rather informal. The most junior administrative officer may be allowed to present his or her case before the minister, even when there is disagreement with a senior officer. The informal administrative culture, and the fact that civil servants remain while politicians come and go, combine to give civil servants a lot of influence on both politically important matters and small administrative questions. Nevertheless, ministers and civil servants are to an extent dependent on each other, and normally it is not the political color of the minister that decides how this relationship will develop. In most cases civil servants care more about whether they have a strong minister than about his or her political orientation. A minister who wins battles in the cabinet, or who has the upper hand in dealing with the minister of finance, is very popular in his ministry and will normally become very influential there. On the other hand, if a minister is regarded as weak, his civil servants will tend to compensate for him in their negotiations with other ministries. In cases like this, civil servants may make deals in which they give away a lot to other ministries in order to save something, instead of risking losing everything at the ministerial level. A weak minister will therefore often be brought into the decision-making process at a much later stage than a strong minister. Generally speaking, if there is a power vacuum somewhere in the management of the ministries, the civil servants will fill it.

In administrative matters, the position of the civil servants is usually very strong. They will of course try to give the minister advice they think he or she will accept, and in nine cases out of ten the minister will follow their advice. From the minister's point of view there is not so much discussion with civil servants on administrative matters. In most cases the minister simply say "Yes" or "No" to proposals made by the civil servants.

Finally, we should note that the minister may not be the only important politician in the ministry. In many ministries the dominating figure, at least from the perspective of the civil servants, can be the undersecretary. It is well known that the undersecretaries – especially when Social Democrats are in power – can be the real policymakers in the government. Many ministers travel so much and deal with external matters to such a degree that they are more or less forced to leave the work of running their ministry in the hands of the undersecretary or some other political appointee.

POLICY-MAKING OUTSIDE THE CHANCERY

Political society in Sweden is by tradition very open. This openness is even guaranteed in several ways by the constitution. The public is, for example, guaranteed, in a special provision in the constitution, the right to see almost every government document. Very few government documents are supposed to be secret, and much of the content of "secret" documents is in reality not secret at all, since civil servants can and often do tell journalists what is in them (although they may not formally be allowed to tell their wives, children, or best friends). The government has no right to try to find out who has leaked the information unless it is highly classified; the person prosecuted is the publisher.

Another article in the constitution requires that, before the government makes a decision on an issue, information shall be obtained from all of the authorities concerned. Associations and private individuals shall be given an opportunity to express their views when necessary. Several ways are therefore open to the public, interests groups, the mass media, and others to influence the government if they want to.

Boards and agencies

The central administration in Sweden, as we saw in the introduction to this chapter, is divided into two parts: ministries on the one hand, and boards and agencies on the other. The former are deemed to direct the latter by way of general guidelines, but not to rule over them in detail. Boards and agencies are responsible to the cabinet as a whole, not to individual ministers. Looking at the formal constitutional role of Swedish ministers this way one might conclude that they are much weaker than their counterparts in other countries. In reality, however, one could probably argue that a Swedish minister has more power than a minister in most other countries when it comes to managing the bureaucracy. The reason for this is a combination of the formal right of the cabinet to give general guidelines, with the right of ministries to have informal contacts with boards and agencies before they make decisions.

If, for example, the Swedish Immigration Board is about to make a decision on whether an individual should be allowed to stay in the country, nobody outside the board has the right to try to direct that decision. It is up to the board to decide. However, if the decision is negative, the applicant can appeal to higher authority, which in some cases is the cabinet. Before the board makes its decision, furthermore, the minister or one of his civil servants has every right to inform themselves about the case. In these discussions they have every opportunity, in gentle and informal terms, to express what they wish the decision to be. The director-general of the board may of course refuse to listen to this "friendly advice" but, since it is the cabinet that every year decides on each board and agency budget, issues general instructions on how parliamentary laws should be interpreted, and also (every three years) appoints the head of the board or agency, the director-general would be a fool not to listen. In other words, one way or another, a minister has a pretty good chance of getting his wishes through on an agency or a board if he or she really wants something done.

On the other hand, a minister is not responsible to a great extent when things go wrong in the bureaucracy. The directors-general are first in danger of losing their jobs. Sometimes they may drag a minister with them when they fall, but this is far from the rule. In most cases the minister comes across as the person who tries to sort things out. In other words, the Swedish administrative system could be described as one in which ministers have as much influence over the bureaucracy as in other countries, but without the corresponding responsibility that elsewhere goes hand in hand with that influence. This may explain why the government has never wanted to change this system (Larsson, 1991: 140–1).

For the most part, however, the relationship between the ministries and the administrative boards and agencies is one of interdependence. Most of the knowledge about how the administration works, and how public-policy programs operate in practice, is in the boards and agencies. The ministries and the ministers therefore need the help of the agencies to formulate new policies; but the agencies need the help of their ministries in order to get money out of the Ministry of Finance (Jacobsson, 1984). The civil servants in the chancery also have an advantage over the agencies because they have a broader perspective on matters, since their area of responsibility is larger. This interdependence is facilitated by the fact that most civil servants in the chancery are recruited from agencies of boards, and most of the heads of agencies and boards have previously worked in the chancery. People in ministries, agencies, and boards therefore tend to know a great deal about each other – an understanding that facilitates all kinds of informal contacts. As a result, boards and agencies tend to have the same perspective on a specific problem as the ministries they are associated with. Conflicts between ministries and agencies or boards are thus quite rare. When there is a conflict between agencies associated with different ministries (and these are much more common), each ministry usually takes the side of the agency or board they are associated with (Linde, 1982).

Royal commissions

Almost every government bill of any importance that is presented to Parliament has been developed in one or more royal commissions. The use of royal commissions has decreased somewhat in recent years, but nevertheless about two hundred royal commissions are at work every year. These commissions are organizationally separated from the ministries. Their relationship to the government is the same as that of boards or agencies: they are given general guidelines from the cabinet as a whole, but are placed under one specific ministry. The guidelines given by the government of a royal commission are often rather detailed, describing the problems that the commission is expected to propose a solution to. Sometimes, however, a commission is primarily set up to get a "hot" political issue off the cabinet agenda, not to solve any specific problem. The cabinet also determines the duration, budget, and membership of the royal commissions. Interest groups, agencies, and representatives of boards are often invited to sit on these, as are politicians from the parliamentary opposition (Johansson, 1992). When complete, the commissions' proposals are distributed to the different groups and authorities that the cabinet considers to have an interest in the matter.

The commission chairman usually has some – in many cases much – informal contact with the ministry under which the commission is placed.

Another way of controlling royal commissions are through civil servants from the ministries, who sit in 75 percent of the commissions. These civil servants are, of course, the eyes and ears of the minister; a chair who is leading a commission in ways unwanted by the minister or the cabinet may soon be called in for an informal discussion with the minister (Petersson 1989: 87–96).

Interest groups

An interest group can affect cabinet policy in many ways. It can sit on an agency, a board, or a royal commission; respond to the proposals of a commission; or negotiate directly with a minister or with the cabinet. These negotiations may be official or unofficial. Almost every investigation of the relationship between government and interest groups in Sweden shows a close relationship that has sometimes been described as neocorporatist. Recently, however, there has been a tendency for at least some of the major interest groups to take a step back from their close cooperation with the government, and even the latest Social Democratic government had a new attitude about the integration of interest groups into the government bureaucracy (Petersson, 1989: 112–37).

Nonetheless, it is still not unusual for interest groups to be invited to give opinions on a matter before it is finally decided by the cabinet. In cases in which proposals for bills or directives for royal commissions are being shared among the ministries, relevant interest groups may also be given a say. Interest groups also keep a close watch on ministers and ministries that operate in their area of interest.

The mass media

The mass media play an increasing role in Swedish policy-making. The work of ministers is closely watched by journalists, who quickly report every breath a minister takes. A politician who becomes a minister is exposed to something that best can be characterized as "media shock." What an ordinary MP says in Parliament is usually of little interest to the national mass media (although on local level the picture is a bit different); but if that person suddenly becomes a minister, everything is of interest. Once a minister learns how the mass media operate, however, he or she often finds them useful in promoting public policy, which gives the minister every chance to get the message out – if the minister has a message to sell the public, that is. Many ministers thus try to have close contact with journalists they know to be favorable to them or their party. At every minister's side is an information officer, whose job it is to help tame the mass media (Petersson, 1989: 148–56).

The public

Even the person in the street has a chance of putting a case personally before the relevant minister. Many of the decisions a minister in Sweden has to make concern individuals who are appealing some kind of decision made by a board or agency. In many cases the cabinet is the supreme court for administrative complaints. Sometimes, when an individual case is up for decision, the individual concerned may be allowed to present the case directly to the minister or undersecretary in charge of the matter. This is not as common today as in the past, but there are many old stories about how personal appeals to the minister had a decisive effect on the decision that in the end was made by the cabinet (Rainer, 1984).

Another type of contact between the public and a minister is by way of the letters that every day are sent to the office of ministers, most of which are addressed to the prime minister. All of these letters are given a reply; the prime minister has at least three civil servants working full-time to answer them. The tiny extent to which these letters affect decision-making in ministries or the cabinet is, however, best forgotten.

The Parliament

A minister must of course appear in Parliament and defend his or her proposals in the name of the cabinet. He or she must also be prepared to answer questions, and in other ways keep in close contact with Parliament. Table 11.2 shows, however, that the proportion of government bills passing the legislature without any substantial change is quite high. (The position of a standing committee will almost always be confirmed by Parliament when the final vote is taken.) And as might be expected, if a cabinet is backed by only a small minority in Parliament, then changes to its bills are more frequent. Nevertheless, even the liberal government of 1978–9, with the support of only 39 of 349 MPs, managed to get 57 percent of its bills through Parliament without any change at all.

This pattern has led many to regard Parliament as something of a conveyor belt, but this is far too simplistic a picture. Many members of Parliament sit on royal commissions and/or boards of agencies, or have informal contacts with the ministries, which means that they have already had a lot of influence over government policy before it reaches Parliament (Isberg, 1982). In other words, MPs exercise a much greater influence on Swedish politics than one would be led to believe by looking at changes to governmental proposals in the Parliament. That influence, however, is not to any large degree practiced within Parliament itself, but rather by virtue of an MP's more general position in the policy-making process.

Table 11.2. *The proportion of bills in which changes were suggested by the majority in standing committees (in percentages)*

| | Palme | | Fälldin | Ullsten | Fälldin | | Palme | Carlsson |
	1972	1975	1977–8	1978–9	1980–1	1981–2	1983–4	1986–7
Changes suggested by standing com.								
No changes	74	66	72	57	67	58	71	71
Details only	16	16	20	19	22	17	19	15
Real changes	10	18	8	24	11	26	9	14

Cabinet/Year

Source: Sannersted and Sjölin, 1990: 124.

The minister's party

Party discipline is usually very strong among Swedish parties. If the government controls only a minority of legislators, then the MPs of the parties play a crucial role in getting the cabinet's proposals through the standing committees of Parliament. This means that a minister is eager for MPs in the same party to support his proposal as strongly as possible. One way to ensure this is to involve these MPs in the decision-making process at an early stage. An able minister may also get approval in advance from his own party congress before starting something big. There do exist, however, cases in which a minister has drastically deviated from decisions made by a party conference.

CONCLUSION

One basic question has been asked in this chapter: what can a person do once he or she has been appointed a cabinet minister in Sweden? It is important in answering such a question to distinguish between offensive and defensive ministerial power. Offensive power is linked to the minister's ability to force other actors in the political system to heed his or her wishes and play according to the minister's own rules. In an offensive capacity the minister becomes a policymaker, someone who can and will make drastic changes to issues within his or her area of responsibility. In this capacity the minister can bring two crucial instruments: the right to initiate new policies and a high profile for public campaigning.

Ministers can put issues on the political agenda and initiate royal commissions – with a little help from their civil servants. Once the decision-making process is in motion, the minister and relevant department may find it hard in practice to get their ideas adopted; but in this event the process can always be halted, reversed, or redirected.

The other important instrument is high visibility in the public eye. What a minister says or does is almost always regarded as important news by the mass media. Therefore a minister's message will almost certainly be made known to the public with minimal delay. On the other hand, there is an ever-increasing demand on the minister to represent his or her ministry, cabinet, or country in local and global circles. The amount of time that can be devoted to ministerial work and policy planning is rapidly becoming a scarce commodity. Ministers thus find they are more and more becoming traveling salesmen, purveyors of ideas formulated by others. Gone are the days when ministers could sit down and write most, or at least parts, of the bills to be presented to Parliament. Today, most of them do not even write their own speeches or the articles published in their names.

In his defensive capacity, a minister can prevent other political actors from enforcing their plans or suggestions. Carrying out a particular political change is almost impossible if the minister in charge of the issue is not in favor of the scheme. This strategy is sometimes used in coalition governments, where political parties have been known to request a certain ministerial post simply to prevent another party from changing policy in a particular area.

Thus, the power of a Swedish minister is closely linked to the ability to put proposals on the political agenda, and to block others. Once the decision-making process has been put in motion, however, the minister has much less ability to control the outcome. In an open society such as Sweden, where interest groups and the bureaucracy have traditionally been allowed to influence the policy process, and where minority governments are common, ministers do not always play a dominant role. This has led some observers of Swedish politics to talk about the minister as more of a reactor than a ruler (Jacobsson, 1989: 142–5); on balance, however, the preceding discussion suggests that a Swedish minister has a pretty good chance of being influential and of being a real policymaker as long as he or she stays well within the orders of formal ministerial responsibilities.

REFERENCES

Bergström, H. 1987. *Rivstart? Om övergången från opposition till regering.* Stockholm Studies in Politics. Södertälje: Tide.

Carlsson, I. 1990. 30 år i regerinskansliet. In *Att styra riket.* Stockholm: Departementshistoriekommittén, Allmänna Fölaget.

The Constitution of Sweden, 1989. Stockholm: Swedish Riksdag.

Feldt, K-O. 1991. *Alla dessa dagar: I regerinen, 1982–1990.* Stockholm: Norstedts.

Isberg, M. 1982. *The First Decade of the Unicarmeral Riksdag.* Stockholm: Forskningsrapport.

Jacobsson, B. 1984. *Hurs styrs förvaltningen – myt och verklighet krin departementens styrning av ämbetsverken.* Lund: Studenlitteratur.

1989. *Konsten att reagera: intressen, institutioner och näringspolitik.* Stockholm: Carssons.

Johansson, J. 1992. *Det statliga kommitéväsendet: kunskap, kontroll, konsensus.* Stockholm: Akademitryck AB.

Koalitionsregerandets Villkor (1983). In *Makt och Vanmakt.* Stockholm: SNS.

Larsson, S-E. 1986. *Regera i koalition: den borgerliga trepartiregeringen, 1976–1978 och kärnkraften.* Stockholm: Bonniers.

Larsson, T. 1986. *Regeringen och dess kansli: samordning och byråkrati i maktens centrum.* Lund: Studenlitteratur.

1990. Regerings och regeringskansliets organisationsstruktur, berednings – och beslutsformer under 150 år. In *Att styra riket.* Stockholm: Departementshistoriekommittén, Allmänna Förlaget.

Linde, C. 1982. *Departement och verk: Om synen på den centrala statsförvaltningens och dess uppdelning – i en förändrad offentlig sektor.* Stockholm: Studies in Politics.

Petersson, O. 1989. *Maktens nätverk: en undersökning av regeringskansliets kontakter.* Stockholm: Carlsson.

Rainer, O. 1984. *Makterna.* Stockholm: Carlsson.

Ruin, O. 1986. *I välfardsstatens tjänst: Tage Erlander, 1946–69.* Kristianstad: Tiden.

1990. Statsministerämbetet: frän Louis De Geer till Ingvar Carlsson. In *Att styra riket.* Stockholm: Departementshistoriekommittén, Allmäna Förlaget.

Tarschys, D. 1990. Regerinens styrformer. In *Att styra riket.* Stockholm: Departementshistoriekommittén, Allmänna Förlaget.

12

The political role of cabinet ministers in Italy

Annarita Criscitiello

INTRODUCTION

Any analysis of the political role of ministers can stress either the constitutional boundaries that constrain ministerial activity or the actual behavior that takes place, both behind and beyond the formal constitutional framework. When dealing with the Italian experience (1946–92), we must remember that a wide gap exists between certain constitutional provisions and the actual governmental process. Indeed, much scholarly debate centers on this discrepancy (Calandra, 1986; Capotosti, 1986; Cassese, 1980; Lavagna, 1974; Paladin, 1970). Furthermore, actual political behavior obviously changes over time, and in the Italian context this change is especially significant. In particular, it is necessary to distinguish between two historical phases: the first, lasting more or less up to the mid-1960s, was characterized by a high ministerial autonomy; the second, lasting from the mid-1960s until the present, is characterized by a stronger – albeit "restricted" – collegiality.

The formal governmental framework has also undergone important modifications during this period. There have been changes in the organization of the government and its relationship with Parliament; this can be seen in the new law concerning the prime ministership, under which an inner cabinet was set up and new parliamentary regulations overturned the existing legislative–executive relations. Furthermore, many constitutional reforms implying a radical modification of the Italian governing model have also been discussed over the last ten years.

I divide my analysis of the political role of cabinet ministers in Italy into five sections following this introduction. The next section addresses the issue of ministerial autonomy, analyzing the extent to which heads of departments can function as independent political actors, both formally in terms of constitutional provisions and empirically in terms of the actual organization of government. One major obstacle to full-blown ministerial

187

autonomy is the need to reach some form of political collegiality when managing governmental affairs. This need arises at both a prescriptive level (to assure a common political responsibility at the top) and a normative level (to make the governmental process conform to certain major constitutional requirements). I address this in the remaining four sections, in which conditions favoring greater collegiality are analyzed. The Italian case is interesting in this regard, as both scholarly and political debates have long concentrated on the need to strengthen collegiality in order to counteract the excesses of ministerial autonomy.

The discussion of the search for greater collegiality has four distinct elements. The third section deals with intracabinet decision making, in particular the search for formal and informal ways of strengthening collective as opposed to individual decision making within the cabinet. Section 4 examines the role of the cabinet in legislative–executive relations. A strong Parliament was characteristic of the first period in this analysis (1945–65), so much so that the Italian form of government was tagged *integral parliamentarianism* (Miglio, 1984). A high degree of ministerial autonomy, resulting in weak collective decision making, was strongly correlated with the preeminence of Parliament over the cabinet. The second period, on the other hand, saw an increase of the role of the executive, both as a collegial body (represented by the cabinet, or *Consiglio dei Ministri*) and as a monocratic one (represented by the prime minister).

The fifth section concerns the strengthening of the role of the prime minister within the cabinet. This role was seen in the early years of the republic as a hindrance to collective decision making; most constitutional thinkers consider a strong prime minister an obstacle to true collegiality. Recent developments have, however, shown that the growth in prime ministerial power and leadership has in fact contributed to the emergence of a more unitary cabinet, both in form and substance.

The sixth section deals with a feature that falls outside formal constitutional procedures: the so-called majority summits (*Vertici di maggioranza*). These extracabinet devices might be considered the "efficient secrets" of the Italian model of government, contributing a great deal to coordination and collegiality at the top of the executive branch. These majority summits – gatherings of certain high-ranking politicians and party secretaries – take place on average every four months (I have identified and analyzed seventy majority summits over a period of twenty years). Although such summits were not unheard of in the early years of the Italian Republic, in the past two decades they have become much more institutionalized. In general, majority summits serve as a reminder that, strong as the executive office might have become in recent years, its strength has remained to a large extent dependent on the role of political parties as the dominant governmental actors.

188

Cabinet ministers in Italy

THE BASIS OF MINISTERIAL AUTONOMY

The basis of ministerial autonomy is in the formal wording of the Italian constitution, which makes provision for the cabinet (Council of Ministers). In addition to the president, the cabinet consists of ministers who participate under the principle of full collegiality. The prime minister's role is to manage the government's affairs by promoting and coordinating the activity of the ministers. He is more a primus inter pares than somebody placed over individual ministers. Ministerial autonomy stems from the fact that each individual minister is considered a constitutional body, political representative, and ministry head, and is also personally responsible for his ministry (Calandra, 1986).

Each minister carries out the following functions as an autonomous constitutional body: he countersigns presidential bills; he has the right to be heard by the legislative chambers whenever he requests; he is responsible to Parliament for the actions of his department; and he participates in determining the government's collegial direction. Moreover, he derives autonomy by wielding a range of executive powers within his own jurisdiction.

The autonomy of each individual minister may also be analyzed in terms of what happens when there is disagreement within the cabinet. In such situations, the constitution gives the prime minister no real power to dismiss a minister. The only constitutionally sound way to resolve a political dispute, should a dissenting minister not resign voluntarily, is to enlist the help of Parliament (Cicconetti, 1991). This entails a form of legislative sanction—the so-called individual motion of no confidence – that obliges individual ministers to resign. Needless to say, this measure is rarely used, as cabinets generally stand by their ministers in order to show unity.

One cannot be surprised that, given such a formal constitutional basis, the result was strong ministerial independence. By placing the prime minister, the cabinet, and individual ministers on the same level, while providing no organizational instruments for internal coordination, the Italian constitution set the stage for what scholars would later define as a "government by ministries" or "multidirectional dissociated government" (*governo a direzione plurima dissociata*).

We can distinguish three main aspects of ministerial government (Serrani, 1979) that, as mentioned, characterized Italian politics in the early decades of the republic. The first concerns the government's internal organization. The second concerns the minister's relationship with his or her own departmental bureaucracy. The third is related to the extragovernmental arena, in particular to the electoral basis of ministerial power.

In relation to intragovernmental organization, the collegial model of governing, as we have seen, makes provision for several department heads, each responsible for his or her own jurisdiction. In practice, the subsequent division of the executive into ministries, and the handing over of government responsibility by the cabinet as a whole to individual ministers, has led to a fragmentation of the government. Every jurisdiction has come to be considered a type of fief – a set of powers at the disposal of each minister and, by extension, of his party or party faction (Ristuccia, 1980).

One major indicator of the weight of individual ministers vis-à-vis the cabinet as a collegial entity can be found in the growing number of ministerial appointments, both ministers and deputy ministers. Until the early 1970s, the trend was steadily rising, bringing the total number of ministerial appointments from forty-four to eighty-seven (Calise and Mannheimer, 1979: 54). This made cabinet coordination and collegiality all the more difficult and led to a form of administrative hierarchy – a predominance of ministers holding "strategic" departments, such as those dealing with the economy, public order, or international relations. It is interesting to note that one key factor in determining the autonomy of "superministers," in relation to both the cabinet and the prime minister, consisted in their privileged access to information vital to more systematic intragovernmental coordination (Rodotà, 1977).

The "sectorization" of governmental decision making can be also noted in the workings of interministerial committees. These bodies were originally established to tackle multisectoral problems and to coordinate the actions of a number of ministries. They comprised a number of ministers while allowing for the possibility of including technicians and experts. However, as many of the functions of these committees overlapped with those of the cabinet, a conspicuous shift of activity took place from the general collegial body (the cabinet) toward a series of specific collegial bodies (interministerial committees). The proliferation of these committees facilitated coordination between smaller numbers of ministers, but it also reduced the level of collegiality between ministers as a whole.

The sectorization of governmental decision making did not necessarily coincide with a more effective steering of specific policy areas, however. As a result of the coalitional and highly competitive composition of Italian governments,

Some of the most important policy areas (for instance external relations and financial and economic affairs) have been fragmented into more than one ministry and allocated to the representatives of different parties. This has meant, in the best case, that the policy of the government in that area has been the result of long consultations between the Ministers (and also the parties and the ministerial bureaucracies) responsible for that area. In the worst case it has meant that each Minister went his own way and that there has been more than one government policy in each area. (Cotta, 1988: 131)

Moving on to consider the minister's relationship with the departmental bureaucracy, I shall confine my observations to the appointment of top civil servants and *grand commis* of the state (the managing directors of public bodies). Traditionally, contrary to what the law formally provides, the cabinet hardly discusses such proposals from certain individual ministers (for example, the minister of the interior, of defense, or of foreign affairs). Relevant as top-level appointments may be for major policy decisions, one should also not forget that Italian ministers have long been known for their intrusions into the lower levels of the pyramid of bureaucratic power, as well. *Clientelismo* and *sottogoverno* can be best understood, in administrative parlance, to refer to an extensive spoils system that makes each individual minister the head of a powerful politicobureaucratic machinery. Structural analysis of the bureaucratic connection, however, found in specific case studies of the relationships between politics and administration (Cazzola [ed.], 1988), demonstrates that there are also consequences of an opposite sort in which each minister's individual decision making is affected.

In considering the third aspect of ministerial autonomy, the extragovernmental arena, empirical research on the relationship between individual-preference votes at elections and subsequent portofolio allocation (Calise and Mannheimer, 1982) shows that each minister's electoral success strongly influences the composition of the cabinet. Each of the major portfolios (the prime ministership, Interior, Foreign Affairs, Defense) is associated with a minister winning a higher number of individual-preference votes than average. Indeed, the whole structure of ministerial careers (from deputy minister to minister, and from less important to more important ministries) appears to be closely related to the number of electoral votes each politician has been able to accumulate through his or her past political activity (Calise and Mannheimer, 1982: 69–107).

On the whole, therefore, ministerial autonomy has had strong roots in the Italian constitutional model. These roots have had a clear normative basis, in that a constitution drafted by those fearful of previous authoritarian legacies (Rotelli, 1972) did very little to facilitate the emergence of a unified center of power. Yet such roots have also rapidly acquired real political strength, as the Italian party system based on highly competitive coalition cabinets and election campaigns quickly turned individual ministers into the true bearers of governmental authority. The reasons such a fragmented system of governmental authority could not last forever are the subject of the following sections.

TOWARD A STRONGER (RESTRICTED) COLLEGIALITY

According to the Italian constitution, the issues to be decided by the cabinet are determined by the political programs of the parties forming the government coalition. The unity and consistency of this program must be guaranteed by the prime minister. In formal terms, the cabinet's collective decision making is a majority vote, and no member has any kind of veto. Such decisions are internal affairs, however, as every decision appears from the outside to have been made by the cabinet as a whole, in accordance with the collective responsibility provided for by the law. Every cabinet decision must be considered unanimously approved, even when it has been passed only by a majority, since cabinet members are collectively responsible for it. In practice, this collegiality is only for appearance' sake – a formal rule that in most cases simply ratifies decisions made elsewhere. It is thus a *deliberative* collegiality as opposed to an *active* collegiality, which limits itself to sanctioning a decison at the end of its natural path (Bonanni, 1978).

As we have seen, the period prior to the 1980s was characterized by a debate about a form of collegiality that gave individual ministers equal status with the cabinet as a collective entity. The so-called government by ministries did not allow any collegial action on the administrative front; instead, ministers presided over their departments almost like barons. From the 1980s onward, however, attention was paid to a more restricted collegiality that appeared to be increasingly characterizing the Italian government.

This was, and still is, considered a solution to two unresolved problems of Italian government: the plethora of ministers and consequent undermining of collective decision making; and the relationship between the cabinet and the coalition parties, given that each minister is bound to his own party.

The development of restricted collegiality is associated with the rise in importance of an inner cabinet of key ministers. The proposal to form such an inner cabinet (*consiglio di gabinetto*) was indeed one of the objects of the assembly that originally formulated the Italian constitution. Nevertheless, the first inner cabinet was informally established only in 1983, as the first act of the cabinet during the Craxi government. In the beginning, it was limited to seven ministers. Their appointment was not necessarily related to the importance of their office but rather to the need to include at least one representative of each party in the government coalition. The presence of the party secretaries made the inner cabinet a stable link between the cabinet and the coalition parties.

After the Craxi government the experience of the inner cabinet, still functioning as an informal political consultation body, was repeated three times, in the second Craxi government, in the second Goria government, and in the De Mita government. Finally, in August 1988, a law concerning the *discipline of governmental activity and the organization of the prime minister's office* was approved. This made formal provision for the establishment of an inner cabinet, with members directly nominated by the president (Bagnai, 1991).

Apart from the function of representing the coalition parties, the inner cabinet has served to organize government decision making more efficiently. Decision-making power has been concentrated in the hands of a smaller number of people, greatly simplifying the decision-making process. This has led to ministers being depoliticized except when they are inner cabinet members (Manzella, 1991).

However, the extent to which collective decision making has been changed by the inner cabinet is extremely difficult to estimate. The press releases from the premier's press office, usually made available after inner cabinet meetings, give an indication of the regularity of meetings and the issues discussed (Del Vescovo, 1988). During the Craxi government, the first to set up an inner cabinet, there were at least fifty meetings. The issues addressed concerned public finance, justice, industrial politics, trade-union relations, and education. In addition to this, considerable importance was given to the problems of international politics, for example, relations between Italy and Libya, the Lebanon issue, and the crisis in the Gulf of Suez.

The inner cabinet did not, however, have the same importance under the successors to the Craxi government. According to many observers this resulted above all from the fact that both the first informal provisions and the 1988 law deliberately omitted the burning issue of specifying the number of ministers and their functions (Bagnai 1991). Other observers concluded that the inner cabinet failed because it was in effect a device for institutionalizing conflict between the coalition parties, rather than a government body in any real sense:

The contradiction stems from here; an inner cabinet should gather together those responsible for the most important sectors of cabinet decision making, but it ends up containing the most important exponents of the coalition parties because of their political role as party exponents rather than the political role they have in the government. (Onida 1991: 26)

Thus, the very requirement that the inner cabinet serves as a mechanism for the representation of each party in the coalition led, in this view, to its failure (Cotta, 1988: 130).

However, the most recent experience of the Italian government with the innovation of the inner cabinet would seem to indicate that a certain degree of collegiality can prevail, albeit in a restricted way, over individual ministerial responsibility. This becomes clear when we consider recent changes that have occurred in the relationship between legislature and executive.

LEGISLATIVE–EXECUTIVE RELATIONS

Once the government has been formed it must have the confidence of both chambers of Parliament. This means that the parliamentary majority gives its consent to the formula, program, and composition of the cabinet. Governments must resign if they lose a vote of confidence. A motion of no confidence must be proposed and signed by at least 10 percent of Parliament members, and voted on by roll call. It cannot be debated until three days after it has been presented. The no-confidence motion must indicate the reasons the political direction of the government in office can no longer be supported. There have been only a few cases wherein a cabinet fell because it did not obtain the initial confidence of the legislature when it first appeared before Parliament. Since the writing of the constitution, no incumbent cabinet has had to resign following a no-confidence motion by Parliament (Martines, 1990). In this sense, every cabinet crisis that has occurred so far has been extraparliamentary (Andreotti, 1991). The government may also request a so-called majority check to see if it still has the confidence of Parliament. Only the prime minister, with the consent of the cabinet, can make this proposal, since the issue of confidence affects the general policy of the government. However, the government does not have to resign until an explicit motion of no confidence is presented and voted in Parliament.

Despite that no explicit no-confidence vote has ever been lost, the anticipated loss of such a vote may, of course, encourage a government to resign voluntarily if it realizes that it no longer has the confidence of Parliament. This has happened on more than one occasion when Parliament repeatedly voted against a particular government bill in what amounted to a tacit no-confidence vote. Beyond investiture and confidence requirements, the relative power of the legislature and the executive in Italy depends in part on formal constitutional provisions, and in part on the resolution of practical politics. Formally, the cabinet may take over the powers of Parliament in certain exceptional circumstances within limits set by the constitution. This happens in two precise situations. In the first, Parliament confers the law-making power on the cabinet through so-called delegated laws on issues that it considers too long for the normal voting process in the two chambers. In the second, the government can autonomously assume legislative power by replacing Parliament in extreme cases of necessity or urgency. This action is only temporary in that government bills, the so-called law decrees, become definitive only when they are made law by Parliament. The power to issue law decrees is the duty of the cabinet as a whole and not just that of individual ministers.

In order to analyze the practical evolution of the relationship between government and Parliament it may be useful to consider five historical phases (Chimenti, 1992). During the first two legislatures of the Italian Republic (from 1948 to 1958) the government prevailed over Parliament. In the second phase, which began with the third legislature and lasted approximately twenty years, Parliament was commonly held to have gained power, a change reflected in the increase in law making. The strengthening of Parliament was facilitated by the lack of homogeneity of the coalition governments of those years. As we have seen, during this period of government by ministries and multi-directional dissociated government, ministers did what they liked, even independently of the cabinet and the prime minister. In 1971, parliamentary reform was at the top of Parliament's agenda. Indeed, these years saw many debates on the centrality of Parliament and can be thought of as the era of "decision-making Parliament, executive government." The third phase, representing the further strengthening of parliamentary decision-making power, began with the seventh legislature (1976–79). Andreotti's "grand coalition" government, a strongly oversized majority including the Communist Party, was the best example of this. The fourth phase began in 1979 and marked a reversal of the previous trend. Parliament gradually became weaker, as can be seen by the increasing number of government bills taking the place of parliamentary legislation.

In 1988, relevant modifications to parliamentary regulations and a law concerning the prime ministership led to the fifth and current phase of the relationship between legislature and executive, the "directing government, ratifying Parliament" phase. There are numerous indicators of this phase: the abolition of secret legislative ballots in order to expose any member of the legislative majority who did not support the cabinet; the programming of the parliamentary agenda so that proposals by the cabinet must have priority; the "privileged path" granted by the legislative chambers to government initiatives; the reorganization of the cabinet office; and above all, the strengthening of the prime minister's role. In fact, most of these changes also created a more powerful role for the prime minister, who can now no longer be considered a primus inter pares.

THE PRIME MINISTER

From the early days of the republic until the mid-1970s, constitutionalists were divided into two main types. Some placed greater emphasis on the strenghthening of collegiality. Others stressed the formal supremacy of the prime minister over individual ministers and the cabinet as a whole. At the beginning of the 1980s a more active consideration of the role of the prime minister became a basic concern for both scholars and politicians. The main innovation in this debate consisted in accepting that the strengthening of the role of the prime minister was not necessarily inimical to the collegial functioning of the cabinet. Thus, it was observed that "by recognizing the position of the prime minister, which is autonomous and supreme compared to the cabinet members, there is less fear that the typical collegial nature of this body is per se diminished; indeed, some observers agree upon the opposite conviction, according to which the principle of collegiality may actually become effective in the presence of a body that, within the complex structure of the cabinet, is able to contrast particularism and slow down the sectoriality of the interests that the officials of the various ministeries appear to have" (Rolla, 1982: 379).

In a farsighted analysis (Cassese, 1980), it was suggested that Italy was no longer a republic surviving without a government, as others had previously indicated (Allum, 1973; Di Palma, 1977). The government could be found in the premier's office, where the prime minister's key role was beginning to emerge. This was no longer a role played within the cabinet, as provided for by the constitution, but outside it, as a result of the prime minister's greater control over the two vital sectors of public expenditure and security. Not only was control over public expenditure under de facto supervision of the prime minister, but also the prime minister was the head of the interministerial committee for information and public security, controlling all data processed by the secret services. Thus, "the seat of government can be found in the premier's office, for it has acquired a unique status. The premier is able to assume the necessary powers and to control the necessary jurisdictions in order to give some central direction to the government" (Cassese, 1980: 181).

The end of the 1970s marked another watershed for the role of the premiership. Effective cabinet decision making increasingly took place in a series of informal subgroups that sprang up alongside the cabinet, in which the prime minister was always present either with other ministers or with party or administrative representatives. In these restricted decision-making bodies, the prime minister took on an unquestioned role of preeminence.

Law number 400 of 1988 affirms that it is the prime minister who convenes the inner cabinet and can invite other ministers to its meetings according to their authority. Thus, the inner cabinet has an auxiliary role in relation to the prime minister. Furthermore, the same law confirms the primacy of the prime minister in relation to interministerial committees. The agendas of these committees must be communicated to the prime minister, who can also make specific proposals to the cabinet establishing the terms of reference for the committee in question.

Thus, we can talk of the practice in recent years in terms of the prevalence of the cabinet as a whole over individual ministerial responsibility, and of the prime minister's new level of autonomy. Indeed, some observers see the old formula of "government by ministries" evolving into "government by a limited-sovereignty prime minister" (Manzella, 1991). Nevertheless, although the prime minister's powers within the cabinet have increased, they remain limited by the need for coalition bargaining, and by the power of party leaders. More specifically, the prime minister's sovereignty is limited by external decisions made by the leaders of the governing parties in the majority summits, extraconstitutional bodies only formally outside the sphere of cabinet decision making. In effect, all of the formal institutions of the government have become seats of administrative management for decisions negotiated and determined during a majority summit.

MAJORITY SUMMITS

Majority summits are meetings between the prime minister and the leaders of parties in the government coalition, often with several other ministers present. The original raison d'être of majority summits is that they are necessary for forming a coalition government in a fragmented multiparty system. This type of summit, which we shall call a crisis summit, is attended by the prime minister of the proposed new cabinet and other party representatives – party secretaries, parliamentary group leaders, or larger delegations. Coalition bargaining concerns the structure of the new government, its political program, and its portfolio allocation.

However, if a majority summit is called when the government is in office, the situation is quite different. In this case the summit replaces the more formal governmental institutions. These summits, which we shall call ordinary summits, are concerned with decision making on strategic issues for which a political agreement could not be found within the cabinet. They can be divided into single-issue summits and multi-issue summits according to the number of key issues on the agenda.

A total of seventy-three majority summits took place from 1970 to 1989. Twenty-five summits were devoted to single issues, whereas thirty-one summits took place to discuss several issues; there were seventeen crisis summits. Not all cabinet crises had a crisis summit (Andreotti, 1991), as in some cases coalition bargaining took place in bilateral meetings between the coalition-party secretaries and the prime minister, who was in charge of the new cabinet.

The Christian Democratic (DC) Party was the main proposer of majority summits, followed by the Socialists (PSI) and the Republicans (PRI). Except for a few cases, most of the summits proposed by these latter parties took place when Spadolini (PRI) and Craxi (PSI) were prime ministers. We thus find a strong relationship between the role of prime minister and that of promoter of a majority summit, and note that 70 percent of these meetings took place in the prime minister's main offices. This relationship grows stronger with the advent of a non–Christian Democratic premiership: for the summits held during Craxi's tenure, the proposer of the summits was always the prime minister; Spadolini, despite his avowed aversion to majority summits, called them twice in only two months when he was prime minister. If we consider that both Craxi's and Spadolini's periods in office "are illuminating in the context of attempts to rehabilitate the prime-ministerial role in the 1980s" (Hine and Finocchi, 1991: 87), we can conclude that the extra-governmental device of the majority summit was found to be useful in strengthening official prime-ministerial authority.

Turning to the composition of summits, most have only party participants. In the single-issue summits there tend to be equal numbers of both party and government representatives, whereas most of the multi-issue summits comprised politicians with party positions only. Obviously, during a government crisis, the participants of the crisis summit are only party representatives.

It is also interesting to note that until 1977, participants were more or less evenly distributed between governmental and party representatives, whereas since 1978 there has been a clear prevalence of summits with only party representatives. All multi-issue summits and most single-issue summits have, in effect, become restricted meetings for the prime minister and the party secretaries.

A final finding concerns the outcomes of the summits, which are an indirect indicator of the health of the cabinets concerned. More than 80 percent of the summits ended with an agreement between the coalition parties. Very often there is an official final bulletin that lays out the terms of cooperation. So, if we consider the summits from the perspective of their outcomes, they appear an important instrument to make a complex system of coalitional government work better. In conclusion, therefore, majority summits appear to both strengthen and constrain the collegial executive. They strengthen it by offering a highly effective way to reach decisions that in turn are binding on the cabinet as a whole; yet majority summits also impose a serious constraint to cabinet supremacy.

However, it may be that the gap between the formal constitution and the working constitution needs to find a more straightforward solution than the one the parties have been able to create (Calise, 1992).

REFERENCES

Allum, P. 1973. *A Republic Without a Government.* London: Wedenfeld & Nicolson.

Andreotti, G. 1991. *Governare con la crisi.* Milano: Rizzoli.

Bagnai, F. 1991. Il consiglio di gabinetto: problemi di compatibilità con la costituzione, analogie e differenze con i comitati di ministri e i comitati interministeraili. *Diritto e Società* 2: 227–45.

Bonanni, M. 1978. *Governo, ministri, presidente.* Milano: Edizioni di Communita.

Calandra, P. 1986. *Il Governo della repubblica.* Bologna: Il Mulino.

Calise, M. 1992. Il governo tra istitvzione e politica. Paper presented at the International Convention of Study in honor of A. Spreafico, Firenze, 30–1 October 1992.

Calise, M., and R. Mannheimer. 1979. I governi misurati: il trentennio democristiano. *Critica Marxista* 6: 47–62.

– 1982. *Governanti in Italia: un trentennio repubblicano, 1946–1976.* Bologna: Il Mulino.

Capotosti, P. A. 1986. Presidente del consiglio. In *Enciclopedia del diritto*, vol. 25. Milano: Giuffrè.

Cassese, S. 1980. Is there a government in Italy? In R. Rose and E. Suleiman (eds.), *Presidents and Prime Ministers.* Washington, D.C.: American Enterprise Institute.

Cazzola, F. (ed.). 1988. *Le relazioni tra amministrazione e partiti.* Milano: Giuffrè.

Chimenti, C. 1992. *Il reppazto parlamento-governo nelle legislature repubblicane.* Milano: Giuffre.

Cicconetti, S. M. 1991. La richiesta parlamentare di dimissioni nei confronti di un singolo ministro. *Diritto e Società.* 3: 417–35.

1988. Italy: A fragmented government. In J. Blondel and F. Müller-Rommel (eds.), *Cabinets in Western Europe.* London: Macmillan Press.

Del Vescovo, P. 1988. Il consiglio di gabinetto: un tentativo di rafforzamento del governo. *Rivistatrimestrale di diritto pubblico* 4: 112–25.

Di Palma, 1977. *Surviving Without Governing: The Italian Parties in Parliament.* Berkeley and Los Angeles: University of California Press.

Hine, D., and R. Finocchi. 1991. The Italian prime minister. In R. Jones (ed.), *West European Prime Ministers,* London: Frank Cass.

Lavagna, C. 1974. Maggioranzo al governo e maggioranze a prlamentari. *Politica del Diritto* 6: 283–97.

Manzella, A. 1991. *Osservazioni sulla legan: 400/1988 sulla presidenza del consiglio dei ministri.* Milano: Giuffrè.

Martines, T. 1990. *Diritto costituzionale.* Milano: Giuffrè.

Merlini, S. 1982. Presidentedel consiglio e collegialità di governo. *Quaderni Costituzionali* 1: 7–32.

Miglio, G. 1984. Le contraddizioni interne del sistema parlamentare-integrale. *Rivista Italiana di Scienza Politica* 14: 209–22.

Onida, V. 1991. *Alcune riflessioni sulle tendenze della forma governo in Italia.* Milano: Giuffrè.

Paladin, L. 1970. Governo italiano. *Enciclopedia del diritto,* vol. 19. Milano: Giuffrè.

Ristuccia, S. 1980. Iniziativa e collegialità: per una riorganizzazione del governo. *Queste Istituzioni* 35: 237–54.

Rodotà, S. 1977. La circolazione delle informazioni nell'apparato di governo. In S. Ristuccia (ed.), *L'istituzione governo.* Milano: Fondazione Olivetti.

1981. La categoria "governo." *Laboratorio Politico,* 1, no. 1.

Rolla, G. 1982. Il consiglio dei ministri tra modello costituzionale e prassi. *Quaderni Costituzionali.* 2: 367–98.

Rotelli, G. 1972. *La presidenza del consiglio dei ministri.* Milano: Giuffrè.

Serrani, D. 1979. *L'organizzazione per ministeri.* Roma: Officina.

Part III

MAJORITY PARTY GOVERNMENT SYSTEMS

13

Ministerial autonomy in Britain

Anthony King

This chapter explores, with regard to Britain, the proposition that cabinet ministers have a good deal of autonomy within their own departments, the implication being that to know what views are held by the ministers in the most important government departments is also to know which policies the government as a whole is likely to pursue on the major issues confronting it.

The proposition is, on the face of it, a plausible one. Suppose, for example, that a country with a very high level of defense spending also happens to be in the midst of a deep recession. Political debate in the country concerns whether defense spending should be cut or maintained to avoid further deepening the recession by putting people in the defense industries out of work. If the defense minister is a hawk and the finance minister is a Keynesian, the outcome is almost predetermined: defense spending will be maintained. If, on the other hand, the defense minister is skeptical about the existing size of the defense establishment, and the finance minister is a neoclassical economist, the outcome is likewise almost predetermined, but different: defense spending will be cut. If the two ministers have opposing views, the outcome is indeterminate. Of course, other factors (the prime minister's views, the state of party feeling, public opinion, etc.) will always have an effect, but the central insight is an important one: cabinet ministers matter, or at least one should not assume that they do not.

Moreover, much of recent British history attests, or appears to attest, to the truth of this proposition. Iain Macleod as colonial secretary in the 1950s greatly accelerated the movement toward colonial independence in Africa. Roy Jenkins was a reforming home secretary in the 1960s. In more recent times, Lord Carrington, Margaret Thatcher's first foreign secretary, almost single-handedly achieved the Lancaster House agreement that brought an end to the civil war in Rhodesia; and Nigel Lawson and Sir Geoffrey Howe in the late 1980s persuaded Thatcher to agree in principle to Britain's joining the European exchange-rate mechanism. More generally, it is an axiom of British politics that the chancellor of the Exchequer, for example, has a good deal of autonomy in drawing up his annual budget, and the Northern Ireland secretary has a considerable amount of freedom in deciding how to govern Northern Ireland.

The question, therefore, is not whether certain British cabinet ministers have a degree of autonomy. Some of them do. The question is how many of them have it, how much of it they have, and the circumstances under which they are able to exercise it. But before we tackle this question we need to answer what in some ways is a logically prior question: do British cabinet ministers *want* to make policy autonomously? In other words, do British cabinet ministers *want* to plow their own furrows? Do they have policy preferences and commitments (or even ideologies and ideals) that, if they were known in advance, would permit the outside observer to make an informed judgment about the probable future course of policy?

INDIVIDUAL MINISTERS: A WILL TO AUTONOMY?

Most British politicians are career politicians (King, 1981). Most of them are not specialists. They do not come from specialist backgrounds, and they do not devote themselves, as American congressmen do, to service on specialized committees, in the course of which they often build up considerable specialist knowledge. On the contrary, British politicians take pride in having a reasonable degree of knowledge across a remarkably wide range of subjects. They can and do talk about almost anything. They are generalists par excellence. Indeed, the rare subject specialist in British politics is considered something of a freak. He or she is unlikely to be appointed to ministerial office. If appointed, his assignment is likely to be in some field remote from that of his specialization. Richard Crossman, for example, was thought to know too much about education; when Labour came to power in 1964 he was made minister of housing and local government.

British prime ministers are not looking for specialists when they make ministerial appointments; indeed they are probably less interested in specialized knowledge and expertise than heads of government in any other democratic country (Blondel, 1985: 277). Instead they are looking for intelligence, political acumen, a capacity for hard work, acceptability to the governing party, presentability on television, at least a minimal level of competence in the House of Commons, and possibly personal loyalty – all stocks in trade of career politicians. This lack of interest in subject specialization is reinforced by the British practice of moving ministers from one department to another at frequent intervals. To cite a single example chosen almost at random, between 1985 and 1992 a man called John

MacGregor served successively as chief secretary to the treasury, minister of agriculture, secretary of state for education, leader of the House of Commons, and transport secretary. In 1992 the Department of Trade and Industry – sometimes as two separate departments, but more commonly merged – had had thirteen cabinet heads in thirteen years.

Being career politicians, most British politicians naturally want to make a career. They want to get ahead and are concerned less to advance causes than to advance themselves. Having become junior ministers, they want to become cabinet minsters. Having become cabinet ministers, they want to move steadily upward in the ministerial hierarchy. As Rose puts it in *Ministers and Ministries* (1986: 74), "From the perspective of an individual politician, what a ministry can do for his career is as important as what he can do for the ministry." For many it is even more important.

To get ahead as a minister – to climb the ministerial ladder – means doing a politically adept and competent job; but it also means making a favorable impression on the person who hires, fires, and relocates cabinet ministers: the prime minister. Prime-ministerial favor is a necessary condition of promotion (and nondemotion). Peter Walker served as a cabinet minister under Margaret Thatcher for almost the whole of her eleven and a half years in office. He was known to dissent from the main thrust of many of her policies; yet he was not dismissed (for reasons to be discussed), nor did he resign. In his memoirs – called, with conscious irony, *Staying Power* – he describes the position that most cabinet ministers found themselves in throughout the Thatcher era (1991: 232):

We were all, at different times, antagonized by the way Margaret rode roughshod over Cabinet, but outsiders do not appreciate fully the patronage power of a Prime Minister who won a General Election in 1983 and then again in 1987. The only way you get into Cabinet is if the Prime Minister decrees it. The only way you can move up from being Minister of Agriculture to Foreign Secretary is if the Prime Minister ordains it.
The politician who keeps in favour is not being unprincipled. He or she has to recognize that the Prime Minister will decide.

Margaret Thatcher was an unusually dominant prime minister, but the underlying relationship of superordination and subordination that Walker describes is far from being unique to Thatcher. It is the modern British norm.

Most British politicians are thus career politicians and nonspecialists; but in addition they possess another attribute that is important in the present context. Most of them do not have strongly held views about public policy; most are neither ideologues nor crusaders. To be sure, the great majority adhere to the values and broad policy preferences of their party – Conservatives favor free enterprise and Labour politicians want to create a more egalitarian society – but beyond that most of them tend to be pragmatic and adaptable. They are zealots in pursuit of their own and their party's interests, but they are not zealots in much else. Partly because most of them are nonspecialists, they are not likely to have developed specific policies or proposals – in the fields of, say, taxation, health, or housing – that they wish to carry forward. Moreover, most British politicians, however senior, are not publicly identified with strong issue stands. On the contrary, if a politician wishes to get ahead and adapt to changing circumstances, it is in his or her interests to maintain a low political profile in policy terms.

The cabinet appointed by John Major following his victory in the April 1992 general election is a good example. It consisted of twenty-one members apart from the prime minister himself. Some, like Douglas Hurd, the foreign secretary, and Virginia Bottomley, the health secretary, were vaguely associated with the "wet" or more "caring" wing of the Conservative Party; others, like Peter Lilley, the social services secretary, and Michael Portillo, the chief secretary to the treasury (in charge of public expenditure), were of a more rigorous Thatcherite persuasion. Nevertheless, all four of them had served under Thatcher; all seemed content to serve under Major; and all four's views were a matter of tendency and generalized ideological preference, not one of profound convictions on specific issues. None had nailed his or her flag to any specific mast. Most of the remaining seventeen were, so to speak, "policy indeterminates," career politicians simply, like Peter Walker, pursuing their careers. That said, there was one exception: Michael Heseltine, the trade and industry secretary (or, as he preferred to be called, the "president of the Board of Trade"). He was an important exception, and we shall come back to him later.

The point is this: if individual cabinet ministers are to exert a degree of autonomy in their capacity as ministers and heads of departments, and if, more precisely, the probable use of their autonomy is to serve as a reliable predictor of government policy, then the individual ministers in question must have both distinct policy views and what might be called a personal will to autonomy. They must want space in which to move in policy terms, and they must have views about how they want to move within that space. Recent British experience suggests that, at most, only a small minority of cabinet ministers fulfill either of these conditions. Most British ministers get along by going along. They are not, and do not aspire to be, major policy actors in their own right.

Suppose, however, that an individual cabinet minister does have views and seeks a degree of autonomy in order to be able to advance them. How successful is he or she likely to be? Do British institutions tend to promote ministerial and departmental autonomy, or are they inimical to it? The demand side of individual ministers' desire for autonomy having been looked at, it is time to look at the supply side.

INDIVIDUAL MINISTERS: A CAPACITY FOR AUTONOMY?

One important feature of the British system undoubtedly promotes a degree of ministerial and departmental autonomy. It is the doctrine of individual ministerial responsibility, the idea that each individual cabinet minister is responsible for, and can be held accountable for, everything that goes on in his or her department. The minister answers for his own actions and decisions; he also answers for the actions and decisions of all the civil servants who work under him. Ministers in the British system have their own statutes to administer, their own annual budget allocations to spend. The doctrine of individual responsibility gives them, in effect, a warrant for keeping other ministers off their turf. As in other countries, there is a tacit agreement in Britain that individual departmental ministers will not gratuitously interfere in each other's affairs. To try to deprive other people of their autonomy is to risk being deprived of one's own.

The doctrine of individual ministerial responsibility is reinforced by the fact of big government. Britain is a reasonably large country with a unitary political system, a tendency toward activist governments, and a well-developed welfare state. As a result, government departments are often large, and the problems they deal with are often (indeed usually) specialized and complex. Not surprisingly under the circumstances, individual departments develop their own institutional mores and subcultures – a tendency reinforced by the fact that movement between departments among civil servants, as distinct from among ministers, is relatively rare. Ministers' views tend to be influenced by those of their departments ("where you stand depends on where you sit"), and ministers are expected to go to bat on their department's behalf. Within the government, the transport secretary is less a member *of* the cabinet than the Department of Transport's ambassador *to* the cabinet. The secretary to the cabinet wrote in 1970: "The first thing to be noted about the central government of this country is that it is a federation of departments" (quoted in Hennessy, 1989: 380). As in all federations, the subunits, and their heads, have a good deal of operational autonomy.

So far as individual ministers are concerned, their autonomy is further increased by the character of their relationship, especially in recent years, with the senior civil servants in their departments. Ministers have always been constitutionally dominant; civil servants have always been their nominal, and sometimes their actual, subordinates. Nevertheless, the practice of British government during most of the twentieth century has been a more collegial one, with ministers and senior civil servants collaborating on more or less equal terms in the development of policy. Civil servants never had a veto over ministerial initiatives, but their views were taken seriously, and they had a right to express those views in an authoritative manner. Neustadt described British government at the top in the 1960s as "a virtual duopoly" (1985: 159). Since then, however, and despite the satirical television series "Yes, Minister," the balance of influence has tilted more in the ministers' direction. Thatcher, in particular, expected her ministers to develop their own policies and, if need be, to override civil-service objections. Senior civil servants found themselves cast less as advisers to ministers on policy and more as top-level managers of the government's programs (Hennessy, 1989). The shift in emphasis is subtle and has certainly not been total; but it has taken place and has correspondingly expanded the scope of ministerial autonomy.

Individual ministers in Britain also benefit from the limited roles played by Parliament in the fields of both legislation and legislative oversight. The House of Commons can be a maker and breaker of ministerial reputations, and ministers cannot afford to neglect the chamber or to perform less than competently there. Nor can they afford to ignore, or to be cavalier in their dealings with, their own backbench supporters, the majority party's MPs in the House of Commons. Subject to those two provisos, however, most British cabinet ministers most of the time are not unduly constrained by Parliament. As in most Westminster-model countries, the government of the day can count on Parliament to pass most of its legislation; and Britain's select committees are not notably effective as a means of legislative oversight. The goodwill of Parliament, or at least of the majority party within it, needs to be maintained; but it is normally relatively easy to do so.

Departments, in other words, are to a considerable degree autonomous, and neither civil servants nor members of Parliament impinge significantly on the autonomy of individual ministers. This very substantial degree of individual ministerial autonomy cannot be gainsaid, and ministers are conscious that a great deal of the time, and over a considerable range of issues, they can go their own way. However, at the same time there are four features of the British system that tend to reduce the autonomy of ministers. One of them might be described as political; the other three are more strictly governmental. All four are extremely inhibiting in their effects.

Ministers' limited bases of political support

The first and most political of the four factors concerns the position of the great majority of British ministers within their broader political environment. Other things being equal, a cabinet minister's autonomy, his capacity to influence government policy and act independently of the rest of the government, could be expected to be at its greatest if the minister in question happened to be the leader of his own political party, whose continued support was essential to the survival of the government; or if he had a substantial personal following in the country, such that his resignation would adversely affect the government's standing or put its life in danger; or if he had a substantial personal following within the ranks of the majority party, such that his resignation might threaten either the government's or the prime minister's hold over the House of Commons. In modern Britain, almost no ministers fulfill any of these conditions.

Since the Second World War, there have been two minority governments in Britain (March–October 1974 and 1976–9), but there has never been a coalition government – that is, a government not all of whose members belonged to the same party. It follows that there has never been a situation in which a member of the government, being the leader of one of its constituent parties, could threaten to destroy the government by withdrawing himself and his party from it. By ensuring that no one minister is able to threaten his or her colleagues in this way, majority-party government, in and of itself, derogates from ministerial autonomy.

Nor do most British ministers have a substantial – or even an insubstantial – personal following in the country. Most cabinet ministers are unknown to most members of the general public. Even when individual ministers do achieve a minimal level of face or name recognition, they seldom succeed in eliciting strong feelings one way or the other, let alone feelings of personal loyalty or identification. On the relatively rare occasions when individual ministers are held in high public esteem, as Douglas Hurd was during most of his tenure at the Foreign Office under Margaret Thatcher and John Major, it is an esteem that is most unlikely to be translated directly into votes. Prime ministers apart, there have probably not been more than three or four individual personalities in any British government since World War II who have had an independent capacity to attract votes to the governing party on a significant scale – and have therefore also had the capacity, by threatening to leave the government, to influence its policy and ensure their own autonomy.

The situation with regard to ministers' personal standings, not among the public at large but within the governing party, is broadly similar, but is also a little more complicated. It is often said that British prime ministers feel it incumbent on them to include and retain within their cabinets leading politicians who have substantial followings within the governing party, the idea being that faction leaders within one-party governments are in a position not dissimilar to that of party leaders in multiparty governments. If they go, then others are likely to go; if they stay, then the government and the prime minister are likely to be strengthened.

This proposition is broadly true. Politicians with substantial party followings are likely to be included and retained in British cabinets. The fact that these politicians have such followings probably increases their influence and autonomy within the cabinet. Nevertheless, two qualifications need immediately to be entered. The first is that not all prime ministers choose to appoint and retain all such politicians. Edward Heath in 1970 felt strong enough to exclude Enoch Powell from his cabinet, even though Powell had a large and vociferous following in the Conservative Party of that time. Margaret Thatcher in the 1980s likewise felt able to dismiss a number of the leading cabinet "wets." The second, more important, qualification is simply that, in modern Britain, there are very few faction leaders. Few individuals enjoy a high personal standing within the governing party, whichever it is. Even the ones who are personally popular and well regarded seldom have supporters who could reasonably be described as "followers."

The 1992 Major cabinet is again a good, because typical, illustration. To list the members of the cabinet – Norman Lamont, Kenneth Clarke, John MacGregor, Malcolm Rifkind, Tony Newton, John Gummer, Michael Howard, David Hunt, Peter Lilley, Ian Lang, William Waldegrave, Peter Brooke, Sir Patrick Mayhew, John Patten, Virginia Bottomley, Gillian Shepherd and so on – is to list men and women who, irrespective of the importance of the offices they hold, are not in any sense movers and shakers within their party. Some of them have friends and admirers. None has followers. The departure of any one of them from the cabinet might well be a temporary political embarrassment to the prime minister. It could, depending on the specific circumstances, be a serious embarrassment; but it would be most unlikely to involve the withdrawal from him or her of the support of any substantial section of the Conservative Party. Again, Michael Heseltine constitutes the single exception; and, again, we shall come back to him.

In other words, ministerial autonomy in Britain is limited by the fact that in practice very few individual cabinet ministers have sufficient political clout to be able to claim that autonomy – even if most of them were disposed to claim it, which, as we have seen, they are not.

Prime-ministerial power

The British prime minister is, within his own domestic sphere, one of the most powerful heads of government in the Western world, far more powerful than most prime ministers in Europe. He owes his power to his position as the leader of the majority party, to the historic prestige of his office, to the fact that he chairs the cabinet and its major committees, and to his control over the structure of government (he can at will create and destroy government departments). Above all, the prime minister owes his power to two circumstances that bear directly on the question of the autonomy of his cabinet ministers.

One is the prime minister's virtually total control – referred to earlier in connection with Peter Walker – over ministerial appointments. The British prime minister does not have to bargain with other party leaders or with faction leaders within his own party over who will or will not be assigned to what offices within his government; he and he alone decides. This would be a powerful weapon under almost any circumstances, but it is especially powerful when so many backbench MPs, being career politicians, desperately want to become ministers, and when so many ministers, also being career politicians, desperately want to rise in the ministerial hierarchy. Accordingly, prime ministers are usually in a position to extract, if they want to, a very high price from ministers both in policy terms and in terms of a more generalized ministerial obedience. Ramsay MacDonald, the incoming Labour prime minister in 1929, complained that he had had would-be ministers "in here weeping and even fainting" (Dalton, 1953: 217). A politician who can make fellow politicians weep and even faint has, to say the least of it, a certain hold over them.

The second circumstance bearing on ministerial autonomy is the British prime minister's position as the person who is almost universally identified with the government of the day (it is "his" or "her" government), who is held responsible for almost all the government's actions, and who therefore makes sure that, to a considerable extent, he or she *is* responsible for all the government's actions, or at least those that are controversial or likely to prove politically embarrassing. "The chancellor of the exchequer is not held responsible if something goes wrong in the Northern Ireland Office; the home secretary is not held responsible if something goes wrong in the Health Department. But in the British system the prime minister is held responsible for everything that goes wrong in everyone's office" (King, 1991: 36). Despite the doctrine of individual ministerial responsibility, the buck increasingly stops on the prime minister's desk.

The immediate and obvious consequence of this centralization of responsibility is that the prime minister in the British system has a license to interest himself in the affairs of every government department – a license to enquire, to intervene, to goad, to check, to prod, to remonstrate, even to dominate. The warrant that rank-and-file cabinet ministers have to keep other cabinet ministers off their turf does not apply to the prime minister. On the contrary, the prime minister has a warrant to roam wherever he likes. Ministers are expected to keep 10 Downing Street informed of all major developments in their field. They are also expected to consult Number 10 before making all important decisions, even those strictly within their field, and to ensure that the prime minister does not find out about important developments affecting his or her administration by reading about them in the newspapers (or even in routine government papers being circulated to other ministers).

The combination of the prime minister's power to appoint, promote, demote, and dismiss other ministers, together with his or her open license to intervene in departmental business, has, of course, the effect of considerably limiting individual ministers' autonomy. The prime minister is a constant, if unseen, presence, with considerable power advantages and an effective veto over a wide range of ministerial actions and initiatives. Gerald Kaufman, who served under Harold Wilson and James Callaghan, gives in *How to Be a Minister* a whimsical account of the advantages, if you are minister, of being able to call upon the prime minister to intervene on your side; but he then continues (1980: 86):

The converse, of course, is that the Prime Minister may also intervene when you do not want him to. He may feel that your handling of a problem, though impeccable in theory, is not going to get the result that he needs politically. He may even inject . . . [one of his friends] into the situation. If he does, do not get cross. Remember that he is looking after the interests of the whole Government while you, like all your colleagues, are subject to fits of Departmentalitis, a disease to which he is constitutionally immune. Sit back and enjoy it.

It needs only to be added that prime ministers' capacity for interference is inevitably restricted by their limited time and their many other preoccupations. It is also the case that some prime ministers are readier to give their cabinet colleagues greater autonomy than others. Thatcher was notorious for regarding her cabinet colleagues as, in effect, her agents. Major, her successor, is by all accounts a considerable delegator. Merely by virtue of Major being prime minister, the quantum of ministerial autonomy in the British system has gone up.

Collective responsibility

British cabinet ministers' autonomy is limited by the fact that most British ministers are not "freestanding"; they lack independent political strength. Their autonomy is further constrained by the prime minister's power over them, and it is still further limited by the doctrine and practice in Britain of something called collective responsibility.

Although ministers in Britain are supposed to be responsible as individuals for everything that goes on in their individual departments, the central thrust of British constitutional doctrine and practice emphasizes collective decisions collectively arrived at. The best and most authoritative decisions in the British system are decisions of the cabinet, a collective body; and ministers are supposed to regard one another as colleagues, as fellow participants in a joint political enterprise. They are meant to act together and to stick together (at least in public). Even if this were not so, it would still be the case that in British government, as in all modern governments, a great deal of business has to be transacted in a collegial manner. Departments are not politically and administratively isolated; they abut one another in all kinds of ways. The building of a new motorway may be the primary responsibility of the Department of Transport, but it has major implications for the Department of the Environment, and quite possibly for the Ministry of Agriculture and the Department of Trade and Industry, as well as for the Treasury.

The existence in Britain of both the doctrine of individual responsibility and that of collective responsibility is apt to give rise to a somewhat misleading picture of how the system actually works. It is tempting to suppose that the great majority of government decisions are either the collective decisions of the whole government or the individual decisions of individual ministers acting autonomously within their own departments. Likewise, it is tempting to suppose that at any given time the individual cabinet minister is operating either as a member of the cabinet, attending a meeting of the cabinet or one of its committees, or as a departmental minister, making autonomous decisions elsewhere in Whitehall.

But of course a dichotomy of this kind is too simple. In the first place, ministers take their departmental concerns along with them to meetings of the cabinet and its committees (some take only their departmental concerns). In the second place, ministers developing policies and making decisions, even within their own departments, do so in the light of their acceptability to the prime minister and cabinet colleagues ("It is the collective view which is at the back of the mind of the individual minister all the time" [Powell, 1964: 60]). In the third place, the institutions and practices themselves are more complicated than the dichotomy suggests. Ministers do not simply sit in their departments or attend cabinet meetings. Rather, in Britain they are caught up in a world of phone calls, interministerial correspondence, bilateral meetings between cabinet ministers, meetings of ministers and officials, cabinet committee meetings, cabinet meetings and, not least, negotiations with the Treasury. The appropriate image is not one of two separate boxes, one labelled "collective," the other labelled "individual," but rather of a dense, complicated network or lattice.

The upshot of a system in which government is a federation of departments, but in which departments constantly bump up against one another, is a further diminution in the autonomy of most ministers. Not only are they, as politicians, rivals for promotion and the public limelight; they are also, as departmental ministers, rivals for resources, turf, and parliamentary time.

The Treasury

The fourth factor tending to deprive ministers of autonomy in the British system is, in a sense, a derivative of the one just mentioned – the effects of collective responsibility and interdepartmental relations – but is nevertheless worth singling out for separate mention: the dependence of most departments on the Treasury in particular, and the process of decision making about public expenditure in general.

The Treasury, in fact if not in form, is the premier department in the British system. It is at once a finance department, an economics department, and an expenditure-controlling department. In this last capacity, it is both the prime minister's and the cabinet's principal adviser on the total amounts of money that should be allocated to public expenditure each year, and also their principal agency for determining the precise ways in which the total amounts should be allocated to specific departments. "The Treasury never sleeps" (Michael Heseltine quoted in Hennessy, 1989: 392). Almost every former British minister who has written about his working life has testified to the Treasury's intimate knowledge of the individual programs of the spending departments and to the way in which the Treasury's efforts to control expenditure inevitably impinges on the substance of policy – whether the decision is to raise the school graduation age or to order a new fighter aircraft.

Norman Fowler, who, like Peter Walker, served under Margaret Thatcher for most of her eleven and a half years, makes his battles with the Treasury over spending one of the subthemes of his memoirs. The relevant index entry reads: "Treasury: constraints and limitations by" (1991: 371). He writes at one point (206):

My baptism of fire had been with Leon Brittan who was Chief Secretary [to the Treasury] until the 1983 general election. Friendship, I fear, counts for very little when the fur really begins to fly. Ken Clarke, having listened to one of our more heated exchanges, wondered if we would ever speak to each other again. I also had fierce battles with Peter Rees, while Peter's successor, John MacGregor, maintained that I was the only minister who almost walked out of one of his 'bilaterals.'

Fowler adds (207), "It is possible to make light of the [public expenditure] process but, be under no illusion, it is a deadly serious affair."

It is also an affair that further limits ministers' autonomy. Seldom politically very strong in themselves, British ministers find themselves surrounded by ministerial colleagues who are actually their competitors, with the prime minister in front of them and the Treasury at their backs.

DEPARTMENTAL AUTONOMY

So far we have been approaching the question of autonomy from the point of view of individual cabinet ministers. How autonomous do they want to be? How autonomous are they able to be? Although these are undoubtedly the main questions, it is nevertheless worth pausing to look at another dimension of autonomy: that pertaining not to individual ministers but to whole government departments. The personalities and ambitions of individual ministers aside, it would be somewhat surprising if some government departments were not more independent of the rest of the governmental machine than others.

Certainly that is the way it feels to ministers and officials. Roy Jenkins, who served twice in the Home Office, later described (1975: 210–11) how the department struck him when he first went there in the mid-1960s:

In 1965 the Home Office was surprisingly detached from the rest of Whitehall. To some extent, this was a result of the nature of its work. Very large sections of this can be and are done without any inter-departmental or inter-ministerial consultation. This meant that senior officials met their opposite numbers elsewhere somewhat less than was the case in most other departments. And the effect of this was considerably fortified by a deliberate policy of exclusivity. There was very little cross fertilisation. Home Office men had a strong tendency to end where they began.

By contrast, Parry in his account of the Scottish Office (1986) emphasizes how tightly enmeshed the Scottish Office is with the other Whitehall domestic departments. "Scottish Office officials," he says (129), "are often much more aware of the behaviour of the corresponding functional department in Whitehall [say, Health, Education, or Agriculture] than of other parts of the Scottish Office."

No one seems to have felt the need to measure departmental autonomy, and for that reason there are no agreed (or even disagreed) indicators of autonomy. The number of contacts between officials in one department and those in other departments might be one such indicator; the number of contacts between ministers in different departments on departmental business might be another. Be that as it may, it is not difficult to identify four factors that might be expected to be conducive to greater departmental autonomy.

One is simply the nature of the department's business: whether or not its activities bring it into frequent contact with other departments and the prime minister. As Roy Jenkins indicates, most of the Home Office's business – such matters as immigration control and the management of prisons – can be conducted without any significant involvement by outsiders. At the other end of the range, departments like Environment, Employment, and Transport operate in fields where other departments' interests are constantly, and often profoundly, engaged. The ministers and officials of these departments will constantly be in and out of other ministers' and officials' offices (and at meetings with them, and on the telephone to them). The Home Office, despite its name, is a sort of offshore island in Whitehall; Environment, Employment, and Transport are, so to speak, continental powers.

Second, a department is likely to be granted a considerable degree of autonomy if it has, or manages to acquire, a low political profile – if its political business does not very often engage the attention of the prime minister and other ministers. The Welsh Office would be an extreme case of "autonomy by virtue of invisibility"; it is doubtful whether other ministers think about Welsh Office affairs more than once or twice a quarter, if that. By contrast, ministers like the chancellor of the Exchequer, the home secretary, and the foreign secretary are constantly in the news; the decisions they make can at any moment become the stuff of political controversy (and therefore of potential embarrassment to the government). The prime minister, in particular, is likely to take a continuing interest in those three ministers' doings. "Political business" of course includes legislation. The less a department needs to legislate, the less politically visible it is, and the less it needs to compete with other departments for parliamentary time.

Third, a department is likely to be autonomous in the present if it has been in the past. There are Whitehall traditions of autonomy, not unrelated to departments' standing in the Whitehall pecking order. Other ministers are traditionally wary of telling the chancellor of the Exchequer how he should manage the economy or reform the tax system. Other ministers almost never give the home secretary advice about how he should advise the queen in the use of the royal prerogative. The Foreign Office does not invite other departments' views about how it should conduct Britain's foreign policy. The prime minister is more or less unique in being able to occupy substantial parts of these ministers' territory. By contrast, other ministers have no compunction about expressing views in the fields of health, education, or the arts.

Finally, departments will acquire a degree of autonomy if they are not pressing for substantial increases in their annual budgets or, conversely, if they are not being pressed (usually by the Treasury) for decreases in those budgets. A department like Social Security can have an enormous budget, yet remain reasonably autonomous provided it is content with the budget it already has, and the Treasury is not pressing for reductions. By contrast, the Home Office has a relatively small budget, but it will find itself forced to engage with other departments – not just the Treasury but all other spending departments – if it wants more money for, say, prison building or the employment of more immigration officers. The Defence Department's

Table 13.1. *Rank of British government departments according to their degree of autonomy*

High	Medium	Low
Foreign Office	Agriculture, Fisheries and Food	Employment
Home Office	Defence	Environment
Lord Chancellor's Department	Education	Scottish Office
National Heritage	Health	Trade and Industry
Northern Ireland	Social Security	Transport
Treasury		Welsh Office

budget, needless to say, is permanently in contention. The point, to repeat, is not so much the absolute size of a department's budget as the pressures on it to change. As in the case of legislation, to seek change (or oppose it) is to make oneself vulnerable.

As soon as one considers the potential sources of departmental autonomy in this way, a number of points become obvious. One is that departmental autonomy varies to a considerable degree, of course, depending on time and circumstances (and the style of the prime minister). Another is that these four potential sources of departmental autonomy by no means all point in the same direction. The Scottish Office, for example, has a low political profile (at least in England) but otherwise has business that brings it into constant contact with the rest of Whitehall. The Foreign Office is a staunch defender of its own autonomy but can scarcely avoid having a high political profile; and so on. Yet another point, the most important, is that no department is completely, or even largely, autonomous. The great majority are impinged upon by other departments. All are impinged upon by the prime minister.

That said – and ignoring all the qualifications that would need to be made in an ideal world – it is tempting to try to construct a rank ordering of British government departments in terms of their institutional autonomy. Table 13.1 attempts such an ordering. Some departments may be in the wrong column; but few departments, if any, are probably more than one column adrift. What stands out from the table – and must have been obvious from the foregoing – is that departmental autonomy and departmental importance are only very loosely correlated. The Ministry of Agriculture, Fisheries and Food probably has more effective autonomy than the Department of Trade and Industry, but the DTI, by almost any measure, is a more important ministry than MAFF. The Lord Chancellor's Department may well be the single most autonomous department in Whitehall (almost no one anywhere else in government knows what goes on in it), but its influence scarcely extends beyond its own very narrow boundaries.

CONDITIONS OF AUTONOMY

Readers will long since have picked up the main message of this chapter: that ministerial and departmental autonomy are in very short supply in the British system. Ministers typically do not strive for it. They and their departments by and large lack the resources and political independence to achieve it. The British system is highly collegial and interconnected. Everybody lives on top of everybody else. Autonomy may in some cases merely betoken impotence and isolation.

Nonetheless, readers will probably also have noticed that the chapter has been developing, implicitly, an informal theory about the circumstances under which individual ministers may acquire a degree of autonomy, and at the same time, a degree of political individuality and influence. The basic ingredients of the theory are simple. A cabinet minister in the British system is likely to be autonomous in a politically significant way if: (a) he holds strong political views that he shows some determination to advance; (b) he is highly regarded by a significant section of the electorate; (c) he has many admirers and a large following in the majority party, whether the party in the country or in the House of Commons; and (d) he holds one of the more autonomous offices listed in Table 13.1 (though this last element is probably the least important).

Those are the basic ingredients; the more of them the minister possesses, the more formidable he or she is likely to be. Nevertheless, two other elements are required to complete the picture. One is that other ministers, especially the prime minister, believe that (a), (b), and (c) or some combination of them are true; it is other ministers' assessments of an individual's political will and standing that are important. The other, related to (a), is that other ministers, especially the prime minister, should believe that the minister in question is sufficiently proud and willful to advance himself and his causes even at some risk to his own career. A minister who is thought to be cautious is likely to be taken less seriously than one considered bold. A minister viewed as nice is likely to be taken less seriously than one thought capable of being brutal. It does a politician no good to be thought to "lack the last six inches of steel." To be credited with a capacity for political roughhouse is not absolutely essential in a minister who seeks a degree of autonomy, but it helps.

Against this background, it is possible to draw a sketch or template of the kind of minister who is likely to want to, and be able to, assert his autonomy. He has always had a strong set of political opinions and has never been afraid to express them. He has probably been a controversial figure in his time, possibly defying the party whips or taking on some important section of the party establishment. He is highly visible to the general public and is well regarded by a majority of voters. His speech at the annual party conference is always eagerly anticipated, and is usually accorded a standing ovation. He is not only admired by his own party (and probably the other party) in the House of Commons, but has a genuine following there – identifiable individuals who see him as their leader and are willing, even eager, to help him fight his political battles. He is known to be a proud person, dangerous to cross. There is a degree of unpredictability in his character.

The Conservatives in Britain have a term for such men (they have always been men: Margaret Thatcher did not fall into this category until she became party leader): they call them "the big beasts of the jungle." On the grounds that, as ministers and potential ministers, they are the politicians most likely to be able to exercise effective autonomy, they are worth identifying, partly to see how many of them there are and partly to see whether they have had a discernible effect on public policy. The whole point of enquiring into ministerial autonomy is, after all, that it is thought to have policy consequences.

THE BIG BEASTS OF THE JUNGLE

Table 13.2 sets out the writer's best estimate as to who have been (and who, by implication, have not been) the big beasts of the ministerial jungle since the Second World War. The table includes only ministers; opposition politicians such as Aneurin Bevan have been excluded. A few of the names have been put in parentheses for reasons to be explained. The name of Michael Heseltine has been placed in square brackets for the 1979–90 period because, although he was a big beast of the jungle, then-prime minister Margaret Thatcher did not seem to recognize the fact – a mistake for which she subsequently paid a heavy penalty. Some of the beasts – for example, Edward Heath during the 1957–64 period – became big only toward the end of the period. The judgments about inclusions and exclusions are solely the writer's; anyone who wants to do so can check his list against the full list of post-1945 ministers published in the latest edition of Butler and Butler's *British Political Facts* (1986: 32–64).

The number of names in the table, as can be seen, is very small – a mere eighteen out of the more than four hundred men and women who have served in British cabinets since the war. The big beasts of the British jungle could be contained in a reasonably small zoo. It is interesting to note that only three of the eighteen – Sir Anthony Eden, Edward Heath, and James Callaghan – subsequently became prime minister. The remaining five prime ministers who served in postwar cabinets before attaining the highest office – Harold Macmillan, Sir Alec Douglas-Home, Harold Wilson, Margaret Thatcher, and John Major – were not big beasts of the jungle as ordinary cabinet ministers (though the exclusion of Harold Macmillan

Table 13.2. *Big Beasts of the Jungle*

1945–51 (Labour)
Ernest Bevin (d. 1951)
Sir Stafford Cripps
Herbert Morrison
1951–7 (Conservative)
R.A. Butler
Sir Anthony Eden (prime minister, 1955)
1957–64 (Conservative)
R. A. Butler
Edward Heath
(Iain Macleod)
(Reginald Maudling)
1964–70 (Labour)
George Brown (resigned 1968)
James Callaghan
Roy Jenkins
1970–4 (Conservative)
Iain Macleod (d. 1970)
1974–9 (Labour)
(Tony Benn)
James Callaghan
Anthony Crosland (d. 1977)
Denis Healey
1979–90 (Conservative)
[Michael Heseltine (resigned 1986)]
Sir Geoffrey Howe
Nigel Lawson
(Peter Walker)
1990– (Conservative)
Michael Heseltine

from our list could be disputed). It seems that the qualities that enable someone to become party leader and prime minister are not necessarily the same as those that enable someone to assert his or her autonomy within an existing government.

What the eighteen have in common is that they were taken exceptionally seriously by the prime ministers under whom they served and by their cabinet colleagues. They were largely left free to run their own departments; they were given wide latitude in commenting on the affairs of other departments and the government as a whole; and their support had to be ensured – they had to be "got on board" – before the prime minister or other ministers undertook major new policy initiatives.

For example Alan Bullock, biographer of Ernest Bevin, Clement Attlee's foreign secretary in the postwar Labour government, writes (1983: 56–7):

At the end of Cabinet meetings it was Attlee's habit to keep Bevin behind when the other ministers left and settle in private with him what was to be done. As Attlee cheerfully admitted, there was no record of these talks, but the constant exchange of notes between the two men shows that it extended to the whole range of Government business, and bears out Attlee's statement that he was as careful as Bevin was not to take any important decision without first making sure that he had the other's agreement.

Bevin was responsible for all aspects of Britain's external relations, not only those nominally covered by the Foreign Office. In addition, he was chairman of the cabinet's Manpower Committee and a member, sometimes acting as chairman, of its Economic Policy Committee and its Socialization of Industry Committee. "Even when he was not directly involved," his biographer tells us (Bullock, 1983: 57), "no minister was more frequently consulted by his colleagues." For example, the chancellor of the Exchequer discussed his 1945 and 1946 budgets in detail with Bevin. He would not have done so with any other minister.

On the Conservative side, the relations between R. A. Butler and successive postwar prime ministers were by no means as close as those between Attlee and Bevin; but Butler was universally regarded as "the indispensable man." He often deputized for Churchill, Eden, and Macmillan when they were ill or abroad, sometimes for several weeks at a time. One of his colleagues recalled that if Butler was absent from his function as chairman of the cabinet's Home Affairs Committee and someone else took his place, "It was as if the government itself came to a standstill" (Horne, 1989: 80). When Harold Macmillan as prime minister was contemplating British entry into the European Community in 1960–1, one of his constant preoccupations was that Butler, who had a solidly agricultural constituency and rather traditional attachments to the crown and the Commonwealth, would lead a parliamentary revolt in defense of the Commonwealth and British farmers. The revolt, had it happened, would have been serious, possibly fatal, for Macmillan. The prime minister was clearly relieved when Butler finally declared his backing for his policy – at a dinner to which he, not the prime minister, issued the invitation (Howard, 1987: 295–6; Horne, 1989: 353). It was a measure of Butler's political standing that, when Macmillan retired in 1963, Butler could almost certainly have prevented his nominated successor, Sir Alec Douglas-Home, from taking office by declining to serve in Home's cabinet.

In more recent times, Michael Heseltine is the archetype of a minister with a substantial degree of political and departmental autonomy. He is left largely alone to make policy within whichever department he currently holds. He has a license, not given to any other minister, to intervene in cabinet meetings on any subject he chooses. The prime minister in the early 1990s, Major, would be extremely reluctant to embark on any line of policy likely to encounter Heseltine's opposition. Shortly before the 1992 election, the *Economist* (15 February 1992) quoted one cabinet minister as saying of Heseltine that he was "absolutely romping," and another as describing him, in effect, as the deputy prime minister, someone who won all his interdepartmental battles. Another Conservative MP remarked, "If you ask who in our great party has the intellectual force and executive ability to stand up against Michael these days, I have to say there is nobody." Like Butler, Heseltine is not as close personally to the prime minister as Bevin was to Attlee; but, like both Butler and Bevin, he occupies a manifestly superior position in the cabinet to that of almost all – probably all – of his colleagues.

Those listed in Table 13.2 all had, or have, a substantial degree of ministerial autonomy; that is why they appear in the table. But it is also worth noting that the great majority of them fit reasonably well the sketch already described. Most of them held strong views on the substance of policy (though sometimes only in specific policy areas). All of them, with the exceptions of George Brown, Tony Benn, and (at times) Nigel Lawson, were highly regarded by the electorate. And all of them, without exception, had substantial followings within their own party; they did not speak only for themselves. Several of them – Sir Stafford Cripps and Sir Anthony Eden in the 1930s, Iain Macleod in the 1960s – had been rebels, and Tony Benn was constantly at odds with the Labour establishment. Many of them, unlike most career politicians, were willful men, either not caring desperately about their careers or being willing to take chances with them. Macleod refused to serve under Home; Brown was constantly threatening to resign (and finally did); Heath took terrible risks with his career in insisting on the abolition of resale price maintenance over the protests of many Conservative backbenchers; Jenkins had resigned as the Labour Party's deputy leader (and later formed a new party); Heseltine's resignation from Thatcher's cabinet in 1986 was one of the most spectacular in British history.

There are two reasons for placing some of the names in the table in parentheses. The first is simply that some of the cases are marginal (there may, since the war, have been even fewer than eighteen big beasts of the jungle). It is arguable that neither Iain Macleod nor Reginald Maudling quite achieved that status in the 1960s, and Sir Geoffrey Howe had often been a somewhat recessive member of the cabinet until his resignation in 1990. The other reason is that some of those listed – notably R. A. Butler, Tony Benn, and Peter Walker – forfeited a considerable portion of their potential influence in the cabinet by giving the impression that they were not quite turbulent enough. Macmillan would have been afraid to sack Butler; Wilson and Callaghan were afraid to sack Benn; Thatcher was afraid to sack Walker. All three men stood for something and had a substantial party following; the political price of sacking them would have been too high. At the same time, however, all three allowed themselves to be sidelined. Butler did not insist on the Foreign Office when Macmillan became prime minister in 1957, and four years later allowed himself to be deprived of the leadership of the House of Commons and the Conservative Party chairmanship. Benn, although a powerful member of the Labour Party's National Executive Committee, allowed himself to be demoted from the Industry Department, where he could influence important aspects of government policy, to the Energy Department, where he could not. Walker's ministerial declension took him from Agriculture to Energy to Wales (where he was given a certain amount of departmental autonomy provided he confined his attentions to the principality). They were, or were capable of being, big beasts of the jungle; but they all "built their own cages" (Gilmour, 1992: 35).

The undisputed beasts of the jungle have usually had significant effects on public policy (insofar as it is possible to measure individual politicians' effects). Bevin largely framed Britain's foreign policy in the immediate postwar years. Herbert Morrison largely framed the Labour government's nationalization policy. Butler and Jenkins left an indelible stamp on the Home Office. Macleod reoriented British policy in colonial Africa. Callaghan played a large part in sinking the first Wilson government's plans for reforming the trade unions. Denis Healey was the first chancellor to turn British economic policy in the direction of monetarism. Lawson and Howe were, as mentioned earlier, largely responsible for Britain's membership of the European exchange-rate mechanism. Heseltine was responsible for abolishing the Thatcher government's "poll tax." The list could be extended. It is doubtful whether more than a handful of other cabinet ministers have had comparable influence. The British system, in short, does leave some room for ministerial autonomy.

CONCLUSIONS

It is time to return to the original proposition, the one that is being tested in the British context: namely, that cabinet ministers have a good deal of autonomy within their departments, and that government policy is, therefore, to a considerable extent determined by, or at least influenced by, which ministers hold which portfolios. The proposition, in sum, is that cabinet ministers matter.

As we have just seen, this proposition does guide one toward an understanding of one important aspect of the British political system that might otherwise go unremarked (or simply be taken for granted): the presence within the system of certain politicians who, while not themselves prime minister, nevertheless have an almost prime minister–like capacity to in-fluence events. The big beasts of the jungle constitute this category, prin-cipally because of their personal standing with the general public and (even more important) within the majority party. These are the people who, if the British had a coalition system, would feature largely in all coalition making. Indeed, Ernest Bevin did play a large part in Winston Churchill's coalition making in 1940. He was not even at that time a member of Parliament, but he was the leader of the Transport and General Workers' Union and, partly for that reason, a powerful figure in the Labour Party. When John Major sought to reconstitute the Conservative Party's internal coalition following Margaret Thatcher's fall in 1990, he felt it prudent to include in the cabinet that other big beast of the jungle, often depicted as a lion, Michael Heseltine.

That said, however, our general conclusion must be that the proposition is not an accurate description of routine British government and politics, and is not even an accurate description of most British government and politics at the highest level: most chancellors of the Exchequer, foreign secretaries, and home secretaries are not big beasts of the jungle. British politicians, being career politicians, are by and large content to go along with the majority. They are not policy advocates. They do not have sub-stantial personal followings in the country or in their party. They know that their future depends on the prime minister. Even the chancellor of the Exchequer, although accorded a good deal of autonomy vis-à-vis other ministers in the preparation of his annual budget, in practice prepares it in very close collaboration with the prime minister. The foreign secretary, although he heads a department that, by Whitehall standards, is unusually freestanding, also works closely with the prime minister of the day. A confident prime minister with a secure power base as the leader of the majority party – and most British prime ministers fall into this category – can even prevent someone from becoming a big beast in the first place. Enoch Powell would undoubtedly have been a big and dangerous beast in Edward Heath's cabinet after 1970. Precisely for that reason, Heath ex-cluded him. Powell never held office again.

The proposition that cabinet ministers matter is worth testing in the British context. It directs attention to features of the British system that are important and deserving of analysis and explanation. Nevertheless, it is falsified by the great bulk of Britain's recent experience with a system of single-party majority government.

REFERENCES

Blondel, Jean. 1985. *Government Ministers in the Contemporary World*. London: Sage.

Bullock, Alan. 1983. *Ernest Bevin: Foreign Secretary, 1945–1951.* London: Heinemann.

Butler, David, and Gareth Butler. 1986. *British Political Facts, 1900–1985.* 6th ed. London: Macmillan Press.

Dalton, Hugh. 1953. *Call Back Yesterday: Memoirs, 1887–1931.* London: Frederick Muller.

Fowler, Norman. 1991. *Ministers Decide: A Personal Memoir of the Thatcher Years.* London: Chapmans.

Gilmour, Ian. 1992. *Dancing with Dogma: Britain under Thatcherism.* London: Simon & Schuster.

Hennessy, Peter. 1989. *Whitehall.* London: Secker & Warburg.

Horne, Alistair. 1989. *Macmillan, 1957–1986.* London: Macmillan Press.

Howard, Anthony. 1987. *Rab: The Life of R. A. Butler.* London: Jonathan Cape.

Jenkins, Roy. 1975. On being a minister. In *Cabinet Studies: A Reader.* Valentine Herman and James E. Alt, (eds.). London: Macmillan Press, pp. 210–21.

Kaufman, Gerald. 1980. *How to be a Minister.* London: Sidwick & Jackson.

King, Anthony. 1981. The rise of the career politician in Britain – and its consequences. *British Journal of Political Science* 11: 249–85.

1991. The British prime minister in the age of the career politician. In G. W. Jones (ed.), *West European Prime Ministers.* London: Frank Cass.

Neustadt, Richard. 1985. White House and Whitehall. In Anthony King (ed.), *The British Prime Minister.* London: Macmillan Press.

Parry, Richard. 1986. The centralization of the Scottish Office. In Richard Rose (ed.), *Ministers and Ministries: A Functional Analysis.*

Powell, Enoch. 1964. Enoch Powell. In Norman Hunt (ed.), *Whitehall and Beyond.* London: British Broadcasting Corporation.

Rose, Richard. 1986. *Ministers and Ministries: A Functional Analysis.* Oxford University Press (Clarendon Press).

Walker, Peter. 1991. *Staying Power: An Autobiography.* London: Bloomsbury.

14

Collective cabinet decision making in New Zealand

Matthew S. R. Palmer*

New Zealand is the most streamlined example of a Westminster parliamentary democracy in the world.[1] The plurality or first-past-the-post electoral system yields single-party majority governments. The cabinet dominates the government caucus. The government caucus dominates Parliament, which is small and unicameral. Parliament has supreme lawmaking power. There is no federalism. The courts may not strike down legislation. Once in power, a New Zealand government may govern as it chooses, constrained primarily by the incentive to be reelected. Laver and Shepsle have recently developed their portfolio-allocation approach to illuminate the formation of coalition governments (1990; in press). As they suggest in the Introduction to the present volume, however, collective decision making within both the cabinet and the governing party may be much more important in single-party majority governments than in coalitions.

The first section of this chapter provides a brief description of the New Zealand system of government. The second section examines the relevance of the portfolio-allocation approach to single-party majority governments and analyzes the theoretical importance of collective decision making. Using this framework, the third, fourth, fifth, and sixth sections examine interrelationships between individual ministers, the cabinet as a collective, the governing party, and Parliament. The seventh section concludes that the theoretical background provides an interesting perspective on the practical operation of New Zealand politics as well as a useful framework for viewing this streamlined Westminster constitution in a comparative perspective.

NEW ZEALAND GOVERNMENT – BACKGROUND

New Zealand, a nation of three and a half million people, inherited the Westminster system of government and common law legal system. (On the New Zealand constitution and politics see Gold, 1992; G. Palmer, 1987, 1992; Ringer, 1991.) The Constitution Act of 1986 brought together several constitutionally important statutory provisions. Otherwise, New Zealand's constitution is "unwritten," and constitutional conventions play a significant role. The doctrine of parliamentary sovereignty still underlies the New Zealand constitution. The Bill of Rights Act of 1990 expressly forbids courts from striking down legislation. Other important conventions, such as collective cabinet responsibility and individual ministerial responsibility, have evolved along lines similar to those in Britain.

New Zealand has had representative government since 1853. The governor-general is still the representative of the queen in New Zealand, but almost all of her or his powers are exercised on the advice of the ministers of the crown. Provincial government was abolished in 1876 and the largely inactive upper house, the Legislative Council, was abolished in 1950. The electoral franchise of the House of Representatives was extended in the 1870s and (with respect to women) in 1893. A separate Maori electoral roll, electing four representatives, has existed since 1867, though the Maori now have the option to run and vote in general elections if they so choose.

Organized party politics developed in New Zealand from the late nineteenth century, crystallizing in the 1930s into the modern two-party system that exists today. Elections are held every three years using a simple plurality formula. Since 1935 either the New Zealand Labour Party or the New Zealand National Party have formed successive single-party majority governments.[2] New Zealand thus has a small unicameral Parliament, dominated by a majority governing party that in turn is dominated by the cabinet.

THE PORTFOLIO-ALLOCATION APPROACH AND SINGLE-PARTY MAJORITY GOVERNMENTS

In order to win an electoral majority under the plurality system, each of the two main parties attempts to appeal to a broad spectrum of opinion. A number of subgroups can be expected to reflect this breadth of opinion within each party (Boston, 1990: 69). Indeed, during the past fifteen years, the two main parties in New Zealand have uneasily encompassed both interventionists and avid believers in market forces simultaneously. Some elements of the extraparliamentary parties, especially in the Labour Party, have at times developed a degree of organization around particular issues and interests, but neither party in New Zealand has achieved the degree of institutionalization of left, right, and center factions shown by the Australian Labor Party (Wilson, 1989: 27). Rather, the dominant view of the cabinet and the government caucus is formed by a number of elements that coalesce around particular issues.

What distinguishes the different elements of a single-party majority government from those of a coalition government? Intraparty negotiations over policy, and the consequent importance of portfolios, might be expected to have the same characteristics as they do in interparty coalition building. Organized factions should form, negotiate, and use portfolio allocation to assure each other of their commitment to policy deals. What difference does it make that the units that negotiate on cabinet policy and portfolios are constituent parts of the same organization?

The difference has to do with electoral incentives. A single party can form a majority government only if the party as a whole wins a parliamentary majority from the electorate. In plurality systems with single-party majority governments, the electorate seems to place a premium on party unity (e.g., White, 1992). Certainly, the existence of a strong electoral preference for party unity is clear in New Zealand. It is regarded by the New Zealand media and political actors as an implicit and often dominating fact of political life.[3] This chapter argues, furthermore, that the New Zealand system of single-party majority government provides parties with strong electoral incentives to maintain their unity (cf. Greece and Canadian provinces: Koutsoukis, 1994; White, 1994).

The overall structure of New Zealand's Westminster constitution gives a monopoly of the government's coercive power to the cabinet (M. Palmer, 1992). The significance of this power and the small size of the cabinet impel cabinet ministers to try to maintain party unity. Indeed, the small size of the government caucus has generally maintained strong pressure on caucus members to preserve caucus unity. The incentive for unity is weaker among extraparliamentry party activists, but it still exists. Incentives for party unity are not always dominant, however. Their efficacy is particularly dependent on the length of an individual's time horizon and the consequent value of short-term opportunism. Unity incentives may also be attenuated if individuals or elements within a party value policy outputs more highly than the attainment of office, or if they fundamentally disagree with their party's judgment about the electorate's policy preferences.

Despite these caveats, New Zealand cabinets face strong incentives to maintain party unity. One of the primary ways of doing this is through a commitment to collective cabinet decision making. Certainly, the members of single-party majority New Zealand cabinets may be expected to be more committed to collective cabinet decision making than would members of coalition cabinets, which do not face such incentives for unity. This provides an interesting organizational distinction between coalition and single-party majority governments.

In the language of the economics of organization (Moe, 1984; Williamson, 1985), the polices of a coalition government are the subject of incomplete *ex ante* contracts between member parties, enforced by the allocation of portfolios of exclusive jurisdiction. Exogenous shocks may cause the initial contract to be renegotiated – represented by a cabinet reshuffle or the formation of a new coalition. The policies of a single-party majority government are determined, not by contract, but through an organizational governance structure – the governing party. The party's collective decision-making structures and procedures are used to consider and adjust to exogenous shocks, including the emergence of new policy issues. This governance structure needs to be flexible, discreet, and effective in order to accommodate changing circumstances, to preserve the image of party unity, and to implement agreed policy.

In the language of the portfolio-allocation approach, bargaining credibility among the members of a coalition government exists to the extent that a portfolio implies exclusive jurisdiction by each individual minister over an area of policy. Greater use of collective cabinet decision-making procedures in a coalition government would undercut individual ministerial autonomy and thus impair the equilibrium-inducing qualities of portfolio allocation. The converse is true with respect to single-party majority cabinets. Here, the integrity of the governing party qua party rests on the use of, and commitments to, collective cabinet decision-making procedures. Rather than fixing policy attitudes *ex ante,* a single-party majority government preserves the ability of its elements constantly to bargain over policy issues as they arise.

The relationship between collective cabinet decision-making and individual ministerial autonomy is just as crucial in an account of single-party majority government as it is with respect to coalition government. This chapter canvasses the constitutional conventions, the social norms and the structures and procedures of the cabinet, the caucus, and the extraparliamentary party in New Zealand's constitution that help to maintain commitment to collective party decision making and thus party unity, thereby inducing equilibrium in government decision making.

INDIVIDUAL MINISTERIAL AUTONOMY

The tension between individual ministerial autonomy and the cabinet as a collective is exhibited in the tension between the fundamental constitutional conventions of individual and collective responsibility. Individual ministerial autonomy constitutes the underlying legal, administrative, and constitutional basis for New Zealand's form of Westminster government. The constitutional doctrines, structural mechanisms, and political incentives that override individual autonomy are examined in later sections.

229

Cabinet portfolios

Currently there are twenty ministers in the New Zealand cabinet and several ministers outside the cabinet, who together hold fifty separate portfolios. A minister's designation may reflect varying degrees of status (Cabinet Office, 1991: 2C). The prime minister defines the portfolios and designates ministers' status according to the machinery of government, the politics of the various policy issues, and the politics of cabinet making.

As a matter of law and prerogative, the crown in New Zealand has the rights, powers, and duties of a natural person, and ministers may therefore undertake any action or omission that is ordinarily within the law, including the establishment of bureaucratic machinery (Legislation Advisory Committee, 1989). These powers are supplemented and confined by many statutory powers and duties, including powers of administrative action, regulatory decision, and appointment. Administrative law imposes procedural constraints on the exercise and fulfillment of statutory powers and duties, whereas the recent New Zealand Bill of Rights Act of 1990 covers ministerial actions based on the crown's prerogative.

Perhaps the most important source of an individual minister's power is the constitutional convention of individual ministerial responsibility and its corollaries (M. Palmer, 1992, 1993). In essence, individual responsibility empowers the minister to administer matters of government policy that fall within his or her portfolio(s). It obliges the minister to report to Parliament regarding those matters and to investigate and remedy errors of administration therein. Important corollaries to individual responsibility provide that public servants forming part of a minister's portfolio owe a duty of loyalty to their minister; the minister is in turn obliged to protect the anonymity of public servants. New Zealand's public service has been politically neutral since 1912 (Ringer, 1991: 71–7; and see for theory M. Palmer, 1992).

The public service

Of any single factor, the public service probably adds most to the "power" of a minister's portfolio. It is also an inherent constraint on a minister's power. This chapter does not pretend to assess definitively the balance between minister and department. However, there is evidence that, on average, senior New Zealand public servants are not generally as conservative or reactive as counterparts in other countries, and are more tolerant of popular participation in government (Gregory, 1991: 310–13). It is clear that a department can have a significant influence on a minister's decision making, depending on the minister. A department has many advantages over a minister, for example institutional memory and experience of issues and process, and a position of access that allows substantial opportunity to present the information and frame the arguments considered by a minister. Against this is pitted a minister's ability, experience, and willfulness, his or her small personal office, his or her colleagues, the information generated by the new accountability and financial-management regime, and the traditional public-service culture of loyalty backed by a code of conduct (State Services Commission, 1990). The weaker the minister in terms of will, ability, knowledge, and experience, the easier it is for a department to manipulate him or her into advocating departmental interests and arguments. On the other hand, the stronger the minister, the easier it is for him or her to ignore the expert information and policy advice available from the department.[4]

Selection of cabinet ministers

The only legal requirement with respect to the selection of a cabinet minister is Section 6 of the Constitution Act of 1986: he or she must be an MP (or have been a candidate at the immediately preceding general election and become an MP within forty days). However, as recognized in the *Cabinet Office Manual* itself (Cabinet Office, 1991: 2B4), the two main parties in New Zealand provide interesting contrasts in the process of selecting cabinet ministers. The fact that the selection of cabinet ministers is a matter for each party's internal rules highlights the endogeneity of a constitutional mechanism vital to the ongoing operation of New Zealand's constitutional politics.

The leader and deputy leader of both parties are elected by secret ballot in their caucuses. They are members of cabinet ex officio as prime minister and deputy prime minister. The other cabinet ministers are selected by the prime minister in a National government or elected by the caucus in a Labour government (see McLeay, 1987). In both parties the prime minister may appoint ministers outside the cabinet, designates the formal ranking, and allocates portfolios. In exercising his or her discretion, a prime minister of either party will always consult closely with the deputy prime minister and will usually take careful soundings of the views of the members of caucus, especially the most senior members. In both parties, the prime minister has the discretion to sack ministers. Conceptually, this decision is based on similar grounds to the appointment decision.

The two selection processes of the main parties may or may not produce different results. The Labour process risks either a deadlocked cabinet or an alienated, excluded minority. The National process may emphasize personal loyalty to the leader over other factors. If the argument in this chapter bears weight, a National prime minister and, to a lesser extent, a Labour government caucus, should each be aware of the electoral need to ensure party unity and a commitment to collective decision making within the party. This seems to have been reflected in recent cabinet making. In 1980, several senior members of the National cabinet retained their cabinet positions after a failed leadership coup. The second-term Labour caucus elected new ministers, who were seen as ameliorating the dominance of a market-oriented economic policy, but later reelected the chief architect of that policy in the face of opposition by the prime minister. The current National prime minister, Jim Bolger, appointed Winston Peters to the cabinet, someone who had often been at odds with the prime minister and minister of finance, but who was the only senior National MP of Maori descent and was more popular with the electorate than the prime minister.[5]

In both parties, representational and personal factors can be relevant in the selection of cabinet ministers and the allocation of portfolios (McLeay, 1987: 290–8). Previous parliamentary experience is generally seen as an essential precondition for cabinet selection. Otherwise, ability and personability may be the most important factors in selection. Personal background may be relevant to allocation of some portfolios, such as agriculture or that of the attorney general. Race, gender, age, and geography can be relevant to selection, as well as to the allocation of portfolios such as Maori Affairs, Women's Affairs, Youth Affairs, and Regional Development.

In a few instances the policy views of an individual have been important in the selection or allocation decisions. A prime minister often uses associate minister appointments and cabinet committee structures to balance individual ministerial appointments. Following the 1987 reelection of the Labour government, the prime minister, David Lange, broke up a trio of finance ministers (the minister and two associate ministers) who had been effective in advocating free-market economic policies within the cabinet. In 1989 a majority of the Labour government caucus reelected to cabinet the former finance minister most closely identified with the government's free-market policies, Roger Douglas. Following this, Lange, who had previously sacked Douglas, resigned as leader of the Labour Party and as prime minister. The succeeding Labour prime minister, Geoffrey Palmer, appointed Douglas to the Police portfolio – ameliorating to some extent Labour fears of the effect of his return. A National prime minister refused to appoint a former prime minister, Robert Muldoon, to an important portfolio due to the negative image of the Muldoon administration's policies.

These incidents occurred with respect to very powerful members of the cabinet, people with reputations that were unusually well established in the cabinet, the party caucus, and the electorate at large. They also usually involved the powerful Finance portfolio. In general, however, the policy positions of an experienced member of caucus may often be known only in a general way – a left/right label could often be applied, for example. Perceptions of an MP's more precise policy views are not always accurate, a person's views may not be ideologically consistent across all issues, and those views may change over time, especially after their holder takes office. The decision on whether to confer cabinet status on an MP, with the consequent inclusion in collective decision making, is usually more important than (and in both parties sequentially prior to) the decision to pick an MP for a particular portfolio.

In practice, the different methods of cabinet selection may not make much difference. The small size of the New Zealand Parliament, and thus the government caucus, inherently limits the available choice of ministers, especially after a change of government. In 1975 the new National government caucus had thirty experienced personnel available to fill twenty-seven positions, and in 1984 the new Labour government made thirty appointments from thirty-nine with experience (Jackson, 1989: 173). Around fifteen of the twenty members of cabinet are virtually automatic selections.

In considering cabinet-making decision processes, it is useful to bear in mind the different arenas in which a minister must operate, often simultaneously. A minister must often predict the potential consequences of action or inaction in the cabinet, in the government caucus, in the governing party, in Parliament, in the electorate, and even in terms of history. A minister will respond to incentives in each arena and assign priorities among the arenas according to that person's individual makeup. However, it is useful to regard the minister as possessing a potentially valuable reputation in each arena – with the potential, as a capital asset, to mitigate opportunism just as a reputation does in the commercial sphere (Klein and Leffler, 1981).

COLLECTIVE CABINET DECISION MAKING

Mechanics of collective decision making

It is important for cabinet dynamics that the offices of all New Zealand cabinet ministers are together in one building – the "Beehive" – adjacent to the Parliament buildings. Established cabinet procedures exist from the moment a new government is sworn in. The *Cabinet Office Manual*, which is now publicly available, represents an authoritative accumulation of cabinet practices and procedures (Cabinet Office, 1991; also see Boston, 1990). These are administered by the secretary of the cabinet (who reports to the prime minister) but may be changed and updated by each administration.

The full cabinet is chaired by the prime minister or, in his or her absence, the next-most-senior minister. It is attended by all cabinet ministers and, with the express prior permission of the prime minister, by ministers outside the cabinet with respect to specific items. The cabinet meets every Monday morning and considers an agenda drawn up on behalf of the prime minister by the cabinet office. During the 1984–90 Labour government, cabinet meetings usually included the following categories of items: an informal discussion of current policy or political issues; coordination of ministers' activities and speeches in the coming week; statutory regulations; ministers' requests to attend functions and travel overseas; cabinet committee reports; twenty to thirty submissions from ministers; and bills for introduction into Parliament (Palmer, 1987; 39–40). Ministers may also, with the prime minister's permission, raise items orally. Sometimes, the cabinet will set aside time for general discussion on particular topics.

Only matters requiring urgent consideration come directly to the full cabinet. Most matters are first considered through the system of cabinet committees, which is the engine of policy decision making in New Zealand government. Cabinet committee decisions of the previous week are reviewed by the full cabinet and are not effective until confirmed (Cabinet Office, 1991; 3C). The number, terms of reference and composition of the cabinet committees are set by the prime minister. There are currently twelve standing cabinet committees, some established on a sectoral basis and some on a functional basis. Committees are chaired by senior ministers and meet at set times each week. Any cabinet minister may attend any cabinet committee, and ministers outside the cabinet may attend with respect to items within their responsibility. Any minister may forward a paper for consideration.

Public servants interact with the cabinet through their own minister, and usually prepare cabinet papers on their minister's behalf. Ad hoc interdepartmental committees of public servants are often established, and the current National administration favors the use of standing committees of public servants to improve coordination throughout government (Boston, 1992: 98). Public servants may not attend full cabinet meetings (Cabinet Office, 1991: 3DP-D11). Recent administrations' practices have differed as to whether public servants attend cabinet committees; they did (and do) under National, but did not under Labour, though they were often called in for questioning.

Form of a collective decision

One of the elements of the doctrine of collective responsibility is unanimity (see M. Palmer 1992, 1993). This deems cabinet decisions to have been made unanimously and provides that all cabinet decisions must be publicly supported by all cabinet ministers. The accompanying confidentiality element of collective responsibility requires intracabinet discussions to be kept secret. The penalty for breach of collective responsibility is resignation – a real penalty that was invoked, for example, in 1982 and 1991.

There are exceptions to unanimity and confidentiality. The New Zealand Official Information Act of 1982 may allow onlookers to identify differences of ministerial opinion. Ministers sometimes leak information to advance their personal interests vis-à-vis other ministers. More subtly, a minister may publicly stake out a personal position on an issue prior to cabinet discussion and decision. Strong differences of opinion within the New Zealand cabinet do sometimes find their way into the media to varying extents, but on the whole the cabinet maintains the unanimity element of collective responsibility – consistent with its electoral incentive for party unity.

It is extremely difficult to flout collective cabinet decisions once they have been made. The cabinet office drafts and disseminates cabinet minutes (known as cabinet "greens"). Where there is a written submission the minutes will usually, though not always, follow the wording of one of the recommendations. Cabinet minutes are reviewed and sometimes amended by the prime minister or the chair of the relevant committee. They go to all cabinet ministers and relevant ministers outside the cabinet, and, via ministers' offices, to appropriate chief executives throughout the public service (Cabinet Office, 1991: 4/11). Consequently, each department is aware of the cabinet's relevant decisions. Cabinet minutes may even be the subject of Official Information Act requests; decisions are often announced publicly by the relevant minister, or in the prime minister's regular postcabinet press conference.

Furthermore, in 1988 the cabinet established a new regime to monitor the implementation of cabinet and cabinet committee decisions (Cabinet Office, 1991: CO(91)26). It systematically identifies the action taken to implement each cabinet and committee decision on a periodic basis, bringing it to the personal attention of the relevant chief executive and, if necessary, to the attention of the full cabinet. Otherwise, detection of deliberate flouting is likely to occur through interdepartmental contact, if not through inquiries by interest groups and media. Public servants have career incentives to refuse requests by their minister to ignore a cabinet decision. A minister may be able to take advantage of his or her department's skill at providing reasonable excuses for delaying implementation of a cabinet decision; but to the extent that other public servants realize what is going on, such action is likely to become an issue with other ministers. As Breton (1991: 24–5) argues with respect to Canada, the public service in this way helps to enforce policy equilibrium within the cabinet system.[6]

ISSUES DECIDED COLLECTIVELY

Four circumstances can be identified as requiring a collective cabinet decision on an issue: when the law requires; when public-expenditure procedures require; when the issue has interdepartmental implications; and when an issue is politically sensitive. Law and expenditure procedures are, in the long run, endogenous to cabinet decisions. Interdepartmental issues occur in any government. Political sensitivity precisely reflects the reasons already suggested for the dominance of collective over individual decision making in New Zealand – the effect on the reputation of the cabinet, especially the image of party unity.

Law. International treaties and agreements require consideration by the cabinet as a whole. The cabinet is also the usual repository of the statutory power to make regulations and appointments (Cabinet Office, 1991: 1 D and 5 A26–31). Since the cabinet has effective control over the formulation of such statutory powers through its dominance of the legislative process, this can be a significant source of cabinet power.

Public expenditure. Overall budgetary priorities and parameters, and many subsidiary issues, are matters for collective cabinet decision (Cabinet Office, 1991: 3/App. 2). Under the current committee structure the Cabinet Strategy Committee establishes the government's total strategic policy and the limits of overall government expenditure, as well as the fiscal limits and general directions for sectoral committees. The Expenditure Control Committee, working with a corresponding officials' committee, makes recommendations to the Strategy Committee concerning the allocation of resources among competing outcomes and sectors. It is able to review proposed levels of resource use (in consultation with the relevant minister) and to scrutinize the proposed mix of departmental outputs. The sectoral committees make recommendations on fiscal limits within their sector in terms of the overall limits, and consider ministers' proposals in excess of their own financial authorities.

Many of the overall parameters set collectively are broad and strategic, reflecting the inherent need to prioritize across portfolios. In these sorts of discussions, which affect the very nature of a minister's portfolio, an individual minister will simply be one voice among many. Collective cabinet decisions may even affect the relationship between programs within the same department. There, the responsible minister often has significant, but not decisive, influence in cabinet decision making, but has comparatively limited scope unilaterally to alter items. Public expenditure is an important collective constraint on individual ministerial autonomy.

Interdepartmental issues. Interdepartmental implications pervade most of the interesting public policy issues in New Zealand. Their resolution is institutionalized through the structure and procedures of cabinet committees. Committee agendas are dominated by papers requiring comment by a variety of interested departments. The *Cabinet Manual* specifies that the onus is on the department and minister initiating a policy proposal to ensure that all relevant organizations are consulted at the earliest possible stage, and that their views are accurately reflected in the submission (Cabinet Office, 1991; 3B2 and 4/2–3). Misrepresentation of others' views can be grounds for the cabinet office returning the submission or noting the variation in its summary.

The need for interdepartmental consultation is inherent in many issues, both significant and trivial. The *Cabinet Office Manual* sets out a list of the broad policy areas in which each of thirty-three departments or ministries has an interest (Cabinet Office, 1991: 4/App. 1). Eleven organizations are identified by the Cabinet Office as having "horizontal responsibilities" across sectoral policy areas. The Department of the Prime Minister and Cabinet has responsibility for "all policy issues likely to have implications for government as a whole or on the coordination of the business of government," and the Treasury is concerned with "all proposals with economic, revenue or fiscal implications." In twenty-two broad policy areas, the smallest number of other government agencies concerned with any area is six, and the average number of agencies per area is eleven. The importance of consultation has been institutionalized in an official form that must be signed by the initiating department and minister with respect to the interdepartmental consultations undertaken for every submission to the cabinet or its committee.

Political sensitivity. The broadest category of potential issues taken to the cabinet or its committees are those with political implications. A minister's identification of an issue as politically sensitive enough to warrant collective consideration is, of course, partly a function of that minister's personality, operating style, and time horizon. Some ministers feel less confident of their own judgment, and some feel more protective of their own independence. However, a number of incentives affect the decision on whether to consult. A former Labour minister for finance, David Caygill, suggests a useful rule of thumb: would the cabinet expect to have heard of this matter before they read it in the newspapers? The *Cabinet Office Manual* suggests that "ministers should put before their colleagues the sort of issues on which they themselves would wish to be consulted" (Cabinet Office, 1991: 3/2 B1).

Using political sensitivity as a criterion for submission of an issue to collective cabinet decision making is related to the weight given by cabinet ministers to electoral perceptions of their party. Actions and omissions by the cabinet are the most important defining elements of the electorate's perceptions of the governing party, and of the governing party's and the caucus's perceptions of the cabinet. The electoral incentive for party unity and the reinforcing mechanism of collective responsibility and cabinet decision-making procedures make it difficult for any individual minister to disassociate himself or herself from a cabinet decision. The cabinet's collective decisions thus affect the reputation of each cabinet minister in the electorate, the party, and the caucus.

Each member of the cabinet thus has a strong reputational incentive to convince the cabinet to make policy decisions he or she agrees with, and to dissuade it from decisions with which he or she does not agree. Otherwise a New Zealand cabinet minister will have to administer a program or implement a decision with which he or she does not fully agree. In turn, each minister has a derived incentive to bring politically sensitive issues to the cabinet. If a minister does not do so, or misjudges the sensitivity, he or she may expect to face criticism from cabinet colleagues, a public reprimand from the prime minister or, potentially, the ultimate withdrawal of the veil of collective responsibility from his or her individual actions. Nevertheless, a minister's persistent recourse to the cabinet with politically trivial issues having no interdepartmental implications will also frustrate colleagues.

In addition to the incentive to make collective decisions, each minister has corresponding incentives to commit to the process of collective decision making. Relitigation and reversal of settled cabinet decisions also affect the reputation of cabinet ministers and the electoral perception of party unity. Ordinarily, all elements in a New Zealand cabinet recognize a cabinet decision as binding and final, when arrived at with deliberation and full information through the normal cabinet processes. When a minister attempts to relitigate an important cabinet decision that satisfies these conditions, or attempts to push through a decision that does not, the potential for public splits and bloodletting rises dramatically. Both of these factors were manifested in the public divisions that lay behind the downfall of the fourth Labour government (see Boston, 1990: 74–6).

Broad strategic policy directions of the government, in economic policy for example, are the most important topics of New Zealand cabinet discussion because of their inherent long-term political effects. At the other extreme, an issue might be trivial in terms of public policy but still be brought to the cabinet because of its political sensitivity. Many routine items on the agenda of the cabinet or its committees seem to be there because of their inherent potential political sensitivity. For example, all significant government appointments go to the Cabinet Honours and

Appointments Committee. Almost any aspect of any issue has the potential to cause political trouble given a particular set of circumstances. Correspondingly, cabinet discussion often focuses on only those aspects of an issue that are politically sensitive.

It is also important to note that political sensitivity can be defined in terms of either electoral or intraparty politics. The New Zealand cabinet devotes significant attention to tactics, and to managing announcements and public events for electoral gain. Nevertheless, some issues may be discussed in the cabinet only because they are of interest to the government caucus or the extraparliamentary wing of the governing party. Proposals to implement party manifesto commitments are required to go before the cabinet (Cabinet Office, 1991: 3E). Indeed, the New Zealand cabinet occasionally deals with purely intraparty squabbles.

Process of collective decision making

Of course, ministers can and do meet at any time, anywhere, in person or by phone, formally or informally. The ultimate forum of decision making is, however, the cabinet (see G. Palmer, 1992). At full cabinet and at cabinet committee meetings, depending on the issue, there is discussion among the ministers present. In committees, public servants are often questioned on particular points. After discussion and in the presence of the other ministers, who may object, it lies with the chair to formulate a decision. The decision, but not the discussion, is recorded by an officer of the Cabinet Office. In the event of strong disagreement between ministers, the chair can formulate a decision that favors one side or that compromises between the two sides; he or she may also defer the decision for further consideration.

The chair's task of formulating the cabinet's decision has been called "the fine art of cabinet government" by a former British prime minister (Wilson, 1985: 39), and indeed involves a complicated calculation of conflicting interests. It is difficult to characterize cabinet decision making in terms of a clear voting rule. Sometimes a prime minister will take a poll of views to help confirm the sense of the meeting, but there are no votes.

A minister will be interested in contributing to collective decision making depending on the issue, his or her portfolio and personal policy interests. When an issue has interdepartmental implications, the ministers concerned will be briefed on their department's views. Some ministers will not advance departmental views they personally disagree with; others will advise their colleagues of their department's views as well as their own. All ministers can be expected to be interested in general public-expenditure decisions and politically sensitive matters.

Not all ministers have equal influence in the cabinet. Four to six senior ministers usually emerge as the crucial decision makers in any cabinet. These ministers are important in setting the strategic political policy directions of the government. They monitor all cabinet decisions, especially in terms of political sensitivity. This group of significant players always includes the prime minister and the minister of finance, and usually includes the deputy prime minister. The minister of finance is most directly concerned with the administration of money, the factor most able to inhibit the implementation of a cabinet's and an individual minister's agenda. Between 1975 and 1984 the National prime minister, Sir Robert Muldoon, allocated himself the finance portfolio and aggregated a tremendous amount of personal power within the cabinet. The deputy prime minister assists the prime minister in coordinating and overseeing the government, and is acting prime minister when the prime minister is out of the country. Generally, the natural role of the deputy prime minister is to complement the prime minister's public presentational role with more discrete attention to intragovernmental administration and firefighting in the cabinet, caucus, and party (Palmer, 1987: 68–9).

The prime minister personifies the governing party for the electorate, for the governing party itself, and to a lesser extent for the government caucus. This makes the prime minister's role vital to the cabinet with respect to every arena simultaneously (see Alley, 1992; G. Palmer, 1992, Chapter 7). He or she has the most acute incentives to advance the party's and cabinet's reputation, including the image of party unity and the corresponding commitment to collective decision making. The prime minister maintains the effectiveness of the collective cabinet decision-making process and monitors policy decisions in all portfolios when they become politically sensitive. For help in this, the prime minister has the Department of the Prime Minister and Cabinet, though it is not large by international standards. With the deputy prime minister, the prime minister must fight fires in the cabinet; hold ministerial hands and occasionally slap them; and monitor all cabinet decisions and present them to the caucus, the party, and the electorate.

The prime minister has the constitutional power to dissolve Parliament and call an election, as well as the political role of leading the governing party in Parliament and election campaigns. The prime minister chairs the cabinet and government caucus, allocates portfolios, designs the cabinet committee structure, and usually chairs an important committee. A National prime minister appoints cabinet ministers, and the prime minister in both parties can sack ministers, although this power is exercised only occasionally.[7] As a matter of institutional power, the New Zealand prime minister dominates his or her cabinet colleagues. However, the extent of this dominance is less than it is in many other single-party majority government systems, such as Greece (Koutsoukis, 1994) or Britain. The New Zealand prime minister works among highly developed norms and procedures of collective cabinet decision making. Like all ministers, the prime minister recognizes that decisions have to be made, and on most issues will accept an unwelcome decision if it clearly reflects the collective will of the cabinet.

The picture of collective cabinet decision making in New Zealand is a complicated one. The electoral importance of party unity enables the cabinet, through the mechanism of collective responsibility and its own procedures, to overrule individual ministers. Each minister faces strong incentives to take certain issues to the cabinet for collective decisions. A minister does have a good deal of policy-making discretion with respect to issues that do not fall within any of these categories and, within his or her jurisdiction, has an opportunity to influence cabinet deliberations on issues that do come up for collective deliberation.

THE CABINET AND THE GOVERNING PARTY

According to the analysis just presented, the electoral incentive for unity operates on the party. The cabinet contains the most senior and powerful party members in Parliament and, while the party is in government, dominates party decision making. However, the government caucus – and to a lesser extent the extraparliamentary party – possesses the ultimate power to end the life of the cabinet. In this sense, these two are parts of the collective decision-making machinery of New Zealand government. It must be recognized that the commitment to collective decision making applies to these institutions as well as to the cabinet (see Chapman, 1989).

The government caucus

The government MPs together constitute the government caucus. Caucus meetings in both parties are held every Thursday morning and are also attended by the most senior members of extraparliamentary party organizations. The prime minister creates caucus committees (eighteen under the current government; Ringer, 1991: 67), which are often structured along sectoral lines and report to the full caucus.

Intracaucus disagreements are often vigorous in substance and expression; yet the government caucus is subject to the same pressures for unity as the cabinet. The weekly proceedings of the caucus are secret, and the prime minister is the only official spokesperson afterward. All caucus members are expected to abide by caucus decisions, which are often made by vote, and are expected to vote the caucus line in Parliament. New Zealand MPs are well aware that public splits in the government caucus will negatively affect the public image of the government, and thus their own reelectability.

Prima facie, the cabinet–caucus relationship is dominated by the cabinet (G. Palmer, 1992: 141–3). Indeed, the twenty cabinet ministers, the four or more ministers outside the cabinet, the two whips, and the chair and deputy chair of committees often constitute a majority of the New Zealand government caucus. One political scientist refers to this development as the "fortress cabinet," with a central keep and outer-works (Chapman, 1989: 22). The small size of the government caucus enhances the efficacy of intracaucus social acceptance and status as selective incentives in producing party unity (McLeay, 1987: 281–3). Related to this, every caucus member aspires to cabinet rank and, with enough experience and ability, has a reasonable expectation of attaining it. Caucus members thus have strong incentives to submit to the judgment of the collective cabinet in matters of policy and electoral strategy.

The prime minister chairs the caucus, and the cabinet often acts collectively in lobbying the caucus. One of the most important weapons held by the cabinet is the power of information. A minister may also influence caucus members by employing minor powers of patronage, by responding favorably to caucus members' inquiries on behalf of constituents, and by drawing on extensive political experience and contacts. Nonetheless, this relationship is not always one-sided. A potentially significant adverse effect on re-electability is often likely to outweigh the persuasive advantages held by the cabinet. Cabinet ministers thus have incentives to engage in a dialogue with the caucus with respect to politically sensitive issues. When a government caucus feels insufficiently consulted by the cabinet on a decision with adverse political implications, it may well revolt and amend or reverse a cabinet decision. This has happened several times in the current large National government caucus, on major items of announced cabinet policy.

The caucus has an ultimate power of appointment over the cabinet – directly in the Labour Party and indirectly, through the leader, in the National Party. Ultimately, the government caucus could defeat a cabinet proposal if sufficient numbers voted against it in Parliament; ultimately, it could bring down the government on a vote of confidence. This is unlikely to happen since this would force an election that might threaten the political survival of those voting, however. Cabinet ministers and caucus members all know this, which helps explain the cabinet's dominance over the caucus in the ordinary course of events. However, the ability to bring down the cabinet can be seen as a source of ultimate caucus power over it.

The extraparliamentary party

The broadest definition of decision-making structures of the governing party includes the extraparliamentary wing, important to both main parties in New Zealand. Party members provide crucial financial and organizational support in fighting election campaigns, and constitute the core of a party's claim to represent New Zealanders. Each main party has organizations in every electorate, and at regional and national levels, in order to select the party candidates for Parliament, to organize and finance the party election campaigns, and to develop party policy platforms.

There is inevitably considerable tension between the extraparliamentary wing of a governing party and the parliamentary wing, especially in cabinet (e.g., G. Palmer, 1992: 143–8). Party election manifestos are inherently incomplete documents, and party policies often appear in a different light to cabinet ministers when analyzed in the circumstances of government; sometimes they even seem impossible for a responsible government to implement. The cabinet usually dominates the extraparliamentary wing of the governing party since the cabinet has the constitutional power to govern, its members are elected as MPs, and its actions define the party's reputation. It has many resources at its disposal. Perhaps most important, the cabinet can invoke the electoral incentive to preserve the appearance of party unity. However, the electoral incentive is much less effective with respect to the extraparliamentary wing of the governing party than it is with respect to elected members of the caucus. At some point, individual party members will value their policy ideals over the damage to the party's electoral fortunes arising from speaking out or resigning.

LEGISLATIVE–EXECUTIVE RELATIONS

Government control, confidence, and caretakers

The governing party in New Zealand is sufficiently disciplined to control the outcome of votes in Parliament, except with respect to the few issues that are treated as matters of conscience (such as abortion, homosexual law reform, and capital punishment). The government caucus has traditionally been small enough to be able to whip effectively. Rule 227 of the Labour Party constitution even requires each party nominee for election to sign a pledge that "if elected, I will vote on all questions in accordance with the decisions of the Caucus of the Parliamentary Labour Party." Historically the National Party has experienced more votes against the caucus line by individual members, but even these have been small in number, and occasions of major controversy. Between 1936 and 1986 only thirty-eight MPs dissented from their party, representing about 1 percent of the total formal votes of the house. Of these, 91 percent were cast by National MPs (Jackson, 1989: 178). The present National government caucus has experienced more MPs crossing the floor than normal, due to its large size.

The cabinet's dominance of the government caucus and the caucus's control of Parliament means that the cabinet dominates Parliament. The cabinet's power can cover all parliamentary decision making, such as the passage of legislation, as well as the composition, chairing, and activities of select committees. Private members' bills, which raise issues of conscience, are perhaps the main exception to otherwise complete cabinet dominance of the parliamentary agenda. Even the formulation of standing orders that govern the procedures of Parliament is subject to the government's majority.

As in other parliamentary systems, a New Zealand cabinet requires the confidence of the majority of the House of Representatives in order to continue in office. The opposition periodically moves motions of no confidence for political reasons, primarily by way of amendment to a motion involving open-ended debate, such as Address in Reply (McGee, 1985: 59–62). Debates involving supply may also constitute an implied vote of confidence, and the government may declare any vote to be one of confidence. However, the prevalence of single-party majority governments in New Zealand negates the relevance of the confidence requirement. For a motion of no confidence to have any real possibility of succeeding, the governing party must be badly split. Such splits are likely to be resolved through the party's collective decision-making mechanism well before such a vote could succeed. The closest a modern government has come to such a split was in 1984, when a National government had to rely on the votes of two independent (former Labour) MPs to win a vote. This was cited by the prime minister as the reason for calling a general election four months early, though commentators suggested other reasons were behind the decision. Apart from this, the New Zealand governing party has not lost a vote of confidence since 1928.

For similar reasons, there have been no real caretaker governments in New Zealand in modern times. The situation most akin to it is the surrender of power after an election in which the government is defeated. This was clarified in New Zealand after a constitutional crisis in 1984 (Palmer, 1987: 34–8). The outgoing National prime minister, Sir Robert Muldoon, initially refused to follow the advice of the incoming Labour government to devalue the currency until convinced by colleagues to follow constitutional convention. The convention was stated as follows: the outgoing government will take no new policy initiatives; and on those matters of such great significance that they cannot be delayed, the outgoing government will act on the advice of the incoming government even if it disagrees with the proposed course of action.[8]

Legislation and select committees

Almost all enacted legislation is part of the government's legislative program (see Cabinet Office, 1991: 5A; Legislation Advisory Committee, 1987). The Cabinet Legislation Committee allocates a priority to each proposed bill. Once cabinet approval has been obtained with respect to the policy and financial aspects of proposed legislation, the responsible minister's department instructs parliamentary counsel in the drafting of legislation on the basis of the cabinet minutes. The responsible minister must then submit the draft bill to the Cabinet Legislation Committee and the full cabinet. The minister of justice or the Cabinet Legislation Committee may refer bills raising public-law issues to the Legislation Advisory Committee (a body of experts that may also make submissions to the select committee once the bill is introduced). If cabinet approval is forthcoming, the responsible minister presents the bill to the government caucus (this step is recognized in the *Cabinet Office Manual* itself; Cabinet Office, 1991: A14–16). At all stages, the content of legislation is confidential. Ironically, premature disclosure to nongovernment organizations is held to imply that the prerogative of Parliament is being usurped (Cabinet Office, 1991: A18).

Once a bill has been introduced into Parliament, it is guided through its stages by the responsible minister, supported by the other cabinet ministers and government MPs. During select-committee deliberation, the responsible minister's public servants ordinarily advise the committee (Cabinet Office, 1991: 5D4–5). The final step required to enact a bill into law is the governor-general's signature – given on the advice of his or her ministers. Throughout the parliamentary process, the responsible minister's guidance is subject to oversight by the cabinet.

The investigatory power of parliamentary select committees was expanded in 1985 by the cabinet (note the institutional identity of the decision maker here). Select committees were restructured; given considerable powers of inquiry into any aspect of policy, administration, or expenditure; and empowered to require a government response to every committee report (see *Standing Orders 1986;* part 33). The Regulations Review Committee has powers to require parliamentary debate of regulations. Ultimately, though, the governing party still has a majority on every select committee and chairs most of them. The relevant minister usually tries to maintain a good working relationship with the chair of the relevant select committee and may view the committee as a useful forum in which other party members and the public can comment on departmentally derived policy. However, the minister may or may not accept select-committee recommendations or legislative amendment, depending on their substantive effect, the motives behind the recommendations, and the effect on the cabinet's electoral strategy. The cabinet's dominance of the government caucus can easily extend to select committees if their activities get out of hand: the government's committee chair can be replaced. In 1985 the government abolished an entire subcommittee when its activities became politically and constitutionally embarrassing (Public Expenditure Committee, 1985).

The opposition

The only way in which an opposition can directly exert a substantive effect on the government is through delay. The parliamentary agenda is always full, and any government depends to some extent on opposition cooperation to get through it, especially at the end of a parliamentary session. However, the opposition must carefully judge the exercise of its rights to oppose. Continuous frustration of the government may cause it to complain that it must be able to implement its program, and may provoke the use of its majority to change parliamentary standing orders to effect that.

Thus, the real political power of the New Zealand Parliament is in the role of the opposition as electoral competitor to the governing party for the power to form a government. Elsewhere I have characterized the opposition role in Parliament as that of an electorally appointed monitoring agent of the governing party (M. Palmer, 1992: 13–14). The opposition seeks to embarrass the government by revealing damaging information and actions, by making electorally popular arguments, and generally by attempting to impose political costs on the government party that will hinder its electoral fortunes. Parliament is the opposition's primary forum from which to amplify the continual electoral competition (Skene, 1992: 255–8). As such, it does deserve acknowledgment as an important element of the Westminster constitution. Electoral competition is the primary check on New Zealand cabinet government (M. Palmer, 1992). Virtually all political incentives are ultimately derived from the electorate – including the incentive for the cabinet not to abuse its power over Parliament, and also including the incentive for party unity.

CONCLUSION

This chapter has suggested that the distinction between single-party majority government in New Zealand and coalition government is the electorally derived incentive for party unity. This incentive is translated into a commitment by individual cabinet ministers to collective party decision making (though note that Müller-Rommel argues elsewhere in this book that coalition governments are more likely to make collective decisions). The underlying premise of this system is undermined by individual ministerial autonomy. The chapter has canvassed the mechanisms by which collective cabinet decision making is adhered to, enforced, and implemented in the New Zealand system of government, particularly with respect to issues that are politically sensitive for the electorate, the party, or the caucus. It has also suggested that the collective decision-making structures and procedures of government include those of the governing party, its caucus, and its extraparliamentary organization. The role of the New Zealand Parliament is to focus electoral incentives on the decision making of the cabinet and the governing party.

The theoretical framework of this chapter derives from, but also differs from, Laver and Shepsle's work on coalition formation. It suggests a simple but powerful distinction between single-party majority government and coalition government, based on unity within the government and commitment to collective decision making. With respect to the New Zealand constitution, the three questions in Laver and Shepsle's introduction must be placed within the context of a single-party majority government. Relative to coalition governments, neither the allocation of cabinet portfolios between different individuals nor between different elements of the governing party makes much difference to policy outputs. The importance of collective cabinet decision making means that who is in the cabinet is more important than who has which portfolio. In New Zealand, at least, one cannot predict a government's policy positions from the allocation of cabinet portfolios.

This chapter also affirms the significance of theory. Laver and Shepsle's analysis of coalition government has impelled a reexamination of fundamental relationships in the New Zealand Westminster constitution. The resulting analysis provides a perspective that advances the understanding of this system, and enhances our ability to compare it with others.

NOTES

* This paper was written while the author was a doctoral candidate and Ford Foundation fellow in Public International Law at the Yale Law School. He has since returned to his position as public policy analyst with the New Zealand Treasury. Of course, nothing herein should be taken to represent the views of the New Zealand Treasury. The author gratefully acknowledges advice and comments from Jonathan Boston, the Hon. David Caygill, the Hon. Peter Dunne, Catherine Iorns, Gary Hawke, Lewis Holden, Michael Laver, the author's father,

the Rt. Hon. Sir Geoffrey Palmer, and Kenneth Shepsle. The author also acknowledges the stimulating dialogue at the Laver–Shepsle workshop at the ECPR's Limerick Joints Sessions, and the funding for his own participation provided by the Center for Studies in Law, Economics, and Public Policy at the Yale Law School.

1 Lijphart (1984: 16–19) cites New Zealand as "a virtually perfect example of the Westminster model of democracy."

2 During 1940–5 two Opposition MPs (who temporarily resigned from the Opposition caucus) were members of the War Cabinet, responsible for decisions relating to war matters (Wood, 1987: 46). Periodically, a third party gains substantial support in opinion polls but no such party has ever held more than two seats in Parliament (Wood, 1987, appendix 5). This may well change in the near future; 85 percent of those participating in a referendum in September 1992 voted to change the current electoral system and, of the alternatives, 70 percent favored the German system of proportional representation.

3 A notable example was the first term of the fourth Labour government, 1984–7. The free-market economic policies implemented by the cabinet were anathema to many party activists, but unity was broadly maintained because this was considered essential to winning a second term in office (Wilson, 1989: 91, 139).

4 The fourth Labour government affected the relationship between minister and public servant by its reforms of the powers and accountability of departments (Goldman and Brashares, 1991; Scott, Bushnell, and Sallee, 1990). The chief executive of each department is now appointed on a five-year contract and is responsible to his or her minister for the department efficiently undertaking its activities. Ministers focus on the policy outcomes they desire and the outputs they want the government to produce in order to achieve them, and provide financial resources to departments to produce them. The aim of these reforms is to allow departments greater flexibility to achieve their objectives and to provide better information with which to monitor departmental performance. The result may be a shift in individual ministers' attention toward broader strategic policy and prioritizing decisions, but it has been suggested that each department's attention has shifted in fact toward servicing their individual minister, thereby creating coordination problems in the government as a whole (see Boston, 1992).

5 The appointment was apparently designed to mute Mr. Peters's criticism of his leader according to Lyndon Johnson's dictate, "I'd rather have him inside the tent pissing out than outside the tent pissing in." Mr. Peters increased in stridence until he was finally dropped in a cabinet reshuffle in 1991 to the comparative freedom of the backbenches.

6 Unlike Breton's account, the New Zealand public-service machinery is geared to enforcing cabinet decisions of any kind, not just those the public service favors. This paper also differs from Breton with respect to his rejection of party as an equilibrating element (1991: 24–5). The public service helps to enforce and therefore equilibrate policy decisions within the cabinet system; but this chapter emphasizes the primary incentive for equilibration as cabinet ministers' incentives to be committed to collective decision making. This emanates from the incentive for *party* unity.

7 The first two National prime ministers, Sid Holland and Keith Holyoake, required their ministers to sign undated letters of resignation for the prime minister to hold during the ministry (Marshall, 1989: 7).

8 The Constitution Act of 1986 clarified the situation by redefining the criteria for

becoming an MP - enabling a new administration to be sworn in immediately after an election if necessary (Officials Committee, 1986).

REFERENCES

Alley, Roderic. 1992. The powers of the prime minister. In Hyam Gold (ed.), *New Zealand Politics in Perspective*. 3d ed. Auckland: Longman Paul.

Boston, Jonathan. 1990. The cabinet and policy making under the fourth Labour government. In Martin Holland and Jonathan Boston (eds.), *The Fourth Labour Government: Politics and Policy in New Zealand*. 2d ed. Auckland: Oxford University Press.

1992. The problems of policy coordination: the New Zealand experience. *Governance* 5: 88–103.

Breton, Albert. 1991. The organization of competition in congressional and parliamentary governments. In Albert Breton, Gianluigi Galeotti, Pierre Salmon and Ronald Wintrobe (eds.). *The Competitive State: Villa Colombella Papers on Competitive Politics*. Dordrecht: Kluwer Academic Publishers.

Cabinet Office, The. 1991. *The Cabinet Office Manual*. Wellington.

Chapman, Robert. 1989. Political culture: the purposes of party and the current challenge. In Hyam Gold (ed.), *New Zealand Politics in Perspective*. 2d ed. Auckland: Longman Paul.

Gold, Hyam (ed.). 1992. *New Zealand Politics in Perspective*. 3d ed. Auckland: Longman Paul.

Goldman, Frances, and Edith Brashares. 1991. Performance and accountability: budget reform in New Zealand. *Public Budgeting and Finance* 11: 75–85.

Gregory, R. J. 1991. The attitudes of senior public servants in Australia and New Zealand: Administrative reform and technocratic consequence? *Governance* 4: 295–331.

Jackson, Keith. 1989 [1992]. Caucus: the anti-parliament system? In Hyam Gold (ed.), *New Zealand Politics in Perspective*. 2d [3d] ed. Auckland: Longman Paul.

Klein, Benjamin, and Keith Leffler. 1981. The role of market forces in assuring contractual performance. *Journal of Political Economy* 89: 615–41.

Koutsoukis, Kleomenis S. 1994. Institutional dynamics and leadership style in cabinet decision making of the Hellenic Republic (1974–1990). In Michael Laver and Kenneth A. Shepsle (eds.). *Cabinet Ministers and Parliamentary Government*. Cambridge University Press.

Laver, Michael, and Kenneth A. Shepsle. 1990. Coalitions and cabinet government. *American Political Science Review* 84: 873–90.

1991. Divided government: America is not "exceptional." *Governance* 4: 250–69.

(in press). *Making and Breaking Government*. Cambridge University Press.

Legislation Advisory Committee. 1987. *Legislative Change; Guidelines on Process and Content*. Wellington: Department of Justice.

1989. *Departmental Statutes*. Wellington: Department of Justice.

Lijphart, Arend. 1984. *Democracies: Patterns of Majoritarian and Consensus Government in Twenty-One Countries*. New Haven, Conn.: Yale University Press.

Marshall, John. 1989. *Memoirs. Volume Two: 1960–1988*. Auckland: Collins.

McGee, David. 1985. *Parliamentary Practice in New Zealand*. Wellington: Government Printer.

McLeay, Elizabeth M. 1987. Selection versus election: choosing cabinets in New Zealand. In Harold D. Clarke and Moshe M. Czudnowski (eds.), *Political Elites in Anglo-American Democracies: Changes in Stable Regimes*. DeKalb: Northern Illinois University Press.

Moe, Terry M. 1984. The new economics of organization. *American Journal of Political Science* 28: 739–77.

Officials Committee. 1986. *Reports: Constitutional Reform*. Wellington: Department of Justice.

Palmer, Geoffrey. 1987. *Unbridled Power: An Interpretation of New Zealand's Constitution and Government*. 2d ed. Auckland: Oxford University Press.
 1992. *New Zealand's Constitution in Crisis: Reforming our Political System*. Dunedin: John McIndoe.

Palmer, Matthew S. R. 1992. The Economics of Organization and Ministerial Responsibility: Towards a Framework of Analysis for Westminster Government. Paper presented at the Graduate School of International Relations and Pacific Studies, University of Calfornia, San Diego.
 1993. The conventional wisdom of ministerial responsibility in New Zealand. In Mai Chen and Geoffrey Palmer (eds.), *Public Law in New Zealand: Cases and Materials*. Auckland: Oxford University Press.

Public Expenditure Committee. 1985. Report on Inquiry into Devaluation. *Appendix to the Journals of the House of Representatives* 12: l.12.C. Wellington.

Ringer, J. B. 1991. *An Introduction to New Zealand Government: A Guide to Finding Out about Government in New Zealand, Its Institutions, Structures and Activities*. Christchurch: Hazard Press.

Scott, G., P. Bushnell, and N. Sallee. 1990. Reform of the core public sector: New Zealand experience. *Governance*. 3: 138–67.

Skene Geoff. 1989 [1992]. Parliament: reassessing its role. In Hyam Gold (ed.), *New Zealand politics in perspective*. 2d [3d] ed. Auckland: Longman Paul.

State Services Commission. 1990. *Public Service Code of Conduct*. Wellington: State Services Commission.

White, Graham. 1994. The interpersonal dynamics of decision-making processes in Canadian provincial cabinets. In Michael Laver and Kenneth A. Shepsle (eds.), *Cabinet Ministers and Parliamentary Government*. Cambridge University Press.

Williamson, Oliver E. 1985. *The Economic Institutions of Capitalism: Firms, Markets, Relational Contracting*. New York: Free Press.

Wilson, Harold. 1985. A prime minister at work. In A. King (ed.), *The British Prime Minister*. 2d ed. Durham, N.C.: Duke University Press.

Wilson, Margaret. 1989. *Labour in Government, 1984–1987*. Wellington: Allen & Unwin.

Wood, G. A. (ed.). 1987. *Ministers and Members in the New Zealand Parliament*. Dunedin: Tarkwode Press.

15

The interpersonal dynamics of decision making in Canadian provincial cabinets

Graham White

Any approach to understanding cabinets in parliamentary systems must address the fundamental tension between cabinets as collegial, collective, decision-making bodies and cabinets as aggregations of individual, autonomous ministers heading government departments.

The interpersonal dynamics of cabinet influence not only ministerial autonomy but the nature and substance of cabinet decisions. If the cabinet is to be viewed as more than a mysterious black box, the interpersonal dynamics of ministers must be treated seriously. Matthew Palmer's chapter in this volume elegantly develops an interpretation of cabinet decision making in single-party majority, Westminster-style cabinets like those found in Canada (both nationally and provincially). In Canada, as in New Zealand, different single-party majority governments clearly produce different policies. Also as in New Zealand, portfolio allocation between different parties in a government coalition does not arise. This chapter is thus premised on a positive response to a third question: does the allocation of cabinet portfolios *within* parties matter? It examines the extent of collegiality and individuality in Canadian provincial cabinets by exploring the interpersonal dynamics of ministers in the decision-making process. It is an attempt to deal with the interplay of personality, friendship, conflict, reciprocity, and the like within the cabinet. A further goal is to understand how these variables are influenced by cabinet norms and structures, by the first minister, by ministerial shuffles, and by other factors.

The data for this study come from 147 personal interviews with ministers, former ministers, bureaucrats (mostly in central agencies) and senior political advisers (mainly in premiers' offices) in four Canadian provinces – Nova Scotia, Ontario, Manitoba, and British Columbia.[1] The period under study is 1969 to the present. Provincial cabinets were chosen for study over the national cabinet because they offered easier access to ministers and to cabinet officials, better comparative possibilities, and a larger field of potential interviewees. Except as they are affected by the larger scale of the national government, the findings of this paper should also apply to cabinet dynamics in Ottawa.

CANADIAN PROVINCIAL CABINETS

Canadian provinces are among the most powerful subnational governments in the world. The only fields in which they are inactive are foreign affairs, defense, and monetary policy. Although the federal government provides a good deal of their funding through shared-cost programs and unconditional block grants, the provinces exercise principal or exclusive jurisdiction over natural resources, education, health, social welfare, labor relations, and local government. Jurisdiction over other fields, such as transportation, justice, economic development, and the environment is shared in varying degrees between the provinces and central government. Few constitutional proscriptions limit the provinces' scope for taxation. In short, the range of activities within the provincial remit is not far removed from that of independent nation-states.

Canadian first ministers are, even by usual Westminster standards, unusually powerful vis-à-vis their cabinets. A premier is chosen not by cabinet or by the parliamentary caucus but by the party. Party leaders in Canada are elected at conventions of party activists; voting delegates may number a thousand or more at such conventions. (In some provinces, leaders are now elected by direct or indirect vote of the entire party membership.) Leaders may be subjected to intense cabinet or caucus pressure to resign, but should they refuse, only their parties, assembled in convention, have authority to remove them. Resort to this avenue is slow, expensive, public, highly destructive to the party, and of uncertain outcome. Premiers' power over their cabinets reflects the limited degree to which they are beholden to their ministers for their position.

Premiers alone appoint, shuffle, and remove ministers, though they face a host of political constraints in making their choices. Most notable of these is the Canadian obsession with representative cabinets. Doubtless prime ministers everywhere choose their ministers with a view to the interests they represent, but in Canada representativeness in cabinet construction has been raised to the status of holy writ (Campbell, 1985). Region ranks as the first and foremost criterion, but language, ethnicity, gender, and ties to economic interests are also important considerations. In addition, of course, a premier must include representatives of the various tendencies and factions in his party.

Pressure to appoint ministers to represent as many regions, groups, and interests as possible makes for provincial cabinets substantially larger than they need to be for administrative purposes. The larger provinces routinely have between twenty-five and thirty ministers, and even smaller provinces have cabinets of fifteen to twenty.

Size of the cabinet has important consequences for cabinet processes and internal dynamics (White, 1990), particularly in light of the limited talent pools from which ministers are drawn (most provincial legislatures have fewer than eighty members). The most able members of the legislative assembly (MLAs) on the government side become ministers but, beyond the first rank, representativeness often outweighs talent. W. A. Matheson's observation about the national cabinet applies with equal force to the provinces: "Every cabinet must contain at least a few dullards or nonentities to represent important interests" (Matheson, 1976: 29).

In terms of structural arrangements, substantial variation is evident across the four provinces and indeed within provinces over time. Throughout the period under study, the Ontario cabinet has had an extensive committee system to review proposals on their way to the cabinet (which often has meant effectively deciding them), supported by several central agencies. Other provinces have had no cabinet committees beyond a Treasury Board for scrutiny of proposed expenditures, so that the full cabinet makes almost all decisions. Turnovers of government have sometimes brought dramatic changes to the cabinet decision-making process. Overall, the long-term trend within all provinces has been toward more complex, institutionalized decision-making processes and away from an unaided plenary cabinet as the exclusive decision-making body (Dunn, 1991).

Two additional features are common in provincial cabinets. First, although an individual cabinet committee (and by extension its members) may become especially powerful, no provincial cabinet has ever been structured – even informally – in tiers, with an "inner" cabinet and an "outer" cabinet. Second, with few exceptions, the business of Canadian provincial cabinets consists of reviewing submissions and proposals brought forward for approval by individual ministers. Thus, ministerial interaction is principally structured around decisions to approve, reject, or amend proposals sponsored by ministers; it is narrowly focused on specifics rather than on nebulous ideas or goals.

COLLEGIALITY, CONFLICT, AND RECIPROCITY IN THE CABINET

Conflict and collegiality

According to the ministers interviewed, cabinets are far less conflictual than is commonly believed. Putting forward strongly held views is, in their opinion, not at all incompatible with a collegial, consensual form of decision making. Much depends on how vehemently ministers are prepared to promote their views, how personally they take disagreement, and whether there are repercussions for future cabinet decisions.

Ministers overwhelmingly agreed that, with relatively few exceptions, they and their colleagues do not harbor grudges or serious ill feelings toward other ministers when they fail to get their way in the cabinet. Disagreements and disappointments, it was widely agreed, are not taken personally. This norm of impersonality in debate means that ministers can and do put their views to the cabinet forcefully, and engage their colleagues in vigorous debate, without having disagreements over particular policies sour a close and essentially harmonious relationship.

A number of factors help explain what may seem a surprisingly low level of conflict in Canadian provincial cabinets. First, politicians are constantly exposed to conflict and may thus come to accept as routine and unexceptional what to others is a significant level of it. Politicians are by nature assertive and often emotional, but at the same time are often thick-skinned and prepared to forgive and forget after a cathartic release of words. More than one minister likened cabinet to a tightly-knit family given to emotional outbursts; "We had," said one minister, "intense feelings but intense loyalties as well." Furthermore, some ministers may be grounding their assessment of the degree of cabinet conflict in an implicit comparison with their legislatures, which are relentlessly adversarial and highly conflictual.

Second, not all cabinet decision making necessarily involves disagreement. It is easy to lose sight of how much cabinet work involves routine, uncontroversial decisions that are not zero-sum situations with winners and losers. Often cabinet discussion is best understood not as conflict between opposing points of view, but as a process by which ministers initiating policy proposals convince their colleagues of the proposals' merits and relieve their doubts. Even for major issues with two irreconcilable options, it may be a misconception to assume that two strongly opposed factions are in conflict; most ministers may well be able to see both the merits of and problems with each alternative, and to struggle toward a better solution.

Nor, third, should one minister's comment that "cabinet conflict is mainly media hype" be discounted. If politicians are quick to blame the media for all manner of ills, it is also true that conflict is the lifeblood of the political media. Ministers argued that, whereas the media like to portray ministers as winners and losers, ministers tend not to think in such terms (though some ministers certainly perceived the cabinet in precisely that way). Moreover, significant conflict within government need not necessarily reflect cabinet conflict. What appear to be conflicts between ministers may in reality be conflicts between bureaucrats; as one premier remarked, "Ministries do the fighting in government, not ministers" (Miller, 1986).

Reciprocity

Reciprocity can involve an explicitly negotiated *quid pro quo* arrangement between ministers – a deal. It can also be a more nebulous process whereby, without even informal communication, ministers extend support to colleagues either in expectation of unspecified future benefits or in return for earlier support.

To a remarkable degree, ministers in Canadian provincial cabinets reject the view that reciprocity plays an important role in cabinet decision making. Several ministers with a decade or more of experience in the cabinet stated that they had never been offered any deals by colleagues; a few others indicated that they had only once or twice been approached by colleagues to trade support for one another's projects. Ministers from all provinces and all governing parties contended, some with considerable vehemence, that very little general reciprocity, let alone explicit horse trading, characterized cabinet processes. They stressed that, contrary to the public perception, ministers respond to policy proposals on their merits rather than on the basis of favors owed to other ministers or of backroom deals. Virtually all ministers said that lobbying colleagues, in order to gain their support for proposals coming before the cabinet, was part of the normal cabinet process. Most maintained, however, that these were attempts to convince colleagues of the proposals' merits and that no debts were incurred in this way.

If specific deals tend to be exceptional, the more subtle forms of reciprocity appear to be rather more common. Although a substantial minority of ministers denied that even a vague sense of reciprocity was present in the cabinet, a larger group indicated that, although there were few explicit deals among ministers, implicit understandings among ministers were common. Even in this group, however, almost all noted that, if tacit reciprocity occurred, it was on relatively minor matters rather than on major policies. Moreover, it was also widely held that ministers would support a proposal in return for an earlier favor only so long as they had no serious objections to it; in the words of one minister, reciprocity "goes on within the framework of one's principles."

Individualism and collectivism

The contrast between individualism and collectivity in the cabinet has two distinct components. First, to what extent do ministers approach cabinet decision making as individuals or as part of a collective enterprise? Second, what autonomy is permitted ministers to develop policy independent of the cabinet? In turn, the autonomy question may be further subdivided into the issue of what scope ministers enjoy to pursue policy without requiring cabinet approval, and the very different issue of ministers willfully disregarding cabinet decisions.

In speaking of the cabinet, ministers repeatedly employed the metaphor of a sports team, in which individual talents and achievements have to be subsumed into a collective effort. Accordingly, they stressed the value of teamwork and team play by ministers. The old bromide about hanging together lest they hang separately was also cited by several of those interviewed. The appreciation of the need for teamwork, however, did not obscure the recognition that pursuit of individual interests often detracted from genuine collective decision making. An Ontario Liberal minister commented that when he first entered the cabinet, "I thought it was a team game, but found out that this was a naive view; some ministers saw their political status determined by what they could get through cabinet or how much money they could get for their ministries." If the cabinet is a team, he explained, it is a track team, in which ministers not only seek to secure team objectives, but also compete against one another for individual recognition.

This minister was by no means alone in identifying ability to get proposals through the cabinet as a central element in ministers' evaluations of one another's success. On balance, however, more ministers portrayed the cabinet as engaging a truly collective process in which ministers were usually willing to compromise and to subsume their interests into the larger good. According to senior bureaucrat with experience in Manitoba and Ontario,

There is always a core group of ministers who form the nucleus of the government who do buy into the idea of making collective decisions . . . they subordinate their portfolio and personal interests to the larger governmental interests . . . there is a second group of purely departmental ministers who are captured very early by their departments . . . [a third group] never get their minds around what it means to be a minister.

The tension between individualism and collectivity is of course not simply a reflection of departmental interests versus government-wide interests. In addition to personal ideological views, the interests of their constituencies promote individualism on the part of ministers.

Although it tends not to be numerically large, in general the core group of ministers who most actively support the principle of collective decision making contains the most able ministers. Almost by definition, the minister of finance / treasurer, who is invariably one of the two or three most powerful and competent ministers, adopts a government-wide perspective. In addition, the attorney general / minister of justice is typically powerful and able but has relatively few, inexpensive line responsibilities, and therefore is usually a strong advocate of collective decision making.

Aside from these portfolios, the best ministers normally hold the largest, most demanding portfolios. Thus, oftentimes the ministers most inclined and able to bring a corporate perspective to the cabinet are those with the least time and capacity to address the issues arising in portfolios other than their own. Virtually all ministers agreed that it was simply not possible to read thoroughly more than a fraction of formal cabinet submissions and their supporting documentation. To a substantial degree, the lack of collegiality in cabinet decision making is a function of the ministers' lack of time and resources to pursue issues outside their own portfolios. An important counterweight to the impediments ministers face in informing themselves adequately in order to take part in a wide range of discussions was pointed out by a veteran Manitoba minister, who observed that "the recall of past experience – both in government and in opposition – is critical" in assisting ministers with heavy portfolio burdens to contribute to collective decisions.

Deciding what is sent to the cabinet

All provinces have formal procedures setting out the types of decisions requiring cabinet authorization. Typically, there is a financial threshold that requires that proposals entailing costs over a certain amount are approved by the cabinet (or at least by a cabinet committee). In addition, regardless of cost, major new policies require cabinet approval. To be sure, these rules eliminate a good deal of uncertainty; yet they go only a certain way toward determining what goes to the cabinet and what does not. Money can often be redeployed from authorized purposes into what are in effect new uses through imaginative massaging of budgets. Similarly, it is all but impossible to establish a comprehensive, operational definition of what constitutes a "major new policy." In particular, decisions that objectively seem exceedingly minor and cost little or nothing, may in fact have enormous political significance. Finally, the existence of formal rules and procedures is no guarantee that they will be followed, raising the question of what happens when ministers ignore or break the rules.

In his *Diaries of a Cabinet Minister*, Richard Crossman states that, in effect, ministers take to the cabinet only those things that they cannot get away with not taking. Canadian provincial ministers, bureaucrats, and politicos who were asked about the validity of Crossman's premise responded in a variety of ways. A number indicated that they avoided the cabinet if they could because the process was so slow and uncertain. Others took precisely the opposite view: "The more you take to cabinet the better because they're your best advisers."

Ministers reported two quite different motivations for taking to the cabinet items that they were not required to bring forward. Some believed that the cabinet worked best when ministers shared information with one another and listened carefully to their colleagues' advice. Simply put, they believed in collective decision making. Others would submit proposals to the cabinet, not for advice and discussion, but for support and protection. Thus, inexperienced or insecure ministers brought to the cabinet minor proposals that they should have decided themselves, thereby needlessly cluttering up the cabinet agenda. Established senior ministers might send to the cabinet proposals that they were entitled to decide themselves if they were concerned that the proposals might generate political difficulty. If things went wrong, the minister's political liability was substantially lessened if the decision had been made by the cabinet rather than by an individual minister. In the words of one minister, "The bigger the issue the more you wanted confirmation from cabinet."

Virtually all ministers agreed that the decision on whether to send a particular matter to cabinet was one of political judgment. Several ministers indicated that their implicit test was whether their colleagues would be embarrassed or unpleasantly surprised if they discovered that the decision had been made without their knowledge or involvement. For others, the premise was that politically sensitive issues should be shared with cabinet colleagues. This might simply mean ministers informally canvassing interested colleagues before proceeding, even on matters within their own competence.

Breaking the rules: "end runs" and "walk-ins"

Collegiality is most starkly put to the test when ministers refuse to observe the rules. On occasion, ministers simply ignore cabinet decisions or directly contravene them. One bureaucrat commented, "I've had ministers who come from cabinet and say, 'you'll be notified that cabinet has decided to do such and such'; don't do it." Ministers and bureaucrats in all jurisdictions mentioned similar occurrences, but it was clear that these were very much the exception and that they were highly risky. Much more common were attempts to circumvent or to short-circuit the usual cabinet process. These ploys are generally referred to as "end runs."

One of the milder forms of the end run is the "walk-in." Exact processes vary but all provinces require that, except in emergencies, proposals for cabinet consideration be submitted some days in advance to the cabinet office (or equivalent) for review and circulation to ministers and departments. Ministers sometimes simply "walk in" to cabinet meetings with submissions claiming they were too urgent for the regular process. Though it is understood that genuine emergencies requiring quick action do occur, ministers are highly skeptical of walk-ins. The general consensus among those interviewed was that, although some ministers are able to get away with them, for the most part walk-ins are unsuccessful. Moreover, it is not simply a case of attempting a walk-in and being refused permission to proceed; offending ministers often lose ground. Not only are their submissions dispatched to negotiate the usual process, but the prospects of their acceptance are also reduced since the cabinet becomes suspicious about why the walk-ins were initially attempted.

By and large, walk-ins are minor irritants that do not fundamentally challenge cabinet collegiality. More serious is bypassing the cabinet to seek authorization directly from the premier, or in jurisdictions requiring formal review of proposals by cabinet committees, skipping the committees and taking an item straight to the cabinet. Even more problematic are end runs in which ministers go ahead with significant policy changes or expenditures without securing cabinet approval, for example by making public announcements that the cabinet is forced to accept as government policy.

Such tactics generate substantial hostility and resentment. Ministers who persist in attempting to end run the cabinet pay a price: their colleagues tend to give their routine, otherwise unobjectionable, proposals a much rougher ride through the cabinet. If they are pet projects of the offending ministers and do not involve major government policy, they may be turned down altogether in retribution. Even in instances where transgressions do not lead to direct retribution, end runs can be costly, for they can lower offending ministers' esteem among their colleagues and damage their credibility.

Ministerial autonomy

Paradoxically, an important element of collegiality is the willingness to permit individual ministers autonomy in the sense of approving with little or no discussion proposals that ministers bring to the cabinet. The Cabinet is far too busy to give anything like full consideration to more than a small proportion of the items that appear on its agenda. Accordingly, a crucial question arises as to how ministers decide which issues to examine closely and which to push through, more or less on the nod. Not surprisingly, highly contentious issues with significant political overtones, and issues that entail either large financial implications or major shifts in policy, are reviewed by the cabinet in some depth simply because they are intrinsically important. More interesting are decisions of minor or intermediate import. Here the very practical question facing ministers is whether to accept, essentially on faith, the recommendation of a colleague as to the best course of action.

Unless some personal or departmental interest is at stake, ministers make this determination from their assessment of the sponsoring minister's credibility, competence, and track record. If ministers are perceived by their colleagues as having good judgment and credibility, their submissions will often be approved with little difficulty. By contrast, ministers whose ability or judgment are not trusted find their submissions looked at with rather more jaundiced eyes, and reviewed much more thoroughly. Often, if ministers appear to have thought out their policy proposals well, and to have anticipated questions and objections effectively, their advice will be accepted; if, however, they are unable to explain or to defend their submissions adequately, acceptance is unlikely.

A key factor underlying ministers' evaluations of one another is the degree to which they observe the formal and informal rules of cabinet; a reputation for attempting end runs can seriously undermine a minister's credibility. Particularly damaging to a minister's credibility is assuring the cabinet that a policy proposal is uncontroversial when, in fact, the issue proves to be highly contentious.

An undercurrent of individualism was reflected in some ministers' tendency to avoid getting in other ministers' way unless their departments stood to be affected. In other words, ministers were permitted autonomy by their colleagues in part out of a recognition that ministers should be allowed individual spheres of influence not normally subject to interference by other ministers. On balance, however, the more important factor was trust among ministers in one another's judgment. Cabinets premised on collegiality are cabinets in which ministers trust one another and respect one another's judgment.

Typically, cabinet debates were described as "free-for-alls" in which any minister might participate. Ministers whose portfolios or constituencies stood to be directly affected by a proposal were most likely to contribute to the discussion, but as one politico put it, "Everyone has an opinion regardless of their portfolio, and they're quite willing to express it." Willingness to express views about a range of subjects was widely seen as part of the general responsibility of ministers to contribute to collective decision making. Indeed, premiers generally encouraged wide-ranging discussion to avoid having only ministers with departmental vested interests debating a proposal. Still, particularly in Ontario, where the press of cabinet business is significantly more burdensome than in other jurisdictions, it was not always possible for all ministers to have their say on all issues. Ministers widely shared the view that offering an opinion on all topics was a good way to undermine one's credibility, and that ministers who did so were not usually taken seriously.

The balance of this chapter seeks to examine factors that affect collegiality, individuality, reciprocity, and ministerial autonomy in the cabinet. These themes are grouped under the following rubrics: cabinet composition, institutional setting, external environment, influence of the premier, and cabinet dynamics.

CABINET COMPOSITION

Ministers' personalities and abilities

Almost by definition, ministers' personalities and abilities, though crucial for interpersonal dynamics within the cabinet, are highly idiosyncratic and thus not readily amenable to systematic analysis. Clearly, self-confident ministers with forceful personalities have an advantage over those who are insecure or reticent. Similarly, friendships and animosities among ministers may be rooted in personality conflicts. Ministers who are well liked may be allowed by their colleagues to do things not permitted less popular ministers.

The question of ministers' abilities is rather less complex and lends itself more readily to generalization. Canadian provincial cabinets tend to be large, but they are drawn from quite small caucuses; except in the larger provinces such as Ontario, it is common for more than half the caucus to be in the cabinet. As a result, cabinets typically include a half dozen or so first-rate ministers and perhaps another six to ten solidly competent ministers; the balance tend to have limited talents. For internal cabinet dynamics, ministers' absolute level of ability is less important than the pronounced inequalities within the cabinet. "Cabinet was not a table of equals," was one minister's widely echoed assessment. The practical up-shot is that weak ministers are reluctant to challenge powerful ministers. What Patrick Gordon Walker categorized as "partial cabinets" – small numbers of key ministers around the first minister who effectively make crucial decisions (Walker, 1970) – are common in Canadian provinces.

Powerful ministers are allowed greater policy autonomy by their colleagues. This is true virtually by definition, since what generally makes a minister powerful is the high degree of faith (from the premier and other ministers) in his or her competence and judgment that is the sine qua non of according autonomy to a minister. More significantly, perhaps, it was all but universally agreed that strong ministers could break or bend the rules (against end runs, for example) with an impunity not possible for weak ministers.

Finally, the interviews suggested that weak ministers with low-priority portfolios were the most likely to engage in explicit logrolling. Weak ministers, it seems, sometimes compensate for their lack of capacity to attract colleagues' support for their projects by attempting to strike deals, particularly with other low-status ministers.

Culture of the governing party

The culture of the party in power may be related to the norms of interpersonal behavior within the cabinet. The most obvious is the greater commitment to collective decision making within the New Democratic Party (NDP) arising from the party's social-democratic ideology as well as from its ties to the trade-union movement and the women's movement. "Ideology makes it easy," one NDP minister argued, "for NDP cabinets to make decisions in a collegial, consensual way." Experienced bureaucrats agreed that NDP ideology and party culture puts a premium on collegiality, especially by comparison with Liberal and Conservative ministers, who tend to adopt a corporate leadership model. NDP ministers also suggested that, as a programmatic party, a defining characteristic of the NDP is intense, protracted, intraparty debate over policy, and that this tendency carries over into NDP cabinets. As one observed, "We thrive on debate in the party and that is transferred to cabinet." NDP ministers, in other words, are used to tough policy debates and, to a greater extent than ministers in other parties, consider them a routine part of political life.

INSTITUTIONAL SETTING

Size of cabinet and complexity of the cabinet process

Increasing the size of the cabinet necessarily leads to added complexity in decision-making processes (White, 1990: 535–6), and can also affect its interpersonal dynamics. In Nova Scotia the Liberal cabinet grew from nine in 1970 to nineteen in 1978, and the Conservative cabinet from thirteen in 1978 to twenty-two in 1990. In both instances, ministers attributed a perceived decline in cabinet teamwork, and in their sense of involvement in policy decisions, to a sheer growth in cabinet size.

Institutional complexity in cabinet decision making means for the most part formalized cabinet procedures, an extensive system of cabinet committees to review proposals before they reach the full cabinet, and a set of strong central agencies to analyze, evaluate, and route proposals coming into the system. The institutionalized cabinet is almost inevitably a more collegial cabinet since most major decisions are reached through a committee process. A veteran minister put it this way: "Cabinet was always a team, but earlier governments had more room for individual ministers to carve out their own agendas." Moreover, a long-serving bureaucrat observed that, as ministers gain access to more information through central agencies, departmental policy-planning units and nongovernmental institutions, it becomes more difficult for them to make quiet side deals; this renders cabinets more collective.

Clearly, committees are important in reducing the difficulties ministers face in finding the time to deal with more than a small fraction of the proposals coming before the cabinet, and to decide whether to trust the recommendation of the sponsoring minister. Committees substitute the collective judgment of several involved, knowledgeable ministers for that of a single minister. Ministers have fewer qualms about trusting a group of ministers than an individual.

In one sense, however, the complexity of the cabinet process enhances rather than reduces individualistic behavior by ministers. In a simple cabinet process, the incentives for end running the system are limited. A complex cabinet process, by contrast, can be cumbersome and time consuming, so that the gains to be realized by circumventing the system are much more substantial. In short, busier cabinets may not be able to afford the time that extensive collegiality requires.

The geography of the cabinet

The physical location of ministers' offices can play a profound role in enhancing or inhibiting cabinet collegiality, and in other facets of the interpersonal dynamics of cabinet decision making.

In Halifax and in Toronto (the capitals of Nova Scotia and Ontario), ministers are physically situated in their departmental headquarters, which are scattered throughout the downtown core. In Winnipeg (the Manitoba capital), all ministers' offices are in the legislative building, and most are in the same part of the building. In British Columbia, ministers are also housed together in the capital, Victoria, and share a large suite of offices in Vancouver (the province's principal metropolis).

Ministers' physical proximity to one another in Manitoba, and to a lesser extent in British Columbia, contributes significantly to collegiality both in crisis situations and in routine decisions. In Manitoba, ministers are readily available to one another for brief impromptu meetings that are simply not possible in Ontario and Nova Scotia. Moreover, ministers are constantly encountering each other in the halls, in the cafeteria, and in washrooms. Much useful information is exchanged – and indeed decisions reached – in this way.

The consolidation of ministers in a single location is important not only for ease of access among ministers but also since it means that ministers are in effect surrounded by, and thus more influenced by, fellow ministers rather than by bureaucrats. As a result, according to a Manitoba bureaucrat, "Cabinet was much more cohesive . . . ministers were not as much at the whim of the department."

Another geographical feature of the cabinet seems to have a bearing on collegiality. Ministers who reside in the provincial capital go home to their families in the evening, whereas ministers whose homes are outside the capital but who live in the capital during the week, often socialize together in the evening. This tends to make for stronger friendships, for more extensive sharing of information, and for greater collegiality among out-of-town ministers.

EXTERNAL ENVIRONMENT

The bureaucracy

Ministers were virtually unanimous in the view that bureaucratic influence is a significant factor in promoting individualistic, conflictive behavior in the cabinet. Bureaucrats were said to encourage ministers to attempt end runs, to make deals with cabinet colleagues, and generally to emphasize narrow departmental interests over broad governmental concerns. Line bureaucrats were, according to ministers, preoccupied with maximizing the money allocated to their departments and with assuring passage of their department's proposals. A good many ministers made it clear that they took seriously the need to approach decision making as members of the government rather than as departmental advocates, but that this required a level of effort that could not always be sustained to counter the effects of the bureaucrats. To be sure, ministers do not always need prompting by their officials to act as single-minded departmental advocates; ego and ambition can play powerful roles, as can insecurity and lack of imagination. It is clear, however, that bureaucrats are an important influence.

Officials of central agencies are important exceptions to the tendency of bureaucrats to promote ministerial behavior that is individualistic, conflictual, and prone to horse trading. Central agency bureaucrats by definition bring a corporate perspective to bear on departmental policy proposals, and are often charged with preserving the integrity of the cabinet process against end runs, by insisting that proper procedures are followed. They dislike deal making among ministers and departments as destructive of collective decision making and as sanctioning bad policy.

Time

Ministers, bureaucrats, and politicos are widely agreed that, over time, ministers come increasingly to adopt departmental interests and priorities as their own. Even ministers who are not captured by their officials assume proprietorial notions of "my department" and "my policies." This inevitably entails a decline of collegiality and cohesion as ministers pursue their own narrowly focused agendas. It often involves heightened propensity to circumvent established cabinet processes (and the ability to do it more skilfully by virtue of experience) as well as greater acceptance of deal making among ministers.

With few exceptions, collegiality and camaraderie among ministers decline perceptibly over time. Not only do ministers become increasingly caught up in their own departments, but the initial esprit de corps diminishes as the team that came into office together (often almost entirely from a small cohesive group in opposition) changes. Comrades "from the old days" leave the cabinet and are replaced by ministers without personal links to the original ministers. With experience and the passage of time, premiers become increasingly powerful vis-à-vis cabinet collectively and individual ministers. In turn, this reduces the importance of cabinet as a collegial body. The initial sense of shared policy goals and ideological ideals tends over time to dissipate into pragmatism and political survival. For all these reasons, cabinets are inclined to lose cohesiveness and collegiality the longer they are in power.

Ministers diverged sharply as to the effect of the electoral cycle on cabinet dynamics. Some said that, as an election draws near, the urge for personal survival inclines ministers to become more self-centered and individualistic, with a resultant decline in cabinet collegiality. Others argued precisely the reverse: that, in recognition of the political necessity for strong teamwork, cabinets become more cohesive and pull together more effectively in the year prior to an election.

THE INFLUENCE OF THE PREMIER

The premier's influence over the cabinet is pervasive. The premier retains undisputed authority to decide any issue as he sees fit; he establishes the structures and rules of cabinet decision making; and his manner of presiding over the cabinet sets the tone for ministers' behavior. Ministers refer to the premier as "the 51 percent shareholder," "the guy who breaks our 9 to 5 ties," and simply as "the boss." Nonetheless, premiers seem not to exercise their power to impose decisions on unwilling cabinets very often, in part because they recognize the need not to usurp ministers' authority, and in part because they genuinely respect the views and the advice of their cabinet colleagues. At the same time, the premier is hardly a neutral force in cabinet decision making; indeed, his views carry great weight.

The premier's personal style and views also affect conflict and reciprocity. One premier stated that deal making was not much practiced in his cabinet "because ministers understood that I would not think well of it." Several premiers were said to be averse to open conflict in the cabinet. A senior Conservative politico in Ontario maintained that "the whole government was dominated by [Premier] Davis's personality and style [which were] nonadversarial and nonrecriminatory."

Maintaining collegiality and ensuring that the cabinet works as a collective are central preoccupations of premiers. Premiers devote a good deal of attention to fostering cabinet collegiality – both positively, by encouraging ministers to act as a team, and negatively, by discouraging ministers from simply behaving as departmental advocates. Manitoba premier Howard Pawley, for example, was said to have "insisted that when you come into the cabinet room you check your portfolio hat at the door." More concretely, an important component of premiers' calculations with respect to ministerial shuffles was concern over ministers identifying too closely with their departments; as Premier Buchanan of Nova Scotia put it, "If a minister was so engrossed in a department that he was losing perspective, it was time to move him out" (Buchanan, 1991).

CABINET DYNAMICS

Cohorts and factions

Although Canadian provincial ministers tend to be spread across a relatively short ideological continuum, many ministers claimed that they could predict with confidence how most of their colleagues would line up on ideological issues. Ideological factions were unusually clear-cut within the Social Credit cabinet in British Columbia during the premiership of Bill Bennett (1975–86). Several ministers who had come into the cabinet from the provincial Liberal Party constituted a distinct cabinet faction, based on adherence to centrist welfare liberalism. By contrast, ministers whose roots lay in the Conservative Party tended to espouse values reflecting free-enterprise conservatism.

Economic interest and region are often more important than ideology in understanding cabinet factions. In Nova Scotia, for example, ministers whose constituency depends heavily on fishing form an informal caucus within the cabinet. In Manitoba, which is dominated to an unusual degree by its capital, cabinets often divide into Winnipeg and non-Winnipeg factions.

In some ways, however, the most critical "faction" within a cabinet is the inner group of powerful ministers who have the ear of the premier. This faction is defined in part by the premier, by the value he attaches to particular ministers' views, and by his allocation of important cabinet posts. Cabinets are typically beset by resentments felt against ministers with the high-priority portfolios, who almost inevitably are the inner-circle ministers.

266

Save at the beginning of a government dominated by a party that has been out of power for a long period, cabinets are composed of various cohorts of ministers: ministers who served in a previous government or under another premier; those who were appointed when the party resumed power or when a new premier took office; and those who were appointed at later stages of the life of the government. These differences need not produce stress and conflict, but they often do. Several ministers in the Buchanan government in Nova Scotia (1978–90) referred to tension between ministers appointed to the original Buchanan cabinet and those who joined it subsequently. Even more pronounced was the conflict in the government of Howard Pawley (NDP Manitoba premier 1981–8) between ministers who had served in the Schreyer cabinet (1969–77) and those who were first appointed to cabinet by Pawley. Ministers from the Schreyer era had been used to a much more freewheeling, individualistic approach to the cabinet than Pawley and the new contingent of ministers were prepared to allow.

Shuffles

Ministers in Canadian provincial cabinets are shuffled with great abandon. Senior portfolios such as Finance / Treasury or Attorney General / Justice are less subject to change, but most ministers can expect to remain in a portfolio for only about eighteen to twenty-four months, and many are shifted within a year (this does *not* take into account the possibility of leaving a portfolio by virtue of the government losing power).

Premiers, ministers, and bureaucrats agree that, on balance, shuffles significantly enhance cabinet collegiality. Ministers who have held several portfolios have a much wider perspective on issues and a greater appreciation for the government's corporate interests than ministers with experience in only one portfolio.[2] Ministers clearly have greater understanding of and sympathy for the problem faced by colleagues in portfolios that they have previously held, and this also makes for a more collegial approach. Having several ministers around the table who have held a particular portfolio improves collective decision making by offering cabinet a range of knowledgeable opinion. Most fundamentally, though, shuffles contribute to collegiality by reducing individuality – by reducing not only ministers' proprietary attitudes toward their departments, but also their tendency to equate their own interests with their departments' interests. Ministers who know that their tenure in a given portfolio will be limited are less likely to be bloody minded about promoting their departments' interests, especially since they may shortly find themselves responsible for other departments with opposing interests.

Overall, the clear consensus was that shuffling ministers substantially improved collective decision making. One politico spoke for many in referring to a "special collegiality" among ministers who had held the same portfolio. A minister commented, "No question it [shuffling] is very useful; you understand issues [in your former departments] and it makes for more intelligent discussions in cabinet." Most ministers looked on former portfolio holders as valuable sources of support and advice, and turned to them readily, concurring with the assessment that "generally you had an ally in the former minister." One way in which former ministers were said to prove especially valuable was in alerting their successors to dubious policy ideas that bureaucrats had earlier tried on them.

CONCLUSION

In 1989 the Liberal cabinet in Ontario moved from meeting weekly to meeting biweekly. This generated a good deal of grumbling among ministers that they were not seeing each other enough. This points out, in the words of a senior bureaucrat, that the cabinet must be viewed as more than a decision-making body: "It is a weekly group therapy session." It is this intangible, yet fundamentally important, aspect of the cabinet that this chapter has sought to examine.

The analysis presented of the interpersonal relations of Canadian provincial cabinet ministers is, to say the least, not parsimonious. Nor, given the difficulty of measuring the component variables and the looseness of the linkages between variables, does it have great predictive value. It does, nonetheless, demonstrate both the possibility and the value of systematically addressing the interpersonal dynamics of cabinet decision making. With relatively few modifications, the approach should be applicable to any single-party cabinet, and could be applied to multiparty coalition cabinets as well.

Some of the substantive findings offer empirical insight into processes that are subject to a good deal of speculation in Canada and elsewhere. In Canadian provincial cabinets, conflict and reciprocity among ministers are significantly less pronounced than is commonly believed, or than might be expected given the strength of individualistic pulls upon ministers. These cabinets are truly collegial in more than name and appearance, though to be sure, ministers can and do pursue their individual interests vigorously. Ministers do adopt within the cabinet a consensual mode of behavior in which they subsume, to some degree at least, their individual preferences and interests into those of the government as a whole. To an extent they do so out of caution and insecurity; but more fundamental is their commitment to genuinely collective decision making.

NOTES

1 Seventy-one interviews were with ministers (ten of whom were premiers), forty-two were with bureaucrats and thirty-four were with politicos. Relevant data on the four provinces is given in the following table.

Table 15.1. *Data on Canadian provincial governments, 1991–2*

Province	Population (thousands)	Size of Legislature	Size of Cabinet	Size of Bureaucracy	Budget (billion $Cdn)
British Columbia	3,127	75	19	37,129	19.0
Nova Scotia	894	52	19	10,817	4.8
Ontario	9,743	130	27	86,705	56.5
Manitoba	1,092	57	18	13,152	6.7

2 Blondel (1988) makes this assumption in his comparative study of Austrian and Belgian ministers, though he does not present supporting evidence.

REFERENCES

Blondel, Jean. 1988. Ministerial careers and the nature of parliamentary government: the cases of Austria and Belgium. *European Journal of Political Research* 16: 51–71.

Buchanan, John. 1991. Interview with author. Halifax, Nova Scotia, 7 November.

Campbell, Colin. 1985. Cabinet Committees in Canada: Pressures and Dysfunctions Stemming from the Representational Imperative. In Thomas T. Mackie and Brian W. Hogwood (eds.), *Unlocking the Cabinet: Cabinet Structures in Comparative Perspective.* Beverly Hills, Calif.: Sage.

Crossman, Richard. 1976. *Diaries of a Cabinet Minister.* New York: Holt, Rinehart, & Winston.

Dunn, Christopher. 1991. Changing the design: cabinet decision making in three provincial governments. *Canadian Public Administration* 34: 621–40.

Matheson, W. A. 1976. *The Prime Minister and the Cabinet.* Toronto: Methuen.

Miller, Frank. 1986. Interview with author. Toronto, 9 October.

Walker, Patrick Gordon. 1970. *The Cabinet.* London: Jonathan Cape.

White, Graham. 1990. Big is different from little: On taking size seriously in the analysis of Canadian governmental institutions. *Canadian Public Administration* 33: 534–40.

16

Cabinet decision making in the Hellenic Republic, 1974–1992

Kleomenis S. Koutsoukis

Western European governments either have coalition cabinets, in which two or more parties form the executive, or majority-party cabinets, in which a single party controls the executive. Although the type of cabinet may appear to be a function of electoral law, it is also associated with a wider popular conception of the way in which societies should be governed. Greece today has a "majority-party cabinet." After the fall of the military dictatorship, the new constitution of 1975 formally recognized the existence of political parties, even providing for their organization under the law, thereby reinforcing their role in the political system. This role is exemplified mainly by a party's ability, once in power, to form a cabinet and implement its own policies (Kontogiorgis, 1986: 43–9). The resulting notion that a party is responsible only when it is in power has led to a series of institutional arrangements undergirding the government party's leader who, as head of both government and party, enjoys an unusual amount of power.

That each of the two big parties, Liberal and Socialist, subscribe to this ethos of single-party government restrains them from collaborating to pass an electoral law that would implement proportional representation. On the contrary, they tend, in silent cooperation, to find ways of granting additional electoral seats to the largest party so that one or the other of them is always able to form a cabinet (Featherstone, 1990).

The ideological polarization of the two parties, perpetuated by their preference for powerful government, reinforces a "majority-cabinet culture" that inhibits cooperation, much less consensus, among parties. This gap between the two parties has become even greater due to the personal infighting and mutual dislike of their respective leaders, who have dominated politics in the past decade. Only in times of national crisis do political forces in Greece tend to cooperate and find, temporarily, ways to achieve consensus on national issues. (Such was the case in 1974, when in the midst of an acute crisis – the country was on the brink of war with

270

Turkey over Cyprus – a national-unity coalition cabinet was formed. Similar coalition cabinets were also formed in the years following the end of the Second World War and during the Civil War.)

It is the thesis of this chapter that this preference for powerful unified government has contributed to an increasing concentration of power in the hands of the prime minister, who is also the leader of the majority party. Despite the system of collective decision making, this arrangement has created a primus solus prime minister able to minimize the role, and limit the autonomy, of his ministers.

THE GOVERNMENT AS A COLLECTIVE ENTITY

According to the constitution of the Hellenic Republic, the government is the Ministerial Council. (Henceforth the international term "cabinet" will be used interchangeably as a synonym for Ministerial Council.) The cabinet in Greece includes the prime minister, also called "president of the government," at least one vice-president, and the ministers. Deputy ministers are not members of the cabinet. "Alternate ministers" (until they were abolished by the present government) as well as "ministers without portfolio" are members of the cabinet.

Under the provisions of the constitution and subsequent laws, the government's profile can be characterized in collective terms, since all major issues of general concern are decided upon by collective governmental organs, the most important of which is the Ministerial Council. The main characteristics of this profile are: the existence and function of various collective governmental organs; that decision making in these organs is collective; and that the members of the cabinet and deputy ministers are collectively responsible for government policy.

The collective organs of government

In terms of formal executive powers, the cabinet is subservient to the president of the republic, who is the head of the executive branch. However, the cabinet is in practice the highest executive organ since it determines both the general policy of the government and its specific program. There is no provision for the participation of the president of the republic in the decision making of any governmental organ, particularly that of the cabinet.

The cabinet is competent to determine and direct the general policy of the country; to decide upon political matters of general concern; and to decide upon any matter within the competence of any other collective governmental organ, or of any other minister, if the prime minister wants to bring it to the cabinet for discussion. Consequently, any decision made by the cabinet substitutes for the decisions of the collective organs of government.

There are several other collective governmental organs. The Governmental Council (KYSYM) has responsibility for deciding on matters of general concern, and for taking necessary steps for the implementation of governmental policies – particularly for assuring that cabinet decisions are implemented by the ministers and other governmental organs. The Governmental Council for Foreign Affairs and National Defense (KYSEA) is charged with responsibility on matters of foreign policy and national defense. The Supreme Council of Economic Policy has, among its responsibilities, the power to decide upon any matter of general economic policy within the guidelines provided for by the cabinet and governmental council. It may also take the steps necessary for the implementation of the government's economic program, and particularly for the coordination and supervision of its implementation. The Committee on Prices and Incomes works out measures related to prices, incomes, and the income policies within the framework provided by other governmental organs, in light of cabinet decisions. With the exception of the latter, which is presided over by the minister of national economy, all other governmental organs referred to are headed by the prime minister. Membership in all these governmental organs is restricted to appropriate ministers (Athanasopoulos, 1988: 87–100; Loverdos, 1991: 127–46).

Collective decision making

Three general principles underline the decision making of collective governmental organs: debate; open voting; and majority rule. In case of a tied vote, the opinion supported by the prime minister prevails. Collective decision making applies to issues, brought to the cabinet by the prime minister or other ministers, that may affect either the entire government or certain ministries. The decision making of the cabinet is regulated by bylaws.[1] The procedures and technicalities regulating the meetings and decisions of the cabinet are critical because, through them, a powerful prime minister emerges. Also, they affect the cohesiveness of the government, ministerial autonomy and collective responsibility.

According to the cabinet's bylaws, a legal majority must sign any cabinet act. Those who dissent may have their reservations registered in the minutes. The meaning of such disagreements is purely political, as are its consequences. If a cabinet member disagrees and his dissent is mentioned in the minutes, as long as he remains in the cabinet he must obey the opinion of the majority and may not publicize this disagreement. By dissenting and going public, a cabinet member attempts to minimize personal political costs of a cabinet decision that he or she may consider unpopular. By doing so he or she undermines the unity and cohesiveness of the government. The prime minister, under these circumstances, may ask the member to submit a resignation. Collective responsibility, therefore, requires all ministers to abide by the decision making of collective governmental organs whether they sign these acts or not.

If a collective decision refers to a minister's jurisdiction and he refuses to cosign, then the minister is obliged to resign or be dismissed. A minister is solely responsible for all personal acts and decisions pertaining to his jurisdiction. He bears political responsibility for any wrongdoing, and the immediate sanction for this is dismissal. If he is felt to bear responsibility for violating the law, he risks facing charges in the Special Court for ministers.[2]

The prime minister's hegemony: from primus inter pares to primus solus

One may conclude from the previous section that, despite the function of so many collective governmental organs, the prime minister presides over almost all of them and emerges as singularly powerful. In addition to his privileges, he has other powers that reinforce his authority in the cabinet. By the constitution and statutory laws, the prime minister is authorized to secure the unity of the government and direct its actions, and the actions of the public services in general, toward the implementation of government policy; to determine precise government policy within the framework of decisions made by the cabinet; to solve disagreements among the ministers; and in general to supervise the implementation of laws by the public services as well as their function according to the law, to the benefit of the state and its citizens.

The above rights, listed in the law and the constitution, supplement those practices and privileges permitted the prime minister after his appointment to the premiership. These are to name ministers, and if appropriate, to sack them; to present to the Parliament the statement expressing the policies of cabinet and ask for the house's confidence; to determine the competences of a minister without portfolio; and overall to represent the government to the Parliament, to the president of the republic, and to the public.

In exercising all of these duties the prime minister is assisted by a series of offices established exclusively for him, and therefore subject to his authority. Among the most important is the Secretariat of the Ministerial Council, the staff of which is organized by his own decisions and therefore obviously loyal to him. Fixing the agenda and keeping the minutes and records of the cabinet's meetings are the main tasks of this service, under the supervision of the prime minister. In addition, there are the national Information

Service and the Central Committee (for the preparation of laws). Most important of all, however, is the prime minister's political office.

The prime minister's political office is a central structure within the overall government organization. Theoretically its purpose, set apart from and above the cabinet, is to enhance the prime minister's capacity to supervise, coordinate, and manage the government's work. Apart from his office, the prime minister is also authorized by law to establish commissions, ad hoc committees, or consulting bodies to assist and advise him on any issue he requires. As a matter of fact, however, his office plays a very important role in selecting and appointing the members of these various committees, councils, and consulting bodies.

Among the other prerogatives of the prime minister are powers to appoint one or more vice-presidents, to delegate some of his powers to them, and to appoint alternative ministers. Overall, however, the crux of prime-ministerial power derives from his dominant position in the ministerial council, which upon the prime minister's recommendation can abolish existing collective governmental organs and replace them with new ones.

THE POLITICAL OFFICE OF THE PRIME MINISTER

The contemporary prime minister's political office emerged under the dictatorship of Papadopoulos who, by his style of leadership, created a strong executive. Thus, although it existed as an institutional entity even before 1974, it took its broader functional and organizational character only in the mid-1980s. The first two postdictatorial prime ministers, Karamanlis and his successor Rallis, arranged the prime minister's office as a handpicked team of persons loyally devoted to the prime minister. This team offered its advice and executed the prime minister's orders, checking on his daily schedule, meetings, appointments, visits, and so forth. This small number of associates, a few of them very close, was easily managed on a face-to-face basis rather than in an impersonal, bureaucratic, or technocratic way. Their number did not exceed twenty.

After 1981, Prime Minister Papandreou's political office not only became an autonomous public service under his absolute authority, but also was enlarged and restructured on a more bureaucratic and technocratic basis to serve the contemporary needs of an enlarged cabinet. In addition to personnel working in the Parliament's premises, where the previous prime ministers had their office, a large part resided in the nearby Maximos Palace, exclusively used by the prime minister's office personnel and staff. In contrast the two previous prime ministers, Papandreou's office exhibited what might be called a White House syndrome, with a staff exceeding 100.

The current prime minister's political office is headed by the prime minister's daughter, a deputy, and former deputy minister. It tends to reflect the prime minister's pragmatic outlook. Being "his eye," as one of his close associates put it, one of its goals is to supervise the work of the ministers in keeping deadlines and implementing work plans and policies. Efficiency oriented, the prime minister is alert to minimizing problems and reconciling possible conflicts among ministers.

The constituent parts of the prime minister's political office are the private office, which gives orders to the other offices; the legal office; the diplomatic office; the economic office; the military office; the security office; and the press office, all of which are specialized to assist the prime minister . In addition, the prime minister has the authority to abolish any of these offices, to establish new ones, to modify their powers and functions, and finally to make any necessary arrangement concerning the internal organization and personnel structure of the political office.

The political dominance of the prime minister in the Hellenic Republic is multidimensional. We have already pointed to a strong authority supported by a huge institutional framework operating through mechanisms such as a political office and a multiplicity of other specialized offices. There is also a series of governmental organizations chaired by the prime minister, who may initiate decision making that can preoccupy the cabinet or other governmental organs. Particularly at the cabinet level the prime minister can exercise influence over the agenda through the cabinet secretariat, which he also supervises. Although under certain procedures issues for the cabinet agenda may also be submitted by ministers, the finalization of the agenda depends upon the prime minister.

The prime minister can keep an eye on party deputies through the spokespersons he has appointed, the speaker of the house who also belongs to his party, and the machinery of party discipline. Important among the last of these is the crucial power as leader of the party to choose the electoral list of party candidates for every constituency in each election. Those on the list are considered the party's official candidates in a specific constituency. The fear of not being in the list makes deputies more careful in their criticisms regardless of whether or not their party is in power. The list thus contributes considerably to the operation of party discipline. The role of the prime minister in choosing his own party's lists considerably consolidates his power.

MINISTERIAL AUTONOMY: DEPARTMENTALISM, INNER CIRCLES, AND THE HIERARCHY OF MINISTERS

In considering the degree of autonomy of an individual minister, we are concerned first with the degree to which the minister is free to make policies within the jurisdiction of his ministry (legally provisioned) and, second, with the degree to which he can influence the formulation of governmental policies in collective governmental organs or disassociate himself from such collectively decided policies.

Each minister is the head of a department. Within the jurisdiction of this department he is competent to exercise all the rights given to him and to be a policymaker. In this regard he is autonomous to act within the limits of law. The more he is aware of his competences, the easier it will be for him to avoid conflict with another minister. Thus, a minister is "autonomous" within his jurisdiction as long as his policies and decisions do not interfere with another ministry.

From time to time, however, he may have to consult with another minister. This is particularly necessary when the issue in question is of financial importance or related to overall economic policy (for example, any bill that generates financial cost must be accompanied by a special report). Any matter dealing with increases of ministry personnel must also be decided in consultation with the minister for national economy and the minister for the presidency (who is responsible for the overall administrative personnel).

There are often policy issues that are inherently interdepartmental and that therefore constrain individual ministerial autonomy (for example, the problem of pollution falls within the jurisdiction of the Ministry for Environment and Public Works, of the Ministry for Industry and Technology, and of the Ministry for Communications). There are also matters relating to the general policy of the government, such as employment, rents, wages, salaries, and so on, and matters on which competence is kept within collective governmental organs, such as the Ministerial Council or more specific organs such as the Committee on Prices and Incomes, and so forth.

Ministerial autonomy may also be restricted when the prime minister appoints to the same ministry either an alternate minister or one or more deputy ministers. The appointment of alternate ministers mainly flourished under PASOK. One explanation might be the ideological suspicion of the party, which kept a close eye on every minister and his policies. The same explanation may apply to the large number of deputy ministers, each representing a different ideological orientation within the party, in addition to all of the personal factors that might influence such an appointment.

The minister as policymaker in his ministry formulates policies within his jurisdiction. The civil service under him should cooperate and follow his guidelines for the implementation of his policy. Constraints on this implementation may be caused, however, by the unchecked discretion of expert technocrats on the one hand and politically hostile civil servants on the other. In part to counteract this, the law allows each minister to have a personal office with a certain number of associates and collaborators. In addition, the minister can move personnel within the ministry as he likes, assigning them to tasks he sees as essential.

The inner cabinet

One of the new developments in decision making and practical politics under the new Greek constitution was the so-called small cabinet. It sometimes appeared formally and sometimes informally as an "inner cabinet" (Koutsoukis, 1982: 216–9). This developed mainly under the two strong leaders Karamanlis and Papandreou, but it is observed today as well. An inner cabinet often includes a small number of ministers or close associates from the prime minister's office, or from outside. These are the people with whom the prime minister most often meets, and who seem to function as an inner think tank for the prime minister. They often present him with possible choices or different policies before he reaches a final decision in the collective governmental organs. The effect of these inner circles, whatever their usefulness in providing information on policy alternatives to the prime minister, is to constrain both collective decision making and ministerial autonomy (Athanasopoulos, 1988: 122–42), thereby increasing the authoritarian character of the regime.

It follows that the autonomy of ministers is not constrained by the Parliament as much as it is by collective governmental organs, collective cabinet decision making, the prime minister's personality and style of leadership, other ministers, the civil service, and inner cabinet circles. Given the partisan nature of the government, the mechanism of party discipline is sufficient to limit parliamentary intrigue against ministerial actions.

The hierarchy of ministers and ministries

The hierarchy of ministries gives priority to specific ministers over others in public appearances, parades, and so forth. Such symbolic gestures often indicate the degree of influence and autonomy a minister enjoys. It is a matter of political prestige for an aspiring political leader to hold a ministry that ranks high in the hierarchy. Given a hierarchy of ministries, one may assume that the higher the position the greater the minister's prestige that may then be translated into greater influence and relative autonomy (Rose, 1987: 87–92). Relatively high ranking often implies proximity to the prime minister, from which flows influence and autonomy. Formally, the cabinet hierarchy becomes obvious to the public from the proximity of a minister to the prime minister around the table in cabinet meetings and other official appearances. Powerful ministers, often under weak prime ministers, have been able to demand the upgrading of their ministries.[3] Indeed, one of the first things that some prime ministers do is change the hierarchy of ministries in accordance with their outlook and priorities.

RESIGNATION AND DISMISSAL

It is characteristic of the differing leadership styles of two political adversaries, Papandreou and Mitsotakis, that they differed as prime ministers in their reaction to public expressions of dissent from their ministers. Under the Socialist cabinets of Papandreou, a disagreement between a minister and the prime minister rarely ended up in the former's resignation, because the prime minister dismissed the dissenter before he could submit his resignation. Ministers were fired either on an individual basis or en masse, and sudden reshuffles took place almost every year. Under Mitsotakis, when a disagreement went public, most of the time it led ultimately to the resignation of the minister (whether or not invited by the prime minister).

Resignations and dismissals typically occur when ministerial views or objectives clash with those of the prime minister. In the recent Mitsotakis governments first formed in 1990, there have been disagreements between ministers – and subsequent departures – over issues related to financial austerity and economic liberalization.[4] Replacements have almost always been more firmly committed to the prime minister's outlook than were their predecessors.

CONFIDENCE AND THE MOTION OF NO CONFIDENCE

According to the constitution, a new government has to appear in Parliament and ask for a vote of confidence within fifteen days after the prime minister takes his oath of office. Before he asks for a vote of confidence, the prime minister presents the program of his government and the general guidelines of its policies to Parliament. After debate, the vote of confidence takes place. The government may also ask for a vote of confidence whenever it considers this necessary or appropriate.[5]

Theoretically, according to the constitution, the Parliament can withdraw its confidence from the government collectively or from one of its members. A motion of no confidence can be submitted at least six months after a previous one has been defeated. Such a motion of no confidence must be signed by a sixth of the total number of deputies, that is, at least fifty signatories are required. If a motion of no confidence is submitted sooner than six months after the previous one, it has to be signed by a majority of the total number of deputies, that is, 151. Debate starts two days after the submission of the motion unless the government asks for immediate discussion. The debate may not last more than three days.

If the government itself asks for a vote of confidence, as it does in the case of a programmatic statement, an absolute majority of the number of deputies present is needed. The majority favoring the government when it asks for the confidence of the house, however, cannot be lower than two-fifths of the total number of the deputies in Parliament, that is, 120.

It is not my intention here to get involved in the detailed technicalities of confidence-voting procedures and legal provisions, mostly discussed by the constitutionalists (Loverdos 1991: 102–13). The emphasis here should rather be on the content of the motion of no confidence and its political meaning. The motion of no confidence against the government collectively is in accord with the system of collective political responsibility provided for by the constitution. A motion of no confidence addressed against one member of the cabinet, if it happens, may be taken as a test of the cohesiveness and solidarity of a partisan cabinet. In this case the cabinet, and primarily the prime minister, will defend the target member, thereby defending the integrity of the government against the tactics of the opposition. So far, no motion of no confidence against a particular member or members of the government has succeeded.

On the other hand, a motion of no confidence against the government is a very serious enterprise for the opposition in its effort to have the government dismissed by presidential decree.[6] It is a politically essential, but delicate, weapon, the use of which must be evaluated in the context of overall strategy of the opposition and the general dynamics of current politics. Due to the effects of party discipline and the polarization of the parties in Parliament, no Greek government or any of its members has yet been obliged to resign as a result of a motion of confidence or no confidence. Such motions, however, allow the opposition to present allegations against the government, such as negligence or wrongdoing in implementing governmental policies, or even of a lack of ethical behavior on the part of some cabinet members (Stamoulis, 1990; Zelemenos, 1989a).

PATTERNS OF CARETAKER CABINETS, 1974–1990

According to the constitution of 1975, when a government submits its resignation because its four-year period has expired, because of defeat in a motion of no confidence, or because of the party's inability to assemble a cabinet, the president of the republic sets in motion a constitutional procedure forcing a general election. One of the choices open to the president is to invite the leaders of all the parties in Parliament to form a coalition cabinet in order to lead the country into elections. If he fails because of the obvious inability of the parties to cooperate in such a coalition cabinet, then he invites the president of the council of state (or alternatively, the president of the supreme court) to form a caretaker cabinet to lead the country into a general election. Only after such a cabinet has formed does the president dissolve the Parliament.

The constitution requires the caretaker cabinet to be "as far as possible, of wide acceptance in order to conduct the elections." In practice this constitutional provision is interpreted to mean that members of the caretaker cabinet should be apolitical and possess no obvious partisan identity. Therefore, these persons usually are found among the three supreme court justices; academics; the economic, legal, and technical professions; retired military officers; bureaucrats; and even journalists. Because of its specific mission to lead the country into elections and its apolitical personalities, the caretaker cabinet administers the state machine rather than governing. It conducts current affairs, attempting to solve pending everyday matters, and prepares the official machinery for the smooth conduct of the election. Although there are no specific provisions of the constitution or laws limiting its jurisdiction or competence, it is widely accepted that in cases of emergency or of major national issues, such a cabinet must consult the leaders of the political parties (Loverdos, 1991: 180–4).

CONCLUSION

This analysis indicates a few characteristics of politics in the Hellenic Republic. The principles of collective cabinet decision making and collective responsibility, established by the founders of the 1975 constitution, have led to the emergence of a powerful prime minister as a primus solus, and a system of "prime minister centrism" (Hennessy, 1988: 94; Nikoloudis, 1977: 62–8; Tsatsos, 1989; Zelemenos, 1989b). The autonomy of cabinet ministers is thus subject to the prime minister's dominance. In all collective governmental organs, the only alternative to submitting to the prime minister is for a minister to dissent and resign, if he is not dismissed first. His autonomy is limited to the matters in his own jurisdiction provided for specifically by law, and is subject to possible restrictions by alternate and deputy ministers or by a politicized civil service. Ministerial autonomy in Parliament reflects his cabinet's overall autonomy vis-à-vis the Parliament. The Parliament is subject to dissolution by the government but, owing to the high level of party discipline, it has never been able to dismiss a cabinet.

Finally, due to the polarization of politics in Greece, coalition cabinets do not seem to work in practice; thus, future governments remain likely to be of majority-party type. These cabinets function within a framework of institutions that reinforce the role of the prime minister, the only officeholder who appears powerful in the political system of the Hellenic Republic. In sum, autonomy is partisan in Greek majority-party cabinets; discretionary behavior within ministerial jurisdictions is the stuff of intraparty politics.

NOTES

1 The content of the bylaws is divided into three chapters, dealing respectively with the organizing of meetings, quorum, and voting; the procedure for introducing subjects for discussion; and the signing and publication of acts and decrees in the government's Gazette. It should be mentioned that all cabinet discussions are secret, and that particular procedural arrangements are made to guarantee their secrecy.
2 Such were the cases of Pan-Hellenic Socialist Movement (PASOK) ministers D. Tsovolas (Finance), G. Petsos (Industry), A. Koutsogeorgas (vice-president) and deputy minister N. Athanasopoulos (Finance). Only the first and the last were convicted by the Special Court.
3 Mitsotakis, as minister of foreign affairs in 1980, demanded that the Ministry of Foreign Affairs become first in the hierarchy of ministries over and above the Ministry of Coordination, first in the hierarchy up to that time. Under PASOK, the Ministry of the Presidency took first place and remains there today, as this post has been held by top party figures.
4 Disagreement on foreign policy, especially over the recognition of the "former Yugoslav republic of Macedonia" led to the dismissal of Samaras from the Ministry of Foreign Affairs in the summer of 1992. He resigned his seat in Parliament that autumn.
5 An absolute majority of those present and voting, which can be no less than two-fifths (120) of the total number of the Parliament's seats (300), is required for the government to enjoy the confidence of the house in the first instance.
6 If a government loses the confidence of the House it has to resign. If it refuses to do so, the president of the republic can dismiss it with a decree not necessarily signed by the outgoing prime minister.

REFERENCES

Athanasopoulos, D. 1988. *Government and Governmental Organs*. Athens: Sakkoulas.
Featherstone, K. 1990. "The party state" in Greece and the fall of Papandreou. *West European Politics* 1: 101–15.
Hennessy, P. 1988. *Cabinet*. Oxford: Blackwell Publisher.
Kontogiorgis, G. 1985. *Political System and Politics*. Athens: Polytypo.
Koutsoukis, K. 1982. *Political Leadership in Modern Greece*. Athens: Athena.
Loverdos, A. 1991. *Government, Collective Function and Political Responsibility*. Athens: Sakkoulas.
Nikoloudis, E. 1977. *Issues of Theory and Practice*. Athens: Papazisis.
Rose, R. 1987. *Ministers and Ministries: a Functional Analysis*. Oxford University Press (Clarendon Press).

Stamoulis, J. 1990. *The Criminal Responsibility of the Cabinet Members.* Athens: Livanis.

Tsatsos, D. 1989. *The Nomination of the Prime Minister.* Athens: Sakkoulas.

Zelemenos, K. 1989a. *The Responsibility in Managing Political Authority.* Athens: Sakkoulas.

1989b. *The Nomination of the Prime Minister.* Athens: Sakkoulas.

Part IV

CONCLUSION

17

Cabinet government in theoretical perspective

Michael Laver and Kenneth A. Shepsle

Anyone who has read at least some of the country-specific chapters in this volume cannot fail to have been impressed by the enormous institutional variety to be found in even a relatively small group of parliamentary democracies. Cabinets may consist of one or of many parties. Cabinet parties may or may not control a legislative majority. The full cabinet may resolve many issues in some cases, few in others. It may be presided over by a strong or a weak prime minister. The cabinet may tightly control its ministers or allow them considerable freedom to act on their own initiative. Ministers themselves may or may not defer to parliamentary parties, extraparliamentary caucuses, or interest groups. They may either use or be used by professional civil servants. The list of aspects of cabinet behavior that differ from country to country could be expanded more or less ad infinitum.

On one reading of this mass of evidence, the possibility of constructing any sort of theory of cabinet decision making might seem an utterly doomed enterprise. An alternative – and we believe more constructive – reading, however, sustains an entirely different perspective. In this concluding chapter we elaborate this perspective and summarize some of the supporting empirical regularities. Amid all of the variation there is, we believe, at least some firm footing on which to proceed toward a more rigorous and systematic analysis of cabinet decision making. Before attempting in subsequent sections to extract a series of empirical regularities from the preceding country chapters, therefore, we lay out in the next section a general theoretical approach to the role of the cabinet in parliamentary democracy.

CABINET DECISION MAKING IN PARLIAMENTARY DEMOCRACIES

Obviously, every individual country has a politics quite different from anywhere else. This is a reflection of its history, its geography, the composition of its population, and a whole host of "large" factors, each with a separate and complicated chain of causality. This means that putting all of the pieces together to tell a sensible and interesting story about a single country, as country specialists do, is a challenging intellectual enterprise. It is an enterprise that often emphasizes unique juxtapositions of events and forces, with the result that the story is told one way in Norway, and somewhat differently in Finland, whereas a completely different story might be told in New Zealand or Britain. This is because, at one level, these are completely different places.

At another level, however, they are not. All of the countries described in this book have things called cabinets with people called ministers occupying jobs thought of as portfolios. All of the cabinets we have looked at are responsible in some sense to something that in each country is called a legislature. The legislature is responsible in some way to voters in regular events that we think of as elections. By the very act of using these same words in different countries, we presume some regularity, and not even the most rigid country specialist would claim that we must think of completely different words for every single thing in each different country, because everything is different, different entirely. In developing and using ideas that we feel have some utility in more than one distinctive setting, we do not necessarily imply that there is some single parsimonious set of organizing principles that apply to everything, everywhere. Such grand theorizing is clearly a hopeless enterprise. It does suggest, however, that there are more modest ways of theorizing about a particular set of cases that can help us to engage in systematic description, explanation, and prediction.

We might think of one such more modest undertaking as "theorizing in one country." The essential task is to produce a logic according to which the phenomena of politics in a particular regime do in fact fit together. The reason to do this, of course, is to be able to account for change, to be able to answer "What if?" questions. Even those who are instinctively hostile to theory rarely claim that this type of theorizing is impossible. In answer to the question, for example, "What if the Labour Party won the next British election?" almost nobody engaged in the serious study of politics would claim that the consequences are completely unpredictable. Indeed, to do so would be to claim that the entire process of democratic politics is pointless, since voters would have no basis for making their decision. Theorizing in one country, therefore, allows us to consider counterfactuals, and this in turn allows us to make systematic choices about the future. What if the next Polish election used a set of rules in which the proportional-representation (PR) threshold were as high as that in Germany? What if language parity were no longer a binding constraint on cabinet composition in Belgium? The point here is that this type of theory is used at least informally by everyone who can defend answers to such questions. It provides an analytical tool for country specialists, a form of argument that is general in its logic but unique to the particular circumstances of the country in question. It is probably better to be systematic about such theorizing than not, and perhaps the best-known systematic body of theory analyzing the operation of a particular set of institutions in a single country is that focusing on the U.S. Congress.

A second type of theoretical analysis that we can use to bring some order to the empirical variation described in the country chapters of this book deals with regularities observed in a group of different countries. Thus, we might theorize about electoral systems. In doing so we do not, of course, assume that every electoral system is the same, but we do assume that different electoral systems are doing the same sort of job in different countries, albeit in different ways. One of the main reasons to do this is to allow us to manipulate something more than counterfactual "What if?" questions when we try to see how well our model works. The essential claim is that we *do* learn at least something about how proportional representation would work in England or New Zealand, for example, by a careful analysis of how it works in other countries. Even the most narrow-minded theorist would never expect PR to work in exactly the same way in two countries. But to introduce PR in one country with absolutely no regard for lessons to be learned from elsewhere is, most would agree, an act of the crassest stupidity. The sense that there are *some* lessons to be learned from what goes on in different countries implies that some sensible cross-national generalizations can be made.

Theorizing across countries is, of course, a dangerous exercise. Unless two countries are utterly identical, information will by definition be lost with every generalization made. Nevertheless, we should never forget that information is also lost when we do not make the links that clearly do exist between broadly similar settings in different countries. Apples and bananas look very different, to be sure, but they are both fruit, and each is more like the other than either is like nuclear war. To call them both fruit and to fail to notice that they are different, of course, loses information; but to fail to notice that they are both fruit and implicitly to assume that an apple is as different from a banana as it is from nuclear war also loses information. *Not* generalizing has costs, too.

In this chapter we hope to uncover sufficient regularities between countries in cabinet decision making, as described in the previous chapters, to allow us to sustain some general statements about how it works in parliamentary democracies. These statements can then be used as the starting assumptions of a theory of cabinet government. Obviously, theories, generalizations, and starting assumptions do not just fall out of the sky whenever we might want them. Every particular analysis has its roots in something else, and the analysis toward which we are working in this chapter is no exception. We are basing what we are doing on a body of theoretical work that says, to put it in a nutshell, that cabinet ministers matter – that different cabinets with different ministers will do different things in ways that make a real difference to politics. It is our firm intention in future work (Laver and Shepsle, forthcoming) to present a far more precise and fully specified model of this. We see ourselves in the present context as working within a general theoretical orientation, the portfolio-allocation approach, which focuses on the idea that cabinet ministers matter.

This volume constitutes something of an experiment in that the editors explicitly asked country specialists to focus their remarks, not on cabinets in general, but on a common set of specific theoretical categories suggested by the portfolio-allocation approach. As we noted in the introductory chapter, we supplemented the arguments and evidence of these chapters with a rather detailed questionnaire, which each author obligingly completed. These data permit us to draw some general conclusions about how the allocation of cabinet portfolios affects the division of labor in policy implementation and administration, which in turn affects the politics of policy formation.

Without for one moment denying the great richness of country-specific variation, we claim in the remainder of this chapter that a modified version of the portfolio-allocation approach serves the broad theoretical purpose of focusing empirical attention, country by country, on the institutional manner in which policy formation, administration, and implementation hang together. Thus, we give a brief characterization of this approach before moving on to explore the empirical regularities that seem to us to be manifested in the preceding chapters.

We begin by considering a set of issues on which parties take positions. These positions may derive from any number of sources – statements by party leaders and other spokespersons, party manifestos, resolutions passed at party conventions, past party behavior, electoral documents – we need not be specific here. We do assume, however, that there are mechanisms of publicity and accountability in place. The first ensures that party positions are commonly known to all relevant actors; the second that party positions are credible in the sense that parties do not wish to deviate from them and that others expect them to act in accordance with their publicized positions if given the opportunity.

Policy issues are assumed to be bundled into mutually exclusive packages; each of these packages falls into the jurisdiction of a particular government ministry with the authority and indeed the responsibility to act in these matters. The allocation of particular issues to particular ministries creates a division of labor within the cabinet. Thus, if a social democratic party is given the employment portfolio, for example, then its minister will proceed, as best he or she can, to implement the policy positions to which his or her party is committed on each policy issue in that jurisdiction. All other actors expect no less and would do the same if any of them were given the chance. This in turn implies that all actors can make predictions about the consequences of assigning politicians from particular parties to particular cabinet portfolios.

Any cabinet minister, of course, operates under a number of constraints. These need not be the same in each country and, even if they are, need not operate with the same force. As a consequence a minister is not a "global maximizer," able to impose his or her party's ideal policies in every policy area in the portfolio concerned. The minister is rather a "constrained optimizer," doing the best he or she can in the circumstances to push the party line and maneuver around whatever obstacles lie in the way. The important point here is that a minister in a specific party is commonly expected to push policies under his or her jurisdiction toward those of the party.

The portfolio-allocation approach is elaborated in considerable detail elsewhere (Laver and Shepsle, 1990 a,b; forthcoming). Its essential concern is with what takes place in the process of forming a government. It is premised on the beliefs of key actors about what will happen to public policy if particular parties control particular ministries. The main claim of this approach, therefore, and one that receives considerable support in the chapters of this volume, is that which parties secure which cabinet portfolios is an important matter.[1] In asserting that portfolio allocation matters, and that cabinet ministers will do their best to implement party policy within their jurisdictions, the approach thereby provides guidance on what policies will be implemented and administered as a result of the formation of particular governments. A model of portfolio allocation, therefore, provides the theoretical glue linking politics to policy.

Such a model focuses our attention on a number of empirical issues that our country authors have addressed. These issues form the basis of the empirical summaries that follow. The first has to do with the constitutional framework of parliamentary democracy. The portfolio-allocation approach does assume, after all, that cabinets make a difference, that countries are not run by their parliaments. At the same time, cabinets are responsible to their parliaments, and can be dismissed by them. Thus, we need to know about relations between legislature and executive, the subject matter of the next section. The remaining sections deal with various aspects of the role of cabinet ministers, asking how free ministers are to act in areas over which they have jurisdiction. The third section considers this issue in general. The section after that looks at the extent to which ministers are constrained by collective cabinet decisions. The fifth section looks at the extent to which they must bow to the discipline of the parties to which they belong. The sixth section looks at the role of the civil service. The seventh section looks at the extent to which the prime minister, formally "first among equals" but typically much more powerful, can constrain the behavior of individual ministers in their own departments.

RELATIONS BETWEEN LEGISLATURE AND EXECUTIVE

The intimate relationship between legislature and executive in a parliamentary democracy highlights a number of important matters, and thus is a good place to begin our empirical assessment. A number of features of this relationship bear upon the extent to which the legislature can control the executive, and the extent to which the executive can control the legislature. Here we elaborate upon four specific types of question:

- What are the procedures for proposing and voting upon motions of confidence / no confidence in the government? Can the government control these procedures? Can any legislative actor propose such a motion at will?
- If a cabinet is defeated by the legislature, what replaces it?
- Can the legislature unilaterally impose policy decisions upon an unwilling cabinet? Can it unilaterally impose decisions upon an unwilling individual cabinet minister?
- To what extent does the cabinet control the substantive legislative agenda?

Procedure on confidence motions

The fundamental basis of Western European parliamentary democracy is that the executive must retain the support of the legislature. The "executive" is almost invariably operationalized in particular constitutions as the set of cabinet ministers chaired by a prime minister. "Support of the legislature" is usually operationalized procedurally in terms of votes of confidence (proposed by the government) or no confidence (proposed by the opposition) and also, in some countries, in terms of votes of investiture. Governments may *choose* to resign for all sorts of reasons, of course, including losing votes on particular pieces of legislation. But they are *constitutionally obliged* to resign if they lose a legislative motion of confidence / no confidence.

The procedure for getting a vote of no confidence onto the legislative agenda is thus a neglected but vital part of the mechanics of parliamentary democracy. Obviously, such a motion cannot be debated while the parliament is not in session. (Thus, in most Western European countries, parliamentary democracy is effectively suspended when the legislature is not in session, notably during the long summer recess.) Even while the legislature is in session, however, it may be more, or less, difficult for different actors to get a motion of no confidence onto the legislative agenda. If the incumbent government can use its agenda power to block or delay such a motion, then it can effectively prolong its own life. On the other hand, if every legislative actor can costlessly propose such a motion at every possible opportunity, then parliament will effectively sit in a permanent debate on the future of the government.

The empirical situation in the countries covered in the preceding chapters can be summarized relatively straightforwardly. Although there are minor variations, procedures for getting no-confidence motions onto the legislative agenda are permissive in every country. The most liberal provisions of all can be found in Norway and Finland. In Norway, for example, although there are no formal constitutional provisions on no-confidence motions, even in standing orders, any member can by convention propose a no-confidence motion at any time, even without a seconder. In Finland, two proposers are needed, but in both cases the government has no effective means of controlling the procedure. In other countries, the number of proposers may be somewhat higher – five in Austria and the Netherlands, for example, and 10 percent of deputies in Italy and Sweden. The least permissive procedure in the countries covered is in Greece, where fifty deputies must sign the motion – a majority must sign if a second motion is proposed within six months. Once more, however, the government has no effective control over the procedure.

Overall, therefore, procedures for proposing motions of no confidence do not undermine legislative control over the executive. Provided that the legislature is in session in each of the countries surveyed, a majority of deputies can defeat the government at any time they choose to do so. In practice it does appear to be the case, therefore, that the legislature sits as a more or less permanent tribunal on the fate of the executive. The executive really does need to retain the continual support of a majority of the legislature.

Government defeats and caretaker cabinets

If a cabinet loses a vote of confidence in the legislature, then, as we have seen, it must resign. Presumably, rational legislators will have some alternative in mind before they vote to defeat the incumbent government, but this alternative typically cannot be put in place the instant the outgoing cabinet is defeated. Alternatively, a government may lose its parliamentary majority as a result of an election defeat, or some of the government parties in a coalition cabinet may resign their portfolios, generating a governmental crisis. In the period before a new government can be formed, somebody has to hold on to the formal levers of power. During this period, a "caretaker" cabinet typically runs the country. Obviously, if the various parties cannot agree on a new government, the caretaker cabinet continues to remain in office, and represents the status quo from which government formation takes place. It is important, therefore, to be aware of the policy implications of having a caretaker cabinet in power. Surprisingly, this is a matter that has been more or less totally ignored by the literature on government formation, so we rely in the remarks that follow almost entirely on the judgments of our country specialists.

With only a couple of exceptions, the position is quite uniform in the countries covered by our authors. After a cabinet has lost its parliamentary basis, it remains in office as a caretaker until a new cabinet is sworn in. It is a strong constitutional convention that no important decisions are made in the meantime. The exceptions are Germany, where a "constructive" vote of no-confidence procedure means that an alternative government is proposed as part of the no-confidence motion; the French Fourth Republic, in which the government was in effect taken over by the legislature; and Ireland, where the outgoing government continues with more or less undiminished powers until an alternative is sworn in.

For the most part, however, once a government has resigned or been defeated, the existence of a caretaker cabinet means that there can be no deviation from the policy status quo that was in place when the outgoing government lost its parliamentary basis. Actually, there is a sense in which the caretaker government represents less than the policy position of the outgoing government: This is because the caretaker cannot react to new issues and problems in innovative ways that might reasonably have been the forecast responses of the outgoing government, had it survived.

Overall, therefore, we can take the status quo in the government-formation process to be the policy position of the incumbent government, if this has not been defeated, and to remain the position of the outgoing government, even if this has been defeated and a caretaker has taken over, until a new full-fledged cabinet has been installed. There is no particular benefit, therefore, in the opposition parties combining to defeat an incumbent government if they do not expect to be able to agree on an alternative, since the outgoing government's policy position effectively remains in place until an alternative is sworn in.

Legislative control of the cabinet

Over and above the role of the legislature in making and breaking governments, most legislatures do also legislate. Obviously, if every detail of public policy were to be settled by parliamentary legislation, then the role of the cabinet would be limited to the mechanical oversight of policy implementation. The partisan composition of the cabinet would be irrelevant, since substantive policy outputs would be determined by the balance of partisan forces in the legislature. (As we indicated in the introductory chapter, certain models of government formation do implicitly make this assumption.) At the opposite extreme, a legislature might have almost no power to set de facto policy. This might result from a permissive approach to the ministerial interpretation of legislation. It might also result from tight government control over the legislative agenda, a matter to which we will return.

Before we can model the political role of the cabinet in any given setting, we need to know if cabinet ministers are constrained by the legislature in their ability to set policy. We need to know if parliamentary action in a particular policy area can force the hand of an unwilling cabinet or minister. If so, then the legislature can let a minister occupy a portfolio in the knowledge that he or she can be controlled should the need arise, and the minister has no effective political discretion. If the legislature cannot realistically bind a minister in this way, then the minister has some discretion vis-à-vis the legislature, at least within his or her jurisdiction.

Making an empirical judgment about the degree of legislative control over the cabinet in the parliamentary democracies we consider forces us to confront some intriguing contrasts between constitutional law and practical politics. Most of the country specialists agree that, although parliament formally has the power to force the government's hand on a particular issue using legislation, the government's majority support in parliament makes this very difficult to achieve in practice.

Formally in almost every parliamentary democracy, the parliament is sovereign. Its legislation is constrained only to be consistent with the constitution as interpreted by the highest court in the land. If a constitutionally valid law is passed that binds an individual minister or the cabinet as a whole, then so be it; such people are not above the law.

In terms of practical politics, however, a cabinet retains majority support in the legislature – testable, as we have just seen, in terms of a motion of no confidence – otherwise it would be defeated and replaced. If there is a "majority" cabinet in which the government parties themselves control a majority of seats in parliament, then we rarely observe an open confrontation between legislature and executive. In such circumstances it is tempting to regard the executive as being in control of the legislature, since the government parties, if appropriately disciplined, can summon up a legislative majority whenever they care to do so. Even so, the possibility of the legislature attempting to impose its will on the executive can still arise, notably in cases where party discipline breaks down and dissident members of a government party join forces with the opposition to pass legislation on some particular issue. In such cases, the key political action takes place within political parties.

The possibility fo. confrontation is far more clear cut if the government parties do not between them control a parliamentary majority; that is, when the government comprises a "minority" cabinet. (Indeed minority governments in parliamentary democracies are in many ways analogous to situations of "divided government" in the U.S. political system; see Laver and Shepsle, 1991.) Although a minority government must still retain majority legislative support in the sense that no credible alternative government is preferred to it by a legislative majority, this certainly does not mean that a minority government can legislate at will. A majority of legislators may prefer to keep the minority government in office, yet impose their will on it in particular instances by passing particular pieces of legislation. Indeed, legislators' anticipations of being able to do this may well form part of the logic of supporting a minority government in the first place.

Analyzing confrontations between a legislature and either a minority or a majority cabinet takes us deep into the realms of strategic interaction, since any cabinet can threaten to resign if it does not get its way on a particular vote, even over a minor piece of legislation. Moreover, if the legislature prefers the incumbent cabinet to any alternative, as it must do in equilibrium, then this threat must be taken seriously. We do not wish to explore such situations here – this is done in great detail in Laver and Shepsle (forthcoming) – but rather want only to point out that the possibility of legislative action of this sort is an important element in the strategic calculations of key actors. The outcome is more likely to be the result of practical politics interacting with formal constitutional constraints than of the latter alone. This highlights that the key to cabinet control of the legislature is not the government's ability to win or defy legislative votes, since the legislature can, if the politics are right, impose its will on the cabinet. Rather, perhaps the most important procedural aspect of the cabinet's power concerns its institutionally determined ability to control the flow of parliamentary business, and thereby to control the issues that can be considered by the legislature.

Cabinet control of the legislature

One of the most striking manifestations of cabinet control of the legislature is the constitutional power, wielded by most governments, either to dissolve the legislature directly or to recommend a dissolution to a head of state, who is almost certain to comply. This power effectively enables governments to get rid of legislatures and call elections at will. (Norway is the only serious exception to this rule among western European parliamentary democracies; Norwegian elections take place according to an immutable four-year cycle.)

Cabinet government in theoretical perspective

The power of the incumbent government to call an election at will allows it to threaten to impose the costs of an election on its opponents. It also gives a vital role to opinion polls, both published and private. The government is continually provided with such polls, and hence with an estimate of the distribution of seats in the legislature that will result from an immediate election. This means that the government can calculate its strategies either on the basis of legislative weights as they currently exist, or on the basis of those forecast to result from an election, whichever are the more favorable. Each of these factors means that the executive's power to dissolve the legislature loads the relationship between legislature and executive in favor of the latter. A popular government can always call an election and improve its legislative position. An unpopular government can remain in office, no matter what the opinion polls say, provided it does not lose its legislative majority.

The second important element of cabinet control over the legislature, as we saw in the previous section, has to do with the flow of legislative business. If the government has a tight grip on the parliamentary timetable and a near-monopoly of both the information and the drafting skills needed to prepare legislation, then it may be very difficult for opposition parties to get significant draft statutes onto the legislative agenda. This will effectively prevent the legislature from imposing specific policies on an unwilling cabinet. In such situations, incumbent governments may effectively legislate at will, as long as they retain the confidence of a majority of the legislature. In this respect, cabinet ministers have discretion relative to the legislature that is subject only to the constraint that they cannot implement policies so unpopular with the legislature that they provide a majority of legislators with the incentive to defeat the government as a whole.

In general in the countries that we consider, cabinet control over the legislative agenda is very firm. At one extreme we find countries such as Ireland, in which cabinet control over the legislative agenda is almost total, and guaranteed by the standing orders of Parliament. The situation in most of the countries we consider is similar, with government effectively controlling the flow of parliamentary business. The only clear-cut exceptions seem to be in Austria and Norway, as well as the French Fourth Republic. In each of these cases, the legislative agenda is at least partially determined by some organ of the legislature itself.

Overall, despite the fact that the legislature may be able to impose its will on the cabinet once a matter is up for decision, the government's opponents in the legislature can find it almost impossible to get something on the agenda in the first place. Firm cabinet control over the flow of legislative business thus vastly reduces the opportunity for a parliament to leave a cabinet in place and yet use its legislative power to impose policy on the government on an à la carte basis. In effect, the only way for the legislature to effect a substantial change in government policy is to change the government, or at least to mount a credible threat to do so.

THE ROLE OF INDIVIDUAL CABINET MINISTERS

A cabinet minister fills two vital roles in a parliamentary democracy. One is as a member of the cabinet, the body with collective political responsibility for governing the country. The second is as head of a major department of state with overall responsibility for the development and implementation of government policy in his or her jurisdiction. The latter role would, on the face of it, appear to give a minister considerable influence over policy.

Within each government department, the minister in charge is able to draw upon a considerable pool of professional expertise that is focused intensely upon the policy concerns of the department. The reverse side of this coin is that any given minister has very little access to the professional expertise and advice needed to develop, evaluate, and implement policy that lies within the jurisdiction of some other department. Each minister, furthermore, faces a very heavy workload within his or her own department – and this is typically superimposed upon the busy life of a full-time politician. Given the intense pressure of work and the lack of access to civil-service specialists in other departments, it seems unlikely that many cabinet ministers will be able successfully to poke their noses very deeply into the jurisdictions of their cabinet colleagues. This should give each minister considerable discretion to act, in his or her own department, independently of other members of the cabinet. Since each minister will have a partisan agenda, each also has the incentive to exercise this discretion. There is thus a potential tension between the collective decisions of the cabinet as a committee, and the individual decisions of its members as department heads. Any model of cabinet decision making must take account of this. Once more, important questions require systematic answers:

- Can ministers ignore collective cabinet decisions without other cabinet members realizing this? What happens when ministers publicly defy such decisions?
- In what circumstances, both in theory and in practice, can cabinet ministers make policy decisions within their jurisdiction independently of the collective views of the cabinet? In what circumstances must they seek cabinet approval for such decisions?

Each of these questions relates to the ability of an individual cabinet minister to go against the collective wishes of his or her cabinet colleagues.

Cabinet government in theoretical perspective

Our model of cabinet decision making will be very different, depending upon whether we assume that government policy is influenced by the fact that cabinet ministers have discretion in their own departments to act independently of other members of the cabinet, or whether we assume that government policy simply reflects a process of collective decision making in the cabinet as a whole.

Ignoring or defying the cabinet – not on

Obviously, if individual cabinet ministers can ignore cabinet decisions without this being realized, or even openly defy them, then they will be very powerful within their own departments, and collective cabinet decisions will mean little. The authors in their chapters are quite unequivocal on these matters, however. In the first place, it seems that it is not possible for a minister simply to ignore a significant cabinet decision relating to his or her department without this being realized and publicized, by either the media, the civil service, or cabinet colleagues. Often there is a cabinet office within the civil service with responsibility for monitoring the progress of cabinet decisions; but even where there is not, our authors agree that it is just not possible for a cabinet minister to ignore a collective decision made by the cabinet.

If, instead of ignoring a cabinet decision, a minister chooses to defy it, our authors are equally adamant about the consequences. The minister concerned must resign, or will be sacked. In some countries – Austria, Germany, and Sweden, for example – it is claimed that a minister never defies the cabinet in this way, presumably as an equilibrium response to the inevitable consequence. In all other countries such defiance almost invariably results in the minister's departure, though the position appears to be slightly less clear-cut in Belgium, Italy, and the Netherlands.

The implications of these empirical observations are straightforward. Ministerial discretion, if it is a factor in government policy-making, does not result from the ability of a minister to go against explicit cabinet decisions.

Ministerial discretion

It follows from the previous discussion that, if ministerial discretion is important, it must result from the ability of a minister to do one of three things. The first is to act on matters that are not decided by the cabinet. The second is to influence which matters come to the cabinet for decision and which do not. The third is to affect the substance of specific proposals on those matters within his or her jurisdiction that do come to the cabinet for decision. Ministerial discretion, in short, must result from the minister's ability to shape collective cabinet decisions rather than to defy them. Once more some empirical patterns do clearly emerge in the countries covered by this book.

Probably the most important of these relates to which issues are to be decided by the cabinet and which by individual ministers. The empirical position seems to be that certain types of decision are almost always formally reserved to the cabinet. These include decisions requiring legislation, involving interdepartmental conflict, with major financial implications, with "hot" political implications, and decisions not in any departmental jurisdiction. Obviously, this list appears to cover most of what is important and interesting about government policy-making. Thus, the power of a minister to act outside the formal jurisdiction of the cabinet seems to be quite low, being confined more or less to routine matters of administration and policy implementation.

The formal position in relation to the cabinet agenda seems also to be rather straightforward. In most of the countries we cover, the prime minister is responsible for the cabinet agenda – though formal rules are important in Austria and Finland, as are individual ministers in the Netherlands, Norway, and Sweden.

The most interesting question about the role of individual ministers in setting the cabinet agenda, therefore, relates to the ability of a minister to determine whether there is a proposal to be put on the agenda in the first place, as well as to his or her ability to shape the substance of proposals that do ultimately find their way onto the agenda. The prime minister can use his or her agenda power only on substantive raw material that is generated for the most part by the cabinet members with jurisdiction over the policy area in question. Most of our country authors confirm that other members of the cabinet will have even less inclination or ability than the prime minister to shape the substance of policy emanating from the department of a ministerial colleague. It is at that point in the decision-making process that the substance of a policy proposal is being shaped, therefore, that the discretion of an individual minister is most effective.

COLLECTIVE CABINET DECISION MAKING

Most parliamentary democracies operate on the basis of a doctrine of collective cabinet responsibility that in many cases is enshrined in the constitution. It is important to bear in mind, however, that maintaining the collective responsibility of members of the cabinet for government decisions is quite different from using a process of collective decision making to formulate those decisions in the first place. Individual cabinet ministers might even be dictators within their respective jurisdictions, for example, making decisions without regard to anyone else, but the cabinet might still bear collective responsibility for those decisions once they have been made.

In certain circumstances, as most of our country specialists point out, collective cabinet decision making is inevitable. Most obviously, if different government departments come into direct conflict with one another, then it will not be possible for each of the ministers concerned to act independently, and such conflicts must be resolved if deadlock is not to result. In addition, certain policy problems, for example urban regeneration, will be intrinsically interdepartmental in character and will require coordinated policy-making and implementation. Last but not least, new issues will emerge that do not automatically fall within the jurisdiction of an existing portfolio. These must be disposed of somehow, directly by the cabinet, indirectly by assigning the problem to the jurisdiction of some particular portfolio, or even by creating a new portfolio or engaging in radical departmental reorganization as, for example, has often been the case for issues involving the environment.

We therefore need to have a clear idea about the procedures a cabinet uses for making collective decisions. If collective cabinet decisions are made by simple majority vote, for example, then the cabinet is in effect a second-order legislature. This would have a number of consequences, including making the smaller partner in a two-party coalition very weak, leaving it with no more than the ultimate threat to resign and bring down the entire government. For three-or-more–party coalitions, a simple majority decision rule would set up a second-order coalition game within the cabinet.

In practice, however, two concepts are used extensively by our country specialists to describe collective cabinet decision making. These are unanimity and consensus – though consensus is used far more commonly. All are agreed that actual voting is very rare in cabinets, and takes place only to dispose quickly of relatively unimportant issues. Whereas a unanimity rule is unambiguous enough, implying that each minister has a veto over every decision, the notion of consensus is more complex. Nobody seems very willing to give an explicit definition to consensus, though there seems to be quite a strong feeling among country specialists that "you know it when you see it."

Most accounts of consensual collective decision making by cabinets agree on two things, however: consensus has to be built, and it has to be "called," or summed up. In these senses, consensus goes far beyond unanimity, which implies agreement among cabinet ministers as to the right course of action. Rather, a consensus is something that receives the general acceptance of all cabinet ministers, even when they have started their

299

deliberations with radically different points of view. The implication is that, since cabinet ministers will be collectively responsible for the decision, it should be something that they are prepared to go along with, even if it is by no means their first choice.

The reasons a minister who begins a discussion opposing a particular position ends up going along with it are, of course, many splendored and far too complex to detain us here. It seems likely, however, that quite a few of these reasons have to do with informal reciprocity norms. Given the enormous number of things that any cabinet must decide during its lifetime, there is simply not enough time to fight everything out to the bitter end. The result is that each minister comes to feel that there are certain issues that he or she can take a stand on, and that others will "go along" on these issues in exchange for reciprocal cooperation on other matters. If people who disagree with each other do not behave like this, then it is hard to see how they can build a consensus. This in turn implies that cabinet ministers are likely to pick certain things that are "their" issues – potentially introducing an association between particular cabinet ministers and specific issue areas, even in pure collective decision making.

The "calling" of the consensus is something that most of our country specialists agree gives a special role to the prime minister. A typical cabinet decision-making process allows for sometimes extensive discussion of a particular issue, during which ministers reveal as much or as little as they choose about their point of view. After this, the prime minister states whether or not a consensus has been reached and, if so, what the substance of this consensus is. If a consensus has not been reached, or if a cabinet member takes serious objection to the prime minister's calling of the substance of the consensus, then the matter is deferred and the process is iterated. If nobody demurs from the prime minister's summing up, then this becomes the collective cabinet decision. This is clearly a very sophisticated decision-making process, and it is one that appears on the face it at least to give quite a bit of power to the prime minister. It also, however, gives more of a say on a specific issue to those with a particular interest in it, and may thereby give something of a departmental structure even to collective decision making.

THE ROLE OF PARTY ORGANIZATIONS

As we saw in the Introduction, the "party government" model of cabinet decision making, developed to account for decision making in one-party majority cabinets, especially in Britain, is based on the premise that the "real" policy decisions are made at some level within the government party organization and implemented via one-party control of the cabinet and legislature. The notion of party government is less straightforward when there is a coalition cabinet, but is developed quite extensively by Müller in his chapter in this book. The basic idea behind his discussion is that there is a two-stage decision-making process in coalition systems. First, each coalition party works out a strategy for its own "government team"; then the party's government team must reach an agreement with other party teams who are part of the coalition. The essence of Müller's treatment of party government, therefore, is that parties function as if they are unitary actors, as far as interaction with other potential coalition partners is concerned. In effect, any differences within the party are re-solved privately, and are not exposed to the outside world.

The answers to two specific questions throw light on the extent to which it seems reasonable to work with a multiparty version of the party-government approach in the present context:

- To what extent is the autonomy of cabinet ministers constrained by the decision-making structures of the parties to which they belong?
- When a party goes into government, are its nominees to cabinet positions usually the party spokespersons for the policy area involved?

Party constraints on cabinet ministers

Many of our country specialists were at pains when addressing this ques-tion to make a distinction between the parliamentary party and the extra-parliamentary party. Several suggested that ministers were at least to some extent constrained by decisions of the parliamentary party – a pattern noted in Belgium, Canada, Finland, Italy, the Netherlands, New Zealand, Norway, and Sweden. The role of the party was more generally played down with regard to Austria, Germany, and Ireland.

Most authors played down the importance of the extraparliamentary party; these organs seem to have an important role only in Belgium and Italy. Party constraints on the cabinet are thus generated within the nexus of legislative relations, and do not in general derive from sections of the party (radical rank-and-file activists, for example) that have no direct stake in legislative–executive relations. To the extent that senior party figures dominate both the parliamentary party and the cabinet, the ability of parliamentary parties to dominate their cabinet ministers may be more apparent than real. This does not, of course, gainsay the role of the parliamentary-party machine in enforcing party discipline, and hence in enhancing the party to function as a single monolithic actor. Indeed, there is strong support among country specialists for the argument that cabinet ministers do in practice tend to operate as more or less reliable agents of their respective parties.

301

Party spokespersons or experts as cabinet nominees

The general response of the country specialists to this question was quite clear-cut. There is no obvious link between a politician being party spokesperson for a particular policy area and being the party's nominee for the cabinet portfolio with jurisdiction over the same area. In general, seniority within the party seems to play a much greater role in being selected as a cabinet minister than does policy expertise, and there were only a few exceptions to this. When a French civil servant is nominated as a cabinet minister, this person is usually an expert in the policy area concerned. There also seems to be some tendency for cabinet members to be the relevant party spokespersons in Norway and Sweden. Barring these exceptions, however, a far more important criterion for being nominated as a cabinet minister is to be a senior party politician of cabinet rank – a "ministrable."

Taken together, the answers to the two questions we have just discussed give strong support to the party-government view of cabinet decision making. Cabinet ministers do indeed appear to be functioning as agents of their party rather than as independent actors in their own right. This pattern is far more consistent with the party-as-unitary-actor view than it is with the view that a party is a diverse coalition of politicians, selecting from this diversity to promote different policy positions in different contexts.

There is a third matter that throws a rather more indirect light on the same issue. This concerns the manner in which a new cabinet minister is nominated, during the life of a cabinet, to fill a vacancy that might have been created by death, illness, resignation, scandal, or whatever. Here, a very clear pattern is reported by our country specialists. When a portfolio becomes vacant, it is almost invariably filled by a minister from the same party. Replacing one cabinet minister with another from the same party, therefore, does not seem not to be a major strategic decision, whereas replacing a minister with a politician from another party does seem to have major implications.

All in all, there is a substantial accumulation of evidence from answers to all of these questions that intraparty policy differences do not play an important role in interparty interactions over cabinet formation and maintenance.

THE CIVIL SERVICE

As we saw in the introductory chapter, if the career civil service can constrain the minister in charge of a particular government department, then we have an example of "bureaucratic government" in the jurisdiction concerned. If this happens in all departments, then we need to know the policy position of senior civil servants rather than those of politicians if we want to forecast government policy.

Our country specialists suggest that the real-world situation in this regard is broadly similar in many countries. The power of the civil service is acknowledged almost everywhere. In particular, it is hardly surprising to find that the civil service has much power over routine decisions, dealing more with the implementation than with the making of policy. It is also acknowledged that the civil service has more power over new and weak ministers than over long-serving and strong ones. However – and contradicting the "Yes, Minister" caricature – it seems generally agreed that most senior civil servants prefer a strong minister who can win battles for the department in cabinet, to a weak one who can be manipulated but who cannot defend departmental interests in the outside world. If senior civil servants tend to back a strong minister who fights for their department, this should serve to increase the degree of departmentalism in cabinet decision making.

Nonetheless, there is clearly some variation in the extent to which the civil service figures in the policy-making process. At one end of the spectrum is France, which not only has a highly specialized elite corps of senior civil servants, but in which senior civil servants may be nominated as cabinet ministers. The other countries in which the civil service seems to have relatively more power over policy making are the Netherlands, Norway, and Sweden. In each of these cases, a professionalized senior civil service becomes very expert in particular policy areas, and it can for this reason be extremely difficult to make policy in the face of determined civil-service resistance.

A final important matter in this regard concerns the role of the political "cabinets" that ministers in some countries set up inside their departments to act as ministerial advisers. Members of these *cabinets* may be policy professionals attached to the party, civil servants in the department concerned whose views are known to be sympathetic to those of the minister, or trusted friends and associates of the minister – a typical ministerial cabinet includes all three types of individual. The ministerial cabinet functions as a politicized inner civil service, able to monitor what is going on in the bureaucracy and to warn the minister if senior career civil servants are holding out in any way. The very existence of these cabinets – important in countries such as Belgium, France, and Greece – shows that ministers feel concerned about the constraints on their freedom of action that might be imposed, without their knowledge, by the civil service. It is almost impossible to evaluate, of course, how successful this strategy is in practice at counteracting constraints imposed by the civil service.

THE PRIME MINISTER

One of the things that is quite clear about most parliamentary democracies is that the prime minister is a very important figure. As we noted in the first chapter of this book, many countries have a government-formation procedure that involves first investing a prime minister, who then presents a cabinet to the legislature. Indeed, in many countries, it is a change in prime minister, not any other change in the cabinet, that formally signifies a change in government. In this sense, the prime minister is an unambiguous constitutional symbol of the government. The prime minister also typically has the formal power to hire and fire cabinet ministers at will, although this power will obviously be constrained by practical politics. Within the cabinet, as we have already seen, the prime minister is almost always the person with the power to set the cabinet agenda, chair cabinet meetings, and call the consensus decision at the end of the discussion of each agenda item.

As well as having a major constitutional role, the prime minister is often the head of a major political party. Indeed, in countries such as Britain with one-party majority governments, the prime minister's role as party leader compounds strikingly with his or her role as leader of the government. Thus, a strong prime minister in firm control of a majority government party, in the manner of Margaret Thatcher in her heyday, can come to look almost like an elected monarch. Certainly, the power of the prime minister does seem to be greater in those countries that have a tradition of single-party majority governments – in New Zealand, Canada, and Greece, as well as in Britain. Even in these countries, of course, the prime minister is not all-powerful. As Margaret Thatcher found to her cost, a prime minister who loses the backing of his or her party can be toppled very quickly.

Prime ministers can also be very powerful in coalition cabinets, although the fact that they are not in control of the other government parties cannot but undermine their position. There is clearly considerable variation here, with the Norwegian prime minister, for example, having relatively weak powers and the French and Finnish prime ministers often being overshadowed by a president of the same party. The German chancellor, in contrast, is without doubt a major force in government decision making.

The general pattern, with a few notable exceptions, is for the prime minister, while formally primus inter pares, to be a central figure in cabinet politics with an effective veto over many aspects of government decision making. In one important respect in coalition cabinets, however, there is a major constraint upon the role of the prime minister. Formally, as we have seen, the prime minister can hire and fire other ministers at will, although

Belgium, Italy, and the Netherlands are exceptions to this. (In practice, the prime minister's position as party leader can often allow him or her to get rid of ministers who are party colleagues, even when the formal power to dismiss them is not available.) However, practical politics can also constrain the formal power of the prime minister to sack ministers, typically making it very difficult to replace ministers from other government parties without the consent of the leader of the party concerned. This is nowhere a constitutional provision – indeed, few constitutions recognize any of the exigencies of life in a coalition executive. Rather, it reflects the very important role of political parties in the equilibrium processes that underlie government formation and maintenance.

IN CONCLUSION

We set out to gather a theoretically informed set of case studies dealing with the political role of cabinet ministers in parliamentary democracies. Our purpose was twofold. First, we hoped that if country specialists wrote about the cabinet within the theoretical framework suggested by the portfolio-allocation approach, then this might not only uncover interesting new aspects of the political role of cabinet ministers, but also cast a new light on some received wisdoms. Second, we hoped to get some empirical feedback on the assumptions that are fundamental to the portfolio-allocation approach, before developing a more explicit and rigorous formal model of cabinet behavior. As is typical of this type of enterprise, each of these interacting objectives has been partially fulfilled.

The portfolio-allocation framework clearly has helped us to assemble systematic empirical information on a range of matters we consider important, but that have hitherto been neglected by those who have written about cabinet formation in parliamentary democracies. These matters include the role of investiture and confidence procedures, the role of caretaker governments, and the extent to which a minister is able to influence policy outputs in areas under his or her departmental jurisdiction. Our general conclusions on these matters can be found in the empirical summaries earlier in this chapter.

Second, we have clearly received some forthright empirical feedback from country specialists about the assumptions of the portfolio-allocation approach. It is to this feedback that we devote our concluding remarks.

We should begin with the observation that the discussions in the preceding chapters have indeed caused us to change our views about certain aspects of the portfolio-allocation approach, as we had earlier elaborated it. In the theoretical briefing paper we sent to all authors before they prepared the first drafts of their papers for the European Consortium for Political Research (ECPR) workshop in Limerick, we expressed our key

305

assumption about the political role of cabinet ministers in the following way:

Regardless of what is formally decided at cabinet meetings, it is possible to forecast government policy in a given area from the identity of the cabinet minister with jurisdiction over this area. The most extreme version of this assumption is that ministers are policy dictators in their own jurisdictions, but it is not necessary to go this far. It is simply necessary to assume, taking account of constraints such as the power of the civil service and existing contractual obligations, that having a particular politician in charge of a particular ministry has particular consequences that can be forecast, and that having a minister with different preferences in charge of the same ministry is forecast to have different consequences.

We also talked quite a bit in this briefing paper about the autonomy of cabinet ministers, and the role that this has on the policy-making process. A number of our country specialists have reacted quite strongly to the most extreme conception of ministerial autonomy quoted in the previous paragraph. Some have then used these objections to conclude that the portfolio-allocation approach may not be very useful in "their" country. We hasten to emphasize, however, that the portfolio-allocation approach does not hinge upon this extreme conception. In the remainder of these remarks we concentrate upon how the evidence of the previous chapters strongly delineates a reconceived notion of ministerial autonomy, one that accommodates the experience of most parliamentary democracies.

Our revised conception of the political role of cabinet ministers is informed by a number of strong regularities in the empirical discussions in the preceding chapters. These regularities can be stated quite simply. First, cabinets do matter. No country specialist disagreed fundamentally with the proposition that government policy is affected by the partisan composition of the cabinet. Second, government departments matter. Although many important policy decisions are formally made in the cabinet, most of these important policies are in fact formulated by government departments – and most interdepartmental conflicts are resolved informally between the departments themselves, rather than being taken to the cabinet. Third, cabinet ministers can have a strong impact on the activities of their departments. Although civil servants may bully or manipulate a weak minister, none of the country specialists gave much credence to the "Yes, Minister" caricature in which the typical minister is run by his or her civil servants. Fourth, cabinet ministers cannot have a strong impact on the affairs of other ministers' departments. Leaving on one side for the moment the matter of collective cabinet decision making, all country specialists concur with the argument that pressure of work and the distribution of civil-service expertise mean that an individual minister cannot successfully influence the processes of policy formation and implementation in another department, against the wishes of the head of that department. These four statements can be taken together to imply that there is a strong degree of departmentalism in the formulation and implementation of government policy, and that cabinet ministers, in their role as heads of government departments, play an important part in this.

This leaves us with perhaps the most difficult area to consider, which is whether the cabinet as a collective body not only makes collective decisions, but can in effect collectively decide to implement any policy it chooses on any issue. The portfolio-allocation approach is predicated on the assumption that this is not the case; rather, that cabinet decision making is constrained by the departmentalism of the policy-formulation and implementation processes. The difficulty of assessing this argument empirically is that it depends to a large extent upon counterfactuals. This is because, if politicians are assumed to be sophisticated actors (and there is every reason to assume that they are), then the effects of the constraints on their freedom of action may never actually be observed in practice.

We can draw an analogy with the game of chess. The rules of chess say that one player wins by putting the other player in the position that every possible move leaves the losing king in peril of being taken – checkmate! Yet it is almost unheard of for there to be an actual checkmate in a game played between even halfway serious players. The checkmate is invariably anticipated and the losing player resigns before reaching this point. Even though we never observe a checkmate, however, the checkmate rule has a massive influence on the course of every serious game of chess. It would clearly be idiotic to say that, because we never observe a checkmate in a game of chess, checkmates are not important. The empirical frequency of checkmates is no guide whatsoever to their importance.

The same basic problem applies to assessing the importance of ministerial discretion in collective cabinet decision making. Many of the authors in the preceding chapters mentioned ways in which collective decisions made by the cabinet are important, and may bind ministers in their departments. Some took this as evidence against the portfolio-allocation approach, although this does not necessarily follow. The fact that a cabinet makes collective decisions does not mean that it can collectively decide to implement any policy it chooses on any issue. Assuming that politicians do not wish to make decisions that have no meaning because they cannot be implemented, the set of credible collective decisions that can be made will be heavily conditioned by the implementation process. As we have just shown, many of our country specialists do in fact accept that the implementation of government decisions is heavily departmental in character, with a minister able to influence what goes on in his or her department. From this it follows that the "collective" decisions of a cabinet will themselves be heavily constrained by the departmental structure of government – a structure in which the minister, as head of a government department, figures strongly. That we do not observe the operation of these departmental constraints in the formulation of, say, a coalition treaty between parties, or in some other collective policy document, is perfectly consistent with the possibility that sophisticated actors anticipate and take account of such constraints when deciding what it is sensible to agree to. It is just not possible to gainsay the strong departmental structure of policy formulation and implementation, so these constraints clearly exist.

Where does this leave us? As we have just indicated, we remain convinced that there is a strong departmental structure to government in parliamentary democracies. Abundant evidence for this can be found in the preceding country chapters and elsewhere. Moreover, we remain convinced that cabinet ministers are important in this structure. We strongly suspect, furthermore, though the counterfactual nature of the proposition makes evidence hard to muster, that many superficially "collective" decisions are in fact heavily constrained by strategies anticipating the effects of this departmental structure. Nevertheless, we do accept that sweeping assertions about the autonomy of cabinet ministers are ill-founded.

Reading the country chapters carefully, the real reason cabinet ministers are not as autonomous as we had alleged is that they are heavily constrained by party politics. Parties are important in parliamentary democracies because they structure the electoral game. The portfolio-allocation approach to cabinet government does not yet incorporate any account of the electoral game, so we can do no better than treat electoral considerations as external constraints on the government-formation process. What the portfolio-allocation approach has hitherto not emphasised enough, therefore, is that cabinet ministers are for the most part also members of political parties, subject to party discipline if they wish to retain their positions after the next election.

All of our country specialists agree, explicitly or implicitly, that politicians are not autonomous agents who just happen to be associated with a political party. Rather, politicians are held to operate in the government-formation process as agents of their party. If this is true, then we do not need to know the personal policy preferences of an individual cabinet minister, or to be able to forecast the effect of installing some particular minister in a department rather than a party colleague, before we can model government formation. These were claims to which our country specialists took particular exception. What is clear from all of this is the need to assume that political parties in parliamentary democracies are well disciplined – an assumption that country specialists seem for the most part much better able to live with.

Our reconceived notion of the political role of cabinet ministers in parliamentary democracies thus sees them as operating within the executive as agents of well-disciplined political parties. We have not gone into the mechanisms of party discipline, since this is not at all our main concern, but it seems likely that the prime minister and other party leaders will figure prominently in these. The strongly departmental nature of policy formulation and implementation seems to us to be well established, both in the preceding chapters and elsewhere. This implies that a reconstructed version of the portfolio-allocation approach should concentrate upon the role of cabinet ministers, acting as agents of their party, in the departmental processes of policy formulation and implementation. It is this role that ultimately links politics to public policy.

NOTES

1 A stronger claim, articulated in early versions of this theory, asserts that *intra-party* reassignments of a portfolio will also make a difference. Putting aside the idiosyncracies of ministerial personality and competence, on which little systematic can be said, the country specialists, both in their chapters in this volume and in their questionnaire responses, unequivocally challenge this claim. Though such a challenge does not initially stop the theorist (we have developed such an intraparty model in Laver and Shepsle, 1990b), it does suggest when a theoretical route may be a dead end. We have incorporated this judgment into the subsequent development of our approach and are grateful to them for steering us right on this matter.

REFERENCES

Laver, Michael, and Kenneth A. Shepsle. 1990a. Coalitions and cabinet government. *American Political Science Review* 84: 873–90.
  1990b. Government coalitions and intraparty politics. *British Journal of Political Science* 20: 489–506.
  1991. Divided government: America is not 'exceptional.' *Governance* 4: 250–69.
  forthcoming. *Making and Breaking Governments: Cabinets and Legislatures in Parliamentary Democracies.* Cambridge University Press.

Index

Index

313

Index

Index

Belgium, 106–12, 119–20
Britain, 208–13, 218–19, 223–4
Canada, 252–3, 262
Finland, 90–8, 102
France (Fourth Republic), 128–9, 133–6
France (Fifth Republic), 141–2
Germany (Federal Republic), 153, 160–7
Greece, 270–1, 274–5
Ireland, 75–6, 79, 82
Italy, 188, 191, 194–5, 197–8
Netherlands, 63–5
New Zealand, 227–8, 231–3, 240–3, 246
Norway, 50–2
Sweden, 184
See also coalition agreements; government caucus, New Zealand; parties, parliamentary; parties, extraparliamentary; party government; party policy; public policy
politicization, Netherlands, 63–4
Portelli, Hugues, 141
portfolio allocation
approach to institutional functions, 288–9
as approach to cabinet government theory, 288
model, 289
within and between political parties, 8–10
Austria, 31–2
Belgium, 106–10, 116–19, 121
Canada, 261
Canadian provincial, 251, 256–7
Finland, 91–3, 103
France (Fourth Republic), 130–2, 136
Germany (Federal Republic), 165, 167
Ireland, 80–1, 85–6
Netherlands, 69–71
New Zealand, 227–30, 232
Norway, 54
See also coalition agreements
Powell, Enoch, 213
premier
Canada, 252, 256, 265–6
Greece, 273
president
Finland, 96–7, 102
France (Fourth Republic), 126
France (Fifth Republic), 139, 143–5, 148
Germany (Federal Republic), 151
Greece, 271, 279
Ireland, 80
prime minister

in parliamentary democracy, 304–5
role in collective cabinet decision-making, 300
Austria, 20–3
Belgium, 107–8, 115, 120
Britain, 205, 210–12, 218–19
Finland, 98–9
France (Fourth Republic), 126–7, 130–2, 136
France (Fifth Republic), 146–8
Greece, 271–5, 280
Ireland, 81
Italy, 188–9, 195–7
Netherlands, 59–60, 69
New Zealand, 231, 234, 240–2
Norway, 41–5, 48
Sweden, 170–3, 175–6
prime-ministerial government
cabinet decision making model, 6–7
Austria, 19–23, 30–1
Britain, 205–6
Public Expenditure Committee, New Zealand, 246
public opinion
role in calling an election, 295
New Zealand, 227
Sweden, 182
public policy
conditions for cabinet role in making, 8–10
formation in parliamentary democracy, 292–4
issues in portfolio allocation theory, 288–9
link to politics, 309
Austria, 21–2
Belgium, 106–7, 113–22
Britain, 203–4
Canadian provincial, 257–9
Finland, 97–8, 103–5
France (Fourth Republic), 128–9
France (Fifth Republic), 140–1
Germany (Federal Republic), 154–65
Greece, 275–8
Ireland, 82, 85
Netherlands, 56–7, 69
New Zealand, 236–9
Sweden, 169–70, 172–84

Quermonne, Jean-Louis, 141, 142, 146

Rainer, O., 182
reciprocity
in collective cabinet decision making, 300
Canada, 255, 261–8
responsibility

317